MW00639505

MOONACHIE, NJ

PARSIMONY
AND OTHER RADICAL IDEAS ABOUT JUSTICE

ALSO BY JEREMY TRAVIS

Exploring the Role of the Police in Prisoner Reentry

But They All Come Back: Facing the Challenges of Prisoner Reentry

Toward a New Professionalism in Policing

ALSO BY BRUCE WESTERN

Punishment and Inequality in America

Homeward: Life in the Year After Prison

PARSIMONY

AND OTHER RADICAL IDEAS
ABOUT JUSTICE

EDITED BY JEREMY TRAVIS
AND BRUCE WESTERN

NEW YORK
LONDON

© 2023 by Jeremy Travis and Bruce Western

All rights reserved.

No part of this book may be reproduced, in any form, without written permission from the publisher.

Requests for permission to reproduce selections from this book should be made through our website: https://thenewpress.com/contact.

This collection of pieces originated in the Square One Project (squareonejustice.org).

Chapter 19, "What Makes a City Safe? Strategies That Don't Rely on Police or Prisons" was published, in a slightly different form, in the *Boston Review* in 2021.

Published in the United States by The New Press, New York, 2023

Distributed by Two Rivers Distribution

ISBN 978-1-62097-755-2 (hc)
ISBN 978-1-62097-775-0 (ebook)

CIP data is available

The New Press publishes books that promote and enrich public discussion and understanding of the issues vital to our democracy and to a more equitable world. These books are made possible by the enthusiasm of our readers; the support of a committed group of donors, large and small; the collaboration of our many partners in the independent media and the not-for-profit sector; booksellers, who often hand-sell New Press books; librarians; and above all by our authors.

www.thenewpress.com

Composition by Dix!

This book was set in Garamond Premier Pro

Printed in the United States of America

10   9   8   7   6   5   4   3   2   1

CONTENTS

PARSIMONY
AND OTHER RADICAL IDEAS ABOUT JUSTICE

INTRODUCTION: REIMAGINING JUSTICE

Jeremy Travis and Bruce Western

Every society faces a fundamental question: How should it respond to harms committed by its members? One answer could be mechanical: A government must define as crimes those acts that warrant the imposition of punishment on the person causing harm. A process of investigation, apprehending wrongdoers, and adjudication must be established to determine whether crimes have been committed and by whom. Punishments must be defined and authoritative institutions must be established to implement these policies on behalf of this society. We might even call this collection of agencies "the criminal justice system."

Yet this description leaves much unspecified. Profound values are implicated at every stage, from the design of punishments to the institutions that implement them. Most fundamentally, the design of a criminal justice system that defines criminal behavior and metes out punishment for violations of those laws embodies a relationship between the citizen and the state. Granting the state power to exercise coercive control over a member of that society immediately raises questions about the limits on that power. What sanctions are allowable? How does this society balance the liberty and autonomy of citizens against the value of redressing harm? Creating an adjudication process for claims of wrongdoing requires a balance between the search for truth and a forum for challenging those claims. How much will this society tolerate error in determining whether an individual engaged in prohibited behavior?

Such a system of clearly articulated criminal laws, efficient law enforcement, neutral fact-finding courts, and principled sanctioning authorities exists only in theory. In the real world, the criminal justice systems created by modern societies are deeply embedded in long-standing conflicts and inequalities, and subject to resource scarcity. Throughout history, the exercise of the state's power to define criminal conduct has been wielded against the political enemies of the current regime. The state's police powers have been used to crush political opposition, terrorize ethnic and racial minorities, drive religious sects into exile, compel adherence to the doctrines of a ruling party, and protect economic interests of the powerful. The philosopher's vision of a society adopting laws that operate in a neutral fashion quickly crumbles when viewed in the harsh light of history.

This has been the contested story of the criminal justice system in America since the founding of the country. One need only recall the Salem witch trials; the use of fugitive slave laws to subjugate enslaved Africans; the deployment of police and criminal prosecutions to quash labor, civil rights, and anti-war movements; or the complicity of law enforcement agents in the terroristic lynching of Black Americans post-Reconstruction to underscore the reality that the enforcement of criminal laws has often been an instrument of oppression in American history.

For the past half-century, however, a new, uniquely pernicious American reality has taken hold. By any measure, the reach of police and prisons into society has exploded. By the first decade of the twenty-first century, the United States had accumulated more laws, police, arrests, higher rates of incarceration in jails and prisons, and more people under supervision by the state than at any time in its history, and to an extent greater than any other contemporary Western nation. Also, the system's reach is not equally distributed across all sectors of society: the realities of over-criminalization and mass incarceration fall disproportionately on communities of color, especially Black men. What in theory should be a process for redressing harms is in reality a juggernaut that undermines the most fundamental aspirations of American democracy. Most tragically, the punitive policies adopted during the "tough on crime" era in the name of public safety yielded intergenerational damage that far outweighed in significance any minimal short-term gains in safety.

The harms attributable to this new reality run deep. In a society marked by stubborn and growing economic inequality, this system exacerbates and perpetuates poverty. In a society long defined by white supremacy and durable racial hierarchy, this system rubs salt in the wounds of slavery, Jim Crow, anti-immigrant policies, the erasure of Native Americans, and the persistent resistance to aspirations for a multicultural democracy.

In a society that fails to protect those members who are vulnerable, marginalized, struggling with poor health, or suffering from stigma, the system, in its everyday operations, violates the dignity of all persons. In recognition of these realities, many observers, critics, and practitioners choose to refer to America's "criminal legal system," not its "criminal justice system," underscoring this history of injustice in the enforcement of criminal laws in America.[1]

To some critics, this reality calls upon reformers to cut back on the excesses of the system and repair the dysfunction, while retaining the fundamental architecture of the system. Today's justice reform discussion often articulates the aspiration to "shrink the system" or "reduce the footprint of the system." Rarely, however, does the reform discussion lead to a description of how much the system footprint should be reduced, much less how to determine the scale of the ideal system.

To other critics of the status quo, this reality calls for the total abolition of police and prisons and the creation of a new approach reflecting a reimagined relationship between the state and communities seeking safety and justice. The abolitionist position casts aside any notion of shrinking or limiting the reach of the criminal law, and starts instead with the premise of a clean slate. In this view, communities should be empowered to develop responses to harm that do not rely on state power or authority.

But neither reformers nor abolitionists feel that violence and law-breaking should go unanswered. What is required for the construction of a new and better system to address harm and support the aspiration for justice in a framework based on fundamental values? This book sets forth a new agenda, rooted in values of parsimony, healing, and shared power that anchor an emerging vision of justice: a vision that seeks to protect public safety and demand accountability for wrongdoing, but in a context of limited state power with the aim of repairing harm.

The principle of parsimony provides a valuable framework for approaching the crucial question of the reach of state power. The cornerstone proposition of the parsimony principle is that the state is entitled to deprive its citizens of liberty only when that deprivation is reasonably necessary to serve a legitimate social purpose. Any liberty deprivation beyond that minimum is gratuitous and constitutes state cruelty. A parsimonious approach to justice therefore insists on the least restrictive intervention to achieve societal goals. This core value then has implications for every aspect of the justice system.

By placing a premium on individual liberty and erecting a high bar for the legitimate exercise of state power, the parsimony principle would dramatically shrink the criminal justice footprint. Virtually all the realities of the modern justice juggernaut—mass incarceration, mass supervision, high rates of pretrial detention, excessive financial penalties, far-reaching collateral consequences of criminal convictions—would be called into question. Which of these is "reasonably necessary" to serve a "legitimate societal purpose"? "How can we prevent government overreach?" "What is the least intrusive action that can be taken in any given situation?" Serious pursuit of this logic would require the development of a regime of alternative sanctions that do not entail excessive liberty deprivations. It would unleash the creative process of finding new ways to achieve accountability for wrongdoing and the repair of harm.

Fidelity to the parsimony principle is not tantamount to an embrace of the abolitionist position. The parsimony principle, rooted in classic social contract theory, recognizes the legitimacy of the exercise of state power in the administration of the criminal law. The state would still have the power to define certain behaviors as criminal. Sanctions for violating those laws would still be permissible. Individual liberty could still be constrained. But each state action depriving an individual of liberty would be closely scrutinized to determine whether the goal of the sanction was legitimate, and whether the sanction in question constituted the least restrictive means of achieving that goal. If taken seriously, these guideposts would point the way to a fundamentally new vision of justice.

This book explores the application of a parsimonious approach to different aspects of the criminal justice system. Parsimony, taken together with other key measures—an honest reckoning with historic harms, respect for human dignity, transparency, and shared governance—offers a concrete framework for rethinking and redesigning the way we respond to criminal behavior.

Over the past decade, the clarion call to "end mass incarceration" has gained political traction. Yet calls for criminal justice reform have been ringing out from the onset of "the era of punitive excess." [2] In 1971, incarcerated people in the Attica prison uprising led the demand for humane treatment in incarceration. During that same period, the American Friends Service Committee argued for short, fixed sentences to counteract racial bias. Scholars, including the Norwegians Thomas Mathiesen and Nils Christie, named prison abolition as a goal for public policy. But these voices were drowned out by the chorus calling for more and more punishment. The incarceration juggernaut continued to grow, notwithstanding the ballooning costs, the rising human toll, the accumulated evidence of ineffectiveness, and the international condemnation of America's punitive policies as outliers among Western democracies.

By the late 1990s, when mass incarceration had fully emerged, a diverse range of voices across the political spectrum sounded the alarm that the country had gone off course. Political progressives on the left pointed to the deep harms of mass incarceration. Libertarians from the right decried the excessive reach of state power, pointing as examples to the unbridled criminal codes and the criminal forfeiture of private property. Fiscal conservatives spotlighted the seemingly unstoppable rise in the costs of incarceration, which were squeezing out other public expenditures at great expense and minimal benefits to taxpayers. Evangelical Christians and other religious leaders asked how the deprivation of liberty could be squared with scriptural commands to honor human dignity and support one's personal journey to salvation.

The political bedfellows in this chapter of our history were indeed odd. Social activist Van Jones and Republican firebrand Newt Gingrich joined forces to call for a 50 percent reduction in America's prison population, dubbed #Cut50—a goal supported by a $50 million grant by liberal financier George Soros to the American Civil Liberties Union. Grover Norquist, tax reduction advocate and head of Americans for Tax Reform, joined the call for fewer prisons as a cause for conservatives, largely as a cost-saving measure. Efforts to reduce the prison populations by stalwart Republicans such as Texas governors George W. Bush and Rick Perry were applauded by prison reformers. A new organization— Right on Crime—was formed in 2007, and by 2014 had attracted over seventy conservative leaders to sign onto a statement of principles emphasizing a cost-effective justice system that "protects public order, restores victims, and reforms wrongdoers."[3]

In the late 1990s, the call for prison abolition was renewed by Angela Davis, Rose Braz, and Ruth Wilson Gilmore, who together led the movement organization Critical Resistance. In 2003, Susan Tucker and Eric Cadora, leaders of The After Prison Initiative at the Open Society Foundation, called for a commitment to "justice reinvestment," a radical reorganization of fiscal priorities designed to reduce prison budgets and reinvest those funds in communities damaged by mass incarceration.

More incremental reforms were also being implemented during this period. Police departments were experimenting with "community policing," which held out the promise of more effective policing strategies and improved relationships between police and communities. Around the turn of the century, the Clinton administration's Department of Justice also launched an initiative to provide support for people leaving prison. This federal commitment to support prisoner reentry was crystallized in the Bush administration's Second Chance Act of 2007.

By the second decade of the twenty-first century, the time was ripe for change. The global financial crisis of 2008 had gutted state budgets, and, after reaching a peak in 2008, imprisonment rates began to fall. Rates of violent crime, which had risen steadily starting in the early 1960s, peaked in 1991 and declined sharply through the early 2000s. The 2010 publication of *The New Jim Crow: Mass Incarceration in the Age of Colorblindness* by Michelle Alexander, which vividly traced the ways that American justice policies had created a new racialized caste system, galvanized opposition to the status quo. The administration of Barack Obama, under the leadership of Attorney General Eric Holder, embraced the goal of reducing the nation's prison population. Law professor and social activist Bryan Stevenson launched the Equal Justice Initiative to increase awareness of the history of lynching in the U.S. and expose the linkage between the history of enslavement and mass incarceration.

The philanthropic sector—including legacy foundations such as Ford and MacArthur as well as new entrants funded by Silicon Valley titans and hedge fund entrepreneurs—also made substantial commitments to reducing the footprint of the justice system. Even the administration of Donald Trump, who loudly pronounced a law-and-order agenda, counted some progress in justice reform, most notably the enactment of the First Step Act, which resulted in the release of thousands of people from federal prisons.

Candidates running for the office of prosecutor, a role traditionally aligned with the conservative status quo of law enforcement, were elected in major urban jurisdictions as champions of reform. They ran on platforms committed to ending cash bail, declining to prosecute minor crimes, reducing prison sentences, investigating police abuses, and establishing units dedicated to reviewing old cases to determine whether their offices had unjustly put people in prison.

By all outward measures, the left-right coalition supporting significant reforms held. During this period of promise a National Academy of Sciences report was released in 2014, determining that, among other things, the growth in incarceration had done little to control crime but was closely associated with the many hardships of American poverty, and also concluding that the unprecedented expansion of state power was driven by politics and policy, not crime rates. The report's call for significant reductions in prison populations resonated with the tenor of the times.

In 2020 the landscape of the justice reform movement changed dramatically. The murder of George Floyd and the widespread outpouring of anger and demands for deep changes realigned the terms of political engagement on criminal justice issues. The Movement for Black Lives trumpeted its commitment to "ending the criminalization, incarceration and murder of African Americans."[4] Activists adopted a new rallying cry to "defund the police," and several cities responded by reducing police budgets and investing in community-led responses to crime. A number of cities developed new responses to individuals facing mental health crises or substance use disorder that did not rely on the police. In even more radical language, activists rallied again to abolish police, prisons, and jails. More broadly, movement leaders proposed to reduce the power of the state in responding to community harms, while building community capacity to perform these functions.

Every major candidate for the 2020 Democratic presidential nomination pledged to reduce the prison population and reduce racial disparities in the justice system. The Movement for Black Lives, channeling outrage over the police killings of Black men and women, had unleashed unprecedented street protests and demands for community-led safety strategies and reduced reliance on the police. A widespread call for a racial reckoning with the legacy of white supremacy had led to a series of public events such as the toppling of statues of Confederate generals, the renaming of military bases, and the somber commemoration of the Tulsa Race Massacre. The national response to the opioid epidemic, which favored treatment over punishment for substance use predominantly among a white population, stood in stark contrast to the far more punitive response in the 1980s to crack cocaine that predominantly targeted Black Americans.

The new demands for abolition and for shifting resources from police budgets to community organizations emerged, however, at an inauspicious time. Amid the COVID-19 pandemic, rates of violent crime, particularly homicides and shootings, rose sharply. In a few short months, the balance of the reform discourse shifted radically, and the justice reform movement, which had made steady if modest gains for two decades, was facing significant headwinds. Mayors were elected in New York City, Atlanta, Buffalo, and Seattle promising to crack down on crime and explicitly rejecting calls to reduce police budgets. Voters in Minneapolis, once the epicenter of anti-police protests following the murder of George Floyd, soundly defeated a ballot amendment that would have abolished its police department and created a Department of Public Safety. Some progressive prosecutors who were elected to office on reform platforms faced recall petitions. Other reform-minded prosecutors had their powers limited by conservative state legislatures or faced active resistance from law enforcement unions.

The Biden administration has straddled the debate, providing more funding for police while also supporting a ten-year, $5 billion investment in community-led anti-violence initiatives. As this volume was being assembled, the debates over criminal justice reform were further reshaped by the troubling spike in gun homicides that hit the country during the pandemic. The forces resisting reform pointed to this trend as proof that the reforms had gone too far. The consequence of this new reality—whether it represents a durable blockage of the forward momentum needed to redesign the American approach to crime and safety or is only a temporary setback—remains to be seen.

Calls for the abolition of police and prisons raise the question of what would stand in their stead. Similarly, reformers' calls to rein in an overreaching government require the articulation of the contours of a new and just regime. This book seeks to navigate the tricky terrain between the extreme calls for abolition and the minimalist calls for system reform, guided by some simple truths. We are clear-eyed about the historical narrative that the state, without democratic safeguards, will tend to abuse its powers. We recognize the harsh reality that the criminal law has been an instrument of white supremacy throughout American history. We also acknowledge that adherence to the principle of parsimony to reduce the current footprint of the criminal justice system does not easily translate into a new vision of justice. Yet the contributors all embrace the challenge posed by abolitionists to start over, in the words of Angela Davis, by "creatively exploring new terrains of justice where the prison no longer serves as our major anchor."[5] Respect for the principle of parsimony can provide an anchor to this process of exploration. Yet the task of reimagining justice requires looking beyond the traditional criminal justice system to find new ways to provide safety, justice, and healing.

Historical Reckoning

To galvanize a public and professional community around the principle of parsimony requires an understanding of the long history of harms and injustice that have been perpetrated in the name of law and order. This reckoning with history helps reveal how institutions that are charged with the task of safety have operated as instruments of control and isolation. History explains why the demographic contours of mass criminalization and incarceration align so neatly with racial exclusion and extreme poverty. Understanding the history of slave patrols, convict labor, Black codes, the terrorism of lynching, the violent suppression of Black political power after Reconstruction, and the role of police and courts in enforcing white supremacy propels the demand for a new vision of justice. Such a process may share more with the trials at Nuremberg, or truth and reconciliation in Johannesburg, than with the sausage machine of policymaking in state legislatures.

Historical reckoning is a truth-telling about the past—about the harms that have been suffered and the actions of those responsible. Truth-telling yields a new kind of politics. Those who have been harmed by police and prisons have often been further dehumanized at the hands of the justice system. A new politics rejects simple moral distinctions that divide the world into good and bad. "Nonviolent drug offenders" and the wrongfully convicted have suffered egregious injustice, but a politics grounded in truth-telling must be capacious enough to rail against the years of imprisonment for someone who has robbed a neighbor at gunpoint, or even taken a life. A politics of truth-telling must be able to say that hurting others is wrong, but piling on the pain of excessive incarceration only doubles the injustice.

Healing with Dignity

The machinery of the American justice juggernaut too often engages in systematic and gratuitous degradation of the individuals it is designed to serve. Victims of crime are frequently traumatized by their interactions with the police and other justice officials. Participants in court proceedings—whether victims, witnesses, defendants, family members, or simply observers—are rarely treated with dignity and respect. Observers of modern criminal courts find the proceedings alienating and opaque. The facilities where individuals are held awaiting trial, the courtrooms where cases are processed, and the prisons that house people convicted of crimes are typically old, poorly maintained, and dehumanizing. American prisons have been marked by high levels of violence, poor health care, rampant illnesses, and extensive use of solitary confinement, all of which reflect official disdain for the dignity of the incarcerated population.

Throughout American history, police have used their arrest powers to target racial minorities and immigrants, denying them their individual humanity. The processes of arrest, fingerprinting, detention in a police cell, followed by an appearance in a courtroom surrounded by bureaucratic officials who speak the foreign language of criminal procedure and make decisions on liberty in a matter of minutes, all represent a brutal psychological assertion of state power.

If the individual's guilt is established, the formal diminution of citizenship status takes hold. Convicted individuals can be denied welfare benefits, student loans, public housing, and eligibility to work in wide swaths of the labor market. Individuals convicted of felonies can be denied the right to vote, thereby ratifying the reality of second-class citizenship. The reality that these rituals of degradation are routinely deployed against people of color, immigrants, and individuals struggling with

poverty and other hardships underscores the power of the justice juggernaut to sustain and exacerbate racial and economic hierarchies.

The antidote to degradation is healing, and the motivating value is human dignity. A system that honors the value of human dignity attends
to the actual harms suffered by victims. This means attending to their
physical and emotional injuries, compensating them for economic losses,
and helping them find a pathway back to everyday life. The value of human dignity must also be extended to those who have harmed others.
Accountability that respects human dignity should not involve the dehumanization and humiliation that are now baked into the court process and incarceration. Human dignity also demands respect for human
agency, and the accompanying capacity for change and redemption. Finally, respect for human dignity requires recognition of the reality that
many people who harm others have themselves been harmed. Recognizing and addressing the trauma in their lives would serve the cause of justice by setting aside the damaging polarity of victims versus offenders and
provide new opportunities for personal growth and redemption.

There is widespread agreement among the contributors to this book
that causing harm to another incurs a debt for which a process of accountability is the remedy. But accountability is not synonymous with
punishment, and relieving the effects of trauma must also be paramount
in response to a punitive regime that has responded to violence by multiplying it. The principle of human dignity would transform prisons and
jails.

Respect for human dignity requires community investment, so the
untreated mental illness, drug addiction, and homelessness that often
lead to jail are alleviated in a non-blaming way. Public policy has a special
obligation to young people in this context. For those youth who might
otherwise face detention, human dignity would call for the creation of
off-ramps to a network of community support, with special attention
given to addressing childhood traumas, especially early exposure to
violence.

Correctional staff also live with deep trauma, and a healing institution oriented to safety would minimize the violence of incarceration
and provide for the humanization of incarcerated people and staff alike.
The same commitment would be extended to all other professionals who
work in the justice system.

The reimagination of the modern criminal justice system to honor the human dignity of all individuals involved, respond effectively to the trauma they experience, and provide opportunities for healing and the restoration of damaged relationships would be fundamentally transformative.

Power Sharing

Running through the ideas of parsimony, reckoning, and healing is a shift in the balance of power. Justice should not be *done to* communities of color and poor neighborhoods in which incarceration is concentrated. Instead, communities should be the authors of their own safety, where their remedies for their family and neighbors are not degrading and exclusionary but rather are socially integrative. Building and sustaining community power are as critical to reimagining justice as reducing harsh and retributive punishment.

In a liberal democracy, the state's capacity for violence through its police and prisons should be subject to control by civilian authority based on popular representation. Police are often deployed as an occupying force, respond to protests equipped with military gear, and are rarely held accountable for their actions. Prosecutors and courts wield enormous power with little regard for the impact of their decisions on public well-being. Jails and prisons are closed institutions that resist the external scrutiny of journalists, courts, and governmental oversight. Community residents who are sentenced to prison terms are shipped to remote facilities, losing connection with family and neighbors. In the era of punitive excess, the agencies of the justice system have largely operated with minimal transparency or civilian oversight. As a consequence, democracy is diminished and community power is depleted.

In a reimagined justice system, communities themselves would have a much stronger hand in designing how and for whom safety is achieved. The pursuit of justice would draw upon community strengths to advance the goals of healing and forgiveness. The accountability of public officials would be obtained through a commitment to transparency and civilian oversight. Sanctions for community members who harm others would show unwavering respect for their value and dignity and be proportionate to the harm they've committed. These changes would represent a new politics of justice.

Skeptics will say that we romanticize community voice as a force for fundamental change. We recognize that community residents want safety above all else and regularly turn to police and prisons for help. But this reflex operates in a context where residents are offered few alternatives. Power sharing is needed because police and penal institutions who claim responsibility for safety have often failed to provide it. Power sharing enlarges the menu of strategies for safety. Better education, health care, and housing, for example, can all help provide security and routine in daily life. In the absence of strong community voice, punishment is the only dish being served, despite the public appetite for improved public health, material well-being, and economic opportunity.

The essays in this volume reflect the thinking of a remarkable, forward-looking group of activists, government officials, foundation executives, academics, and lawyers who came together at a moment when the modern American approach to safety and justice was under intense challenge. The contributors all demonstrate the importance of identifying principled limits on the exercise of state power, an approach with the potential to create common ground across ideological boundaries, as conservatives and progressives delve into the implications of aggressive adherence to the presumption of liberty, and find perhaps surprising alignment on the notion of limited government in the context of the justice system.

The opening chapter of this volume applies the principle of parsimony to a range of criminal justice practices—long prison sentences, the use of solitary confinement, and the extensive network of collateral consequences of criminal convictions. A chapter on violent crime looks at the broad definition of the "violent offender" and uses it as a cautionary case study in unspeakably gratuitous deprivations of liberty and overreach of criminal law. Lest the reader think that no progress is possible in curtailing these abuses of state power, a chapter on youth prisons adds an encouraging case study of a context in which this deprivation of liberty has already been significantly reduced.

Other chapters explore examples of the power of historical reflection and the potential for liberation that it provides. In Portland, Oregon, county criminal justice officials worked with community representatives to probe a virulent history of racial exclusion. Learning and documenting the history set the stage for the development of a local housing program that provided shelter and support for Black women leaving prison and returning to neighborhoods around Portland. From their seats on the bench, the judiciary, as other contributors assert, also face a reckoning on the nation's shameful history of lynching, and the countless mandatory sentences that have been meted out to overwhelmingly Black and brown defendants. The realm of education also provides a truth-telling opportunity. The denial of education has been a cudgel subjugating African Americans, beginning in the era of enslavement and now continuing to the era of mass incarceration. The only way to counter this history, as one chapter argues, is to recognize affirmatively that education is a path to liberation.

Several chapters explore the theme of power sharing and its wide-ranging implications, including the transformation of city budgets, and the involvement of community organizations in resolving conflicts among young people and helping them to heal in the aftermath of harm. These forms of power sharing are underway in real and substantial ways in communities around the country, and, as these chapters show, represent a democratic resurgence at a time when the political process has placed community power under acute stress.

The book's final chapters wrestle with practical questions and suggest answers drawing on the contributors' research and experience. As these chapters illuminate, the politics of transformation involve unbridled community activism, coalitions between the right and the left, cooperation between community leaders and criminal justice practitioners, and feasible policy change. Creating a different kind of justice will disrupt the connections between harsh punishment on the one hand, and race, poverty, and violence on the other. Bail reform, relief of fines and fees, curtailing pretextual police stops, drug decriminalization, prosecutorial reform, community-based anti-violence initiatives, housing and health care support for people leaving prison, and the reexamination of long sentences are among the long list of concrete steps dictated by a parsimonious approach. Taken together, they can disrupt the logic of punitive excess.

Each of these efforts at justice asks that we acknowledge the awesome power of the state to cause harm. Most fundamentally, to reimagine justice, we must envision a new role for the state in promoting safety and justice. History teaches that the traditional role in which the state defines criminal conduct and punishes those who violate the law has proven inadequate to achieving true justice and has been deeply harmful to individuals and communities. In a new vision of justice, public policy should empower communities, respect the liberty of individuals, and promote a vibrant and healthy society.

The opportunity—and obligation—to advance this vision rests with all of us. This new vision requires that we confront the urgent problem of community safety. Harm is a central problem to solve for which accountability is necessary, but punitive excess provides no solution. Racial injustice and poverty must be reckoned with if violence is to be meaningfully addressed. In this vision, the values of punishment, retribution, division, and fear are replaced by the values of parsimony, healing, power sharing, and human dignity.

We are invited then to turn toward forgiveness, empathy, fairness, respect, and love, so that our institutions might do the same.

PART I

PARSIMONY

1

THE POWER OF PARSIMONY

Daryl Atkinson and Jeremy Travis

Daryl Atkinson is the co-director of Forward Justice, a law, policy, and strategy center dedicated to advancing racial, social, and economic justice in the U.S. South.

Jeremy Travis is executive vice president of criminal justice at Arnold Ventures, where he leads a team that is implementing reform strategies focused on policing, pretrial justice, community supervision, prisons, and reintegration.

As our country comes to terms with the damage caused by excessive reliance on punishment as a response to crime, by the use of the criminal law to sustain racial hierarchies, and by the ways the justice system has undermined our democracy and weakened communities, we must ask: What principles should guide our transition to a more just America? In this chapter we propose that the principle of *parsimony*—if reconsidered while recognizing the historical racist underpinnings of the American criminal legal system—can facilitate a critique of our history, an acknowledgment of the racist underpinnings of our criminal legal system, and an elevating aspiration for a reimagined approach to justice.

The parsimony principle holds that the state may exercise no more than the lightest intrusion into a person's "liberty interest" needed to achieve a legitimate social purpose. (We define a person's "liberty interest" as their right to be left alone by the state.)[1] Intrusion beyond this is inherently illegitimate and may even constitute state violence. Determining the extent to which any intrusion is necessary, ascertaining the legitimacy of the social purpose, and recognizing the value of beneficial state support all require pragmatic calculations. But the power of parsimony lies in its emphasis on the primacy of the liberty interest and its limitation on state power.

Social contract theory envisions a mutuality of obligations—a "contract"—between the state and its residents. The social contract compels the state to provide people with safety, security, and an opportunity to thrive. In return, residents must cede some of their sovereignty, pay taxes, and abide by state laws. Under the social contract, the state—within constitutional limits—is granted the authority to define as "criminal" conduct viewed as inimical to the safety and security of society. The state is also authorized to hold its inhabitants accountable for committing those crimes, following a determination of legal culpability. The state may impose a deprivation of liberty on someone who breaches the contract. Deprivations can range from mild—such as minor conditions of probation—to more severe, such as a prison sentence and, under some legal regimes, the death penalty. The principle of parsimony, which prioritizes residents' liberty interests, forces us to determine whether any deprivation of liberty, mild or severe, is necessary to achieve a legitimate social purpose. In doing so, it can operate as a check on the exercise of state power.

As we consider the connection between the principle of parsimony and social contract theory, however, we cannot ignore the distance between theory and reality. State power has, throughout American history, upheld a social contract only for some members of society; countless others have been denied its benefits, rights, and privileges. Our country's biggest quarrels have been, and continue to be, over precisely who is included in the proverbial "We" in "We the People." Beginning with the genocide of Indigenous people and the enslavement of Africans, the forces of white supremacy have for centuries leveraged state power to crush the liberty interests and aspirations of Black, brown, Latinx, immigrant, and other dispossessed communities.[2] If social contract theory entails mutual obligations between the state and its inhabitants, the state has failed tragically to keep its end of the bargain in relation to these communities. Put bluntly, there has never been a binding social contract between the United States and these marginalized groups.

Moreover, since the country's founding, the criminal law has been wielded to deliberately undermine the social contract. Laws have propped up oppressive racial hierarchies, advanced the economic interests of a powerful few, stifled political dissent, and protected the status quo. The use of state power to diminish the status of some inhabitants while privileging that of others is a clear violation of the social contract.

As such, the criminal law has undermined the country's trust in, and aspirations for, an effective social contract. This has called into question the legitimacy of the state's authority to enact and enforce the criminal law, particularly among people who have experienced the abuse of state power. The historical harms exercised by the government have corroded trust. They have fostered doubt that the state can be trusted to adopt the fundamental reforms necessary to create an inclusive and equitable social contract.

An honest and explicit reckoning with the use of criminal law as a tool to oppress and marginalize is a precondition to establishing legitimacy in the exercise of state power. Such a reckoning will enable all inhabitants of this country to believe that the state will honor the social contract and grant rights, protections, and liberty to everyone. This process of reckoning could give rise to a trustworthy and legitimate state, one that has the moral authority to uphold the social contract by consistently and justly applying state power. Without a reckoning, the exercise of state power will always be suspect.

Parsimony provides an analytical framework to understand how criminal law has been weaponized to distort the social contract. If reckoning with these historical state failures can help create a new vision of justice, the principle of parsimony can support this ambition. It requires that society affirm the centrality of individual liberty, limit the application of state power, acknowledge our history, and reconstruct a social contract to include communities that have been excluded. The vision of justice that emerges would be grounded in human dignity, social justice, an honest understanding of our past, and vibrant community life. The principle of parsimony, and the reckoning we believe it compels, can make a powerful contribution, as reformers, abolitionists, activists, legislators, and system stakeholders alike bring new energy to the urgent challenge of creating a more just America.

Parsimony is a double-edged sword: it recognizes the legitimacy of state power while asserting the importance of limits on its exercise. State power can be exercised beneficially, as in providing social supports such as health care, public education, housing, and security from harm. These exercises of state power represent what French philosopher Pierre Bourdieu called the "left hand" of the state.[3] Here, however, we are concerned with the state's "right hand": the coercive exercise of state power in ways that limit individual liberty, especially in response to criminal conduct.

Social contract theory holds that the state may impose consequences on people who harm others. To be legitimate, however, this coercive exercise of state power must be limited. Modern Western philosophical reflections on this topic date back to the eighteenth century. Philosopher Cesare Beccaria, for example, wrote that retributive sanctions imposed by the state must be *proportionate*, both to the offense itself and to the goal of deterrence: "Punishments are unjust when their severity exceeds what is necessary to achieve deterrence."[4] Philosopher Immanuel Kant similarly described punishment as an evil to be used only when necessary. Philosopher Jeremy Bentham articulated the parsimony principle even more strongly—"All punishment is mischief: all punishment in itself is evil. . . . If it ought at all to be admitted, it ought only to be admitted in as far as it promises to exclude some greater evil."[5]

Legal scholars have also debated the principle of parsimony, discernible in many of this country's foundational political documents. The constitutional amendments ratified in the Bill of Rights were explicitly designed to limit the power of the federal government while guaranteeing personal rights and freedoms to members of society. The Eighth Amendment, for example, codifies parsimonious principles by prohibiting cruel and unusual punishment and barring excessive bail and fines. The Fourth Amendment, which protects people from "unreasonable" searches and seizures without probable cause, also reflects the parsimony principle.

In "The Future of Imprisonment," a 1974 law review article, legal scholar Norval Morris defined the principle of parsimony as "the least restrictive or least punitive sanction necessary to achieve defined social purposes."[6] Morris explained the principle's roots in moral precepts: "It is utilitarian and humanitarian; its justification is somewhat obvious since any punitive suffering beyond societal need is, in this context, what defines cruelty."[7] He viewed the parsimony principle as the "Hippocratic criminal justice oath," requiring that criminal sanctions do no more harm than required to achieve legitimate social purposes.[8] Relatedly, legal scholar Michael Tonry considers parsimony as grounded less in principles of punishment than in more general values of justice. Parsimony demands that people be treated with equal respect and concern, in a way that affirms their fundamental human dignity.[9]

Parsimony also undergirds legal scholars' efforts to guide the enforcement of the criminal law. The Model Penal Code of 1962, for example, argues that courts should impose the "least restrictive alternatives" as a condition of pretrial release and criminal sentences.[10] Legal scholars at the American Law Institute recently reaffirmed parsimony as a guiding principle. In 2017, after a fifteen-year reexamination of the Model Penal Code, the American Law Institute approved an expansion of the application of the parsimony principle to include decisions to defer prosecution, impose collateral consequences, and adopt sentencing guidelines.[11]

Notwithstanding this historical tradition, the principle of parsimony does not have a high profile in today's debates over the reach of the criminal justice system, including regarding mass incarceration. As criminologist Mary Bosworth notes, "Criminology has a rich tradition of valuing restraint, tolerance, and 'peacemaking,' and has many times extolled the virtues of a minimum necessary penal system. But such literature is today dimmed, if not altogether disappeared from sight."[12] Yet the parsimony principle still has its advocates. Jamie Fellner, senior counsel in the U.S. program at Human Rights Watch, recommended that parsimony be centered in sentencing debates. She notes that while "few may use the term parsimony, many have come to understand that unnecessarily harsh sentences make a mockery of justice."[13]

A landmark 2014 report of the National Research Council—*The Growth of Incarceration in the United States: Exploring Causes and Consequences*—affirmed the importance of parsimony. After reviewing the history of the four-fold expansion of incarceration rates in the United States, this interdisciplinary consensus panel concluded that an "explicit and transparent expression of normative principles has been notably missing as U.S. incarceration rates dramatically rose over the past four decades."[14] The report recommended that future justice policy should reflect four normative principles: proportionality, parsimony, citizenship, and social justice. Parsimony, according to the panel, "expresses the normative belief that infliction of pain or hardship on another human being is something that should be done, when it must be done, as little as possible." [15] The report also linked the concept to the larger concern for social justice, noting, "Parsimonious use of punishment may not only minimize unnecessary use of penal sanctions, including imprisonment, but also limit the negative and socially concentrated effects of incarceration, thereby expanding the distribution of rights, resources, and opportunities more broadly throughout society." [16]

Despite parsimony's historical presence in our philosophical and legal traditions, we acknowledge again that practice has frequently strayed far from theory. The punishment meted out by U.S. courts has often been more severe than required to achieve a legitimate social purpose. The criminal law has been used to suppress free speech, protect the interests of corporations and other powerful actors, limit opposition to the status quo, and further marginalize those already denied the state's benefits. This use of the criminal law as a tool of oppression strains the social contract, seemingly beyond repair.

Viewed against this history, the values that should limit state power—including the principle of parsimony—can appear inadequate to the task of restoring a legitimate relationship between government and the governed. But this is the work that lies ahead. By reinvigorating the legal and policy discourse to once again emphasize parsimony, we can illuminate how far our modern criminal legal system has strayed from its own Hippocratic oath to do no more harm than absolutely necessary to achieve a legitimate social purpose. An honest reckoning with our country's history of abusing state power through the criminal law is the first step on the long path toward reimagining justice.

Given modern punitive excess, the unequal enforcement of the social contract, and the racist use of the criminal law throughout U.S. history, there are few examples of the successful application of the parsimony principle. Yet, at a time when advocates are demanding fundamental reforms and activists are calling for the abolition of police and prisons, the principle of parsimony can provide more than a critique of current realities. Perhaps, as we build a more equitable and effective approach to criminal conduct, parsimony—with its affirmation of the primacy of human liberty and its insistence on limits to state power—can provide new models for the core functions of the justice system.

A two-pronged analysis allows us to apply the principle of parsimony to specific justice practices: first, to determine whether the deprivation of liberty serves a "legitimate social purpose," and second, to ascertain whether it is "reasonably necessary" to achieve that purpose. If either of these two standards is not met, the practice is, in Beccaria's words, "unjust." As Morris notes, "Any punitive suffering beyond societal need is, presumably, what defines cruelty." [17]

What does the principle of parsimony say about prison sentences? The aforementioned National Research Council report asked two essential questions about mass incarceration: What drove the four-fold increase in incarceration rates over the past four decades? And what were the consequences of this unprecedented expansion? After an exhaustive review of the research literature on the first question, the panel agreed that the explosion in the prison population owed to three simultaneous trends: the increased use of mandatory minimums, the launch of the War on Drugs, and policy decisions to make long sentences even longer.[18] Mass incarceration, as the report carefully documents, resulted from a series of choices in sentencing policy, fueled by the politics of the "tough on crime" era and grounded in implicit and explicit racism. Importantly, the panel also reached two further conclusions. First, the increase in incarceration in the United States was not driven by an increase in crime rates; second, the expansion of imprisonment produced no significant public safety benefits. Applying the parsimony principle to a fundamental rethinking of sentencing policy could lay the groundwork for a sharp reduction in the prison population.

First, we must ask whether the deprivation of liberty inherent in a prison sentence serves a legitimate social purpose. All criminal sanctions—from least onerous to most severe—can serve three purposes. They can deter future crime, rehabilitate someone found guilty of a crime, and provide appropriate retribution for the harm caused. Deterrence and rehabilitation have a common goal: to prevent future crime. Deterrence can operate at the individual level ("specific deterrence," which either decreases the likelihood a person will engage in criminal conduct, or prevents them doing so via incapacitation) or at the societal level ("general deterrence"). The test of effectiveness is straightforward: Does the imposition of a criminal sanction deter its recipient—and others—from engaging in future criminal conduct? Rehabilitation, in a similar fashion to specific deterrence, operates at the individual level. To assess efficacy, we ask whether providing supportive services via a criminal sanction will prevent the recipient from violating the law in the future.[19] (The retribution rationale is discussed separately below.)

Promoting safety and communal well-being is a core function of the state. Indeed, the expectation that governments provide security for the governed is an explicit part of the "bargain" that constitutes the social contract. Accordingly, because achieving public safety is a legitimate social purpose, the use of the state's coercive power to impose a criminal sanction—in this discussion, a prison sentence—satisfies the first prong of the parsimony test. Too often, however, the public discourse ends there. The second prong of the parsimony test requires a determination of whether the deprivation of liberty is reasonably necessary to achieve this purpose.

The tough-on-crime rhetoric that has dominated American political discourse for the past half-century claims that prison sentences are necessary to produce public safety. Proponents of this view attribute the significant reductions in crime over recent decades to the growth in the prison population. The National Research Council report, however, puts this reasoning to rest. Following an exhaustive research review, the panel of experts concluded that "the increase in incarceration may have caused a decrease in crime, but the magnitude of the reduction is highly uncertain and the results of most studies suggest it was unlikely to have been large."[20]

The parsimony framework, however, requires us to ask whether this penal policy was "reasonably necessary" to promote safety. This shifts the public discussion to consider other, more effective policies that could reduce crime and create public safety. Some may involve only minimal restrictions on liberty, such as effective community supervision instead of a prison term. Crucially, however, a growing list of policies and programs promote public safety with no application of the criminal law and no intrusion on individual freedom. Community-led crime reduction strategies, for example, operate with limited governmental interference to prioritize the rehabilitation and reintegration of community members. The list of proven interventions that reduce crime with minimal—or no—use of criminal sanctions is increasing and the evidence of their effectiveness is promising. Such policies and practices accord with the parsimony principle. They are more effective—that is, more "reasonable"—at achieving a legitimate societal goal and, importantly, intrude less on individual liberty. As we reimagine justice, we should actively promote reforms that are shown to reduce crime with minimal reliance on the coercive powers of the state.

Proponents of prison sentences often claim that they are "reasonably necessary" to promote the rehabilitation of the person convicted of a crime. Rehabilitation is framed as a goal that not only supports public safety, but that promotes individual betterment. Certainly, advancing the well-being of people under criminal justice supervision—especially those who have been removed from the normal cycles of family and community life—is a legitimate social purpose. But is it "reasonably necessary" to deprive someone of their liberty to achieve that goal? Likewise, prisons should offer programs that help incarcerated people realize their potential and prepare them for life in free society. But is it necessary to incarcerate people to improve their lives? We recognize that for some people, time in prison can lead to personal benefits brought by reflection and discovery. But forced removal from society is not how these admirable goals are best achieved. Finally, the goal of rehabilitation is too often twisted into an instrument of control; incarcerated people are coerced to participate in programs "for their own good" and further punished if they do not.

Under the principle of parsimony, the state may advance the legitimate goal of rehabilitation, but must also meet the second prong of the test by demonstrating that this deprivation of human liberty is "reasonably necessary" to achieve that purpose. This is a high hurdle. If someone is already incarcerated for other reasons, providing supportive services in the name of rehabilitation is humane and can be efficacious. But the assertion that rehabilitation is the primary rationale for the deprivation of liberty following a criminal conviction strains logic.

Finally, prison sentences are also justified as necessary to achieve the goal of retribution. Unfortunately, in common parlance, "retribution" is sometimes confused with "revenge" or "retaliation." As a result, it is deemed unworthy of affirmative recognition in our sentencing philosophy. Yet traditional jurisprudential formulations view retribution as a legitimate purpose of the criminal sanction. In this formulation, all criminal sanctions—whether a monetary fine or a prison sentence—are necessary to demonstrate society's disapproval of the underlying criminal conduct, underscoring to society the expectations for good behavior. It also reaffirms the social contract under which people cede to the state the power to determine which harms require formal disapproval. This disapproval can include limitations on individual liberty through imprisonment.

Throughout history, scholars and advocates have debated whether a prison sentence is justified for the sole purpose of expressing public disapproval of a criminal act. Is a prison sentence necessary to hold someone accountable for breaking the social contract? If so, for what crimes, for which people, for how long, and with what opportunities for early release? Is a life sentence ever justified? Should a prison sentence ever be mandatory? Should someone with mental illness ever be sent to prison? How do we ensure that prisons respect human dignity, and that after incarceration, people are restored to full citizenship? How does the criminal legal system acknowledge the harms experienced by victims and survivors?

As these debates continue, the parsimony principle can structure a new dialogue on the role of prisons in our response to crime. This analysis must begin with a recognition of the profound damage that mass incarceration has caused. As the National Research Council report documented, the four-fold increase in incarceration rates has led to untold pain. It has harmed individuals, separated families, weakened communities, hampered economic vitality, and undermined our democracy. The growth in imprisonment has most profoundly impacted young men of color, particularly those who have not graduated from high school. Reversing this damage to our social contract, if possible at all, will take decades. Any calculation of what is "reasonably necessary" to achieve the goals of sentencing must take these harms into account and recognize that they have fallen disproportionately on communities of color.

Public discussions about the harms caused by mass incarceration often move quickly to various reform options. For example, should we repeal three-strikes laws, eliminate mandatory minimums, adopt European-style limits on the length of prison terms, abolish life without parole? These are all worthy goals, but as we reimagine justice, we must ask a more fundamental question: When, if ever, is it appropriate to send someone to prison? This question forces honest confrontation with the place of retribution or "just deserts" in our sentencing philosophy. This question about the legitimate social purpose served by this extreme deprivation of liberty illuminates the fact that our society has for too long worshipped at the altar of punitiveness as a societal necessity. This raises another question: Have we incarcerated so many people because we believe that cruelty to some of us is necessary to affirm the social contract that binds all of us?

Imposing a prison sentence is certainly not the only way to show societal disapproval for criminal conduct. We could follow the lead of the Model Penal Code, which calls for the imposition of "the least restrictive alternative" sanction, and envisions a menu of non-custodial sanctions. This menu of alternatives to incarceration should also be subjected to the parsimony test: Do they advance legitimate societal purposes while imposing the lightest intrusion on liberty? As with proven crime reduction strategies, the list of effective and innovative alternative sanctions is long and growing. Restorative justice practices stand out because they offer new ways to acknowledge harm caused, promote individual responsibility for that harm, and lay a path forward for all parties. But the growth and acceptance of these alternatives has been stunted by the oppressive weight of the tough-on-crime era and our overreliance on prison.

In a thought-provoking departure from the traditional analysis of sentencing policies, a 2017 report highlights the justice goals that long prison sentences fail to achieve: long sentences do not help victims heal, meaningfully hold people accountable, help people change for the better, or effectively prevent violence.[21] The fundamental question of this moment is: Which responses to harms caused in violation of the social contract can accomplish these justice goals—help people heal, hold people accountable, allow for change, promote community health, and prevent violence—while minimizing deprivations of liberty? The parsimony principle points the way to new forms of accountability that rely less on the deprivation of liberty and more on practices that promote healing, human dignity, and community well-being.

A parsimony analysis also proves useful in analyzing another area of justice policy: the collateral consequences of criminal convictions. Over the past four decades, legislatures at all levels of government have enacted restrictions on the lives of people with criminal convictions. These restrictions—called "collateral consequences" or "invisible punishments"—proliferated alongside the four-fold increase in incarceration rates, the doubling of the reach of community supervision, the three-fold growth of pretrial detention rates, and the criminalization of wide varieties of state-defined antisocial behavior.[22] The laws and regulations known as collateral consequences now prevent millions of Americans from participating fully in society.[23]

Collateral consequences can affect every aspect of a person's life—limiting or entirely prohibiting access to public housing, education, and employment opportunities. People with a criminal record may be deemed ineligible for public benefits, like food stamps or government-approved student loans, or restricted from obtaining certain occupational licenses to pursue jobs such as working as a cosmetologist or barber.[24] Statutes restrict where people convicted of sex offenses can sleep, travel, or associate with family.[25] Some statutes also deny people with criminal convictions their right to vote, serve on a jury, or hold public office, creating a second-class of citizens who cannot fully participate in our democracy. Voting restrictions are particularly pernicious because they limit the power of people with criminal convictions to hold their government accountable for the punitive policies that diminish their standing. These legal barriers significantly impinge on liberty interests.[26] Moreover, combined with intrusive probation and parole conditions and the financial burdens of court-imposed fines and fees, collateral consequences are another reminder to justice-involved people that their debt to society can never be fully paid.

The impact of these liberty intrusions is not confined to individuals. The vast reach of the modern U.S. criminal justice system means they have a collective impact. When, for example, a large percentage of a neighborhood's residents have felony records and are excluded from sectors of the labor market, "invisible punishment" has a far-reaching economic impact. Along with state-imposed exclusions, many private employers refuse to hire people with felony records. The net effect is not only diminished lifetime earnings at the individual level, but also a depressed community-level "gross domestic product" in neighborhoods with high rates of justice involvement. The damage is compounded by the restriction on political power as felon disenfranchisement laws reduce the percentage of residents eligible to vote. When we consider the history of racial segregation, redlining, voter suppression, and other manifestations of white supremacy, a clear picture emerges: these restrictions extend the long history of the criminal law as a tool of oppression.

Before considering whether this intrusion on liberty is necessary to achieve a legitimate social purpose, we first recognize a fundamental flaw inherent to these restrictions. In many cases, they were created by irregular legislative processes. Unlike policies that authorize prison sentences, collateral consequences are rarely debated in the legislature or subjected to oversight hearings. They are seldom codified in a state's criminal code. Some were enacted at the federal level yet apply to people with state convictions. Some are embedded in complex statutes governing federal public benefit programs. Many lawyers are not even aware of the full range of possible restrictions, so cannot advise their clients on how their felony conviction might hobble their autonomy.[27] This invisible network of criminal sanctions represents an insidious contortion of traditional democratic processes.

These exercises of state power—which limit liberty, autonomy, and full participation in civil society—are qualitatively different from criminal sentences, fines and fees, and arrests. Their imposition is virtually automatic. There is rarely any adversarial process to challenge these invisible punishments, or a framework for an independent jurist to tailor the sanctions to the needs of the individual. How does one challenge these deprivations of liberty? Which government official is responsible for the regulations? Which legislative committee will consider the implications of collateral consequences?

The framework of the parsimony principle can help critically examine the application of collateral consequences. In virtually every case, they will fail the parsimony test. The test first requires a determination that collateral consequences serve a "legitimate social purpose." The goal of promoting public safety—so often cited as justification for other criminal sanctions—is rarely relevant in the case of collateral consequences. Perhaps this rationale is plausible in a narrow set of circumstances, such as prohibiting an individual convicted of child sexual abuse from working in a childcare capacity; but beyond a few specific cases, it is difficult to articulate a link between these sanctions and the goal of promoting public safety. Moreover, to serve a "legitimate social purpose," collateral sanctions would need to demonstrably reduce crime. In contrast to prisons, however, no significant body of research tests whether these punishments have a deterrent effect. In 2019, the U.S. Commission on Civil Rights found no evidence that collateral consequences are effective beyond those narrowly tailored to prevent future crime, and no evidence that they have a societal benefit.[28] On the contrary, laws that create what Michelle Alexander in *The New Jim Crow* memorably terms a lower "caste" of American citizens seem unlikely to constitute an effective crime reduction strategy. If anything, limits on opportunities for employment, education, stable housing, civic participation, and family stability are likely to create conditions that contribute to crime.

The parsimony framework reveals the truly pernicious nature of these rules and restrictions. The fact that they are called "collateral consequences" perpetuates the myths that they are not themselves real punishments and are only minimally intrusive. Granted, they are less intrusive than other punishments such as prison, probation, parole, and financial penalties. Yet they undeniably constrain individual autonomy. Although their individual and social impact is difficult to document, recent research and storytelling has shed light on their impact. Beyond dispute is the fact that people with criminal convictions are constrained, sometimes for the rest of their lives, from full participation in society. Also beyond dispute is that these state-imposed limitations on freedom fall disproportionately on communities of color, further undermining the legitimacy of the social contract.

This leaves retribution—punishing people for antisocial behavior and signaling social disapproval of criminal conduct—as the primary legitimate social purpose behind these sanctions. But this goal is complicated by the "invisible" nature of these sanctions. They are rarely imposed in public settings such as a courtroom, where a judge—as the agent of the state—can articulate societal disapprobation. Moreover, these sanctions are typically long-lasting, involve few opportunities for relief, are often disproportionate to the offense, and are not tailored to a person's circumstances. Collateral sanctions add retribution upon retribution— they are gratuitously and automatically imposed in addition to other criminal sanctions. To limit this example of punitive excess, we must call on core values of our democracy. These include the right to due process in the application of the law, the need for proportionality between offense and punishment, and the right to challenge state actions. It is difficult to reconcile these values with the insidious web of collateral consequences.

Collateral consequences underscore the need for guardrails on the

state's punitive powers. The collateral consequences enacted by our legislatures are not "reasonably necessary" to express this disapproval. They
do not constitute the "least restrictive alternative" as demanded by the
Model Penal Code. They do not reflect the "do no harm" aspiration of
Morris's criminal justice Hippocratic oath. Collateral sanctions fail the
parsimony test and harm marginalized communities, undermining the
legitimacy of the criminal law and weakening the social contract.[29]

The parsimony principle also has strong implications for the use of
solitary confinement within prisons. As the number of incarcerated
people grew rapidly through the tough-on-crime era, the United States
failed to invest in more humane facilities that could accommodate larger
populations. The well-established correctional principle of "one man,
one cell" gave way to double- and even triple-celling people who were
incarcerated.[30] As overcrowding grew, prison conditions deteriorated,
recreational programs were discontinued, and prison programming was
significantly cut. Many states restricted family and conjugal visits. In
1994, federal funding for college education programs was stopped. State
and federal governments curtailed programs designed to facilitate successful reentry into free society such as halfway houses, educational and
work-release programs, and compassionate release.[31]

The increasingly punitive conditions of confinement are perhaps best
captured by the growing use of solitary confinement. Although precise
numbers are hard to come by, the practice has become common. Between
1995 and 2000, the number of people in solitary confinement grew
by 40 percent, outpacing the 28 percent growth in the overall prison
population.

Solitary confinement, sometimes called "administrative segregation,"
is a long-standing practice in the corrections field. First used in the
Pennsylvania prison system in the nineteenth century, the practice was
thought to promote penitence and thus rehabilitation through isolation.
It was used sparingly and only for short periods of time.[32] In the 1970s
and 1980s, however, solitary confinement became a popular technique to
"keep prisons safe."[33] In the modern version of the practice, a person is
confined to an eight-by-ten-foot cell, about the size of a car parking spot,
twenty-three hours a day, with an hour outside the cell for recreation or
other activities.[34] Typically, periods of confinement are short, measured
in days. But the U.S. context is noteworthy for its long periods of solitary;

a survey found that 18.6 percent of people in restrictive housing were held 15–30 days, 27.5 percent were held 31–90 days, 16 percent 181–365 days, 14.5 percent one to three years, and 9.6 percent more than three years, of which 5.7 percent were in restrictive housing for six years or more.[35] Louisiana holds the record for the longest solitary confinement stay of a single person at forty-four years.[36]

The detrimental effects of solitary confinement are well documented. Studies find that just a few days in segregation can cause increased anxiety; hypersensitivity to stimuli; hallucinations; diminished impulse control; severe and chronic depression; appetite and weight loss; heart palpitations; talking to oneself; problems sleeping; nightmares; self-mutilation; difficulties with thinking, concentration, and memory; and lower levels of brain function, including a decline in electrical activity in the brain.[37] Self-harm, including suicide, is significantly more prevalent in populations subjected to solitary confinement.[38]

Moreover, these serious individual-level harms do not account for the practice's broader impact both within the prison community and beyond the prison walls. Research rarely considers the stress suffered by families worrying about the well-being of their incarcerated loved ones, or the damage and scars carried home by returning citizens who have been confined in these inhumane conditions. In this era of mass incarceration, firsthand experience in an eight-by-ten-foot isolation cell is no longer rare. A research team led by sociologist Bruce Western made this stunning finding: 11 percent of African American men in Pennsylvania have spent time in solitary before the age of thirty-two.[39] Solitary confinement "remains a mainstay of prison management and control in the United States."[40]

The parsimony framework demonstrates that solitary confinement, as currently practiced in the United States, cannot be justified. Not only does it severely intrude on people's autonomy and liberty interests, but also inflicts psychological pain, damages physical health, and deprives people of basic human needs like sensory stimulation and human connection.

The first step in our analysis is to ask whether the practice of solitary confinement serves a legitimate social purpose. The purpose generally used to justify the practice is safety within the prison. In this view, the institution's ability to isolate someone from the general population— either in response to a rules infraction or to interrupt a cycle of violent behavior—is an essential tool to provide a safe and secure environment. Certainly, administering prisons that are safe and humane is a legitimate and necessary function of government. To do so, correctional administrators create rules for appropriate conduct and, as with criminal codes, also specify that violations may lead to certain sanctions. They often prescribe removal from the general population in response to the most serious breaches.

Yet even this generous interpretation of a rationale does not begin to justify the excesses of the current practice. How could this explanation ever support years or decades in isolation? While a limited period in solitary confinement—with ample due process guarantees—could be seen as proportional to egregious misconduct, analogous to a short prison sentence for someone convicted of a serious crime, how can we justify the degrading conditions that characterize administrative segregation in American prisons?

The parsimony framework requires us to ask whether solitary confinement is reasonably necessary to promote safety within a prison. Borrowing language from the Model Penal Code, we can ask, "Is solitary confinement the 'least restrictive' sanction that can be imposed for institutional infractions?" To answer this question, we need to consider other ways prisons can maintain order. We could learn from other countries' principled limitations on the use of solitary confinement. Germany, for example, has a two-week limit on solitary confinement, though the practice is rarely invoked. Domestic examples can also be informative. For instance, the Maine Department of Corrections reduced the population held in solitary confinement by more than half while experiencing no significant change in levels of institutional violence.

If current forms of solitary confinement far exceed what is "reasonably necessary" to achieve safe and secure prisons, is there another justification for the practice? Perhaps it helps reinforce a prison's rules of conduct, just as criminal sanctions are justified as expressing societal disapproval of crime. But punishments imposed by punitive institutions have few guardrails. They represent a virtually unfettered expression of vengeance by a government agency—the prison—with enormous power to preserve its own rules and hierarchy. And, as with collateral consequences, this practice is nearly invisible to oversight. Unlike in Germany, where solitary confinement is subject to judicial oversight,

U.S. courts have rarely applied our Constitution's prohibition against cruel and unusual punishment to limit this practice.[41] If we believe that only the lightest intrusion into individual freedom is permissible by the state, the current use of solitary confinement constitutes nothing less than state violence.

Solitary confinement is, in one sense, an easy target for the principle of parsimony. It is clearly excessive and harms human dignity. But should the practice be totally abolished? As with all criminal sanctions that constrain human liberty, the question is not whether the sanction can ever be justified, but rather whether it is reasonably necessary to serve a legitimate social purpose. Can even the most parsimonious use of solitary confinement ever be justified? We do not resolve that question here, but the parsimony principle clearly demonstrates that current U.S. solitary confinement practices cannot be justified.

Other aspects of the justice system would benefit from a parsimony analysis as well, including the state's decision to criminalize certain behaviors, and to examine the application of criminal law to categories of people. We recognize that these policies do not exist in a vacuum—and neither should the application of the parsimony principle. On the contrary, parsimony draws much of its power from the explicit recognition of historical and social context.

The project of reimagining justice must involve a historical reckoning with the legacy of white supremacy that has dominated the modern criminal legal system in the United States. We believe that we need nothing less than a new social contract based on a recognition of this historical oppression and injustice. We must acknowledge the harms inflicted in the name of the "rule of law" and under the guise of "criminal justice" over centuries, up to and including yesterday's news. This is an imagination project of the first order, requiring fortitude, honesty, and a deep commitment to anti-racist principles. The killings of Breonna Taylor and George Floyd in 2020 and the widespread protests calling for racial justice and police reform have given this undertaking new urgency and energy. We believe that a new vision of justice can emerge only through a process of truth-telling about the harms experienced by dispossessed groups, particularly those of African descent, and through an agreement on how to repair those harms.

This new vision of justice also depends on a radical restructuring of the country's social support systems. We need to provide such basic necessities as universal access to health care, good public education, a strong economy, employment opportunities, security in our homes and communities, and a functioning democracy—the functions conferred by the "left hand" of the state. We believe that a robust, trusted social infrastructure for community well-being will lessen the public demand to use the "right hand"—the state's punitive powers.[42] The COVID-19 crisis exposed the weaknesses in both sets of infrastructure. A new social contract that values compassion and empathy will facilitate the emergence of a new approach to justice.

We acknowledge that parsimony is not the only normative principle that merits support as we reimagine justice. The report of the National Research Council on the causes and consequences of mass incarceration in the United States named, in addition to parsimony, the principles of proportionality, citizenship, and social justice as values that should shape a more just and humane response to crime. Each of these is powerful in its own right. Like parsimony, the principle of proportionality—the idea that penalties should be proportionate to the harm caused—limits the state's power to impose criminal sanctions. The principle of citizenship—which we characterize as the imperative to respect human dignity—centers the humanity of all involved in the criminal legal system. The principle of social justice compels us to ensure that state power, including the criminal legal system, is never used to favor one societal group over another, or to defy the notion of equal treatment before the law.

As reformers, abolitionists, activists, legislators, and system stakeholders seek to define a new future for justice in the United States, these building blocks—historical reckoning, a new social contract, and essential normative principles—provide a powerful platform. The principle of parsimony can catalyze the creation of a new model for criminal justice through the questions it compels us to ask: Why do we allow the government to limit human liberty beyond the degree reasonably necessary to achieve a legitimate social purpose? Why do we allow the state to inflict so much pain with no compelling justification? Why do we tolerate state violence that weakens respect for the rule of law, undermines community well-being, and threatens the legitimacy of our democracy? Why do we allow our government, in our name, to pursue law enforcement policies that have perpetuated racial hierarchies and excluded marginalized populations from full social participation? By demanding answers to these questions, we will hasten the end of a shameful era in American history. Only then can we imagine and create a new vision of justice in our country.

2

PRESUMPTION OF LIBERTY: REDUCING PRETRIAL INCARCERATION

Tracey Meares and Arthur Rizer

Tracey Meares is the Walton Hale Hamilton Professor at Yale Law School. She is one of the leading national theorists on police legitimacy and, in particular, how racial narratives influence police relationships with minority communities and how deliberate attention to these issues can influence community engagement with legal authorities and compliance with the law.

Arthur Rizer is the founder of ARrow Consulting, a criminal justice and legal consulting firm. Arthur is also a former police officer and federal prosecutor. Before forming ARrow, he was the founding director of the R Street Institute's program on criminal justice policy.

"It was the smell of . . . death, it was the death of a person's hope, it was the death of a person's ability to live the American dream." This is how Dr. Nneka Jones Tapia described the Cook County Jail, where she served as warden from May 2015 to March 2018. This is where we must begin.

We begin here to make a critical point: subjecting citizens, who are presumed innocent of the crimes they are charged with and whose cases may never go to trial, to pretrial detention is to subject them to a form of social death.

American history is replete with failures to live up to one of the country's basic founding principles: the presumption of innocence. We failed to uphold this principle to enslaved people and, after the Civil War, to those who were emancipated. We failed after Reconstruction and well into the twentieth century, when thousands of Black Americans, mostly in the Jim Crow South, were lynched without proper trials.[1] And today, we continue to ignore this principle when we unnecessarily hold people who are presumed innocent—disproportionately people of color, and overwhelmingly people without means—in pretrial detention, depriving them of liberty. Subjecting citizens who are presumed innocent of the crimes they are charged with, and whose cases may never go to trial, to pretrial detention is subjecting them to a form of social death.

In one devastating example, Kalief Browder spent three years of his life in pretrial detention at Rikers Island in New York City. He was confined in jail on the basis of probable cause that he had stolen a backpack containing money, a credit card, and an iPod, even though the police did not have any physical evidence tying him to the theft. Two of those years he spent in solitary confinement. After he was released, Browder committed suicide. Despite the outrage his death generated, pretrial detention remains common. In fact, during the COVID-19 pandemic, which could have provided a humanitarian justification for release of those confined to jail, defendants spent even *more time* in jail as courts lengthened the allowed window between a defendant's arrest and their bail hearing.[2]

In the face of contemporary practices across the United States, the presumption of innocence appears more like a radical idea than a bedrock principle. To make the presumption of innocence real, we must replace pretrial detention with the presumption of liberty. Detention looks and feels like punishment to those who are detained. Furthermore, detention can make it much harder for someone to defend themselves in court. To ensure that pretrial detention is rare and limited to cases where there is a substantial chance of harm, the state should seek pretrial detention only when it can present evidence that the defendant poses a specific risk to the trial process (different from a generalized harm to society), such as threatening harm to a witness or a victim, juror tampering, or a likelihood of flight. A threat to an individual who is key to the adjudication process is fundamentally different from a generalized harm to society. Detaining a defendant for generalized "dangerousness" is rooted neither in law nor even in public safety when it is based merely on probable cause that the defendant committed the crime of which they are accused.

We can commit to this country's founding principles aided by advancements in technology that allow the state to use other, less intrusive ways to ensure the defendant shows up to trial. Alternatives to pretrial detention include multiple strategies, from confiscating passports and freezing assets, to electronic monitoring, supervised behavioral health treatment, and, in certain circumstances, high monetary bail.

The scale of pretrial detention is staggering and should shock the conscience of all Americans. Of the approximately 547,000 people who are currently being held in local jails, the vast majority, about 445,000, are still awaiting some type of adjudication of their cases and thus are presumed innocent.[3] Importantly, those who are locked up before trial often are not the most dangerous or the highest flight risks—the two rationales often given for pretrial detention—but are simply our poorest citizens.[4]

A huge number of these people face misdemeanor charges. National jail data from the 2010s suggests that roughly four in ten felony defendants in the largest urban counties are detained pretrial. There are no national data on pretrial detention rates for people charged with misdemeanors, who make up roughly 80 percent of the country's 10.3 million annual arrests. But researchers have estimated the rate of misdemeanor defendants detained for more than a week to be 53 percent in the Houston area and 35 percent in New York City. In Philadelphia, roughly 25 percent are detained for at least three days. A study of the Miami-Dade court system reveals that misdemeanor defendants were detained for an average of six days and felony defendants an average of forty-three days.[5] The longer lengths of stay among felony defendants means they make up a greater proportion of those jailed pretrial on any given day, but those with shorter stays "churn" through jail more quickly, meaning many more misdemeanor defendants are detained overall. While exact numbers, especially considering misdemeanants, may be hard to come by, the problem of pretrial detention is clearly massive, affecting hundreds of thousands of people across the country. It is not site-specific, isolated, or limited to the highest-risk people.

Given the current reality of pretrial detention, we are deliberately being ironic in describing the presumption of innocence as "radical." Every American child learns that the presumption of innocence is a bedrock principle of our system of law. Common law has long recognized this principle, with the eight-hundred-year-old Magna Carta declaring that the sovereign could not imprison a citizen "or in any other way ruin [him] . . . except by the lawful judgment of his peers or by the law of the land."[6] We can trace the presumption's lineage back 1,500 years to the Roman Corpus Juris Civilis, enacted by Emperor Justinian.[7] Even the eye-for-an-eye Code of Hammurabi, older still than Roman jurisprudence by 2,200 years and maybe the oldest written law, included this principle by making the unfounded accusation of another an offense punishable by death.[8]

For generations, the presumption of innocence has been touted in the United States as essentially sacrosanct, with its supporters often citing founding father and second U.S. president John Adams: "It's of more importance to the community, that innocence be protected, than it is, that guilt be punished."[9] Although not located in the Constitution itself, the presumption nonetheless plays a major role in American law. The presumption was primarily an informal assumption at the beginning of American legal history, but the principle gained greater weight in *Coffin v. United States* (1895), when the U.S. Supreme Court acknowledged that the presumption of innocence for people accused of crimes is "undoubted law, axiomatic and elementary, and its enforcement lies in the foundation of administration of our criminal law."[10] It is hard to find a criminal justice concept with deeper roots or more solid footing.

In contrast, the broad use of detention for safety's sake has evolved as a new principle for bail decisions over the past few decades, and is an exception without solid foundation in traditional legal philosophy. In 1970, the District of Columbia Court Reform and Criminal Procedure Act established the first legal basis for detaining someone because of the risk they posed to the community. A little over a decade later, the District's approach became the national standard for federal courts under the Bail Reform Act of 1984.[11] When it was challenged, the U.S. Supreme Court upheld the notion of pretrial, preventive detainment in *United States v. Salerno*. According to the Court, the Act did not intend preventive detention as a punishment, which clearly would violate the right to due process in the Fifth and Fourteenth Amendments. Rather, the Court held that pretrial detention functioned merely as the regulation of dangerous people. In this way, the government is able to act on behalf of the community's interest even if it conflicts with individual liberties.[12] In practice, since the 1990s, defendants in federal cases have had to overcome the "presumption of detention"—a burden that is akin to having a trial at which the presumption is guilt and a person must prove their innocence. Not surprisingly, today the federal pretrial detention rate is around 75 percent.[13]

This approach has generated a dangerous precedent. As posed by legal scholar Michael Louis Corrado, "What of any violent offender who has been convicted several times? Does dangerousness alone give the state the right to regulate the freedom of those individuals?"[14] A government that is able to detain its citizens for an act it has not yet proved beyond a reasonable doubt is a capricious government, vulnerable to the whims of policymakers and judges' fears and beliefs about who may be a threat to the community.

The presumption of innocence has not fared better at the state level, despite forty-eight states still having presumptions of pretrial release for all but a few specified types of defendants. The Connecticut constitution is representative when it states that defendants have a right to be released on bail "except in capital offenses, where the proof is evident or the presumption great."[15] In most states, though, the presumption of pretrial release is ignored when capital offenses are charged regardless of the quality of evidence, and some states specify other charges as exceptions, including murder and treason (Indiana), offenses punishable by life in prison (Hawaii), and violent offenses and various drug-related offenses (Louisiana).[16]

And someone who is on probation or parole and charged with violating their supervision can fare even worse in the court system. Often found guilty of technical violations on the say-so of a probation or parole officer, they too can be detained and, if the violation alleged is a criminal charge, usually automatically. In many states, such as New York, a criminal charge is not even needed for automatic and mandated pretrial detention. Simply an additional *arrest*—not even a guilty verdict—violates the terms of supervision. In other words, if you are arrested while supervised, even if your charges are immediately dropped, you will still face a stay in detention until a judge decides whether you will be incarcerated further just for having been arrested—although the state has already determined you didn't commit the crime.

Pretrial detention practices vary widely from state to state, from what bonds they require, if any, to whether they use risk assessment tools, to the conditions placed on those released pretrial. For example, in Connecticut, police have wide discretion—and no statewide guidelines—to release the accused on recognizance or to require secured or unsecured bonds.[17] In Kentucky, on the other hand, it's illegal to profit off bail—so there are no private bail bond corporations.[18] New Jersey made great strides in 2017 by expanding the use of summonses rather than bonds and limiting preventive detention hearings only for those whose charges fit certain criteria.[19] As a result, more than 90 percent of people are released pretrial, and those who lose their liberty do so after a hearing at which the burden of proof is on the state.[20] By 2018, thousands fewer people were in pretrial detention in New Jersey on any given day compared with a few years earlier, with no notable increase in pretrial crime or failure-to-appear rates.[21] Despite what this example suggests, and the ideals set forth in their own constitutions, other states have not followed suit.

This must change. Incarcerating people indiscriminately before they are found guilty erodes basic liberties and cheapens the public perception of jail cells as a form of punishment. When both the innocent and guilty alike are held behind bars, jails also lose their power even to attempt to rehabilitate those who are sentenced between their strained resources and the cynicism this approach breeds in the community. Reforming pretrial detention is essential to convincing the public, and especially those whom the criminal justice system aims to deter, that its punishments are just.

The importance of the presumption of innocence goes beyond its historical provenance. It is a hedge and protection against arbitrary rule. In criminal law, Blackstone's ratio—which states it is better to protect one innocent man from false imprisonment and let multiple guilty people go free rather than harm an innocent—is axiomatic.[22] Presuming innocence is the practical outgrowth of this sentiment. Both see the legal system's priority as minimizing undeserved suffering while attempting to hold the guilty accountable. But there is a trade-off: to protect the liberty of the innocent, society may have to live with potentially dangerous individuals going free prior to conviction.

A different era of history shows the value of the presumption of innocence, and the protection it offers from the "mob rule" of a society that is quick to assume guilt, especially when the accused is a person of color. The horrific "trials" by lynch mob of Black people in the South led to a rewriting of American legal procedure in the 1920s and 1930s, building the modern system upon a foundation of due process and the presumption of innocence.[23]

At the beginning of every jury trial, jurors are instructed to presume the defendant's innocence unless and until the state has proved their guilt "beyond a reasonable doubt."[24] As the U.S. Supreme Court underscored in *Taylor v. Kentucky* (1978), "the ordinary citizen may well draw significant additional guidance" from this reminder.[25] The burden of the proof must always be on the state. To presume someone guilty rather than innocent exacerbates the power disparity between a person and the state, as the burden of proof falls on the person whose resources pale compared to the state's. The presumption of innocence stands not only as a cornerstone principle of American law but as one of its foremost protectors of equality and liberty.

While history and practice may imply that the presumption of innocence is accepted as a part of trial procedure, the principle clearly has not been fully embraced at all points in the legal process—especially prior to trial. One prominent legal scholar has argued that if we truly presumed innocence until proven guilty, it could very well "invalidate" the mainstream use of pretrial detention and bail.[26] In many states, defendants may have their bail set by a lay magistrate with minimal legal training and education—if any at all.[27] Incredibly, bail hearings in which a person's liberty is at stake may occur over video conference and can last a few minutes or even less than a minute. Defendants are not always represented by counsel in these hearings, and the decision to detain, to assess cash bail, or to release—a decision with far-reaching consequences for a defendant's life—is made on the spot, after cursory analysis or discussion.[28] Current failures to presume a person's innocence through all parts of the legal process—including determinations of bail and pretrial detention—directly undermine core American values of justice.

Risk assessment tools, which have recently become prominent, can also determine whether someone's presumption of innocence is respected. Approximately a quarter of the U.S. population lives in a jurisdiction that uses a validated pretrial risk assessment tool.[29] These tools were developed to help courts follow state statutes requiring them to consider a host of factors beyond the charge in making pretrial detention decisions. The tools encourage judges to determine bail conditions based on the tool's prediction of someone's likelihood to make scheduled court appointments without a new arrest. In many places, this judgment of whether a defendant is "high risk" results in courts holding people in jail, typically by setting a high secured money bond.

But while these tools may provide a theoretically objective method to help inform judicial decisions, they don't overrule the presumption of innocence nor lessen the impact of pretrial detention on a defendant's life. When we impose punishment—and this is what pretrial detention is in practice—on people who have not been convicted and are presumed innocent, we must have a good reason grounded in legal jurisprudence and practical realities. Risk assessment tools too often simply codify existing beliefs about "dangerousness" that are at odds with the presumption of liberty, providing an objective veneer to practices that are deeply at odds with important historical legal principles.

Indiscriminate pretrial detention is a clear violation of the presumption of innocence. Defendants are held behind bars pretrial (often in the same place they will be incarcerated if they are found guilty) because of a cursory assessment of their predicted or possible future behavior. Importantly, they have been brought into that assessment process based on a minimal amount of evidence: nothing more than probable cause that they have committed a crime.

While concerns about flight risk are grounded in the court's concern for due process and the right to a speedy trial, pretrial detention on account of perceived danger to the community is orthogonal to the presumption of innocence. It goes almost without saying that one can be "dangerous" yet not involved in the criminal justice system at all; there may be other people in the community that present a risk of "danger" just as high (or low) as the average detainee, but courts clearly have no jurisdiction to grab those people off the street and assess them for potential danger.[30] Procedures exist for detaining, in very limited circumstances, a person who has not been charged with a crime but is nonetheless considered a danger to themselves or the community at large. Those procedures provide substantially more due process protections than a typical bail hearing. But the simple fact of having been arrested allows a court to reach into a person's life and restrict constitutionally protected liberties in a fundamental way. The evidence required for an arrest is insufficient to warrant these kinds of liberty deprivations, and short, assembly-line bail hearings certainly do not solve the problem.

The issue of pretrial detention extends beyond innocent people being temporarily locked away. There are additional costs to this practice. Pretrial detention, already denying liberty, also severely impedes the accused person in defending their case. Practically speaking, a jailed defendant has a limited ability to communicate with or assist their attorney. Many defendants are impoverished and, when detained, lose their jobs, further increasing the likelihood that they will be forced to use under-resourced court-appointed attorneys, many of whom are juggling a myriad of other cases. And the COVID-19 pandemic highlighted how being held pretrial could be a threat to one's health and even one's life: social distancing is impossible behind bars, and prisons and jails have struggled with high case rates throughout the pandemic.[31]

Even if someone who is detained is ultimately found not guilty, the fact that they were held pretrial may still interfere with their reputation, relationships, and place within the community. Because of government transparency rules, booking photos and identifying information may be publicly available, causing significant, permanent collateral damage to the individual's image. Beyond the loss of liberty, detention often brings the mental anguish of being separated from one's loved ones and a loss of income or housing, which are punishments that ripple beyond the defendant to impact their family as well. This anguish may lead to anxiety and depression—as shown poignantly in Kalief Browder's case—as defendants behind bars are held in limbo with little certainty about the timeline and outcome, and with a plea deal as their only apparent way out.[32] Pretrial confinement places extraordinary pressure on defendants to accept plea bargains, even when the government's case is weak.[33] This pressure is especially strong for those awaiting trial on misdemeanor charges, as they typically face shorter sentences than those accused of felonies and may be released for time served while detained.[34] It should not be surprising, then, that study after study shows that pretrial detention increases a defendant's chance of conviction—in part owing to a greater number of plea deals, at least some of which are likely wrongful convictions of innocent but desperate people.[35]

Those detained before trial for felonies often receive significantly harsher sentences than people in otherwise similar circumstances who were free while their cases moved forward. The main reason for this disparity is predictable: the prosecution wields additional leverage—in this case, the power to offer a plea deal that allows defendants to exit pretrial detention. But there is a deeper reason: those who are free can "prove" their trustworthiness by not committing any more crimes and ensuring they comply with all of their pretrial release conditions. Defendants who are released can show their suitability for probation programs instead of incarceration—something that is categorically impossible for those who are detained.[36] On the flip side, those detained may face additional penalties for misbehavior that occurs during their detention, even if it is connected to understandable circumstances resulting from their detention. For example, if someone struggling with mental health is detained, disconnected from their treatment and prescribed medication, and then acts out, any disciplinary infraction imposed can be used against them during a trial or disposition. Put simply, a defendant detained pretrial is effectively presumed guilty, and detention can negatively affect the outcome of their trial in multiple ways, whereas the presumption of liberty can lead to and be a strong argument for their defense.

Finally, for some, any pretrial detention is a more severe punishment than what they would or even could incur if they were found guilty, since millions of people who are found guilty of a crime go on to be supervised in the community. In a study analyzing more than 165,000 cases from 2012 to 2015 in Miami-Dade County, around 81 percent of misdemeanor defendants were given credit for time served as their sentence, meaning no additional jail time, as were 37 percent of felony defendants, meaning that they likely were incarcerated longer awaiting trial than they would have been if they were found guilty and sentenced right away.[37] And felony defendants were even more likely to be sentenced to probation than those charged with misdemeanors.[38]

For all these reasons, the only way we can live up to one of the United States' guiding principles—presuming every person innocent until proven guilty—is to create and respect every person's right to be presumed free until proven guilty as well. This does not mean that every person goes free on their own recognizance, but it does require the state to meet a higher standard, one in which pretrial detention is a last resort.

Given pretrial detention's incredibly large impact on individuals, families, livelihoods, and the idea of justice more broadly, one would think that the decision to detain would only be made when its benefits appear much greater than the harm it will cause, and after a thorough investigation of its effectiveness. However, a recent economic benefit-cost analysis by economist Michael Wilson suggests that the costs of pretrial detention may outweigh the benefits for all but the highest-risk defendants.[39] Our system relies on cursory assessments of flight risk and dangerousness based primarily upon a finding of probable cause that a crime has been committed, and fails to weigh these individual and societal costs. Bail and detention decisions may take just a few minutes. Magistrates often serve as judicial officials and set bail despite, in some cases, not having law degrees. Monetary bail amounts are often set too high, putting bail out of defendants' reach. So, many people who pose no great risk of flight are detained pretrial in jails across the nation. For example, in a recent study, more than half of those accused of misdemeanors from 2008 to 2013 in Harris County, Texas, were detained pretrial; those detained had an average bail amount of $2,786 that they could not afford to make.[40] In contrast, those who pose similar risk but can afford to pay may remain free. As a number of commentators have observed, this situation has essentially created a new form of debtors' prison, where people are incarcerated because of their poverty. As noted by the U.S. Supreme Court in 1951, "Unless this right to bail before trial is preserved, the presumption of innocence, secured only after centuries of struggle, would lose its meaning."[41]

Before considering if and when there are circumstances when the use of pretrial detention might be appropriate, one must first understand the history of punishment in America.

During the early Republic, many crimes were punished by death, banishment, or the severing of limbs. Our nation was founded in part by people who came to the new country as part of their punishment. Roger Williams, one of the founders of Rhode Island, originally was exiled from England for his religious beliefs.[42] While some early state constitutions allowed banishment, more often the punishment for committing a crime, especially a felony, was death.[43]

Punishment also historically included shaming. During the colonial era, colonists could be held in stockades as targets of public ridicule.[44] A few centuries later, one Arkansas town included stockades as a possible form of punishment for parents whose child violated curfew after they had received written notice of a first violation.[45] Shaming has not disappeared, but taken new forms: in the digital age, something as simple as a booking photo posted to social media can be used to shame a person for decades, whether or not they were found guilty.

Over time, punishment came to be identified with incarceration. In contrast to shaming penalties, incarceration, measured in months of confinement as opposed to various types of public degradation, offered more equality among citizens and, moreover, reinforced the idea that in a democratic republic, a citizen's most sacred treasure was their liberty.[46] In America today, incarceration remains a primary mode of punishment, and the prison cell is the most powerful symbol of justice—and injustice. But the message of equality and the sacred idea of liberty are undermined when the "Land of the Free" is the number one incarcerator in the world, renowned for locking her people up and throwing away the key. Make no mistake: pretrial detention is one factor that drives that reputation for hypocrisy.

Pretrial detention makes clear the conflicts between the operation of this nation's criminal laws and its self-image. When someone is detained before trial, for supposed dangerousness or because they were assessed a bail they cannot pay, the consequence is the same as if they were found guilty and delivered punishment.

U.S. law insists that punishment be imposed only after adjudication. To us, this means that the risk of a defendant fleeing or corrupting the trial are the only bases for setting bail and pretrial detention that have historical grounding. As legal scholar Laura Appleman notes, although we don't know the Constitution framers' intentions on bail, "all available evidence points to the fact that pretrial detention . . . was limited to flight risks."[47] And historically, the amount of bail was only allowed to differ between defendants according to this risk.[48] In contrast, pretrial detention is now imposed as a preventive measure, ostensibly to protect public safety by locking up the defendant so they cannot commit any new crimes. Beyond being improperly overused to restrict defendants' liberty and rationalize the use of high monetary bail, this rationale is problematic for at least two reasons.

First, it is not at all clear that pretrial detention advances public safety. Not only does preventive detention have a long history of being over- and inequitably used; research suggests that those who are detained are more likely to commit a crime in the future. One study found that after only two or three days in detention, those deemed to be "low risk" were, once released, about 40 percent more likely to commit a crime before their trial compared with other low-risk people who were detained for twenty-four hours or less.[49] This sad statistic gets worse with time: low-risk defendants who were held for thirty-one days or longer were almost 75 percent more likely to commit a crime upon release than those whose presumption of innocence was honored by pretrial release.[50] While research has not totally captured why this is the case, it's not hard to fathom some of the factors: a person who is detained may lose their job and stable housing, only to come home to the numerous family problems that are related to being locked in a cell. It's no wonder Dr. Jones Tapia described jail as smelling of the loss of hope and the American dream.

Furthermore, research suggests people who are detained for several days before being deemed low risk and released before trial have a 22 percent higher chance of failing to appear for their court date than those who are in similar circumstances but held for twenty-four hours or less.[51] Here, too, the statistic gets worse with time: those who are held in detention for two weeks to a month before being released are 41 percent more likely not to appear compared with those not held in pretrial detention. Making matters worse, the court and the public then judge a person by their recidivism without considering the ways the criminal justice process has harmed them—isolation from family, loss of employment, stigmatization—taking their behavior as proof that they are incorrigible and cannot be rehabilitated. Pretrial detention clearly is misused under the current system and actually undermines its purported goals. Even in "small doses," it is what those in the medical profession would call "iatrogenic"—a well-intended approach that actually creates disease. And let's not forget Blackstone's theory, a Hippocratic Oath for the legal system: first, do no harm. We all want our institutions of criminal legal processing to help us to feel safer. Pretrial detention does not seem to be advancing that cause.

The second problem with the "prevention" rationale is that it lacks proper legal footing. The prediction of someone's risk of committing a new crime is in part based on the assumption that they are guilty of the alleged offense, violating their presumption of innocence. Additionally, many people who are guiltless may appear to pose an additional risk to society. Imagine, for example, someone with mental illness who sometimes behaves erratically. Even if they are innocent, they may be more quickly detained than a person who has committed a crime but appears to be more mentally competent or stable. Not only is this unjust, but detaining the person with mental illness pretrial rather than getting them help in the community further disconnects them from the services and environment that can address their illness. As a result, we actually increase their likelihood of committing a crime.

We can better assuage community safety concerns without infringing on individual liberty by investing in alternatives to pretrial detention. In addition to being more effective and likely less expensive, many of these other methods do not clearly signal punishment in the way that jail detention does. The government already knows how to make careful determinations of dangerousness by following very regulated procedures before depriving a person of their freedom. There is, for example, a long history and practice of involuntarily committing people with mental illnesses to treatment facilities under much more carefully prescribed criteria than those used for pretrial detention (and usually for much shorter periods of time). In even more specific and carefully regulated situations, the state can quarantine a person with contagious diseases to protect public health.[52] Obviously both of these practices limit a person's freedom for the public good, but they do so, at least in the modern era, in places that typically do not smell nor look like death and, critically, are overtly in the business of treatment disconnected from criminal legal processing. We do acknowledge the dark history of compulsory mental health treatment, and that some contemporary mental health facilities represent an American parade of horribles. But while the hospital and the jail may have overlapping consequences, the logic of the jail is not the logic of the quarantine. Following such familiar practices for pretrial detention would be much more in keeping with a parsimonious approach to justice.

Even in instances where state officials believe that pretrial detention is necessary, other, much less restrictive means of making sure that people show up in court can be employed. We can, for example, send text reminders so people don't forget their court dates. We can have them check in with supervision officers via phone calls or mobile apps, providing them with cell phones if necessary. We can also place people on pretrial

3

LEAST RESTRICTIVE ENVIRONMENT: THE CASE FOR CLOSING YOUTH PRISONS

Vincent Schiraldi

Vincent Schiraldi is a senior fellow at the Columbia Justice Lab and senior research scientist at the Columbia School of Social Work. He is former commissioner of New York City's Departments of Correction and Probation, former director of Washington, DC's Department of Youth Rehabilitation Services, and author of the upcoming Not Quite Free: America's System of Mass Supervision and What Can Be Done About It.

On the horizon, therefore, are tens of thousands of severely morally impoverished juvenile super-predators. They are perfectly capable of committing the most heinous acts of physical violence for the most trivial reasons.

—John DiIulio, 1996

They are often the kinds of kids that are called super-predators—no conscience, no empathy. We can talk about why they ended up that way, but first, we have to bring them to heel.

—Hillary Clinton, 1996

Youth justice policy in America has changed drastically since everyone from John DiIulio to Hillary Clinton vilified young people (primarily those of color) in the 1990s. Youth incarceration has dropped by over half since its peak of one hundred thousand young people in 2000. Among activists, formerly incarcerated people, youth correctional leaders, and prosecutors, a growing movement supports ending the use of youth prisons in favor of community programs and forms of support for young people who have run afoul of the law. For the few still sentenced to custody, many states have replaced large youth prisons set far from the community with small, homelike facilities closer to home. As youth crime continues to plummet, there are now calls for the complete decarceration of young people.

After steep increases in adult and youth crime, particularly homicides, in the 1980s and 1990s, youth justice practices were criticized as soft on crime. Policymakers from both parties described members of America's youth as "super-predators," insisting that remorseless adolescents who "do the adult crime . . . should do the adult time." Researchers issued wild—and, as it turned out, wildly inaccurate—forecasts of a "blood bath of teen violence" unleashed by hundreds of thousands of juvenile super-predators on hapless citizens.[1]

Fear seized the public. In newspapers and other media, young people were pervasively framed as offenders. As a result, 60 percent of California residents surveyed in 1996 believed that "most crime nowadays is committed by young people," though youth were responsible for just 13 percent of violent crime that year. Two years later, 62 percent of poll respondents believed youth crime was on the rise, even though youth violent crime rates were at their lowest since the launch of the National Crime Victimization Survey.[2]

Policymakers responded in kind. During the 1990s, every state in the U.S. eroded core elements of the youth justice system, making it easier to prosecute or jail young people with adults, or rolling back confidentiality protections, or both.[3] Advocates and pundits ruminated about the end of the juvenile court. University of Minnesota professor Barry Feld proposed the court's demise in favor of "youth discounts" for young people in adult courts; the Coalition for Juvenile Justice's annual report to Congress was somberly entitled *A Celebration or a Wake? The Juvenile Court After 100 Years.*[4]

The racial animus behind this assault on the more benign youth justice system was thinly veiled, or sometimes not veiled at all: As DiIulio wrote, "All that's left of the black community in some pockets of urban America is deviant, delinquent and criminal adults surrounded by severely abused and neglected children, virtually all of whom were born out of wedlock."[5] Such rhetoric was remarkably effective at criminalizing communities of color. From 1983 to 1997, 80 percent of the increase in detained youth were youth of color.[6]

Youth incarceration in juvenile facilities exploded, reaching 108,882 young people detained in youth facilities.[7] Another 250,000 young people were tried as adults each year, of whom approximately 12,000 slept in adult prisons or jails each night. Such numbers were unheard of internationally.[8]

And then it stopped.

Punitive policies aimed at juveniles plummeted. The past two decades have seen a 66 percent decline in the number of youths in juvenile custody, and youth incarceration has fallen by double-digit percentages in every state except West Virginia.[9] California, for instance, which had over ten thousand young people in state youth prisons in the mid-1990s, had under eight hundred.[10] As facilities emptied, the taxpayer cost per incarcerated youth exponentially increased, making it even harder to argue for the facilities' utility.[11] In 2020, California governor Gavin Newsom proposed eliminating the state's Division of Juvenile Justice, once the nation's largest youth corrections system, leaving counties to handle youth incarceration.[12]

Nationwide, the number of children locked up in adult jails and prisons also plunged 70 percent—from 17,633 to 4,099—between 2000 and 2018.[13] Eleven states raised the age of inclusion in their juvenile systems to eighteen (and one—Vermont—raised it to twenty), leaving just three states—Georgia, Texas, and Wisconsin—trying seventeen-year-olds as adults. In addition, forty states and Washington, DC, enacted almost a hundred pieces of legislation to remove youth from adult jails and prisons, limit the prosecution of youth in adult court, and/or revise sentencing laws.[14]

This new, less punitive approach to youth punishment did not cause the predicted bloodbath. Instead, youth crime plummeted too, with the juvenile arrest rate declining 65 percent between 2000 and 2018.[15] The sharp declines in youth crime and incarceration meant that between 2002 to 2012, 970—one in three—youth facilities closed. Most large youth correctional facilities have been shuttered.[16] In some cases, money saved from these closures has followed kids from prisons to their home neighborhoods, offering critical services to support their success.[17] How and why did this dramatic change happen?

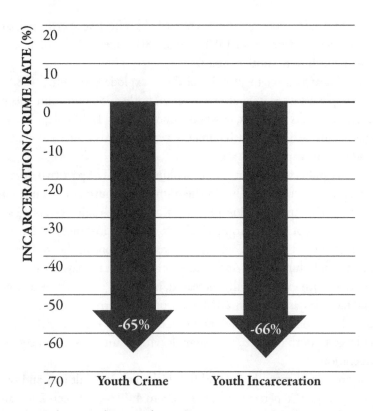

FIGURE 1: Decline in youth crime and incarceration rates, 2000–2018

The failure of youth incarceration to advance public safety should not come as a surprise.

In 2013, the National Research Council summarized research on youth prisons. It recommended against institutionalization and outlined what court-involved young people need to thrive:

• Limiting contact with antisocial peers and encouraging contact with prosocial peers.
• Keeping youth near their communities, to avoid disrupting their development.
• Involving parents and ensuring family engagement.
• Providing a structured social context that supports healthy development and gives youth the tools to deal with potential negative influences encountered in the future.

- Offering opportunities that foster academic success and develop decision-making and critical thinking skills.[18]

These items are not—and have not historically been—available to kids incarcerated in the U.S. Unsurprisingly, these youth prisons have dismal outcomes. Seventy to 80 percent of youth returning to the community from incarceration are re-arrested within two to three years.[19] Researchers used a "natural experiment" to analyze the outcomes of 35,000 court-involved youth over ten years. Whereas nonincarcerated young people accrued human and social capital, incarcerated youth accrued "criminal capital." This both increased their rates of adult offending and diminished their academic achievement, including the likelihood that they would ever return to school when they returned home from incarceration.[20] In other words, the youth justice system fails at its two basic goals: reducing the odds of youth reoffending and setting young people on a path to successful adulthood.

As with the adult criminal justice system, racial disparities in youth incarceration are dramatic. But unlike disparities in adult imprisonment, which have declined slightly of late, racial disparities in youth imprisonment climbed even as overall youth incarceration rates have fallen.[21] Recent studies found that Black and Native youth are incarcerated, respectively, at 5.8 and 2.5 times the rate of white youth, and found Latinx youth 1.7 times more likely to be incarcerated than white youth.[22] Overrepresentation of Black youth increases as they penetrate deeper into the youth justice system from arrest, through preadjudication detention, to ultimate sentencing into youth prisons.[23]

In a meta-analysis about the disproportionate confinement of minority youth, twenty-five of thirty-four reviewed studies (73 percent) found "race effects"—disparities not explainable by current offense or prior record—in the legal treatment of young people.[24] This racial bias emerged in an analysis of probation officers' reports of young people in a large, anonymized county in the U.S. Northwest: probation officers more often viewed crimes by youth of color as caused by internal forces (e.g., personal failure, inadequate moral character, personality), and crimes by white youth as caused by external forces (e.g., poor home life, lack of appropriate role models, environment). Controlling for current offense and relevant background information, youth of color were described as

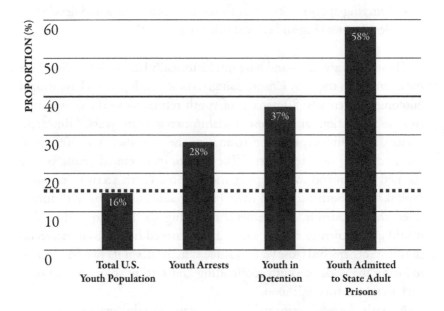

■ ■ ■ Dotted line represents
demographic proportion
of Black youth in the U.S.
youth population

FIGURE 2: Cumulative disadvantage: proportion of Black youth along the justice system trajectory, 2002–2004[25]

higher risk and were more likely to be recommended for incarceration than white youth.[26]

Comparing two boys of different races accused of separate first-offense robberies, probation officers wrote about Ed, a Black youth who robbed a gas station with two friends:

> This robbery was very dangerous as Ed confronted the victim with a loaded shotgun. He pointed it at the victim and demanded money be placed in a paper bag. . . . There is an adult quality to this referral. In talking with Ed, what was evident was the relaxed and open way he discussed his lifestyle. There didn't seem to be any desire to change. There was no expression of remorse from the young man. There was no moral content to his comment.

By contrast, in their description of Lou, a white youth who robbed two motels at gunpoint, probation officers wrote:

Lou is the victim of a broken home. He is trying to be his own man, but ... is seemingly easily misled and follows other delinquents against his better judgment. Lou is a tall emaciated little boy who is terrified by his present predicament. It appears that he is in need of drug/alcohol evaluation and treatment.[27]

At scale and in some jurisdictions, these disparities have completely eliminated incarceration for white youth as incarcerated populations have declined. In New York City in fiscal year 2017, only Black and Latinx youth were committed to Limited Secure (locked) facilities.[28] During the five years I ran Washington, DC's Department of Youth Rehabilitation Services, not a single white kid was committed.

Throughout my four decades in this field, I have worked within and outside the youth justice system. I have seen firsthand how systems intended to protect and support youth have instead enabled the widespread abuse and inhumane treatment of those in their care. When I became director of the DC Department of Youth Rehabilitation Services in 2005, the conditions suffered by kids incarcerated in our nation's capital were shocking. Staff routinely beat young people, occasionally stripping them naked and tossing them into their cells for lengthy periods. Sometimes youth were locked down for so long that they urinated or defecated in their cells. Young people reported removing their shirts at night, using them to stuff cracks in the walls to prevent rats and cockroaches from crawling on them while they slept. Drugs were so pervasive in the facility—even being sold, we learned, by a corrections officer—that youth who had entered custody testing drug-free had marijuana in their systems when they were retested a month later.

Sexual abuse was rampant. I met a new educational aide who had been incarcerated at our youth prison—the Oak Hill Youth Center—as a teenager. She told me that one of the staff still employed there had raped her during her confinement. Our internal investigators and lawyers also uncovered widespread sexual assault of female staff.[29] My colleagues and I replaced Oak Hill with a smaller (although still too large) facility.

In 2010, I became commissioner of New York City's Probation Department, supervising around 2,500 youths and 25,000 adults. Shortly before my arrival, youth corrections in New York State had reached a crisis point. The American Civil Liberties Union and Human Rights Watch had published a damning report about conditions for girls in state youth prisons run by the Office of Children and Family Services.[30] That same year Darryl Thompson, a fifteen-year-old Black boy from the Bronx, was killed after facility staff slammed him to the ground and pounced on him in a "takedown" at the Tryon Residential Center, an Office of Children and Family Services youth prison in upstate New York. His death, which resulted in heightened scrutiny of such youth prisons, was ruled a homicide by the county coroner but never prosecuted.[31] The Justice Department investigated and sued, reporting: "Staff . . . consistently used a high degree of force to gain control in nearly every type of situation. . . . Anything from sneaking an extra cookie to initiating a fistfight may result in a full prone restraint with handcuffs. This one-size-fits-all control approach has not surprisingly led to an alarming number of serious injuries to youth, including concussions, broken or knocked-out teeth, and spinal fractures."[32]

The Justice Department settled its litigation with the state in December 2009. Office of Children and Family Services commissioner Gladys Carrión described conditions in her facilities as "toxic," and a state commission investigating conditions in the state's youth prisons wrote: "New York's juvenile justice system is failing in its mission to nurture and care for young people in state custody. The state's punitive, correctional approach has damaged the future prospects of these young people, wasted millions of taxpayer dollars, and violated the fundamental principles of positive youth development."[33]

The number of youths from New York City imprisoned in state facilities had already dropped dramatically, from 1,896 in 1995 to 642 in 2010.[34] For those left behind, the cost of incarceration per youth mushroomed. Yet state policymakers had been loath to close facilities that were shoring up rural economies.[35]

After his election in November 2010, Governor Andrew Cuomo toured Tryon, which was then fully staffed yet completely devoid of young people. In his first State of the State address in January 2011, Governor Cuomo angrily summarized the case against the state's youth prisons:

You have juvenile justice facilities today where we have young people who are incarcerated in these state programs who are receiving . . . treatment that has already been proven to be ineffective—recidivism rates in the 90 percentile. The cost to the taxpayer is exorbitant. For one child, over $200,000 per year. The reason we continue to keep these children in these programs that aren't serving them but are bilking the taxpayers is that we don't want to lose the state jobs that we would lose if we closed the facilities. . . . An incarceration program is not an employment program.[36]

Likewise, Mayor Michael Bloomberg called the state's youth prisons "relics of a bygone era, when troubled city kids were stripped from their families and shipped to detention centers in remote rural areas."[37] Bloomberg proposed the "Close to Home" initiative, through which all New York City youth would be returned to the city; most of the money the state spent to incarcerate them—up to $41.4 million annually—would follow the young people home and fund in-home and community programs for youth. The few youths placed out of home would be in small, homelike facilities near their communities. Close to Home became law in 2012, with support from Governor Cuomo, Mayor Bloomberg, and the state's politically divided legislature. Within months, youth were placed in facilities run by nonprofit organizations in or near the city.

After four years, Close to Home's outcomes were strongly favorable. The nation's largest city had committed to better serving all young people sentenced through its family courts by removing them from deplorable state youth prisons. By February 2019, there were just 107 youths in custody, housed in local placements ranging in size from six to twenty beds. Only twelve of those youth were held in locked facilities. Moreover, 91 percent of Close to Home youth passed their academic classes while in custody; 82 percent of youth released from Close to Home facilities transitioned to a parent or guardian; and 91 percent of youth exiting Close to Home facilities were enrolled in post-release community programming.[38]

The nation's largest city—in terms of population larger than most states—showed it could remove youth prosecuted in family courts from youth prisons, reinvest most of the savings into community programs, and enjoy record-breaking declines in youth arrests.

It has struck me—throughout my forty years as a juvenile facility staff member, foster parent, researcher, advocate, and department head—that the public sees atrocities in youth prisons as episodic rather than endemic. Horrific conditions flare up in the media for a brief period. Politicians momentarily decry them and call for action. Perhaps a task force is established or a corrections commissioner replaced. The media and political waters calm and attention wanes. Gradually, or sometimes abruptly, conditions deteriorate, resulting in scandals, then a public outcry, and the cycle begins again. Far less often is there a critical examination of the youth prison model itself and even less frequently the elimination of such facilities.

But youth prisons have enforced these types of deplorable conditions since they sprang up in the U.S. in the 1800s. Historian David Rothman chronicles nineteenth-century youth "reformatories" and "training schools" that, from the onset, were plagued with physical abuse and neglect and atrocious practices such as leasing youth out under brutal labor conditions. Summarizing this legacy, Rothman concludes, "When custody meets care, custody always wins."[39]

Over a century after the opening of the nation's first youth prison, Jerome Miller, head of youth corrections in Massachusetts, closed the Commonwealth's youth prisons in the 1970s. As he placed youth into ultimately more successful community programs, he met fierce resistance from staff and elected officials justifying a brutal status quo.[40] Defending his decision, Miller wrote, "Reformers come and reformers go. State institutions carry on. Nothing in their history suggests they can sustain reform, no matter what money, what staff, and programs are pumped into them. The same crises that have plagued them for 150 years intrude today. Though the cast may change, the players go on producing failure."[41]

Unfortunately, Miller and Rothman's dismal conclusions endure. Between 2004 and 2007, the Associated Press surveyed every juvenile justice agency incarcerating youth in the country. Reporters uncovered thirteen thousand allegations of abuse in facilities housing 46,000 youth.[42] Relatedly, a 2018 survey by the Bureau of Justice Statistics found that one in fourteen incarcerated youth reported being sexually assaulted while in custody during the twelve previous months.[43] And, in a pair of reports analyzing youth facilities from 1970 to 2015, the Annie E. Casey Foundation uncovered evidence of systemic maltreatment in facilities in almost all states. Half of this maltreatment—which included high rates of violence and sexual abuse, overreliance on physical restraints, and excessive use of isolation and solitary confinement—occurred since 2000. Violations occurred even when state systems were under court oversight. The data are overwhelming: negative conditions are not episodic. They are not aberrant or facility-specific. Instead, they are a baked-in characteristic of the youth prison model itself.

Beyond the chronic and endemic violence and failure of youth prisons, several factors help explain the steady and profound declines in youth incarceration in evidence since the turn of the twenty-first century.

First, the substantial drop in youth arrests over the past several decades has helped in at least two ways. Most obviously, the crime drop reduced the number of young people available for the system to incarcerate. The reversal of the early 1990s crime spike also gave judges and elected officials the political breathing room to experiment with fewer youth prisons.

At the same time, increasingly sophisticated and well-funded advocates and community organizers launched local and national efforts to close youth prisons and to stop incarcerating youth in adult prisons or trying them as adults. For example, the Youth First Initiative, a "national campaign to end youth incarceration and invest in community-based supports, services and opportunities for youth," has campaigns with youth, families, and grassroots organizers in fourteen states. Its goal is to amass enough decarcerated states to reach a national "tipping point," prompting total elimination of the youth prison model. Importantly, the initiative's efforts to craft justice solutions without youth prisons involve not only community members and families, but also the voices of youth in the system.

The voices of young people and their families have long been an important component of justice reform efforts. In Missouri, for example, youth have testified for decades at annual Division of Youth Services hearings.[44] In 2003, Families and Friends of Louisiana's Incarcerated Children helped close the state's notorious Tallulah Correctional Center for Youth.[45] In 2015, the Annie E. Casey Foundation created a youth advisory council to inform its juvenile justice work.[46] These examples all include positive youth development efforts; by participating in advocacy, system-involved youth use their own knowledge and strengths to build agency.[47]

Youth voices have been joined by litigators, philanthropic organizations, researchers, and reform-minded correctional leaders, together helping drive down populations of incarcerated young people. Litigators—from organizations including the Juvenile Law Center, National Center for Youth Law, Youth Law Center, Southern Poverty Law Center, and ACLU—have not only helped improve conditions, but also highlighted institutional atrocities, increased the costs of running barely constitutional facilities, and created flashpoints for reform.

Philanthropic support has helped create a developmentally appropriate response to youth crime that eschews youth prisons. The Annie E. Casey Foundation's Juvenile Detention Alternatives Initiative, founded in 1994 at the height of the "super-predator" era, helps jurisdictions build experience with, and evidence about, safely and effectively reducing pre-adjudication youth detention populations and racial disparities in detention. It now operates in forty states, three tribal territories, and over three hundred counties. In twenty-three states where it was operative before 2010, detention populations in participating counties fell by 2.5 times more than the state average.[48] The MacArthur Foundation's Research Network on Adolescent Development and Juvenile Justice funded research that profoundly affected U.S. Supreme Court decisions—including about the juvenile death penalty and juvenile life-without-parole sentences—and also influenced system-wide discussions of youth justice reforms.[49] More recently, the Youth First State Advocacy Fund was established to close youth prisons and secure investment in communities most affected by incarceration, working in partnership with the Youth First Initiative and grassroots groups throughout the country.[50]

Such initiatives often influenced, and were influenced by, a burgeoning group of reform-minded youth correctional leaders. In 2019, fifty-seven youth correctional administrators formed Youth Correctional Leaders for Justice; sixty-two people are now signed on. They joined calls by advocates, youth, and families to end the youth prison model and replace it with a youth justice system favoring community programs and small, local facilities for the incarcerated few: "As current and former leaders of youth justice agencies around the country, we believe that the time has come to close down youth prisons, once and for all. Our collective experience 'on the inside' has shown us that separating youth from their families and communities and emphasizing punishment and retribution harms young people and their communities."[51]

Finally, a growing cadre of "evidence-based practices"—such as Multi-Systemic Therapy, Functional Family Therapy, and Multi-Dimensional Treatment Foster Care—were shown to reduce recidivism among young people who shared similar risk and offending profiles with incarcerated youth. For cost-conscious, public safety–concerned policymakers, these practices offered lower-cost, research-backed alternatives to youth imprisonment.[52]

In combination, these factors not only reduced incarceration, but also nudged public opinion toward a less punitive and more supportive youth justice system. A 2019 survey found that 80 percent of people favored financial incentives that reduced youth incarceration by funding community rehabilitative programs. Seventy percent supported reducing racial and ethnic disparities in the youth justice system, and 57 percent supported closing youth prisons.[53] Poll findings of this sort were unheard of in the heyday of the "super-predator" era.

So what comes next? Advocates and community organizers rightly argue that much more needs to be done. With campaigns to close youth prisons growing more common and twenty years of plunging youth incarceration under our belts, now is the time to take stock of where we are with youth confinement, where we should be headed, and the lessons we can apply to adult decarceration.

The first implication is that we must finish the job, overcoming resistance to do so. We must end America's 180-year experiment with youth imprisonment. Consistently brutal conditions, stark racial disparities, dismal outcomes, and high costs have characterized youth prisons since their birth. Jurisdictions have reduced or eliminated youth prisons without jeopardizing public safety. They have funneled some of the savings from deinstitutionalization into programs to support youth who would otherwise have been incarcerated. And there is public support for doing so.

Yet resistance remains. Often, youth prisons provide jobs in the rural communities in which they are generally located. This creates entrenched interests among staff, local elected officials, and business leaders. Public officials in charge of closures encounter harsh public scrutiny. Gladys Carrión, who closed two dozen youth prisons while heading youth corrections in New York, was vilified by her staff and elected leaders in the upstate communities where those facilities were located, despite the facilities' deplorable conditions, racial disparities, and underutilization.[54]

Similarly, Jerome Miller's memoir, *Last One over the Wall*, describes the fierce resistance and outright sabotage he endured closing Massachusetts's training schools.[55] When I closed the Oak Hill Youth Center, I faced numerous votes of no confidence by the Fraternal Order of the Police, the union representing my staff—some of whose members actively sabotaged our efforts.[56]

This resistance makes it difficult to close youth facilities, which feather a variety of well-connected nests. In New York, legislation—passed at the urging of correctional officers' unions and elected officials from rural "prison towns"—mandates that state officials announce the planned closure of any correctional facility a year in advance.[57] These announcements allow local business, political leaders, and correctional officers to organize and protest any closures. This sometimes enables facilities to cling to existence, and facility costs per incarcerated youth to mushroom even as their populations dwindle.[58]

There are lessons here for both youth and adult justice. Within youth justice, policymakers, advocates, and community organizers in states with waning incarcerated youth populations should seek to close—not downsize—facilities. Shrunken prisons consume almost as many resources as full ones, given the fixed costs and the reluctance of elected officials to lay off workers who are often their constituents. Those looking to decrease mass incarceration for adults will similarly need to take on the considerable challenge of wresting resources away from facilities.

Shoring up local economies can help quell objections to facility closures. Early in his administration, New York governor Andrew Cuomo allocated $50 million and additional tax credits to spur economic development in communities where youth or adult prisons have closed.[59] When I closed DC's Oak Hill Youth Center, the District was reluctant to allocate funds to raze it. We did the next best thing. Working with City Administrator Dan Tangherlini, the District leased the facility to the National Guard, which rehabbed it, removed much of the correctional apparatus, and repurposed it to house the Capital Guardian ChalleNGe residential program for at-risk youth.[60]

A second implication is we must capture and redeploy resources; the full closure (as opposed to downsizing) of youth prisons can redirect the exorbitant resources that they consume into efforts that bolster community cohesion and support young people coming home. This investment can build a more durable, "thicker" brand of community safety than the "thin" kind provided by imprisonment.[61]

Over the last two decades, youth justice systems nationwide have moved in this direction, shifting resources away from incarceration and into communities. Efforts including New York City's Close to Home initiative, RECLAIM Ohio, and Redeploy Illinois, along with fiscal realignment in California, Connecticut, Kansas, Texas, and Virginia, have reallocated hundreds of millions of dollars from youth prisons to communities while reducing incarcerated populations and closing facilities.[62] Such approaches have coincided with sustained reductions in youth crime and incarceration.[63] While cause and effect are difficult to establish, it is undeniable that while many states have funneled savings from reduced youth incarceration into community programs, youth crime has dropped.[64] This suggests that policy changes, including reinvesting money into supports for young people, have contributed to dramatic reductions in youth imprisonment. Similar efforts to reallocate funds from adult prisons to community programs, however, have been less successful. Perhaps this is because many youth justice systems contracted with nonprofit organizations to provide at least a modicum of rehabilitative programming, while adult prison systems largely abandoned rehabilitation starting in the 1970s.[65] Put another way, realigning resources from youth prisons may be easier than from adult prisons because adult prisons have a longer way to go.

Third, we must really invest in communities. A lament heard often among youth corrections workers is that some youth do well when they are in custody but reoffend when they return home, even when referred to aftercare services. Still, there are few efforts in the criminal or youth justice system to help highly affected communities improve the environments to which people return after incarceration. Despite recent reinvestment in community programs, more needs to be done to move beyond group homes and individually focused evidence-based practices. We need to build legitimacy in our justice system and support community cohesion—both of which reduce crime rates.[66]

Communities can raise their own safety and well-being when they have neighborhood-based, resident-led institutions that support basic needs and exert informal social control.[67] For example, the addition of ten nonprofit organizations devoted to community development or violence prevention has been found to result in a 9 percent drop in the murder rate and a 6 percent drop in violent crime.[68] As Candice Jones, president of the Public Welfare Foundation and former commissioner of the Illinois Department of Juvenile Justice, stated: "When reinvestment is at its best, it's about reinvesting out of systems and into communities and the places that are being the most harmed."[69]

Services and resources that both improve safety and minimize the need to incarcerate should be shaped by the expertise of formerly incarcerated people and members of their families and communities. Several pilot programs have enabled community members and government to co-design community reinvestment approaches. In 2014, after a spike in shootings in New York City's public housing developments, the Mayor's Office of Criminal Justice directed twelve city agencies—including police, housing, mental health, education, probation, and community development— to work with community residents to co-design neighborhood-based efforts to increase public safety. These efforts, dubbed the Mayor's Action Plan, included hiring formerly incarcerated people to mentor neighborhood kids, expanding the summer youth employment program, and extending community centers' hours until midnight. Within four years, violent crime declined by 8.9 percent in the fifteen housing developments participating in the Mayor's Action Plan, compared with a 5.1 percent decline in developments not participating.[70]

Relatedly, in 2017, the Colorado Criminal Justice Reform Coalition partnered with legislators from both parties to craft a new approach to justice reinvestment. The resultant bill, the Justice Reinvestment Crime Prevention Initiative, reinvested $4 million annually in two communities for an initial three-year pilot period. It funded a microloan program to spur small business development in the two neighborhoods, and a community grants program co-designed by local planning teams who set crime prevention funding priorities.

As justice organizers and policymakers find ways to transfer power and resources to the communities most affected by crime and incarceration, they should tap into the power of formerly incarcerated "credible messengers." In New York City, the Arches mentoring program, adapted from Oakland's Mentoring Center, pairs credible messengers with high-risk eighteen- to twenty-four-year-olds on probation. Young participants work with these credible messengers, most of whom have been incarcerated, in a transformative mentoring model that includes group mentorship, cognitive behavioral therapy, and journaling. Arches participants have 57 percent lower felony reconviction rates within their first two years of probation than similar probation youth not in the program.[71]

Communities can also be enlisted to help house people returning from prison. Reentering people often have a difficult time securing decent housing, which sometimes delays their parole or forces them into substandard accommodation. Family members are often willing but unable to help.[72] Community-based programs—such as the Osborne Association's Kinship Reentry program and Impact Justice's Homecoming Project—can offer individually matched, local housing options that are more desirable than oft-criticized, "one size fits all" halfway houses.[73] Kinship Reentry financially supports family members who house loved ones coming home from prison.[74] The Homecoming Project provides subsidies for homeowners who house returning citizens in spare bedrooms, in an "Airbnb-style" arrangement. It also offers social services and supports.[75]

Along with housing, communities can also undertake some justice system functions normally performed by government. For instance, in Baltimore, when the W. Haywood Burns Institute launched a call-notification project—originally staffed by a mother whose child had been in detention—to remind families of court appearances, detention for failures to appear in court dropped by 75 percent.[76] And in northern New Zealand, members of the Ngāpuhi Iwi (*iwi* means "tribe") created an "invisible remand" program to prevent young residents from being detained at a location up to seven hours' drive from home. Tribal families agreed to hold youth in their homes in lieu of shipping them off to detention. Tribal members were also hired to supervise and engage the youth in cultural activities during the day.[77]

This roster of innovations is not an exhaustive list, nor should policy-makers and activists view the options as something to be airlifted into their jurisdictions. On the contrary, one strength of redirecting power and resources to communities is the collaborative process through which residents co-design their own innovations. Instead of a cookbook, these are a non-prescriptive set of ingredients that mesh well with one another. These ingredients include services, supports, and opportunities that have emerged from communities, involved residents in their development and implementation, and been funded by monies shifted from corrections to communities. Youth and adult justice systems should carefully research and evaluate their innovative approaches, and work with affected communities to learn from their experiences.

This is the opportunity before us today. From a past where young people enmeshed in the juvenile justice system were vilified as public enemy number one, resulting in a massive expansion in youth incarceration, the tide has turned. Youth incarceration has dropped by nearly two-thirds since its peak in 2000, and youth crime has declined by 65 percent. In some places like New York City and Washington, DC, youth incarceration has entirely ended for white young people and almost ended for youth of color. This has happened without increasing youth crime, offering widespread hope for the elimination of the youth prison. This roundly refutes the very foundation of the waning "super-predator" era, under which mass incarceration purported to prevent crime. It offers valuable lessons for those eager to see the end of mass incarceration not just for young people, but for *all* people.

4

MERCY AND FORBEARANCE: A PARSIMONIOUS APPROACH TO VIOLENT CRIME

Vincent Schiraldi, Bruce Western, James Austin, and Anamika Dwivedi

Vincent Schiraldi is a senior fellow at the Columbia Justice Lab and senior research scientist at the Columbia School of Social Work. He is former commissioner of New York City's Departments of Correction and Probation, former director of Washington, DC's Department of Youth Rehabilitation Services, and author of the upcoming Not Quite Free: America's System of Mass Supervision and What Can Be Done About It.

Bruce Western is director of the Justice Lab and is the Bryce Professor of Sociology and Social Justice at Columbia University. He is the author of Homeward: Life in the Year After Prison.

James Austin is the president of the JFA Institute. He has over twenty-five years of experience in correctional planning and research. He is the former director of the Institute on Crime, Justice and Corrections at George Washington University in Washington, DC.

Anamika Dwivedi is the senior manager of research and partnerships for The Square One Project at the Columbia Justice Lab. Previously, she served as manager of The Square One Executive Session on the Future of Justice Policy.

Despite a wave of criminal justice reform over the last decade, the U.S. still has the world's highest incarceration rate, with reform efforts focusing primarily on people considered "low-level" and "nonviolent." Currently, of the almost seven million people incarcerated daily or on community supervision, people labeled violent offenders accounted for 58 percent of the state prison population, and made up large shares of jail, probation, and parole populations. In total, 35 percent of incarcerated people on any given day in the U.S. are labeled violent offenders. Thus, any meaningful effort to reduce incarceration must grapple with and fundamentally reconsider the notion of the "violent offender." And any effort to reduce violence should build more community organizations, not more prisons.

Population	Total admissions	Daily population (violent and nonviolent)	Daily violent offense population	Daily violent offense population (%)
Jails - 2019	10,300,000	741,900	311,598	42
Probation - 2020	1,216,100	3,053,742	763,436	25
Prisons				
State - 2019	530,905	1,221,288	710,790	58
Federal - 2020	27,315	142,028	11,078	8
Parole - 2020	392,400	862,100	310,356	36
Totals	12,466,720	6,021,058	2,107,257	35

TABLE 1: U.S. correctional population and segments of those charged with violence[1]

The criminal justice system has always treated people convicted of violent crimes harshly, but in the four decades of rising incarceration beginning in the early 1970s, punishment of violent offenders intensified disproportionately. Under President Clinton, bipartisan consensus cemented the 1994 federal crime bill, enacting stricter federal sentencing laws for violent offenses and incentivizing similar changes at the state level.

Two decades later, in 2015, President Obama, while calling for a reexamination of sentencing laws, noted, "There are people who need to be in prison, and I don't have tolerance for violent criminals."[2] That same year, in a *Washington Times* opinion piece, former U.S. representative Newt Gingrich described criminal justice reform as a "rare area of bipartisan agreement in an otherwise sharply divided Congress," but added, "we all agree that violent, dangerous criminals should be in prison, and the cost of incarcerating them is money well spent."[3] Following suit, in 2017, then senator Kamala Harris, a self-identified "progressive" prosecutor, stated, "We must maintain a relentless focus on reducing violence and aggressively prosecuting violent criminals."[4]

Historically, demonizing people as "violent" has helped perpetuate policies rooted not in facts but fear. Ultimately, however, the violent offender label is of little utility: it breaches the principle of parsimony, may distort proportionality, exacerbates racial and ethnic disparities, and fails as a predictive tool for future violent behavior, since people do not specialize in violent or nonviolent behavior.[5] The time has come to break from the tradition of punitiveness focused on those convicted of violent offenses, and to embrace instead policies that both mitigate punishment based on an individual's own prior violent victimization, and discount the violent offender label as predictive of future violence. Punishment should be parsimonious. While violent offenses may merit a proportionally greater response than nonviolent crimes, the principle of parsimony still holds that the punishment should be the least coercive response necessary to achieve justice.[6]

Causes of Violence

Much violence is *contextual*, often emerging in families, neighborhoods, and institutions in which informal bonds of guardianship are weak. People who commit violence have often been exposed to violence as both victims and witnesses. These social contexts and experiences of violence and victimization should temper our assessments of culpability and elevate our sentiments of mercy. Parsimony—which urges us to avoid gratuitous harm—should guide individualized assessments of a person's culpability and shape sentencing decisions.

Violent acts are often attributed to their perpetrators' behavioral propensities, yet much violence is situational. Environments depleted of informal social bonds—some poor neighborhoods and prisons— make violence more likely. Research shows that neighborhoods can be violent settings, not because of their residents' innate dispositions, but because of how these contexts shape social life. In poor neighborhoods, high rates of unemployment, single parenthood, limited social services, and low high school graduation rates all contribute to a lack of predictability and neighborhood well-being. The daily routines of young men are less structured by work and school, and residents may be less able to monitor street life. There is limited access to economic opportunities that help people transition from adolescence to adulthood.

Along with neighborhood effects, psychologists emphasize the influence of family life on violence. In disadvantaged families, everyday life can be more unstructured and chaotic. Adult guardians struggle with economic insecurity and may experience untreated mental illness and addiction. In communities struggling with housing instability, households often have complex structures, with unrelated adults often residing in the home. Such instability and chaos are associated with increased violence.

Prisons, too, lack the informal social connections that help regulate behavior and keep people safe. They also lack the sense of collective efficacy that could compel strangers to intervene in the event of trouble. Instead, prisons attempt to coerce order with the threat of sanctions. Hierarchical relations also open the door to arbitrary treatment and the abuse of power; studies regularly find higher rates of violence and victimization in penal facilities than in free society.[7] These institutions— like many less cohesive neighborhoods and families—are social contexts ripe with the possibility of violence. When violence does emerge from such contexts, our response must be parsimonious, proportionate, and informed by a sense of mercy and rehabilitation.

Those who have committed violence are also likely to have been victimized themselves. Growing up in chaotic families and poor neighborhoods elevates the risks of victimization. People who have been incarcerated are particularly likely to have been exposed to violence and trauma.[8] Before levying the strictest punishment for a crime, the justice system must first seek to understand an individual's life history of violence and trauma, and then use that understanding to inform parsimonious and proportional decisions about sentences and confinement.

Data from youth detention facilities and state prisons reveal serious victimization in young people's life histories. For example, the Survey of

Youth in Residential Placement, released in 2010 by the Office of Juvenile Justice and Delinquency Prevention, showed high rates of exposure to violence among youth in custody.[9] Thirty percent had attempted suicide, 67 percent said that they had personally "seen someone severely injured or killed," and 70 percent said that they had "had something very bad or terrible happen" to them. Over 60 percent of youth surveyed suffered from anger management issues, half of incarcerated youth exhibited elevated symptoms of anxiety, and half exhibited symptoms of depression.

Similar patterns of victimization exist among incarcerated adults. In Arkansas, for example, all people sentenced to state prison undergo a "Social History Inventory," or assessment, that asks about prior exposure to violence. The Department of Corrections use data from the inventory to develop a case plan for each incarcerated person, and to make referrals to programs and services deemed most necessary.

Survey question	Percentage (%)
Been in fist fights?	85
Been stabbed/shot/seen someone killed?	49
Been shot/stabbed?	36
Seen someone killed?	30
Under age 25	19
Under age 18	13
Carried a weapon or used to commit a crime?	26

TABLE 2: Percentage of people admitted to Arkansas state prison reporting prior exposure to violence (out of 790 respondents)[10]

In 2018, the inventory was expanded to add questions in the mental health section about histories of exposure to violence as either perpetrator or victim. Topics included involvement in fistfights and stabbings, witnessing murders, and carrying or using a weapon. These questions and other inventory changes were pilot tested on all 790 people admitted between June and July 2018. The sample was mostly male (87 percent) and white (62 percent), with an average age of thirty-five years. Most respondents had been committed to prison for nonviolent offenses including drug use or sales (31 percent), burglary (13 percent), or theft (12 percent).

Only a minority had been convicted of violent offenses, including robbery (9 percent) or assault (6 percent).

Most respondents (85 percent) had been involved in multiple assaults as either aggressor or victim. Strikingly, about a third had witnessed a person murdered; of these, about 40 percent witnessed a murder while they were under age eighteen, and about two-thirds before they were twenty-four years old. Another 36 percent said they had been stabbed or seriously beaten, and roughly a quarter reported carrying a weapon or using a weapon to commit a crime. Of people who had witnessed a murder or been stabbed or shot, half had carried or used a weapon. Overall, those exposed to violence were more likely to be Black (42 percent) and male (90 percent) compared with the total prison admissions population in Arkansas prisons, but there were no statistically significant differences by age and primary offense.

Researchers collected similar data on prior exposure to violence for the Boston Reentry Study, which followed a sample of 122 men and women over the span of a year following their release from state prison in Massachusetts. In the final interview, respondents were asked detailed questions about their exposure to violence and other trauma while growing up. Those with violent convictions were only marginally (and not consistently significantly) more exposed to any type of childhood trauma. Nearly all respondents reported getting in fights in childhood and using drugs or alcohol. About half said they were hit by their parents and 40 percent reported other family violence in the childhood home.[11] Similar to the results from the Arkansas sample, 40 percent of the Boston respondents had seen someone killed in childhood. Some respondents reported witnessing murders, suicides, and fatal car accidents.

Data from incarcerated youth and from adult state prisoners in Arkansas and Massachusetts indicate that histories of victimization and witnessing violence are common among justice-involved people. This supports the idea that violence is contextual, not dispositional. Violence is not a behavioral tendency among a guilty few who harm the innocent. Instead, many people convicted of violent crimes have lived in social contexts rife with violence. Growing up in chaotic homes and poor communities with high rates of street crime, many justice-involved people have

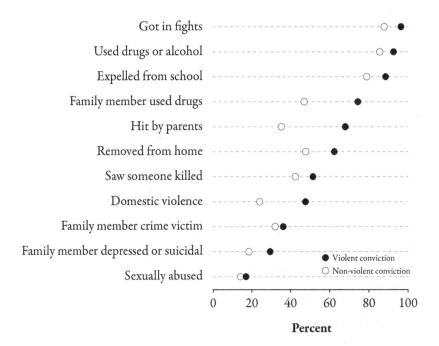

FIGURE 1: Percentage of study respondents in Boston, Massachusetts, who reported exposure in violence and other trauma in childhood by violent or nonviolent conviction (out of 122 respondents)[12]

been swept into violence as victims and witnesses. While violent offenders may have caused serious harm, they are likely to have suffered serious harm as well.

Yet people charged with or convicted of a violent crime are treated more harshly by the criminal justice system, with the violent offender label taking on a significance of its own, resulting in more punitive responses. At each step within the jail, probation, prison, and parole processes, the violent offender label imposes a higher likelihood of pretrial and post-conviction incarceration, and more severe and lengthier periods of punishment. The label's punitive impact distorts our notions of proportionality.

Throughout the legal system, a violent offender label is used if the associated crime is defined as violent, yet many people convicted of violent crimes did not commit any actual violence. State and federal laws regarding violent crimes vary and are often broad, encompassing acts commonly understood as nonviolent. In turn, this inappropriate categorization imposes punishments—including deprivations of liberty, sentence enhancements, and collateral penalties—that are disproportionate to the actual, or even intended, harm.

For example, at the federal level, the constitutionally upheld portion of the law defines a "crime of violence" as "an offense that has, as an element, the use, attempted use, or threatened use of physical force against the person or property of another," commonly referred to as the "force clause." [13] The force clause can encompass a wide variety of acts ranging from murder to breaking into a car. For example, Texas's "burglary of a vehicle" law was found to constitute a "crime of violence," though the statute merely defines it as "if, without the effective consent of the owner, [a person] breaks into or enters a vehicle or any part of a vehicle with intent to commit any felony or theft." [14]

States also use the "felony murder" rule to punish nonviolent behaviors as if they were acts of violence. This rule allows a person to be convicted of murder if they are found to have been an accomplice to a felony that results in death, even if the person neither committed nor intended the killing.[15] Felony murder creates the perverse possibility of life sentences for people who neither acted violently nor had the intention to do so. For example, if someone unlawfully helps a person illegally possess and consume drugs resulting in death, the felony murder rule can apply. In *Hickman v. Commonwealth*, the Court of Appeals of Virginia upheld the second-degree felony murder conviction of a man who ingested a large amount of cocaine together with his cousin who later died.[16]

Use of the felony murder rule is hardly rare, and its impact is far-reaching. Although statistics about people incarcerated for felony murders are inconsistently recorded and reported, a 2016 survey conducted by a coalition of California justice reform groups found that, of the women serving life sentences for murder in the state, 72 percent did not commit the actual murder.[17] And, according to the Juvenile Law Center, of the 511 people who comprise the juvenile lifer population in Pennsylvania,

36 percent have convictions for second-degree murder, which encompass felony murders.[18]

The violent offender label also has negative consequences within the prison system, affecting both incarceration length and classification. The higher classification also means that people convicted of violent offenses experience a more degrading and less programmed prison environment. When people carry the violent offender label, important privileges such as extended visitation hours, canteen purchases, recreation, and access to work details outside of prison are unavailable for a portion of a person's incarceration. If we hold that the punishment of a prison sentence lies in the deprivation of liberty, not the severity of prison conditions, sentencing those convicted of violence to harsher incarceration not only violates the principle of proportionality, but also, in its gratuitousness, violates the parsimony principle.

People convicted of violent offenses face longer sentence lengths owing to a suite of sentencing policies—including mandatory minimums, three-strikes laws, truth-in-sentencing provisions, and life without possibility of parole terms—enacted from the mid-1980s through the 1990s, which both ensure incarceration for a wide range of offenses and also lengthen terms for those offenses.[19] Truth-in-sentencing laws have played a particularly significant role in lengthening incarceration for people with violent offenses. The 1994 federal Violent Crime Control and Law Enforcement Act required states to incarcerate people convicted of violent crimes for at least 85 percent of their sentence as a condition of receiving matching federal prison construction funds.[20] The Crime Act both lengthened sentences for violent crimes and ensured that people with such convictions served a much higher percentage of those longer sentences.

One study found that people arrested for violent crime in the 2000s faced greater risk of entering prison and serving a longer prison sentence than comparable alleged offenders who were arrested in 1985.[21] Research by the Urban Institute supports these earlier findings on the impact of the Crime Act. Since 2000, across forty-four jurisdictions, the average time served in state prison has increased, a trend that is due almost entirely to an increase in time served by people convicted of violent offenses.[22]

	Current prison population (%)	Prison releases (%)	Sentence length (years)	Length of stay (years)	Proportion of sentence served (%)
Violent	56	30	10.8	4.8	53
Murder	14	2	48.8	17.8	58
Non-negligent homicide manslaughter	2	1	14.3	8.2	63
Negligent homicide manslaughter	–	1	10.2	5.3	54
Rape	13	2	18.2	9.6	68
Other sexual assault	–	3	10.4	5.0	58
Robbery	12	5	7.4	4.8	57
Assault	11	12	11.6	2.5	47
Other violent	4	2	2.3	3.5	45
Property	16	26	4.9	1.8	42
Drug	14	25	5.2	1.8	39
Public order	12	19	4.4	1.8	43
Other	1	1	9.3	2.6	37

TABLE 3: U.S. prison population, releases, and length of stay for state prisoners by offense, 2018[23]

People convicted of violent offenses represent 30 percent of all releases in 2018 but comprise 56 percent of the current or daily state prison population. The single reason that people with violent convictions comprise a higher percentage of the daily prison population is that their average length of stay—4.8 years—is more than twice that of people incarcerated for nonviolent crimes. Those convicted of violent offenses also serve an average of 53 percent of their sentences, while people convicted of drug or property offenses serve 39 and 42 percent of their sentences, respectively. Importantly, these length-of-stay statistics do not include pretrial jail incarceration, which generally ranges from three to nine months for people sentenced to prison.[24]

Laws and policies including mandatory minimum sentences, three-strikes, truth-in-sentencing, and life without possibility of parole collectively function to make incarceration more likely, extend the length of imprisonment, and adversely affect the conditions of confinement for people convicted of violent offenses. This means that while advocacy groups often propose reforms focused on people convicted of nonviolent crimes, the data suggest that to meaningfully lower America's uniquely high incarceration rates, we must extend reforms to those imprisoned for violent offenses, too.[25]

People convicted of current, or even previous, violent crimes are less likely to be classified to minimum custody regardless of their conduct in prison. This limits their access to work or program credits that can reduce their sentences and support their rehabilitation.[26] For example, the U.S. Bureau of Prisons bars people with current or prior convictions for a violent crime and people convicted of a drug crime involving a weapon (whether or not it was used) from receiving up to a twelve-month reduction in their prison term for completing a drug treatment program.[27] Similarly, South Carolina prevents people convicted of violent crimes from earning special work and education credits.[28] Such sentence reductions are designed to incentivize participation in rehabilitative programs. As a result, laws and administrative rules that deny access to programming cause those labeled violent to serve a greater percentage of already longer sentences, even though they pose the same or less risk as so-called nonviolent offenders.

The violent offender label is intended to identify a discrete group of people who have, purportedly, an unusual propensity to commit violence and harm innocent victims. But little evidence suggests that the term identifies those who commit exclusively violent offenses; people convicted of violent crimes are also likely to have been involved in nonviolent crimes. Although such people may be responsible for a large proportion of all crime, both violent and nonviolent, predictions of highly criminally involved individuals are imperfect.

The absence of criminal "specialization" has been found in a wide variety of contexts. Foreshadowing contemporary policy debates about risk assessment, numerous studies of youth in juvenile courts in the 1970s and 1980s found no patterns of arrests and convictions across offense types, challenging the hypothesis of specialization.[29] Similarly, criminologists Gottfredson and Gottfredson—examining specialization through the lens of recidivism—conducted a long-term follow-up study with a cohort of men incarcerated in California prisons from 1962 to 1963.[30] While just over half were re-incarcerated within three years, members of the cohort—including those originally convicted of violence—were most commonly re-arrested for public order offenses. Of those re-arrested for violent offenses, about half had been previously incarcerated for property crimes. The national recidivism studies conducted by the Bureau of Justice Studies find similar results: the recidivism rates among people incarcerated for violent offenses are lower than those incarcerated for other offenses.[31]

Some evidence suggests that the small number of people involved in serious violence do tend to be highly criminally involved over their life courses.[32] Longitudinal studies have found that about 5 percent of people perpetrate about 50 percent of all crime committed by the cohort. Members of this 5 percent both offend at a higher rate and commit more serious crimes than the rest of the population.[33] But efforts to predict such would-be high-rate violent offenders from early in the life course have failed.[34] As one review of the literature explained, "Attempts to correctly predict the violent recidivist are virtually impossible regardless of the make-up of individual risk and protective factors available to researchers and policymakers."[35] Committing a violent crime is "rare," they note, except for among a very small group of chronic offenders. Yet "chronic offenders" do not specialize in any particular crime type but rather have a higher probability of committing a violent crime simply owing to their high rate of offending.

The Bureau of Justice Statistics has issued three national studies of recidivism rates for people released from state prison in 1983, 1994, and 2005. All three studies measure rearrest, reconviction, and return-to-prison rates over a three- (and, in some cases, five-) year period. Although these statistics are highly aggregated, the results are remarkably consistent over a three-year follow-up period. Specifically, recidivism rates for people convicted of violent crimes are either the same or lower than the recidivism rates for all state offenders (violent and nonviolent).

Among all released state prisoners in the 2005 cohort, only 22 percent were subsequently rearrested for new violent crime charges within

Three year follow-up	1983	1994	2005
Most serious commitment offense			
All released prisoners			
Re-arrest	63	68	68
Re-conviction	47	47	45
Return to prison	41	52	50
Violent offense			
Re-arrest	60	62	62
Re-conviction	42	40	37
Return to prison	37	49	45

TABLE 4: Percentage of state prisoners arrested, convicted, and returned to prison within three years after release, by original commitment charge. Bureau of Justice Statistics release cohorts, 1983, 1994, and 2005[36]

three years. Of these new violent offenses, virtually all were assault or robbery; only 3 percent of total new offenses were homicide or rape/sexual assault.[37] Other studies find that people convicted of murder and sexual assault or rape have the lowest rates of recidivism. Sex offenders, in particular, face extraordinary restrictions, like residency and reporting requirements, which often follow people for the rest of their lives, despite having some of the lowest recidivism rates of any group of formerly incarcerated people.[38]

Within five years after release from state prison, 33 percent of people convicted of a violent crime were rearrested for a new violent crime, a rate only slightly higher than new violent arrests among people previously convicted of property and public order crimes.[39] While these statistics do not consider other risk factors like age or criminal history, they do suggest that people imprisoned for violence pose no greater risk to public safety after leaving prison than those convicted of nonviolent offenses.

Most serious committed offense	Any offense	Violent	Property	Drug offense	Public order
All released prisoners	77	29	38	39	58
Violent	71	33	30	28	55
Property	82	29	54	39	62
Drug	77	25	33	51	56
Public order	74	29	33	30	60

TABLE 5: Percentage of released state prisoners arrested within five years, by type of post-release arrest charge and most serious commitment offense, 30 U.S. states, 2005[40]

Research on pretrial detention dating back to 1994 shows that people charged with violent crimes are *less likely* to fail to appear in court or to be rearrested than people charged with property and drug crimes. Yet they are more likely to be detained until they are convicted.[41] Further, statistics indicate that of those people accused of violent offenses, very few—less than 2 percent—are arrested for another violent crime while under pretrial supervision.[42]

Domestic violence exemplifies the limitations of relying exclusively on a violent offender label to assess pretrial risk. While research shows that domestic violence defendants have the same risk of reoffending as other defendants, they have a lower rate of release and higher bail amounts.[43] Further, these often lengthy pretrial detainments can negatively affect families' financial situations, which may make domestic violence survivors hesitant to report their victimization.

People arrested for violent crimes and detained in local jails often face greater obstacles to securing release pending the disposition of their charges. Bail schedules are generally driven by the severity of the offense, with violence charges having the highest bail schedules. In some jurisdictions, pretrial service agencies screen cases for release without the need to post bail. Yet these agencies often impose restrictions on release recommendations for people charged with homicide, domestic violence, or rape or other sex crime. As a condition of pretrial release, many jurisdictions also require a formal court hearing for people charged with violent offenses instead of granting this authority to a pretrial services agency. This can delay release, sometimes resulting in incarceration for the entire pretrial period. Some jurisdictions also deem people accused of violent felonies ineligible for certain alternatives to detention like supervised release, further jeopardizing their liberty.[44] Collectively, these restraints cause people with violent charges to spend more time in pretrial detention, even though no evidence suggests they are more likely to fail to appear or be arrested for another crime during pretrial release.[45]

The violent offender label also lengthens the supervision period for people on parole or probation. As with prison terms, people on probation or parole who were convicted of violent crimes serve much longer periods of community supervision than those convicted of nonviolent crimes, even though they pose no greater risk to public safety. This, in turn, leaves them more vulnerable to revocation of probation or parole and incarceration for non-criminal technical violations of the terms of their supervision.[46]

Society's response to violent crime must affirm the values of parsimony and proportionality and reject punishments that do not reduce violence. Proportionality is a key sentencing principle. While the violent offender label can help calibrate sentences to harm, proportionality must be balanced with the principle of parsimony to ensure sentences are no longer than necessary to achieve the goals of justice. The widespread life histories of victimization and trauma among correctional populations make parsimony especially important.

To uphold parsimony and proportionality, we must weigh context more heavily, limit individual culpability, and mitigate punishments for adverse contexts. Of course people who commit violence should be accountable to the people and communities they harm. And society has the right to establish laws and policies that treat violence more severely than other types of crime. But current criminal justice laws and practices that impose excessive and ineffective punishment on both people labeled violent offenders and people inaccurately labeled violent offenders are misguided and fail to address the harm and trauma suffered by victims of such crimes.

Research shows that people who commit violent crimes do not

specialize in violent crime; age out of such offending; and are no likelier to fail to appear in court or to recidivate than those who have committed nonviolent crimes.[47] Therefore, our primary recommendation is to rethink the use of the violent offender label in sentencing decisions, and to abandon its use when making correctional decisions including pretrial detention, sentencing, conditions of confinement, prison release, and probation and parole supervision decisions. This would make periods of imprisonment and community supervision more proportional to the severity of harm caused, in turn significantly and safely lowering our correctional populations. Victim services should also be enhanced to better address the trauma faced by those experiencing violent crimes.

For people facing pretrial detention, less significance should be attached to the violent offender label than to factors that correlate with pretrial failure and resources that can help ensure faithful and incident-free court appearance, including reminders, supervision, and supports. Prison and jail systems should classify incarcerated people according to their behavior, rather than the label with which they enter custody. People convicted of violent offenses should not be denied important programming and accompanying merit time sentence reductions. Parole boards should not refer to the nature of the crime when considering parole applications, and there should be a presumption of parole at the earliest parole eligibility date. Since people convicted of violent crimes have already received longer sentences and later parole eligibility dates because of their crime, any further enhancement of their imprisonment is unwarranted, costly, and ineffective.

Historically, punishment has been considered one valid purpose of sentencing. Yet prison sentences for violent offenses have grown out of proportion to such crimes, subverting the ends of justice. Sentences of both incarceration and community supervision should be much shorter. We support policies that cap sentences—including The Sentencing Project's policy proposal to cap sentences at twenty years and Manhattan district attorney Alvin Bragg's requirement of his staff that they not request sentences longer than twenty years because, as DA Bragg wrote, "research is clear that longer sentences do not deter crime or result in greater safety to the community."[48]

A forward-leaning bundle of measures would also include early parole reviews, expanded good time, and "second look" statutes (judicial reviews

after sentencing of especially long prison terms), all of which were important parts of state sentencing policy before the era of "truth in sentencing" and violent-offender enhancements. We also propose that state and
federal agencies do away with truth-in-sentencing laws that force people
to serve 85 percent of their sentences, as well as restrictions on good-
time awards for people with violent convictions. Such policies needlessly
lengthen sentences, and, by denying people incarcerated for violent offenses from earned time credits, inhibit program participation.[49]

Since people convicted of violent offenses have often led lives enmeshed
in violence, their prior victimization should mitigate their sentences. In
2019, New York passed the Domestic Violence Survivors Justice Act,
which mitigates sentences for domestic violence victims.[50] Jurisdictions
should consider a similar policy for other forms of violent victimization.

Contrary to the bright line sometimes drawn in popular narratives between innocent victims and remorseless offenders, people in prison have
often experienced violence both prior to and during their imprisonment. Data show that incarcerated people have typically witnessed, heard
about, or been the victims of violence and trauma.[51] They often grew up
poor in families and neighborhoods where violence was prevalent. Ignoring such life histories tips retribution into vengefulness and undermines
proportionality.

Violence is deeply situational. Thus, to promote public safety, reform
efforts should provide healing and support for the disadvantaged communities to which many people incarcerated for violence will return.
The bloated cost of imprisoning and surveilling nearly two million
people charged with violent crimes could be much better spent. Policies
that help neighborhoods heal from violence and improve their capacity
to support those returning from prison would help make communities
safer. To reduce local violence, partnerships between government agencies and disadvantaged communities should increase collective efficacy.
Studies show that each additional nonprofit organization focused on
violence reduction can lead to a measurable reduction in a city's murder
rate.[52] New York City, for instance, added twenty-five nonprofits per one
hundred thousand residents between 1990 and 2013, and experienced a
large decline in homicides during the same time period.[53]

Curtailing use of the violent offender label, reducing incarceration for violence, and investing in communities challenged by violence would shift the criminal justice paradigm. Reckoning with the empirical reality of violence compels us to affirm the values of parsimony, proportionality, and mercy, a paradigm shift that would chart a fairer and more effective path to safe and healthy communities.

To decrease the United States' historically high incarceration rate, reforms must extend to people imprisoned for violent offenses. Convincing policymakers and the public to change the approach to people charged with or convicted of violent offenses will require a significant cultural change. It will also require active education on the truths of violent offending. Yet affirming well-established criminal justice principles of parsimony and proportionality should take priority over a politics of fear.

5

A CALL FOR NEW CRIMINAL
JUSTICE VALUES

Arthur Rizer

*Arthur Rizer is the founder of ARrow Consulting, a criminal justice
and legal consulting firm. Arthur is also a former police officer and
federal prosecutor. Before forming ARrow, he was the founding director of the R Street Institute's program on criminal justice policy.*

What does American criminal justice reveal about what we value
and who we are? And how can we adjust these values to better reflect
who we are today? Laws are supposed to reflect societal values. Both
the Constitution and the Bill of Rights reflect our belief in inalienable personal rights and the need to safeguard them from government
overreach.

Unfortunately, because of fear and intolerance from some segments
of our society, we also created laws, such as those constituting Jim Crow,
that failed to recognize the inalienable rights of Black Americans. The
legal system, however, has continued to evolve along with new notions of
justice, changing the mission of our criminal justice system and shifting
power to different players within it.

A rehabilitative notion of justice, focused on reforming individual behaviors, has traditionally awarded more authority to judges and parole
officers. Meanwhile, notions of retributive justice, seen as proportional
punishment for those who commit wrongs, have awarded power to Congress and the greater public.[1] Historical changes in values have led to laws
such as mandatory minimums and sentencing enhancements, and those
laws have changed justice outcomes. There are few better examples of this

than the sharp increase in incarceration in the 1970s through 1990s following the passage of "tough on crime" legislation. Here, society's values directly shaped not only the contents of our criminal code, but also the entire mission of the justice system. This was expressed through increasingly harsh enforcement and punishment, and disregard for the collateral consequences of that punishment.

Individual and institutional values are also displayed in the day-to-day rhetoric and decisions of lawmakers and criminal justice practitioners. Compare the language used by former U.S. attorney general Jeff Sessions and former U.S. representative Mia Love (R-UT), for example: Sessions often indiscriminately referred to those who commit crime as "hardened criminals" while Love describes incarcerated people as women and mothers.[2] These word choices can either increase public stigmatization of those convicted of crime or reduce it. Beyond rhetoric, however, values often translate into practice. For example, in an age of tight budgets and competing demands, criminal justice practitioners often use their values to determine what programming to prioritize. A 2009 study of prison and parole administrators demonstrated that prison wardens who felt substance abuse treatment was highly valuable were more likely to adopt evidence-based treatment practices within their facilities.[3]

Local justice officials, such as police officers, prosecutors, and judges, can greatly influence a person's pathway into or exit from the justice system—and thus so can those officials' values. A police officer, for example, may have the choice to arrest a person having a mental breakdown or to escort them to a hospital or public health facility, and may make that choice on the basis of her or his values. While a reform-minded district attorney may decide to send a greater number of people to diversion programs instead of pursuing prosecution, the values of a "tough on crime" judge may cause him or her to refuse to sentence eligible defendants to a local community-based sentencing alternative and insist on giving them the maximum penalty allowed by law. Rather than relying on individuals to mete out justice based on their personal values, criminal justice agencies need a coherent value structure to unite behind in order to create a more effective, transparent, and equitable system.

Our values can also be examined through what we fund. Indeed, if a core value of the justice system is rehabilitation, one would expect major investments in public defense, alternatives to incarceration, rehabilitative programming, reentry services, and mental and substance abuse treatment. In comparison, if a core value is incapacitating people for illegal behavior, one would expect increased funding for prosecution, policing, and incarceration. If the lawmakers who fund justice agencies do not hold similar values to the practitioners who run them, the latter may find themselves without the funding or resources necessary to accomplish their missions, making reform all the more difficult.

The origins of the American criminal justice system in colonial times were marked by a belief in the value of retribution. Punishments for specific crimes were often clearly stated, and the legal code was simple and easily understood.[4] This changed in the early 1900s, when rehabilitation emerged as an important value of the criminal justice system.[5] In 1959, legal scholar Francis Allen asserted that the existing "rehabilitative ideal" was based upon two beliefs: that preexisting and environmental factors influence how humans behave, and that justice serves a "therapeutic function" when it considers how best to respond to those who commit crime.[6] To fulfill that ideal, rehabilitative measures seek to transform the convicted person's behavior both in their own and in society's best interests. Judges and the broader correctional system sought to uphold these ideals. For much of the twentieth century, American judges largely determined sentences with broad discretion and little oversight from legislatures or appellate courts.[7] However, in practice, this system created large disparities in sentencing outcomes, and rehabilitative programming was frequently underfunded and poorly managed, which undermined the chance for positive results for people who offended.[8]

In the 1970s and 1980s, rehabilitation was increasingly replaced by other penal theories, first that of retribution and then that of deterrence and incapacitation.[9] The value of retribution regained prominence during the 1970s and remains one of the most strongly held values in criminal justice. Andrew von Hirsch, director of the Centre for Penal Theory and

Penal Ethics, has noted how the concept of retribution was redefined and applied in that era, with "eye for an eye" being replaced with the concept of "just deserts," in which the level of punishment matched the severity of one's crime.[10] In contrast to rehabilitation, which focuses on correcting criminal behavior and minimizing future harm, retribution looks at past behavior (specifically, the crime itself and past crimes committed by the person) when determining punishment. Believers in proportional punishment, which is supposed to be a key component of retribution, disagreed with the disproportional, severe penalties that would come to be enacted in the name of deterrence. The value of "just deserts" and proportional punishment informed sentencing guidelines in the 1970s and 1980s, which, in turn, helped reduce sentencing disparities among those who committed similar offenses and promoted a more consistent form of punishment.

By the end of the 1980s, however, the values of retribution and proportional punishment had been supplanted by a new value: deterrence. Those who claimed deterrence as a key value believed that when a rational person knows the consequences their actions will trigger, it will influence those actions.[11] Therefore, the criminal justice system should invoke fear of punishment in order to deter future criminal activity. In response, laws, courtroom tactics, and policing practices evolved to increase the certainty, severity, and speed of punishment. Scholars credit the belief in deterrence, along with the belief in removing people convicted of criminal activity from society, with the transition to mandatory minimums, "three strikes" laws, and preventive techniques such as "hot spots" policing.[12] These new deterrence penalties, such as the three-strikes law, often contradicted the previously central notion of proportionality, sentencing people convicted of relatively minor crimes such as misdemeanors, property felonies, and drug offenses to the sorts of punishments once reserved for homicides and other serious acts of violence.[13]

Studies have since suggested that the certainty of punishment may be more effective for deterrence, while the severity of punishment is less effective or completely ineffective. However, even the effectiveness of certain punishment has been questioned and seems to differ widely based on a person's offense, their peers, and previous experiences with crime and the justice system. Research has also significantly challenged the idea of speed of punishment as a deterrent. Overall, deterrence seems to be fundamentally ill suited to be the sole value of our criminal justice system.

Some have argued that the new deterrence policies were responsible for a portion of the drop in the national crime rate throughout the 1990s. Others think the fact that many people were locked up or otherwise incapacitated may have caused this crime reduction, not deterrence.[14] When a society values incapacitation—restricting someone's freedom so they can't commit a criminal offense—it relies heavily on incarceration or supervision. After deterrence and incapacitation policies went into effect in the 1980s, the number of incarcerated people in the U.S. skyrocketed. However, other factors entirely may have influenced the crime drop that followed—during the same decade, both Canada's national crime rate and its use of incarceration decreased.[15]

While incapacitation may prevent someone from committing crime temporarily (at least outside prisons or jails), it is hardly a tenable—or just—long-term solution. There is almost always room to argue that the release of a convicted person may lead to future harm, justifying limitless incarceration in the name of public safety. This is clearly not a commensurate or just punishment for all or most crimes, nor does locking people up forever address the underlying circumstances that may promote criminal activity. A society guided exclusively by the value of deterrence would ultimately be caught in a vicious cycle in which more people sit in prisons, more communities are left broken, and society is only marginally—if at all—made safer. While it might be a temporary fix to crime, clearly incapacitation should not be our principal or foremost value.

These various values have continued to evolve as society's views on criminal justice have changed. Current proponents of the notion of retribution believe punishments must be carefully proportional, while those who argue for deterrence believe punishments should be only as severe as is necessary for effectiveness. The value of rehabilitation has returned to the center of the criminal justice reform movement, followed by a call for more effective rehabilitative, reentry-focused programming, implemented with care. However, American criminal justice lacks a core—and agreed upon—system of values. People across the political spectrum today agree that we must redefine our central principles and reform our institutions to match them.[16]

Our nation was founded on the value of inalienable rights, and the idea that government's primary purpose is to secure and protect those rights—namely, life, liberty, and the pursuit of happiness. In exchange for this protection, citizens give government the power to regulate human activity, "so far as is required for the preservation of himself and the rest of society," and the power to enforce such regulations.[17] Limited government is perhaps the most important value of our criminal justice system, because it is the value upon which every other value is built. Yet current criminal justice policies clearly contradict this principle, from the over-criminalization of human behavior, to the infliction of arbitrary collateral consequences after punishment, to the subsequent disregard for the life, liberty, and happiness of people who become involved in the justice system.

To return to our founding principle of limited government, we would have to roll back the laws that greatly infringe on personal liberties and yield little or no benefit to public safety. Currently, the nation's penal systems often inflict punishments upon people for acts that cause little harm to others, and often the perpetrators aren't aware what they've done is illegal. Former U.S. attorney general Edwin Meese III warned against this over-criminalization in 2010: "We are making and enforcing far too many criminal laws that create traps for the innocent but unwary, and threaten to turn otherwise respectable, law-abiding citizens into criminals."[18]

A simple, widely understood set of laws clarifies the principles of the nation, makes it easier to identify right from wrong, and limits government power so that it can focus on enforcing the laws that matter most to public safety.[19] In contrast, today's legal system, in which a twelve-year-old may be arrested for eating junk food on the subway or an elderly grandmother may be criminally charged for not trimming her hedges, remains opaque to many citizens and gives the government excessive power to regulate and punish.[20]

Even when acting to protect public safety, government should be limited in how it holds people accountable. For example, the shackling of pregnant women, particularly during labor and birth, greatly reduces a mother's personal liberty and human dignity, and causes potential harm to both her and her child while providing little benefit to public safety.[21] This abhorrent practice has already been limited in several states and in the federal penal system, but has yet to be eradicated throughout the country.[22] Similarly, solitary confinement, if allowed at all, should only be employed when someone presents a severe, credible threat to the safety of others, and only for the amount of time absolutely necessary to prevent such harm. Placing a person in solitary confinement has been shown to have many devastating effects, and harrowing accounts from those who have experienced months, years, and even decades in solitary confinement make clear that it is incompatible with human dignity and mental health.[23] Whether the goal of punishment is retribution, deterrence, or rehabilitation, the ways in which we punish cannot justify failure to respect and restore the integrity of the human mind rather than destroy it.

A society that values limited government in criminal justice would seek to be proportional and also local in where it holds people accountable, beginning the justice process at the lowest level of authority first, with decision-making power as close to the people as possible. So, for example, when a teenager runs away or skips school, parents or guardians should enforce the consequences in the first instance, rather than the justice system. This is also reflected today in the concept of community-based programming, which tailors rehabilitative services to the person's needs within their own community instead of removing and incarcerating them in state prisons or local jails. Pre- and post-arrest diversion programs use a similar concept; local prosecutors can assess whether someone is better suited for punishment at the state level or for help through community-based programs. This puts the decision-making power in the hands of the localities that will likely have to live with the consequences of whether or not a given punishment is successful. If the person is rehabilitated, the community benefits from reduced crime and increased safety, more available labor, and greater numbers of reunified families. If they are removed or not rehabilitated, the community suffers from the opposite.

Finally, the concept of limited government should lead us to value how cost-effective a method of accountability is—its return on investment. Over-criminalization and over-incarceration have depleted state coffers across the nation. Indeed, it was the high cost of the harsh and punitive approach to criminal justice that first sparked reform in states that still center retribution, such as Texas. Policies that limit a person's ability to become a productive, contributing citizen upon reentry should be eliminated. For example, the practices of withholding work-related licenses from those with a criminal record that are unrelated to the duties of the position, or that have lengthy or involved supervision requirements, should be reassessed. Moreover, data collection and program evaluation should be the hallmarks of criminal justice, not rare exceptions. Local, state, and federal policymakers should want to know what rehabilitation methods are most effective so they can reduce crime while wisely stewarding taxpayer dollars. Tracking the outcomes of criminal justice policies and programs and measuring their return on investment is essential to promoting a cost-effective, limited justice system.

The criminal justice system is designed to protect our liberty, but in its current form, criminal justice broadly oversteps the bounds of liberty in several ways. Political scientist Carl Eric Scott offers helpful articulations of different types of liberty that illuminate these transgressions. "Natural rights liberty," or the protection of rights we expect from the government, is violated when the right of private property is transgressed by practices such as civil asset forfeiture. Society forsakes "classical-communitarian liberty," or freedom of self-governance, when those who commit a crime are permanently barred from casting a vote. "Economic-autonomy liberty"—the right to make our own labor decisions—is prevented when a criminal record seals off opportunity for those returning to society, as when licensing boards arbitrarily ban them from occupations. It is similarly disrupted when other necessities for employment—such as stable housing and a driver's license—are inaccessible. We fail to realize "progressive liberty," what Scott calls "the social justice of the national community," when large racial disparities prevail in the system, both in whom we choose to prosecute and in how we punish them. Finally, "personal-autonomy liberty," or the right to make decisions according to our own mores, is disregarded when the criminal code prohibits or regulates many acts, such as medical treatment, that should remain in the hands of private decision-makers and public norms, not the government.

When a crime has been committed, society is often justified in enforcing the law and removing several aspects of someone's liberty; however, criminal justice can be reformed to reinstitute the *value* of liberty even when incarceration is a necessity. For example, we can promote economic autonomy by training incarcerated people in new skill sets through work-release programs, removing criminal records via expungement, and helping people who are reentering society to secure stable housing, transportation, and the documentation necessary to find stable employment. Classical-communitarian liberty can be granted through the restoration of voting rights, and progressive liberty through reforms that recognize and counteract racial disparities.

A person's liberties should not be permanently abrogated when they break the law. Rather, our methods of accountability should uphold the value of liberty by removing only those freedoms conflicting with the minimal effective punishment and by preparing people for reentry and granting them all the rights and duties of citizenship upon their release.

Who we are and the values tied to that question are defined by the United States' incredible and storied past. We are a nation born from a revolution of ideals and remade in a civil war rooted in the oppression of those very ideals. We united to stop the horrors of the Nazi empire but, at home, simultaneously subjected many of our citizens to a regime of hate and intolerance. Indeed, America is more often a paradox than a monolith.

But a core set of values can weave together different segments of society with diverse perspectives and biases. These values must be shared from the top levels of policymaking power down to the practitioners whose buy-in is essential for them to be successfully implemented. And ultimately, these policies must also have public backing to enjoy longer-term stability.

In today's America, criminal justice lacks a cohesive set of values from which everyone in the justice system may define their mission and align their purpose. During various stages of our history, rehabilitation, retribution, deterrence, and incapacitation have each been a core value from which laws and practice derived. Yet their outcomes have demonstrated that, in many cases, these values have failed to uphold a true and equal justice, to respect human dignity, and to restore public safety. Instead of solely embracing these traditional principles, people looking to redefine the criminal justice system should integrate the values of limited government and liberty into a new vision of justice—one in which society is safer, those who commit crime are transformed, and liberty is preserved.

PART II

RECKONING AND TRUTH-TELLING

6

TELLING THE TRUTH: CONFRONTING WHITE SUPREMACY, PERIOD

The Reverend Vivian Nixon

Vivian Nixon is a writer in residence of The Square One Project at the Columbia Justice Lab. Previously, she served as the executive director of College & Community Fellowship (CCF), a nonprofit dedicated to helping women with criminal convictions earn college degrees. As a formerly incarcerated woman and CCF program graduate, she has been a leader in the movement to ensure that justice-involved women and their families have a better future.

America incarcerates people at higher rates than any other country, disproportionately impacting people who are Black, brown, Indigenous, or migrant. Other factors that increase the risk of criminalization and its consequences include socioeconomic status, gender, age, ability, health status, religion, and sexual identity. However, identifying disproportionate criminalization does not reveal the root cause of the disparities. Indeed, the problem is not simply a justice problem. Rather, underlying all social policy—including the details of systems like housing, employment, education, and health care, and decisions about who gets to be rich or poor, sick or well, influential or invisible—is a common denominator rarely examined explicitly: *white supremacy*.

White supremacy is an ideology that posits the superiority of white people over nonwhite people, even though the white/nonwhite distinction itself has been historically variable and contested. At times, white people's purported superiority has been justified with debunked pseudo-scientific theories, allegedly endowing whites with higher intelligence, greater self-control, and superior physical beauty. White supremacy has also pointed to imagined character deficiencies among nonwhite people, including laziness, criminality, and promiscuity. An ideology of dehumanization, white supremacy says that nonwhites do not deserve basic respect or dignity.[1] It believes that institutions must preserve the dominant position of whites. It holds that America, at its core, is a white society, owned and controlled by white people.[2]

White supremacy does not need to be explicitly or widely shared to have corrosive effects. Its secret life makes its violence all the more dangerous. The ideology of white supremacy is not trapped inside the minds and bodies of self-proclaimed white supremacists. Few Americans would admit to being white supremacists, or to believing in the superiority of white people. Still, cloaked in reasonableness, white supremacy undergirds social policy nationwide. It leads to policies and practices that appear to be in the interest of the "public good" but significantly harm whole segments of society. "Unintended" harm befalls vulnerable populations: nonwhites, poor people, women, sick or disabled people, other marginalized groups, and so on. Concrete examples that relate to mass incarceration are cities that use excessive fines, fees, and cash bail as guaranteed revenue streams; states that disenfranchise voters with felony convictions or that refuse Medicaid expansion; and the damage caused by the infamous 1994 Violent Crime Control and Law Enforcement Act.

Therefore, even without explicit endorsement from most—or even many—Americans, white supremacy is a belief system that functions implicitly and systematically across society, causing cultural erasure and extreme economic and social inequity for nonwhite people. Before we can reimagine justice, we must understand the beginnings of white supremacy in the United States of America. Until a critical mass of civically engaged people understand and acknowledge the inextricable links between white supremacy, the economic demand for controlled labor, and injustice, we will not be able to create a social policy that reflects a radically different set of values.

State-sanctioned racialized violence in America—including native genocide, chattel slavery, post-Reconstruction terror, Japanese internment, and abuse of migrant labor—is well documented. Less often discussed—and even less understood—is the precursor: indentured servitude. When Europe first colonized Indigenous land in what would become the United States between 1607 and 1617, the decade after the settlement of Jamestown, indentured servants and other indigent populations from Europe provided cheap and plentiful labor before the transatlantic slave trade began. Indentured laborers were told that the debts they owed to society could be repaid through uncompensated labor for a set period. At that time in history, this judicial practice was not a reflection of white supremacist ideology in the same way our current justice system is. Indentured servants were not disproportionately Indigenous or of African descent; although racialized in some ways, they were mostly European.

Ultimately, however, indentured servants began to feel that the terms of their sentence infringed on their citizenship rights. They were, after all, "free-born men."[3] At the same time, the slave trade came to replace indentured servitude.[4] Amid this social and economic upheaval, landowners taught poor whites and displaced laborers—who had, initially, co-organized labor movements with prisoners—that they were superior to the enslaved people now forced to provide free labor. This superiority was owed to their whiteness. Race became economically useful; poor, non-slaveholding white farmers were pacified by the idea that enslaved people would never enjoy full citizenship.

Furthermore, the release of white indentured servants called for more land. With time served, people were owed "forty acres and a musket."[5] Released debtors were told that they could take that land, work hard, and have African slaves of their own one day.[6] This propelled the forced seizure of Indigenous land and perpetuated a cycle of land-grabbing and labor exploitation.

The implications of this brief history are twofold. First, white supremacy was used to justify the immoral seizure and control of native land by white Europeans and the beginnings of chattel slavery. Landholding—the most important marker of social and economic capital at the time—was limited to white people, Moreover, as landholding became a qualifier for the right to vote, access to political power was available only to white landholding men, then women. Second, there was a short period—when chattel slavery was not yet in practice—during which racialized narratives did not permeate national political and economic discourses. Perhaps this brief time in our history offers a sliver of hope that a future not predicated on white supremacy is possible.

To reach this future, we need a sophisticated understanding of how white supremacy functions today. While contemporary white supremacy may often take a more implicit form than forms of explicit racism (such as post-slavery laws that named Black people as targets, or that criminalized being unhoused or unemployed—a common condition of newly emancipated Black people), it continues to shape all spheres of social policy, impacting people's daily lives. For example, modern-day housing markets were formed by decades of racist policymaking, including redlining; racially inequitable access to low-rate mortgages; the use of false charges of eminent domain to rob Black farmers; and the razing of whole Black business districts in the name of gentrification. As a result, proportionately fewer Black people own houses in comparison to white people. For most families, home equity is their largest asset. White supremacy is still at work when stereotypes influence decisions about bank loans or apartment rentals.

Only by acknowledging this history and context can progress be made. Once named, white supremacy loses the superpower of invisibility. Instead of avoiding references to white supremacy, what if we acknowledged it? What if we seriously discussed white supremacy and committed not only to eradicate it but to repair the historic harms the ideology has caused for nonwhite people? We could scrub state laws of arcane statutes that have caused the disparate racial impact. But we can only do this when enough of us, white and nonwhite, agree that white supremacy lies at the root of injustice.

The power of truth—and its connection to community empowerment and better government for all—has been emphasized by nonwhite thought leaders from many ethnicities and backgrounds. Black thought leaders, in particular, have long protested the almost genocidal impact of American criminal legal policy, which was only further compounded by the wholesale slowdown of investments in education.[7] Instead of supporting access to education, states built massive systems and institutions designed for control and punishment. At the same time, policies including racial profiling, the war on drugs, and stop-and-frisk targeted Black and brown youth to justify investing in, staffing, and filling those punitive systems and institutions.

Some activists, scholars, and practitioners foresaw the backlash that followed the passage of the Civil Rights Act of 1964. But hope was kept alive by a generation's "powerful faith in the decency of white people."[8] That hope faded when policies that ushered in the era of mass incarceration arrived in 1970.[9] Recent scholarship by Khalil Gibran Muhammad, Carol Anderson, and Elizabeth Hinton continues to document the repetitive cycle of progress and retrenchment that generations of nonwhites have endured. At the same time, Black Americans continue to ask what more is needed to validate for others what they've witnessed with their eyes, experienced in their flesh, and testified to with their words. Existing research repeatedly confirms that the links between white supremacy and state violence in U.S. systems of justice from slavery to modern-day policing, courts, and corrections have not magically disappeared.

Ten years before the Civil Rights Act, the Supreme Court decision in *Brown vs. Board of Education* also gave Black people hope. When they've been able to access it (often under the threat of severe punishment), education has proven to be a source of attaining some power over their futures. One way to combat the ongoing harm of white supremacy is to invest in education.

From anti-literacy laws in the antebellum South, through the resistance to the integration of colleges and public schools, up until contemporary fights to eliminate affirmative action policies, white supremacist power structures have long sought to deny Black people access to education. But, as literacy helped enslaved people to navigate the Underground Railroad, spread abolitionist thought, and organize resistance, Black people remained undeterred, pursuing education as an essential pathway to freedom despite the threat of punishment. Education that combines academic and civic knowledge with activist culture is a tradition in the African Diaspora. Activist efforts in diverse spaces such as churches, community centers, and behind prison walls have doubled as education spaces, teaching Black history and critical thinking as a way to build solidarity and form resistance.

Education is critically important. In the context of the justice system, education has proven to predict success for people reentering communities after prison sentences. Since 2004, when the Second Chance Act was passed in response to the growing cost of mass incarceration, a focus on supporting incarcerated people as they return to communities to rebuild their lives has created an entire nonprofit industry called "reentry." Reentry began with a focus on housing, addiction treatment, and employment as the pillars of success. These pillars, while important in and of themselves, are strengthened in innumerable ways when education is added. Congress recently acknowledged that fact when it passed legislation in 2021 to restore federal financial aid eligibility to qualified incarcerated people who enroll in higher education programs. But subsistent survival and sobriety are not the only reasons to invest in education for those reentering after prison and others who have historically been valued more for their labor than their intellect.

The benefits of education are not just individual, but communal. Increased involvement of these communities in education can help counter white supremacist ideas by offering new ways of learning and different ways of producing knowledge. Robust civic and political education is a self-perpetuating resource in communities whose cultures are steeped in more intuitive forms of learning, whose traditions are oral and not literary. Teaching oppressed people to counter racism by accepting their plight or changing their behavior—without addressing the realities of systemic harm—upholds the structures that permit mass incarceration and other forms of social and legal exclusion.

Rather, we need to democratize education to bring about radical transformation. In the world's most prosperous nation, public schools should be palaces. Teachers should be well trained and receive salaries commensurate with the crucial nature of their responsibility. Diversity should be the pride of every school faculty, assembling people from various geographies, cultures, gender identities, and ethnic backgrounds into one place. Curricula should elevate knowledge produced by Black, brown, Indigenous, and scholars whose native tongue is not English. To combat white supremacy, the scholarship, ideas, and knowledge production of nonwhite people must have a legitimate place in the education system—from preschool to postgraduate studies. People with different ideas need to be welcomed to speak and given the space to learn.

Ultimately, a sustained engagement with different ideas can help produce meaningful social change. To reach common ground, we must explore assumptions and challenge opposition in a way that works through contradictions and gets to solutions. For instance, in order to radically transform the criminal justice system, America must consider the history of white supremacy in shaping current policies and practices. We need sustained conversations at the systemic and structural level; polarizing arguments about defunding police departments are futile as long as the people who provide the funding believe that any problem lies with individual police. Relatedly, reformers will need to acknowledge that dismantling systems of oppression will take more than demands and a slogan. They will need to embrace a process that does not seek quick and easily reversible solutions. Tinkering with laws and policies will not change the durable and systemic institutions that perpetuate white supremacy. The path to an America where liberty and justice are available to all can emerge only through long, hard discussions about these institutions and our history.

Racial reckoning will begin when a substantial majority consistently affirms that white supremacist ideology has been constructed, strengthened, and codified in the history of American expansionism. Whether or not they are to blame, modern heirs to this legacy are responsible for ending its continuation. For too long, and despite the public and private experiences of people harmed by white supremacy, white people have tended to unite under a banner of denial. Corporate CEOs, elected officials, and religious leaders all appear genuinely shocked and dismayed upon the release of each new video that shows an unarmed Black or brown man, woman, or child being killed by police or by a citizen claiming protection under state "stand your ground" laws. Their public statements decry the horrors of police brutality and denounce racism as if to reassure themselves that "this is not who we are." After a brief period of mourning, everyone can rest easy because it can't possibly happen again.

By contrast, to be Black in America is to be in perpetual mourning. It is to realize that each video is a sign of more to come and proof of those whose names we will never know. Is it any wonder why the reaction of surprise and the accompanying outbursts of vocal allyship begin to fall on deaf ears? This is the conversation as it occurs at millions of kitchen tables and behind the walls of tens of thousands of churches, civic organizations, and prisons. People do not need disciplinary jargon or subscriptions to academic journals to express what is happening to them and what they fear will happen to their children.

Americans across ideological divides seem prepared to relinquish the idea that excessive punishment and incarceration solve social problems, but they have yet to come to grips with what to do about violence. Data confirm that the consequences for nonwhites who kill whites are more frequent and severe than those for whites who kill nonwhites. Also known are the devastating consequences of violence in impoverished areas where Black, Indigenous, people of color, and poor whites live. These numbers tell a story. American systems of justice are imbalanced. They have routinely persecuted, disenfranchised, and endangered certain populations. However, until white supremacy loses its grip on white Americans and on social policy and institutions, this harm will continue to occur. A sustained effort to be truthful about white supremacist thinking—an effort that would inform organizing around its eradication—would be transformative change. An exhaustive confrontation with the truth will reveal that addressing symptoms by changing laws, providing social support, and defunding police systems is not a cure, but a salve. To untangle the current injustices in the criminal legal system, the underlying toxic ideology is the starting point.

After the murder of George Floyd in the spring of 2020, the most influential people in the country publicly claimed to reject structural racism, implicit bias, and systemic injustice. But to mitigate generations of harm, what has to be paid and to whom? What are people due if they've had centuries of labor, blood, and life taken away? America has both the capacity and the mechanisms to supply relief that is both tangible and symbolic. Could it finally expand the massive direct investments that built a white middle class to Black and brown communities? Reforms will be meaningful when past harms are acknowledged and reconciled.

But reckoning is cheapened when blame is its goal. Rather, a process of setting things right so that everyone is made whole offers the promise hope in a reconciling society. Being a member of any society comes with accountability on both sides, and all must be involved. That's the nature of democracy.

It is powerful and affirming to take an abolitionist stance. But what happens when the label becomes a rigid boundary or narrows vision instead of expanding it? Ideally, abolition rejects all forms of oppression, suppression, and exclusion. It teaches us how to live together without human cages, excessive surveillance, and other forms of state violence. But in the current moment, some reformers who embrace the values of abolition do not openly embrace the label because they either are unsure how to reach the explicit goal of building a world without police and prisons, or do not fully understand the criteria for allyship.

Today, debates about how to bring about a more just America are po-larized. Will the law-and-order people break from their dogmatic faith in the police? Will "defund the police" campaigners insist that the solu-tion be all or nothing, instead of helping protect the vulnerable from real violence in an imperfect world filled with imperfect people? Ultimately, no side will win all of their demands. Yet we must all agree on one thing: white supremacy can no longer rule the land. To achieve this transfor-mation, we need to do more than tinker with policy, change org charts, or write new curricula for the police academy. That doesn't mean there won't be any change, accountability, or repair. It means that the process must be a thoughtful one that includes inputs from diverse segments of society. It means that consensus is difficult. It means that reconciliation, not retribution, must be the underlying assumption.

As identity-based hatred and anti-democratic sentiment increase worldwide, I suggest we find the courage to explore new concepts that can bring us toward justice, dignity, and equality. Values such as agape love (unconditional compassionate kindness), present in virtually every world religion, are necessary in movements for social justice. Embracing agape as practice means we acknowledge that even our opponents are hu-man. A commitment to dignity requires the activist to believe that op-pressors can change; it also requires the oppressor to see the oppressed as human and as valuable no matter their differences.

Agape is one of four ancient Greek words for love. It refers to uncon-ditional love. Agape requires action beyond theoretical discourse on di-versity, equity, and inclusion. Activities that draw on the psychosocial impact of agape love can bring about positive change. Thinkers from disciplines including philosophy, psychology, theology, sociology, and political science might agree that the tenets of agape are similar to the tenets of a just society.

Justice, at the end of the debate, is grounded in individual and col-lective well-being. Freedom and safety for communities require a moral commitment to the core belief that no human being is more valuable than another. As polarization increases and the threat of violence reso-nates around a post-pandemic, nuclear-weapon-obsessed, globe, we can no longer afford to mask symptoms with temporary solutions. Attacking harmful disparities and devastating outcomes for communities within the justice system requires addressing the root causes of the problem. White supremacy is the poison at the root. It, as an idea, informs policy and practice in ways that are both visible and invisible. Let's start that work with a sustained conversation deliberately aimed at eradicating white supremacy and repairing the harm left in its wake. Let's start it seeking reconciliation instead of blame. Let's power it with Agape!

7

THE CHALLENGE OF CRIMINAL JUSTICE REFORM

Bruce Western

Bruce Western is director of the Justice Lab and is the Bryce Professor of Sociology and Social Justice at Columbia University. He is the au-thor of Homeward: Life in the Year After Prison.

In a context of low crime rates and renewed criminal justice reform, the United States has seen a sustained decline in the national incarceration rate. While violence has flared in some cities over the past two decades and, strikingly, during the COVID pandemic, the national violent crime rate has generally stabilized at its lowest level since the early 1960s.[1] At the same time, the incarceration rate fell from its 2008 peak of 766 per 100,000 (2.33 million people in prison and jail) to 524 per 100,000 (1.73 million) in the COVID year of 2020.[2] Black-white racial disparities in imprisonment also declined significantly in these twelve years.

Wide-ranging policy reforms contributed to these drops in crime and incarceration. The federal government, for instance, began supporting local reentry initiatives two decades ago. Litigation relieved prison over-crowding. Legislation and ballot initiatives reduced drug sentences. As terms of community supervision were cut, probation and parole agencies limited revocations of probation and parole for technical violations, along with periods of incarceration for violations. At the entry point to incar-ceration, some jurisdictions reduced or eliminated the use of money bail; others reexamined the use of court-imposed fees. Prosecutorial reform is being pressed both by district attorneys and at the ballot box through the election of progressive prosecutors.

Communities have widely adopted initiatives aiming to improve fairness in policing, the courts, and prisons. Police departments across the country now use anti-bias training and body-worn cameras. Quantitative analysis is guiding criminal justice decision-making, including randomized controlled trials that evaluate correctional programs, and risk assessments that decide pretrial detention and classify levels of custody in prison.

Levels of violence and incarceration remain extremely high by international standards, but at this point in America's long history of punishment, the broad trends are toward less crime and punishment. Now, key questions include: Of all the reforms being adopted, debated, and conceived, what will produce foundational change? What will reverse mass incarceration, bury white supremacy, and support communities of color and people living in poverty who have borne the brunt of punitive excess? What will help us approach "a broader vision of liberation"?[3]

Of many possible reform efforts, some are fundamental, disrupting the logic of a system based on harsh punishment. Others are more superficial, and unlikely to yield large reductions in imprisonment. Still others may be positively reactionary, creating the appearance of change while really standing in the way of a qualitatively new approach to making communities safe. The voices seeking to reverse mass incarceration can seem cacophonous, pushing in many directions at once. Often missing from the chorus, however, is an alternative vision of justice.

The idea of social integration—fostering strong connections to community institutions and loved ones—can offer one way of thinking about future justice reform, guiding us to the kinds of changes that might be transformational rather than superficial. The punitive excess of American criminal justice has harmed communities already challenged by racial inequality, poverty, and violence. Piling incarceration on top of neighborhood poverty and segregation only entrenches the social conditions from which violence emerges. A different kind of justice responds to violence in a way that strengthens the social bonds of community life weakened by poverty and racism. To meet this challenge, we must develop socially integrative responses to violence that draw people who have been harmed and those responsible back into community life. We must restore social bonds and build pathways of opportunity for neighborhoods contending with poverty and racial exclusion.

The punitive revolution in American criminal justice has brought us to a unique point in history. Despite recent drops, prison populations remain extraordinarily large, and criminal justice agencies overwhelmingly pursue an agenda of punishment. While the extent of punishment today has come to feel normal, it is actually extreme, departing from both historical and international standards. Moreover, the system inflicts disproportionate harms on already marginalized communities, many of whose members must now cope with incarceration, community supervision, court fines and fees, and collateral consequences on a vast scale.

Yet fundamental change may be on the horizon. The country has entered a period of reform. What should replace America's great experiment with punishment? How can justice be a driving force for human dignity and thriving?

To develop meaningful alternatives to pervasive incarceration, we must understand the social worlds in which punitive criminal justice currently operates. The social world of mass incarceration is defined by three characteristics: racial inequality, poverty, and a high level of violence.[4]

Racial inequality dominates both the criminal justice system and the context in which it operates. Black Americans are six to seven times more likely to be incarcerated than whites; Latinos are about twice as likely to be incarcerated as whites. Owing to racial segregation in housing and the concentration of poverty in minority neighborhoods, contact with the criminal justice system—including jail time, parole appointments, and police interactions—has become a regular part of life in poor communities of color.

This reality has been shaped by history. Racial inequality became institutionalized, woven so deeply into police routines and penal codes that disparities in punishment would endure even if discrimination were eliminated among line officers and sentencing judges. Contemporary racial inequalities in police contacts, sentencing, and incarceration reflect a long history of white supremacy that extends from slavery to Jim Crow in the South and the emergence of deep pockets of neighborhood poverty in northern cities.[5]

Black Americans have faced successive eras of forced confinement. One legacy of a history of racial oppression is segregation in housing. Discrimination in banking and housing excluded Black families from white neighborhoods, and Black residents have been largely confined to Black neighborhoods. Moreover, the poverty rate is much higher for Blacks than whites, meaning that Black people are much more likely to live in high-poverty communities whether or not they are poor themselves. These high-poverty minority neighborhoods have been targets for punitive criminal justice policy, and face the highest rates of arrest and incarceration.[6]

The spatial concentration of policing and incarceration has come to affect entire communities. People who live in neighborhoods with a heavy police presence often grow alienated and cynical about the true intentions of the justice system.[7] Even without mass incarceration, poor minority neighborhoods face large racial differences in labor market outcomes, family structures, and health. But mass incarceration—which is associated with family disruption, poor health, and diminished earnings and employment—has added to these disadvantages.[8] Pervasive penal control in communities of color has become a defining feature of American racial inequality.

Some see little injustice in racial disparities that flow from incarceration. High rates of incarceration among African Americans, they argue, simply reflect racial disparities in crime. As policy researcher John DiIulio wrote, "If blacks are overrepresented in the ranks of the imprisoned, it is because blacks are overrepresented in the criminal ranks—and the violent criminal ranks, at that."[9] But this claim baselessly naturalizes the link between crime and incarceration: policymakers could have responded to the problem of crime in countless ways. But they chose a course that curtailed the liberty of a segment of the population who, from this country's founding, have had to fight for their freedom.

Despite large racial disparities in incarceration, inequalities in criminal punishment have grown most along economic not racial lines.[10] Incarceration rates, through the late twentieth century, increased most among those who had the worst economic opportunities: people with the lowest levels of education.

The term "poverty," which usually refers only to a particular level of income, fails to capture all the accompanying social problems. Untreated addiction and mental illness, housing insecurity and homelessness, and life histories of trauma and victimization are also closely correlated with incarceration. The term "human frailty" describes this cluster of maladies that accompany the harsh conditions of American poverty, maladies that are also well documented in correctional populations.[11] Poor people confronting addiction and mental illness who struggle to find adequate treatment can get into conflicts, or resort to drug dealing or other survival strategies that raise the risks of arrest; jails and prisons become health care providers of last resort.

Research also underscores the links between poverty, homelessness, and incarceration.[12] For those who are insecurely housed or homeless, more of private life is conducted in public, exposing people to police scrutiny. Buying and using drugs, quarreling, and fighting all become risk factors for arrest when unfolding on the street instead of in private homes.[13] And since housing insecurity is acute after incarceration, unstable housing contributes to the process of repeated incarceration.

The social correlates of poverty, including untreated mental illness, addiction, and housing instability, can often give rise to chaotic home lives. Many men and women who have been incarcerated grew up in poor homes and neighborhoods marked by street violence and other crime. They have often experienced serious childhood trauma and violent victimization. In the sample examined in the Boston Reentry Study, 40 percent of the previously incarcerated men and women had witnessed someone being killed in childhood, and a similar percentage had grown up with family violence.

Poverty is about more than being low-income. It is a cluster of life adversities that reflect a lack of state and social support as much as material hardship. Without adequate treatment, addiction and mental illness become corrosive. Without affordable options, housing becomes unstable. Childhood trauma can arise in chaotic homes and poor neighborhoods, where adult guardians are themselves buffeted by economic insecurity. In neighborhoods that lack resources for recreation, education, and employment, young people, especially men, often run into trouble with the police. In these ways and more, mass incarceration stands in the shadow of American poverty.

For those who have been incarcerated, childhood trauma is often just one part of a larger social environment that involves long-term exposure to violence. Violence is often strongly contextual, arising under conditions of poverty. Many people who have been to prison grew up in homes that lacked routine, where adult guardians were frequently at work, and where unrelated men might pass through the household. In such chaotic homes—which emerge not from the "bad character" of their residents but from the material circumstances of poverty—violent victimization frequently occurs.

Violence can flourish at a neighborhood level where poverty has depleted an area of steady employment, community organizations, and a stable population that can monitor street life. What criminologists call the "informal social controls" of family and employment are in short supply. Many poor neighborhoods also lack the community groups that can engage young men, provide adult supervision, bring structure to social life, and reduce the possibility of crime.

Violence rooted in the social environments of poverty—in chaotic homes and unpredictable neighborhoods—is more a product of unchosen circumstances than individual dispositions or character. As such, people living under those circumstances come to play many roles in relation to violence: victim, offender, and witness. Often, those who have committed violence have also witnessed and been victimized by it.

Many incarcerated men and women have lived with serious violence. But has the growth in incarceration curbed this violence, making communities safer? The social costs of mass incarceration might be justified if the punitive revolution significantly reduced violence. It is true that crime rates fell dramatically from the early 1990s as incarceration rates increased. By 2015, the murder rate was historically low. This great decline in American violence significantly improved the quality of life in marginalized communities. But the growth in incarceration appears to have played only a small role in this decline. Researchers find no compelling evidence that high and concentrated rates of incarceration produced large and long-term reductions in violent crime. Given the great fiscal cost, prison has failed to clearly yield a positive return on investment.

But prison's costs are not only fiscal. Research evaluating the effects of incarceration on crime often fails to take into account those other costs, including the unemployment that comes with prison and its aftermath, families' struggles with visitation and reentry, the separation of children from parents, and the cynicism that grows in heavily policed communities. Neither does the research weigh the injustice of mass imprisonment, concentrated as it is among people who have themselves often been seriously victimized by crime, who are poor, and who are mostly Black or Latino. Finally, even the crime reductions for which incarceration can take credit should be judged against alternative responses to crime, not against the politically impossible option of doing nothing. For all these reasons, the punitive revolution failed to clearly bring justice and safety to America's poorest and most troubled communities.

Along with its limited power to reduce violent crime, incarceration itself enacts a kind of serious violence. A forced confinement, often in decrepit and overcrowded conditions, is a form of violence. The most extreme form of incarceration, solitary confinement, isolates people in a eight-by-ten-foot cell for twenty-three hours each day. Research in Pennsylvania, whose incarceration patterns resemble the national average, shows that about 40 percent of incarcerated people are held in solitary confinement at some point during their imprisonment. In Pennsylvania, the median length of stay in solitary confinement is about thirty days, over double the maximum declared by the United Nations for the permissible treatment of prisoners. Around 11 percent of all Black men in Pennsylvania have experienced this extreme isolation by age thirty-two.[14] Beyond being an intrinsic source of harm, prisons and jails are violent places where incarcerated people face high risks of assault, sexual violation, and suicide.[15] This violence is often left out of the criminal justice policy conversation, discounting the welfare of incarcerated people in public discussions about safety. Meaningful efforts to reduce violence must include a reduction in the state violence of policing and incarceration.

Foundational reform to address violence will help raise well-being in the communities in which mass incarceration is concentrated, and in which victimization and other trauma are disproportionately common. We also need new ways to talk about violence, beyond its use as a cudgel by tough-on-crime proponents against those who want to change the system. When homicides and shootings are on the rise, more police and prisons can seem to be the only way to stem the tide of violence. Mass incarceration, which caused tremendous harm, was enveloped in a cultural project that aimed to make at least some people *feel* safe. Often this took the form of rank race-baiting, where the specter of Black criminality was brought to heel by the rhetoric of law and order. But law-and-order rhetoric is often resonant in communities of color, too. As such, a politics of foundational change must do more than tout its anti-poverty and anti-racist credentials. It must build a new kind of peace movement that offers solutions not just to the state violence of incarceration, but also to the very real problem of community violence.

What does this mean for the future of justice? Racial inequality and poverty gave rise to violence in homes and neighborhoods. In this context, incarceration became the ready answer to a range of challenging social problems. Sentencing policy relied on long terms of imprisonment for people convicted of violent offenses, even when they themselves had serious histories of victimization. In the absence of policy alternatives, prisons and jails designed for punishment became de facto shelters, detox units, and mental health facilities for poor people facing joblessness, untreated addiction, and homelessness. The wide reach of the criminal justice system meant that mass incarceration became a significant source of violence in many people's lives.

After decades of harsh sentencing and mounting incarceration rates, criminal justice reforms are gaining momentum around the country. At least three impulses are guiding this emerging criminal justice reform conversation. First, a libertarian impulse seeks to shrink the system and reduce government intrusion into citizens' lives. Appetite for downsizing prisons was sharpened by the 2008 recession, when correctional budgets threatened to plunge states into fiscal crisis. This stance proposes dialing back criminal sentences to their 1980 level, reducing incarceration rates nationwide. Second, a scientific impulse, which resists crime policy populism, seeks to bring data and systematic evidence to bear on correctional management. The goal is to generate and implement evidence-based policy. Third, an ethical impulse emphasizes values of redemption, fairness, and human dignity as counterweights to punitive crime policy that too often divides the moral universe into good and bad, victim and offender.

Each of these three impulses has shifted crime policy in a less punitive direction, but fundamental reform must also grapple directly with the social conditions in which mass incarceration emerged. It must grapple with the racial inequality, poverty, and violence that deeply challenge our politics and public policy.

Racial inequality today—marked by neighborhood segregation, discrimination, and racial disparity in incarceration—is a residue of historical restrictions on Black freedom and citizenship. Justice reform must acknowledge and repair the wounds of this history; by itself, good policy going forward does too little to address the harms of the past. To create legitimate justice institutions that belong to all, we must recognize the historical and collective injuries of mass incarceration. Here the models of accountability central to restorative justice provide a guide. Causing harm incurs a debt; healing from harm requires, in part, that the responsible parties acknowledge to survivors the harm they have caused. Meaningful systemic change will involve the acknowledgment of systemic harm. Police chiefs, prosecutors, judges, and prison wardens will play a role in helping address the injuries of mass incarceration. Some activists may staunchly reject any positive role for the practitioners in a system that has caused so much pain. But mass incarceration rendered whole categories of people disposable, and a new politics of justice should not do the same. Instead, those who staffed prisons and jails can contribute to a public recognition of the damaging effects of punishment and help open new space for creative thinking.

Since violence stems not from offenders' individual dispositions but from social environments marred by poverty, justice will be found more in the abatement of violent environments than in the punishment of violent people. A reimagined criminal justice system will concede some jurisdiction to other agencies—including departments of housing, child services, public health, education, and labor. Criminal justice will become social justice, as the goals of promoting safety and reducing violence are contiguous with providing people with stability, predictability, and material security.

And if prisons are recognized as places of enormous violence, then reducing violence will come from less prison, not more. The past decade of declining incarceration has largely been propelled by policy changes that reduced prison admissions for the possession and sale of drugs. As a result, people convicted of violent offenses now make up a larger share of the incarcerated population. Reversing mass incarceration will require reducing prison sentences for violent crimes, a much deeper political challenge than shifting drug policy. Fundamental change will ultimately involve new ways of thinking about and responding to the problem of violence. Often, our punitive instincts are activated by moral outrage caused by one view of violence: the strong preying on the weak. But the bright line between victims and offenders dissolves when we grasp how conditions of poverty and racial inequality produce violent contexts. People who have lived in these contexts and have harmed others have, in many cases, suffered serious harm themselves. The ethics of punishment must weigh this moral complexity.

Justice reform requires social and political imagination—envisioning how justice institutions might help extinguish rather than fan the flames of poverty, racial inequality, and violence. Mass incarceration failed as public policy precisely because it was divisive, eroding the social bonds of family and community. Justice is the reverse; it sets relationships right and brings people closer together. Research shows that public safety does not depend on police, courts, and prisons. Instead, it is produced by a raft of social institutions—families, schools, employers, churches, neighborhood groups, and community bonds—that regularize social life and promote daily routine.

Social institutions are made up of neighbors, co-workers, spouses, teachers, pastors, civic leaders, and employers who monitor social life and promote stability. The social institutions of community life help children transition into adulthood and prepare them to be citizens and supporters of the generations that follow. Movement through the life course has an important material component, where growing up confers not just independence from family and school, but also the means to sustain oneself and others. Communities rich in institutions and social connection, where residents enjoy predictability and material security in everyday life, enjoy a "thick" kind of public safety. Residents are not only safe from bodily threats, but materially secure in their housing, intimate relationships, and livelihoods. Thick public safety eliminates the need to make perilous choices or rely on survival strategies that may break the law. Thick public safety helps people invest in themselves and their families.

In the aftermath of violence, our courts and correctional agencies should help rebuild this thick public safety. Instead of imposing long sentences of incarceration, they should help restore the full social membership of both victims and offenders. This will involve recognizing histories of victimization and trauma among those who caused harm, and it will involve turning away from the false comfort of retribution to directly attend to the wounds of those who have suffered harm.

Responses to the violence that emerges amid poverty and racial inequality must be socially integrative, helping build the conditions of opportunity and social connection that underpin thick public safety. With social integration as a basic principle of justice reform, we can revisit the libertarian, scientific, and ethical reform impulses currently gaining traction.

The current trend of shrinking correctional populations might contain government policy run amok. By itself, however, it will not restore social and community bonds in the aftermath of violence. Libertarianism alone is insufficient. Instead, public investments must address harms suffered by victims, and lay a path back to the community for those who have hurt others. And in poor communities isolated by segregation, public investment in education, public health, and jobs can promote social integration, knocking down barriers to mobility and sharing opportunity more widely.

Systematic quantitative evidence is indispensable to tempering the hot emotions that have driven harsh sentencing policy. In practice, however, quantitative precision has been used to legitimize individualized assessments of risk and retribution that can in fact threaten social integration. Improved predictions of future criminal behavior have long been an elusive goal of the criminal justice system. "Career criminals," "high-rate offenders," and "super-predators" have been offered up as the targets of "selective incapacitation" and "intensive supervision." Today's predictive analytics for risk assessment are the latest efforts to base punishment on a forecast. Such predictive efforts view criminal conduct as a personal attribute, something that can be individually assessed and managed, and that does not respond to changing social environments. These predictions of risk also often reflect race and class disparities in crime and arrest, and single out poor people of color for intensive attention.

Finally, the ethical impulse. Elevating the values of redemption, compassion, and dignity affirms the common humanity that motivates the project of social integration. Often these values are enlisted to justify mercy or leniency that moderate harsh punishment. But leniency alone is incomplete unless it also provides an opportunity for moral action among those who have harmed others. Just as incarceration strips prisoners of moral agency, leniency can unduly absolve people of their moral obligations without enabling perpetrators to take responsibility for the pain suffered by victims.

The principle of social integration offers a valuable guide for justice reform. It clarifies that no penal policy that adds to poverty and racial inequality can promote community health and safety. Instead, fundamental reforms must cut the historical connections between incarceration, poverty, and racial inequality. The elimination of money bail and legal financial obligations, investments in education and training, and reentry programs providing treatment, housing, and employment are all examples of reforms that erode the criminalization of socioeconomic disadvantage.

A reimagined justice policy offers avenues to social and material security for those who have been harmed and those who have harmed others. Socially integrative measures that provide housing, health care, and education help build opportunity and human capacity. Much of this work will be done outside of traditional criminal justice agencies. The result will be thick public safety, where social integration replaces punishment. The provision of material security and predictability in daily life will establish a virtuous cycle that promotes safety and reduces the harms of violence, while strengthening family and community. In this vision of justice, people contending with violence, poverty, and racial inequality may find new safety and well-being that allows them to imagine a better future for themselves and for their children.

8

RECKONING WITH RACIAL HARM FROM THE BENCH: LEARN, ACKNOWLEDGE, AND REPAIR

Elizabeth Trosch

Elizabeth Trosch is the chief district court judge for Mecklenburg County, North Carolina, where she has served as a judge for thirteen years. She serves as a board member for Race Matters for Juvenile Justice.

In 2019, I was invited to join a racial equity pilgrimage for justice system practitioners to the National Memorial for Peace and Justice in Montgomery, Alabama. The purpose of the trip was to confront the legacy of lynching in America. As the chief judge in Mecklenburg County, North Carolina, I believed my colleagues and I were already doing the work needed to challenge racial disparities across the justice system. I did not understand why we should pause our ongoing work to confront a history we had already been taught. But, persuaded by close colleagues that I had more to learn, I agreed to go.

In Montgomery, we gathered to confront the legacy of racial terror and its ongoing impacts. The first documented terror lynching in Charlotte took place in August 1913, on a street corner that is now the 20-yard line in the Panthers football stadium. At the phrase "terror lynching," I felt myself shutting down, clinging to the sanitized version of lynching taught in high school U.S. history: an aberrant practice carried out by rogue individual bigots in the South. As a white woman in my forties, I grew up in a world transformed by the civil rights movement. I never participated in a lynching and did not see myself as a bigot. Yet the word "terror" implied something more odious, even institutional, about this practice. At the Memorial, I finally saw the direct link between this history of violence and the pain, fear, and anger that burdens so many Black Americans today. I saw the mechanisms that continue to separate white and Black people—including defensiveness, shame, intentional ignorance, and fear of losing the benefits of whiteness—created and maintained by violence and terror.

Terror lynchings, which used fear and violence to control Black Americans, have parallels in the rituals of control and dehumanization in today's justice system. Contemporary killings of Black people by police officers invoke the terror of the lynch mob. Public statements that rationalize such killings echo the cheering white crowds that gathered for rituals of public terror. As the wounds inflicted by the violence of terror lynchings have been transmitted from generation to generation, the nation now confronts a new moment of reckoning prompted by the senseless asphyxiation of George Floyd, the fatal home invasion of Breonna Taylor, the lethal presumption of Jacob Blake's dangerousness, and the police killings of countless others. The failure of prosecutors and courts to hold officers accountable extends a long history of legal complicity. Gatekeepers in the justice system—like me—must act. We cannot let this moment of reckoning pass.

My trip to Montgomery showed me that white supremacy is very much alive in our communities and courts. Judges—who have historically been regarded as society's moral authority, and who have long enforced social values and norms—must, in particular, confront this legacy. Since we are entrusted to make decisions that impact people's lives, we must be willing to learn and to listen. We must reckon with the legacy of racial terror and pursue transformational reform to heal these wounds. As a white woman, I could choose to remain ignorant and dismiss our nation's history as "in the past." But as a chief judge, my efforts to enact justice and promote healing will lack legitimacy until I reckon with the legacy of white supremacy in my own jurisdiction, court policies, and practices.

Over-policing of communities of color, mass incarceration, and the court-ordered extraction of money from poor people of color are practices that trace to the era of racial terror. Although the civil rights movement of the 1950s and 1960s ended many institutional policies and practices that enabled segregation, our nation has never acknowledged the role of the courts in sanctioning racial terror and white supremacy. While landmark civil rights victories may assuage our collective shame for racial subordination and signal strides toward equality, we have not collectively recognized the institutional benefits historically conferred on white people, or reckoned with the state-sanctioned violence that preserved white supremacy under the banner of safety and justice.

Starting in 2020 and 2021, the United States has been forced to confront police brutality and the indifference of the criminal justice system. We watched white nationalists storm the U.S. Capitol Building, but saw a much harsher police response to people marching in Black Lives Matter protests than to rioters seeking to overturn an election. This reflected an ugly truth: our nation is fundamentally organized around the idea that white people are free from the presumption of danger and often lethal legal control that Black people face.

As some police chiefs, prosecutors, and judges pursue justice reform with commitments to implicit bias training, police accountability, bail reform, and more compassionate responses to drug offenses, we must recognize that acknowledging harm alone does not heal wounds. New policies to promote racial equity do not disturb the foundation of white supremacy. Eliminating chokeholds and implementing new bail practices does not place power in the hands of Black people nor recompose their relationship with the criminal legal system.

Our country could be on the cusp of transformative justice reform. But, to achieve this, we must reckon individually and collectively with the legacy of racial terror. We must recognize that systems and structures within our criminal legal system continue to disempower and harm Black, brown, and Indigenous people, and other marginalized groups.

Reckoning is defined as a "settlement of accounts." Yet I pursue and advocate for an even more expansive reckoning process that involves holding institutions accountable for past and present harm through atonement. In this context, racial reckoning is more than a collective acknowledgment of racially disparate punishment. It is action that takes responsibility for—and corrects—historical and present-day racial harm enacted by the criminal legal system.

Inspired by a five-step reckoning framework outlined by author and healing advocate Danielle Sered, I propose a three-step reckoning process for criminal justice leaders.[1] The first action is learning and truth-telling:

justice leaders must seek to understand the specific historical and on-going systemic practices that inflict racial harm on Black people, individually and collectively. The second action is formal acknowledgment that the criminal legal system has legitimized and perpetrated violence on Black individuals and communities. Third, racial reckoning requires atonement through reparative action, informed and guided by the needs and desires of those who experienced the harm, and includes the replacement of harmful policies with new, life-affirming ones.

My individual reckoning work started over ten years ago when our juvenile courts were challenged by the National Council of Juvenile and Family Court Judges to reduce racially disparate outcomes for children of color in foster care. Our clear and measurable goal was to ensure that the chances of entering or aging out of foster care could not be predicted by race or ethnicity. We began by spending nearly two years with several race equity organizations trying to understand what drove disparities. A workshop facilitated by the Race Equity Institute prompted me to reflect on my own life experiences. After an exercise illustrating that the people who live in areas of concentrated urban poverty are disproportionately Black and brown, our facilitators asked our circle of roughly thirty county and state government leaders, "Why are people poor?" Participants offered explanations: lack of opportunity, lack of personal discipline and effort, inadequate welfare systems, and other systemic and individual failures.

I reflected on my own experience as a white woman who grew up poor. My single mother raised four children on a salary that barely disqualified us for free and reduced lunches. She was constantly stressed, and my siblings dealt with the social and emotional problems typical to children growing up in poverty. I began working at the age of twelve to contribute to the household. My parents had not gone to college, and no one in my family had an advanced degree. Yet I wanted something better, and education seemed like the path there. I poured myself into my studies and student leadership, attending school on a scholarship and work-study program, and ultimately became the first woman in my family to graduate from college. I worked through law school, married a "good" man from a "good" family, and started a career I could never have imagined for myself as a teen. I thought I had made the necessary choices to improve my circumstances, and had earned my new life of stability and comfort. Surely, I thought, anyone willing to work hard could do the same.

The facilitators questioned our explanations, especially those that blamed individual factors. "Does it make sense that every 'lazy,' 'unlucky,' and 'inept' person of color came to live in this one neighborhood in Charlotte?" It doesn't. Personal characteristics do not explain why poverty is concentrated in certain areas or why it disproportionately impacts people of color; nor does it explain why white people hold so much of this country's wealth. I considered whether my experience of poverty would have differed if I had not been white. Would my defiance of my high school principal have been celebrated as courageous, or would it have led to detention? Would my middle school struggles with peer relationships have prompted a compassionate referral to school-based counseling, or suspensions? Would it have been as easy to secure those job and college offers? I realized that the barriers to escaping poverty are overwhelming for Black, Indigenous, and people of color. As a judge, I witnessed people trying to overcome difficult circumstances through hard work and discipline, but I began to understand that they were trapped in a way I never was.

The facilitators went on to detail four hundred years of common law, statutes, ordinances, policies, and court decisions that served to maintain white supremacy. This history—different from what most of us had learned in school—showed how the construct of race has intentionally and systemically fostered a hierarchy among humans. While America has deemed itself exceptional, emboldened by the premise that "all [people] are created equal," the reality is that the government has given people called "white" access to resources, while exploiting and subjugating Indigenous, Black, and Latinx people.

Learning this history can be difficult; it requires humility and openness. Yet learning that Black and Indigenous people and people of color face obstacles that I have not encountered does not diminish my personal challenges and achievements; instead, it helps me understand the experiences of others. It helps me—a gatekeeper in the criminal legal system—better enact the ideals of justice, equity, and fairness.

This learning guided me over eight years hearing child welfare and delinquency cases in juvenile court, and working with children in our Youth Recovery Court. I stopped trying to identify families' problems and dictate the services I thought would solve them, instead listening to what parents and children said about what they themselves needed. I talked less, listened more, and asked questions. I heard about the distrust of the government caused by intergenerational harm from "child welfare" interventions that separated children from their grandparents, aunts, uncles, and cousins. Parents in Youth Recovery Court described how the demands of our "helping" services threatened employment and strained resources. Listening helped me see the world through a very different lens.

I have been learning for over a decade and I will continue for decades to come. But I did not come to this learning on my own. The collaborative leadership group Race Matters for Juvenile Justice has created the infrastructure to support change in the court system. I have benefited from their guidance, but I have also made mistakes. Community members have called me out for ways I have caused harm. Friends and colleagues of color have called me in to listen to their truths. Above all, my personal experience with reckoning has been shaped and advanced by building trust and authentic relationships with and among people of color.

Moving from this learning to active acknowledgment, we confronted racial disparities in the child welfare, delinquency, and education systems by collecting, analyzing, and sharing data. Agency leaders committed to teaching the history of structural racism and to using formal racial equity workforce development plans; members pledged to lead change within our organizations. It was novel for government agencies to acknowledge their racist policies and outcomes. It was even more revolutionary to institute practices that addressed racial disparities. We called this "institutional organizing."

I brought this institutional organizing approach to the adult criminal courts. I partnered with law enforcement, the prosecutor, and the public defender to analyze and share data, and to reform bail practices and the use of court fines and fees; finally, my justice system colleagues and I committed to acknowledging that race drove unequal outcomes in the system. Yet while I was proud of our work and promoting new reforms in the local media, my enthusiasm was met—in community forums and among system-affected organizers—by skepticism or indifference. As I wondered why, I realized that institutional reform will be illegitimate as long as it remains an ahistorical project aimed at simply improving outcomes. I came to understand that as a criminal legal system practitioner, I have inherited—and participated in—a long legacy of harmful practices. Merely seeking to improve outcomes is insufficient; I must also formally take responsibility for my harmful role and implement repair-focused actions to atone for and eradicate these systemic practices.

The Reimagining America Project: The Truth, Reconciliation, and Atonement Commission of Charlotte established a formal process in 2020 to "[call] to account the history of racialized oppression in Charlotte, and . . . foster—through testimony, witnessing, and atonement—measurable systemic changes to end systemic racism permanently."[2] The Reimagining America Project holds formal hearings where witnesses testify about the racialization of specific institutions, and I was invited to testify during a hearing about the criminal legal system. At the hearing, "historical witnesses" testified about the origins of racialized criminal justice policy. Next, "impacted witnesses" testified about experiences with police, prosecutors, and the courts, and explained their consequences. Finally, I testified as a "confessing witness," acknowledging my own participation in practices that caused racial harm. The following is my testimony in that proceeding.

Confessing Witness Statement of Chief Judge Elizabeth Trosch to the Reimagining America Project

October 22, 2020

As a white woman who is a gatekeeper in the criminal legal system, I have benefited from, contributed to, participated in, and perpetuated criminal justice policies and practices with deep roots in slavery, Jim Crow, and terror lynchings. As a defense attorney, I advised clients who were Black men to comply and stay quiet during police encounters. As a juvenile court judge, I told Black youth not to stand up for themselves when school faculty targeted them for discipline; failing to see how this diminished their dignity, I advised them to subjugate themselves. In child welfare cases, I failed to ask about fathers, assuming they were not available to parent their children. In criminal court, I dressed down defendants who were late and, even, on occasion, jailed them. I did not ask why defendants were late, or consider that people who do not have cars rely on a bus system that does not operate throughout the county. I threatened contempt sanctions when defendants became stressed and dysregulated while addressing the court.

I deeply regret my actions, which perpetuated racial harm in my community. My efforts to dispense justice were misguided. I regret that I was not more informed about the obstacles trapping people in the criminal legal system and that I stereotyped people instead of seeing their humanity. I am sorry for the harm I have caused.

Confessing the ways that I have caused racial harm served not only the impacted witnesses and the public observers. The practice of confession is both painful and liberating as a means to establish deep truths. Confession—and truth—can liberate victims, perpetrators, and bystanders.

Reforms born in the conference rooms of justice agencies are disconnected from the experiences of impacted individuals. People who have been marginalized, excluded, and oppressed must be given the power and platform to direct change. Impacted individuals and communities must be invited to help examine data and design policies and interventions to improve their experiences. This kind of power sharing opens the door to reconciliation.

Establishing a formal role for community organizers, racial justice activists, and people with lived experience of the criminal justice system requires a radical change to the work of local government and courts. This might be why my vision of partnership and power sharing was not initially embraced by police chiefs, the prosecutor, or the county government. Early "community engagement" initiatives included police-led resource fairs, garden planting, and community forums telling Black, Indigenous, and people of color how to have safe interactions with law enforcement. Yet such activities failed to shift power into the communities most affected by the criminal legal system, or to increase safety and equity. Ultimately, I used my positional authority to break down institutional barriers and ensure full and meaningful collaboration.

Through persistence and the engagement of Black, Indigenous, and people of color organizers, activists, and local elected officials, our county manager finally embraced a vision of partnership on justice reform. We formed a Community Engagement Task Force, whose diverse membership represented the varied experiences of our community members, including Black, Indigenous, and Latinx people; LGBTQ+ people; young people; multinational people; crime survivors; and those who were previously incarcerated. We designed it so community members—whose time and expertise we valued and compensated—would outnumber criminal legal system representatives on the task force. Still, even with this shared goal of altering the power relationship between impacted communities and the criminal legal system, we faced barriers. For instance, local government rules required those contracted for services to be registered vendors with liability insurance. We wrote new rules for this new paradigm of community-government partnership.

The members of the Community Engagement Task Force laid a foundation of humility and partnership before beginning our work, positioning ourselves for transformational reform after winning the support of community members and criminal justice system gatekeepers alike. Law enforcement, the court, the prosecutor, and local government all committed to reconstituting our relationship with community members, to critically evaluating and addressing our harmful practices, and to implementing more equitable policies. But justice system practitioners cannot do this work in a vacuum; we must collaborate with and center community members.

The first step for us was instituting a reckoning with legal financial obligations such as cash bail, court costs, fines, and civil asset forfeiture. The process of learning, acknowledgment, and repair required action to eradicate harmful policies and practices. Putting "institutional reckoning" into practice, I worked with court partners and consultants to uproot our bail system and reshape how we assess legal financial obligations.

Legal financial obligations have long, violent histories with which courts and legislatures must reckon. For centuries, criminal courts have been complicit in profiteering from the dehumanization and criminalization of Black personhood. This began with slavery, and took new forms up to and including contemporary criminal-legal financial obligations. While the nature of dispossession has transformed from labor predation to complex, multilevel systems of financial extraction, poor people and communities of color remain disproportionately harmed. Fines are levied as punishment for breaking the law. Fees are meant to fund the courts and other government activities. Yet these justifications ignore a long history of harm.

As books such as *Slavery by Another Name* by Douglas Blackmon have documented, after the abolition of slavery in the nineteenth century, agriculture-dependent economies in the South suffered. Since wealth influenced power, this economic downturn reduced the political standing of Southern elites and landowners. They sought to offset the failing economy with a new system of free labor. This system—convict leasing—relied both on white supremacy and on a constitutional loophole: people convicted of a crime were exempt from protections granted by the Thirteenth Amendment, which abolished slavery.

The practice of convict leasing meant that Black people were incarcerated and forced to carry out physical labor to "pay off" their sentence. This system, which helped maintain agricultural Southern economies and reinstate political power for white Southern elites, continued through the early twentieth century. The criminal justice system directly sustained America's racial hierarchy. Today, it continues to enable profit extraction and maintain white supremacy by imposing legal financial obligations for people who come into contact with the criminal legal system. State authority is leveraged to incarcerate legally innocent people and subsidize government revenue by stripping resources from poor and Black communities.

Legal financial obligations for people involved with the criminal legal system have become increasingly prevalent over the last three decades. Starting in the 1970s, the rising criminalization of poor people of color contributed to a sixfold increase in the number of people incarcerated in state and local facilities.[3] This entailed significant costs to governments. To defray the growing costs of increased surveillance and incarceration, state legislatures and local governments created new ways to charge defendants, multiplying the fines and fees owed as a consequence of criminal legal system involvement. This led to complex fee schedules that trap defendants and their families in a debt loop of court bondage.

Nationwide, roughly ten million people owe more than $50 billion in criminal legal system debt.[4] Along with monetary sanctions, personal property is routinely seized from poor Black people under police surveillance, under the assertion that possessions are the fruits of criminal enterprise. Fees accompany every step of the criminal legal system process.

Most monetary sanctions are imposed as a consequence of conviction or even accusation of a crime: jail fees for pretrial detention, appointment of counsel fees, court costs, fines, restitution, probation supervision fees, community service fees, fine collection fees, electronic monitoring, and the costs of court-ordered programs. In most states, the offense—and not someone's ability to pay—determines the amount of financial sanctions. The average debt from court-related fines totals over $13,000.[5] And most state legislatures limit courts' authority to waive or remit these sanctions.

Nationally, about 80–90 percent of people charged with a crime are poor enough to qualify for a court-appointed lawyer. Almost a third of defendants are unemployed before their arrest. And Black Americans are stopped, searched, arrested, and incarcerated at higher rates than white Americans. This leads to accumulated court debt that deepens racial and economic inequality.[6] The racist over-policing of minority neighborhoods concentrates the criminal legal system in poor, minority communities.[7]

Legal debt can be catastrophic for people who are already financially insecure. Failure to pay only compounds long-term economic harm. Some states charge interest or additional fees for failure to comply; others report debt on people's credit history, compromising access to credit, rental housing, mortgages, cars, and employment; and many suspend driver's licenses for people with unpaid legal debt.

Although an 1833 federal law banned debtors' prisons in the United States, poor people are still regularly incarcerated because they cannot afford to pay court debts. Many fees are levied to generate revenue for state budgets; and cities with higher Black populations rely more heavily on fines and fees from petty offenses to raise municipal revenue.[8] This paradigm positions the courts as tax collectors for the state, turning residents into potential sources of revenue and undermining the independence and fairness of state courts.

Courts must recognize the harm these practices perpetuate, formally acknowledge them as a legacy of convict leasing, and implement criminal legal system debt reforms. New policies should be accompanied by statements of purpose that articulate this harm, noting that reforms aim to atone for, repair, and prevent racialized harm. Alongside formal acknowledgment, courts should include the history of these practices in curricula used to train judicial officers and court personnel on reforms.

In our court system, we are working to issue an acknowledgment statement to post in the courthouse and publish in a local newspaper, where the broader public can access it in perpetuity. The text would acknowledge that the racialized extraction of billions of dollars from our poorest citizens cannot be justified as a rational scheme to fund fair and impartial courts. It would go on to say that monetary sanctions degrade the courts, framing them as a commercial enterprise in which "user fees" are collected from defendants who are "customers." This practice casts doubt on judges' independence and shifts the burden of funding the judiciary onto already penalized citizens. As explained by Heather Hunt and Gene Nichol, since all citizens have "potent interest in a strong, fair, functioning justice system," all citizens "ought to pay for it, like they do police, or the fire department."[9] Finally, the statement would say that "this court acknowledges that the current system of legal financial obligations disproportionately harms poor and minority defendants, consistent with its historic roots in racial terror and white supremacy. Courts have been complicit in the perpetuation of this racial harm. This policy to reform the imposition of legal financial obligations is instituted to atone for and repair the harm the court has done."

The final step of atonement and repair in our district involved eliminating court costs, fines, and fees resulting from criminal court involvement and forgiving all outstanding criminal legal system debt. Although eliminating legal financial obligations requires legislation, judges can take immediate action to repair harm done and prevent future harm. Judges can work with prosecutors, clerks, and defense attorneys to enact criminal legal system debt relief. Court leaders in Mecklenburg County completed such a debt relief project in 2019. Nearly eleven thousand people in my district whose criminal cases had been resolved anywhere from two to twenty years earlier still had outstanding balances for unpaid legal financial obligations. Criminal legal system debt had interminably burdened them and constrained their freedom. Together, the district attorney, the clerk of Superior Court, and I entered orders forgiving the outstanding debt. Removing the burden of outstanding legal financial obligations unshackles citizens and restores their liberty.

Additionally, judges can act to preserve the constitutional mandate that no one should be jailed because they are poor. They can do this by conducting ability-to-pay hearings and by remitting, waiving, or reducing legal financial obligations where possible. Despite several Supreme

Court rulings that incarceration can only be used to collect criminal legal system debt when a person can afford to pay but willfully refuses to do so, nearly 20 percent of people jailed in the county in 2019 were held for failure to pay court costs and fees.

This prompted two colleagues and me to convene court stakeholders and establish new policies related to legal financial obligations. Now, before establishing a monetary obligation, a Mecklenburg County judge must both determine a defendant's ability to pay and enter an order with findings of fact. We also altered the enforcement of monetary judgments, terminating the practice of issuing bench orders for arrest and setting cash bonds in the amount a person owes for fines and fees. Instead, we provide a procedure for people who have failed to pay to show that they no longer have the ability to do so. We have also ceased imposing sanctions when defendants fail to pay legal financial obligations imposed as conditions of probation. These administrative changes can be made through policy directives from local administrative judges and state supreme courts.

Jurisdictions must do more than reform legal financial obligations. They must address the roots of these practices and the harm done to generations of Black and Indigenous people and people of color. Transformational reform that generates trust in the courts must be built on a foundation of acknowledgment and atonement. This requires deep engagement between system actors and the people these changes seek to serve. To repair and prevent racialized harm, criminal legal system debt reforms must entail collaboration with local community organizations and impacted people.

There has long been a mutually reinforcing link between racialized dehumanization and extreme punishment. Today, courts continue to impose harsh punishments—that serve no public safety purpose—disproportionately on Black and brown people without regard for this history of terror and violence. Too often, discussions of this history obscure the human toll of white supremacy, and fail to acknowledge the names, identities, dreams, relationships, and hopes of people who were harmed. To formally acknowledge our violent history and atone for racist, punitive excess inflicted on people, families, and communities of color, we need a new narrative of crime and accountability that centers human dignity and parsimony rather than punishment. This new narrative must recognize and honor the value of the lives involved. We must focus not on the criminality of a single act, but on human potential and future possibilities.

Racial reckoning requires a recomposition of the power relationship between communities of color and the criminal legal system. Individuals and communities harmed by crime must be empowered to shape the state's response to the damage they have endured. Through formal partnership, court leaders and community members can together craft institutional strategies to reduce racial harm and direct justice system resources to address communities' needs. Only those harmed by the racial violence of the system have the power to release criminal legal practitioners from their debts. Through reckoning, Black Americans can reclaim the dignity stolen by a historically harmful criminal legal process, and white Americans can be released from the shame of this legacy.

Reckoning is not a linear, one-time process. It is ongoing work that requires self-examination at the individual and community level, grounded in honest reflection and humility. It takes constant learning and introspection, focused on the values and goals of our justice work. It's a lifelong confrontation with, and atonement for, past and present racialized harm. As the Reimagining America Project explains, "It is through concrete forms of making right what was wrong that perpetrators and bystanders can be set free from the terrible mistakes of the past, while victims and their descendants can start to see actual, measurable evidence of contrition." From there, true justice can "[build] an utterly new relationship among equals." [10]

9

CREATING NEW NARRATIVES FOR CRIMINAL JUSTICE AND IMMIGRATION REFORM

Matthew Desmond and Greisa Martínez Rosas

Matthew Desmond is the Maurice P. During Professor of Sociology at Princeton University. He is the principal investigator of The Eviction Lab at Princeton, and the author of Evicted: Poverty and Profit in the American City.

Greisa Martínez Rosas is the executive director at United We Dream, a national nonpartisan, membership-based organization of over one hundred thousand immigrant youth and allies. Led by its fifty-five affiliate organizations in twenty-six states, United We Dream advocates for the dignity and fair treatment of working-class people of color. Originally from Hidalgo, Mexico, Greisa came to the United States with her family at a young age as an undocumented immigrant.

How should we tell the story about crime and punishment in America? Justice narratives—stories about criminal legal systems and the people that come under their supervision—are told every day by presidents and neighbors, artists and journalists, police chiefs and prison abolitionists. Whether to frighten or inspire or expand our vision about what is possible, these stories are meant to persuade. They aren't maps, giving us the lay of the land, but compasses: they tell us where to go.

A war story, according to Vietnam veteran Tim O'Brien, has no moral.[1] The violence has no point; it serves no larger purpose. Crime stories are the opposite. There is always a "therefore" declared or implied at the end of a crime story. These narratives have a way of following the logic of the court: after the details comes a verdict.

For simplicity's sake, we distinguish between incrementalistic and transformational justice stories. Incrementalistic stories support incremental change and serve specific, short-term ends, such as a ballot initiative or policy intervention. Transformational stories imagine entirely different kinds of justice systems and often question foundational assumptions that buttress the status quo. Incrementalistic stories ask what can be done. Transformational stories ask what should be. We focus on both kinds of narratives in this chapter.

Transformational stories might not be beholden to a specific policy change; nor are they idealistic tales cleaved from tangible reforms. Whereas incrementalistic stories often home in on specific issues that reformers hope a broad public will likely see as problematic or unjust—e.g., draconian sentences for nonviolent offenders, deporting immigrant young people—transformational stories make a different bet. They wager that a more general or foundational critique will galvanize a social movement and shift the terms of the debate by redefining what is "reasonable." Transformational stories can make radical policy ideas look moderate and moderate policy ideas appear noncontroversial. Next to calls for "abolishing" or "defunding" the police, for example, doing away with qualified immunity appears like the least a city could do. Next to calls for citizenship for 11 million undocumented Americans, shielding 1.3 million from deportation through Deferred Action for Childhood Arrivals (DACA) presents as a policy compromise. As abolitionist organizer and advocate Mariame Kaba once remarked, "This is how I know things shift: when Ferguson happened, and all the demands were about body cameras and things like that to—to come to this moment, six years later, and the demand is to defund and abolish the police for a significant number of people. I mean, my God, that's incredible to me." [2]

Incrementalistic and transformational stories have different audiences, goals, and theories of change. Both kinds of narratives are necessary to reimagining and enacting new justice systems. An organizer might tell an incrementalistic story one day and a transformational one the next, depending on her audiences and intentions. The difficult part is making sure one kind of story doesn't compromise the other.

We worry that one kind of justice narrative—call them the easiest cases—can potentially do harm to long-term, comprehensive reform goals. We have in mind occasions when reformers focus intensively on harvesting low-hanging fruit, targeting what sociologist David Garland has called "the soft middle of undecided voters," in an attempt to engage the ambivalent.[3] The authors of "easiest case" stories select an aspect of the criminal legal system they believe most Americans will find unjust and focus their energy exclusively on that specific target until it moves from margin to center. As a result of such strategies, our national debate about mass incarceration has, through recent decades, in large part been a conversation about locking up "nonviolent offenders," just as the public conversation about immigration has centered "undocumented workers," as if the second word in the phrase justifies, or tidies up, the word that precedes it.

There is no denying that easiest-case narratives have brought about policy change, from presenting alternatives to incarceration and decreasing mandatory minimums for some crimes to deferred deportation and work permits for some undocumented young people through DACA (a federal executive action taken in 2012).[4] Opinions do appear more flexible when it comes to lower-level offenses. This strategy of picking "easiest cases" is, on its surface, practical and straightforward. For instance, one study found that while support for harsh punishments for drug-related crime declined after participants were shown evidence about racial disparities in sentencing, support for the death penalty did not waiver in the face of such evidence.[5] Findings such as this might incentivize reformers to seek smaller victories over more ambitious defeats.

Yet there is still much we don't know about political persuasion. Do Americans' attitudes toward crime and punishment change slowly, then all at once? What effect do traumatic events, such as a terrorist attack or police killing, have on accelerating or stalling reform? How do we account for movements and counter-movements and the uneven course of social change? If the medium is part of the message, what are the implications of the speed at which technological advances shape and reshape modes of communication? To these questions, we add several more about the kinds of stories we promote in the service of criminal justice and immigration justice.

In the United States, those who wish to tell a story about undocumented or formerly incarcerated people are immediately confronted with a dominant narrative that holds those people in contempt. Oftentimes, the identities of those who have committed crimes or crossed borders outside of official checkpoints are condensed from full personhood to one label: criminal.

Responding to stereotypes about people so labeled, some reformers tell easiest-case stories about system-involved people. In the criminal legal field, the "non, non, non's"—nonviolent, nonserious, nonsexual offenders—carry the narrative, presenting the criminal legal system as one of punitive overreach into the lives of those who have committed minor offenses. In the immigration debate, reformers frame undocumented young people as "Dreamers," so named for the DREAM Act, emphasizing deservedness rooted in conventional modalities of upward mobility (e.g., higher education) and assimilation into Anglo-American culture (e.g., English proficiency).

Here, reformers do not reject the basic conceptual formula on which negative stereotypes rely—"A" is x, where "A" is a bounded group (e.g., immigrants) and x its defining attributes (e.g., dangerous). Rather, they merely substitute something more positive for x.[6] This well-intentioned narrative choice attempts to humanize those often painted with a negative brush. However, this maneuver has several limitations.

For one, if we challenge a stereotype by inverting it, that action can always be reversed. For every story published in *Mother Jones* of a hardworking, kind-hearted immigrant, there is a story of an undocumented person charged with a heinous crime published on Breitbart. The *New Yorker* ran stories on Kalief Browder, a young man accused of stealing a backpack who spent three years in Rikers Island and later died by suicide. The *New York Post* reported on Farkell Hopkins, a man accused of killing a pedestrian while driving drunk, who was released "thanks to new soft-on-crime laws."[7]

Moreover, when reformers counter negative "whataboutism" with positive "whataboutism," they can sometimes ignore the concerns of the very audience they hope to persuade: "the soft middle of undecided voters." For example, when criminal justice reformers say little about crime, choosing instead to focus on, say, racial disparities within the prison population or the damage incarceration does to families, they can make an audience member feel akin to a homeowner who hires a contractor to remodel the kitchen only to discover the bathroom gutted. To be sure, there were problems with the bathroom, but the job was the kitchen. In the debate about "crime and punishment," if we focus only on the problems of punishment, at the expense of reckoning with crime, we will both alienate and disappoint Americans for whom the fear of crime is a powerful motivating force.

In addition, reformers who craft stories intended to uplift heroes can be caught unprepared when confronted with morally repulsive (and politically inconvenient) acts. When Kate Steinle, a thirty-two-year-old white woman, was shot and killed in San Francisco by José Inez García Zárate, a forty-five-year-old undocumented immigrant from Mexico who had been previously deported multiple times, conservative pundits and politicians drew on the event, creating an anti-hero narrative. "My opponent wants sanctuary cities," then Republican presidential candidate Donald Trump said at a rally. "But where was the sanctuary for Kate Steinle?" Texas senator Ted Cruz leveraged the shooting to introduce federal legislation establishing mandatory minimums for any illegal reentry offense. The bill was introduced as "Kate's Law." If we reserve mercy only for the good people, when others fall far short of the mark, that failing can be exploited by those championing punitive policies.

All these considerations are backlit by the racial divisions that characterize American institutions and civil society. Recognizing the saliency of racism in justice narratives is critical to understanding their power and reach. The rhetorical use of Kate Steinle's death, for example, was informed by a long, bloody history that justified violence (both vigilante and state-sponsored) against Black and brown men on the principle of protecting the safety and purity of white women. This racialized fear of victimization is regularly exploited for political gain, from the "Willie Horton" ads run by George H.W. Bush's 1988 presidential campaign to Donald Trump's demonization of immigrants.[8] Collectively reaching for new narrative strategies, then, requires critical reflection on how stories of reform are compromised, empowered, or complicated by the central American story, which is the story of racial domination and progress. We need to reconsider how stories are formulated and communicated, creating new structures for both processes that do not rely on racism and othering.

When confronted with a horrific episode or a vile crime, reformers often cite their rarity. Violent crime is rare from a national perspective. But neurological and psychological research also has shown that anger and perceived threats to safety override other reactions based on empathy. That means a positive story about a formerly incarcerated person does not cancel out a negative one, the latter of which has been linked to favoring more punitive sanctions.[9] Other studies have shown that people calibrate their fears not to the frequency of threats but to their potency. This implies that "rationalizing" statements that attempt to contextualize one's risk of being victimized will have limited impact.[10] Indeed, those who most deeply register a fear of crime—or who translate it into political action, like voting for the "tough on crime" candidate—often live in communities with very low actual risk of victimization.

There is also reason to believe that efforts to suppress or supplant stereotypes actually backfire. Psychological studies have shown that people instructed to resist negative thoughts about a stigmatized group end up perceiving that group in a less favorable light than those who were not given such instructions. A review of the research put it plainly: "Suppression is not an effective prejudice-reduction strategy."[11] Americans know people commit violent crimes. Asking them to sublimate that fact in favor of a morally palatable picture of lawbreaking strikes us as unrealistic and potentially counterproductive.

But there is a second, and even deeper, reason not to challenge a negative stereotype by reversing it with a positive one. There are two ways to dehumanize: to strip people of all virtue and to cleanse them of all sin. Narratives of moral panic do the former; narratives of moral uplift do the latter. Neither narrative embraces the full complexity of the lived experience of people.

In 1947, *The Nation* commissioned James Baldwin to review the book *There Was Once a Slave* by Shirley Graham, a well-known author, playwright, and civil rights activist. A biography of Frederick Douglass, Graham's book was well received, winning the Julian Messner Award for the best book published that year combating racial intolerance in America. Baldwin hated it. "I cannot see that Miss Graham has made any contribution to interracial understanding," he wrote, "for she is so obviously determined to Uplift the Race that she makes Douglass a quite unbelievable hero and has robbed him of dignity and humanity alike."[12] Writing nearly two decades before the passage of the Civil Rights Act, Baldwin was upset, not that Graham had been too harsh on Douglass, but that she had been too fawning, following him with "wide-eyed adoration" and portraying his critics as one-dimensional stooges or scoundrels. This stripped Douglass not only of an honest portrait but also, tellingly, of his "dignity and humanity," which comes with full personhood.[13]

Baldwin's critique is relevant today, as some seek to invert stereotypes affixed to justice-involved people and reveal saints where before there were thought to be villains. These "sinners to saints" stories often do not in fact humanize but instead further reduce people to either perpetrator or victim. In fact, many people convicted of crimes have previously been victims of crime. Relatedly, studies estimate that four in five people incarcerated in state prison for "nonviolent" offenses also could be classified as "serious" offenders.[14] In other words, the people who have been most victimized are often also those most engaged in criminal activity, with little meaningful distinction between serious and nonserious engagement. Both sides of identity divisions convenient for political messaging—violent/nonviolent, documented/undocumented, victim/offender—can often be found within the same person, family, and community.

Recognizing this reveals a third vulnerability of positive stereotyping: that doing so props up a contingent morality based on individual performance as opposed to a universalistic morality grounded in widely shared values. A contingent morality extends rights to the good and deserving but denies rights to the evil and undeserving. Historically, poor Americans have had to choose between having access to social welfare programs and being granted full rights that accompanied the independent citizen.[15] In the same way, the politics of contingent morality asks those who may be in need of social provision to forgo such support in favor of a shot at fuller inclusion into the body politic; or, as law scholar Marie Gottschalk has put it, America's criminal legal and immigration systems promise "to give people a second chance, never acknowledging that many of the people cycling in and out of prison and jail"—and immigrant detention facilities—"were never really given a first chance, let alone an equal chance."[16]

Easiest-case stories divide the worthy from the unworthy: those deserving of mercy and citizenship from those deserving of punishment, banishment, and death. Calls for mercy for nonviolent offenders imply that violent offenders are undeserving of that mercy. Likewise, when undocumented young people are characterized as innocent immigrants who "came to the United States through no fault of their own," they are juxtaposed against their loved ones, their mothers and fathers who crossed borders intentionally and courageously. "Historically," writes author Karla Cornejo Villavicencio, "legislators and immigration advocates have parted the sea of the undocumented with a splintered staff—working brown men and women on one side and academically achieving young brown people on the other, one a parasitic blight, the other heroic dreamers." [17]

Divisive narratives that categorize system-involved people—documented/undocumented immigrants; violent/nonviolent offenders—imply that one group is more deserving than the other. Such narratives may contribute to short-term gains at the expense of long-term ones. For one, they can imply, or outright assert, that some people are irredeemable. A similar specter of moral depravity haunts the concept of rehabilitation during incarceration, as it implies that reincorporation into society must be preceded by a fundamental transformation of oneself. The word derives its meaning from the Medieval Latin word *rehabilitare*, meaning "to bring back to a former condition after decay or damage." Those condemned to die in prison are seen as depraved beyond repair; those marked for rehabilitation are seen as depraved and in need of restoration. Both designations train our attention on broken people (not broken systems) or even broken moments. The fact that most people age out of crime demonstrates that the self is far from fixed.[18] When justice narratives neglect to challenge presumptions about the irredeemable nature of certain offenders, they can push reforms targeting those offenders further down the line.

Easiest-case narratives have also led criminal-justice and immigrant-rights reformers to operate in isolation from each other, dividing policy agendas and diminishing their collective voice and organizational capacity. Immigrant-rights groups once rallied around the slogan "We are workers, not criminals." But in doing so, they contributed to the stigmatization of people entangled with the criminal legal system.[19] Likewise, support for criminal legal system reform policies like the First Step Act that explicitly exclude undocumented immigrants contributes to the increased criminalization and punishment of immigrants. Of course, criminal legal reformers and immigrant-rights reformers have different stories to tell and different policy goals. But when each group operates independently of the other, one group's messaging can complicate, even compromise, the other's.

As mentioned earlier, easiest-case narratives have helped increase public support for criminal justice and immigration reform. In 2010, for example, South Carolina legislators established bipartisan reforms that included alternatives to incarceration for certain drug crimes and reduced maximum penalties for other offenses, like burglary. Two years later, California voters approved Proposition 36 by a wide margin, excluding nonviolent offenders from mandatory life sentences under the state's "three-strikes law." At the federal level, Attorney General Eric Holder in 2011 testified in support of retroactive application of the Fair Sentencing Act of 2010, which reduced sentencing disparities between drug crimes involving crack and powder cocaine. Measures such as these were supported by arguments that emphasized the cruelty of racial injustice and punitive overreach, as well as the importance of second chances.[20]

But there was a catch. Each of these reforms was also accompanied either by public statements or public policies supporting harsh penalties for violent crime. In South Carolina, when legislators proposed alternatives to incarceration for some crimes, they simultaneously made more offenses eligible for life-without-parole sentences. In California, proponents of Proposition 36 made it clear, in the words of one spokesman for the campaign, that people considered "hard-core criminals" would "get no benefit whatsoever from the reform, no matter what third strike they commit." Similarly, when Attorney General Holder decried sentencing disparities, he asked the U.S. Sentencing Commission not to apply his recommendations to violent offenders[21]—despite strong evidence that Black defendants receive harsher sentences for violent crime than white defendants.[22] It is telling, moreover, that most of the above-cited reforms excluded undocumented immigrants from any relief.

Immigration policy has been characterized by a similar push-pull of progress and regression. After the September 11th terrorist attacks, many political pundits and federal lawmakers began framing immigrants, especially from South Asian and Muslim countries, as national security threats. The political gains that immigration advocates had achieved up to that point were not enough to secure the congressional votes needed to pass an immigration bill that had been years in the making. In response to this defeat, advocates adopted a new narrative strategy, one that framed immigrants as striving "Dreamers."[23] Young immigrant organizers built on this rhetorical foundation and began referring to themselves as "undocumented and unafraid," a narrative stance that led to substantial policy gains. In 2014, President Obama announced the Deferred Action for Parents of Americans and Lawful Permanent Residents (DAPA) program, staying the deportation of some parents of United States citizens. When he announced this program, the president relied on another set of binaries, emphasizing that enforcement resources would target "felons, not families. Criminals, not children. Gang members, not a mom who's working hard to provide for her kids."[24] At the same time, however, the Obama administration simultaneously ramped up Secure Communities policies, eventually deporting more than five million people between 2009 and 2016.

Gottschalk calls these "split policy verdicts."[25] With split policy verdicts, criminal legal and immigration reforms often take one step forward and one step back, the backward step sometimes considered politically necessary to secure forward momentum. Yet securing mercy for some while solidifying and expanding severity for others can increase the overall harshness of criminal legal and immigration systems simply because those extended mercy typically are in the numerical minority. The number of people serving time for violent crime in state prisons exceeds that of people convicted of drug crimes by a rate of 3.7 to 1.[26] Likewise, DAPA—which was blocked by the courts—would have protected roughly 3.7 million undocumented immigrants, a fraction of the undocumented population, estimated to number around 11 million.[27]

To be clear: the DAPA program would have been nothing short of a historic victory for immigrant rights, and rolling back harsh sentencing for nonviolent crimes has resulted in considerable reductions in prison and jail populations. For example, when Jerry Brown's governorship ended in 2019, roughly 34,000 fewer people were incarcerated in California state prisons than in 2011, when he was sworn in. This reduction was driven mainly by reforms to address nonviolent offenses without relying on incarceration.[28] Our point isn't that easiest-case justice stories are ineffective. They have helped to usher in tangible, even sweeping, reform. But split policy verdicts remind us that the overall utility of such narratives cannot be assessed in isolation—on the basis of a single policy change or ballot measure. Rather, they must be assessed on a system-wide basis. A "win" today may make one more difficult to attain tomorrow.

Sometimes, a changing national tolerance and political climate can lead to the passage of new legislation whose success is misattributed to the impact of easiest-case narratives. In the criminal legal system, notable recent decreases in incarceration could be attributed to America's discursive shift away from "tough on crime" rhetoric and toward a less punitive viewpoint in the public debate about incarceration and inequality. But the prison population has fallen, not because of policy changes reflecting newfound public sentiments, but because of "the great crime decline."[29] Jeffrey Butts, executive director of the Research and Evaluation Center at John Jay College of Criminal Justice, observes that juvenile confinement dropped by more than 40 percent since the mid-1990s not because of policy reform, but because juvenile crime has dropped by 40 percent in the last fifteen years.[30] It was not narrative change that resulted in policy reform, causing increases in safety and decreases in harsh punishment. It was because crime fell that elected officials and advocates could promote narrative change about criminal offending and criminal legal reform. As the crime spikes that occurred in several cities during the COVID-19 pandemic revealed, the public's tolerance for reform is contingent on how safe it feels. Safety can be swiftly erased by even small crime bumps or an isolated incident that is particularly heinous or threatening.[31]

A distinction between narrative and legislative change does not blunt the power of stories, but emphasizes how narratives, as engines of social transformation, must attend to structural constraints and opportunities. The "great crime decline" expanded the possibilities of reform narratives and engaged new audiences. Those narratives, in turn, could take advantage of the structural transformations that empowered them, leading to further structural change. This dynamic explains why warring narratives often compete over the very nature of social reality. During the Trump administration, conservatives observed that there was a surge of immigrants at the Southern border, while progressives observed that net immigration was zero. Both camps were factually correct—the surge at the border was accompanied by more deportations—but winning the debate about the fundamental character of the issue enables different rhetorical and political strategies.

How then can we make justice narratives more powerful and effective? The science of political persuasion is still in its infancy and is made all the more difficult as modes of communication evolve. Poetics still lives in the temple of art, not science, and perhaps always will. Yet we believe that the following guidelines—informed by community organizing, research, and lived experience—can help craft new narratives. Specifically, we suggest justice narratives should move from people to systems, rising above specific cases or crimes to consider the thing entire; from distance to proximity, bearing witness and promoting the experiences and leadership of justice-involved people; from separate to united contexts, recognizing that the criminal legal and immigration systems are linked; from contingent to universal morality, pitching reform in alignment with shared values and not individual deservedness; and from fear to trust, asking more of our audiences.

Question the Terms of the Debate

The power to shape an argument lies not with one's response to questions but with one's ability to decide which questions are asked in the first place. Reformers often find themselves crafting reactive narratives. If we offer the mirror images of negative stereotypes, we bind ourselves within a narrative frame that was employed to motivate repressive policies. New narratives promoting dignity, fairness, and justice could attempt to avoid this trap. This could entail posing different questions; transferring the locus of attention from people to systems; employing different tones, terminology, and points of emphasis; and experimenting with different mediums. The law professor john a. powell emphasizes that the stories we tell need to move beyond an "us versus them" framework without minimizing differences between people.[32] To do so, powell has advanced the concept of "bridging," which "is about creating compassionate space and practices where we can acknowledge each other's stories and suffering. We have to construct stories that allow space for others. Our story cannot just be about us in the narrowest way, nor can it reproduce othering by consigning an other to be just a villain in our story."

Consider the example of Frantz Fanon and his singular ability to summon up a different language, addressing himself to a different audience, when discussing colonialism and racial inequality. Jean-Paul Sartre, in his preface to Fanon's 1961 book *The Wretched of the Earth*, homes in on this new voice. Addressing white European readers, Sartre writes, "And if you mumble, sniggering awkwardly: 'He's really got it in for us!' you have missed the true nature of the scandal, for Fanon has got nothing 'in for you' at all; his book, which is such a hot issue for others, leaves you out in the cold." [33] Fanon does not respond to "the white gaze," to use Toni Morrison's term; he does not speak back to it, correct it. He ignores it. In the same way, new narratives for criminal legal and immigration reform could avoid supplying new answers to the same questions—questions about recidivism or deservedness or behavior pitched as predatory. Rather, it would leave those questions "out in the cold." [34]

Or consider James Whitman's distinction between the "presumption of innocence" and the "presumption of mercy." [35] In an adversarial justice system, like the kind developed in the United States, the accused is presumed innocent and obstacles are placed in the state's way, making prosecution difficult. In an inquisitorial system, like the kind found in Western Europe, the accused is not assumed to be innocent; rather, court actors work together to ensure that, if guilt is in fact established, the convicted does not undergo excessive punishment.

Whitman argues that presuming mercy has led to the construction of a more humane justice system, even if it has introduced other complications. Moreover, with the advent of prosecutorial power and the fact that over 90 percent of U.S. cases are resolved by a plea bargain, the presumption of innocence occurs more as legal theory than legal practice. [36] For our purposes, the presumption of mercy shifts the narrative terrain of the debate by sidestepping questions of guilt to ask: What is the most compassionate and parsimonious way to hold accountable someone who has harmed another?

Tell Personal Accounts

A 2016 study published in the journal *Science* reported the results of a field experiment that found that transphobic prejudice was reduced after canvassers went door-to-door, engaging people in a ten-minute conversation. During the conversation, canvassers encouraged people to take the perspective of others by discussing a time they were judged for being different. The effect of this intervention was still detected three months after the conversation.[37] These results suggest that reformers could encourage civil society to take the perspective of system-involved people. This would entail telling longer, more complex and multidimensional stories about immigration and crime, stories that dismiss conventional binaries (e.g., victim/perpetrator) and provide larger context about the lives of those often represented in a monochromatic light. Moving past the logic of the court, which focuses on personal agency during a discrete event such as a border crossing or burglary, perspective-taking narratives could focus on trauma, poverty, racism, and forms of correlated adversity that often contextualize the experiences of those processed through judicial systems.[38]

Who should tell new justice stories? The *Science* study suggests an answer: although both transgender and cisgender canvassers were effective, transgender canvassers were significantly more so.[39] This provides empirical support to the slogan that "people closest to the problem are closest to the solution." Another implication, then, is that those who have direct experience with justice and immigration systems should play key leadership roles in developing and deploying new narrative strategies. We believe narrative change campaigns should prioritize supporting and elevating the voices and leadership of formerly and currently incarcerated people as well as undocumented immigrants, so long as those sharing their story feel that doing so promotes their human dignity. Outlets such as United We Dream, The Marshall Project, and the Economic Hardship Reporting Project have modeled ways to support and promote art, poetry, reporting, and other modes of storytelling led by those with firsthand experience of the problem their work addresses.

We also believe that a more personal touch is likely essential to narrative change. After all, the *Science* study documented the effects of in-person conversations, not, say, an editorial written by a transgender journalist. Reaching large audiences through conventional means requires a privileged skill set—from writing and talking competencies to connections to media outlets—often unavailable to system-involved people. Civil rights activist Rashad Robinson notes that "narrative builds power for people, or it is not useful at all."[40]

A related principle is that justice stories are empowered when we gain intimacy with the issue, when we strive for "proximity," as social justice activist Bryan Stevenson has put it.[41] Bearing witness to immigration, crime, and punishment is a way to cut through simple and overheated takes based on abstract fear or political strategy. "An enemy is someone whose story you have not heard," the saying goes.[42] If we tether our stories to lived experiences, basing their authority on what anthropologist Clifford Geertz called "I-witnessing," we have a better chance of representing the full complexity of the issues at which justice narratives direct their attention.[43] This necessarily requires genuinely listening to and learning from those who have harmed others and those who have been harmed. When it comes to the latter group, this should not be mistaken for leveraging victims' anger and pain to achieve political ends—or assuming we speak for victims when we promote punitive retribution.

As author and advocate Danielle Sered has written, "When we hear victims attest to the unremitting intensity of their pain, we should not hear it as a straightforward justification of more incarceration—we should hear it at least in part as an indictment of our reliance on incarceration to help them heal."[44] When reformers center crime survivors' experiences, they often discover a desire to hold people accountable and promote public safety through something very different from incarceration.[45]

At the same time, as the activists Daryl Atkinson and Hernán Carvente Martinez have noted, consistently having to retell personal narratives to different publics can inflict its own kind of trauma. The most intimate details of a person's life can be used as tools to motivate political will, which for that individual can be experienced as constricting and reductive: one's whole personhood reduced to a convulsive moment or decision. In psychiatrist Bessel van der Kolk's classic definition, trauma emerges through a double disconnection: the first occurs when our bodies disconnect from our minds, such that noncognitive functions respond in a different way than our cognitive functions to the same painful event; the second occurs when we are disconnected from a community, isolated with feelings of shame or rage.[46] In the same way, rituals of public storytelling can disconnect the narrator's full self from their story and alienate the narrator from the community (through the process of caricature, for example). To counter this, we must focus both on the narrator and the narrative, being careful to avoid severing the relationship between the two.

Sharing personal experiences and bearing witness to problems is one way to move away from myth and toward proximity when it comes to questions of crime, punishment, and fairness. Another way is to lean on science. The National Research Council's 2013 report *Reforming Juvenile Justice* offers a good example.[47] The report drew on extensive research about brain development, developmental psychology, and the life course, establishing that adolescent involvement in crime is "part of the normal developmental process" and that young people's brains function differently than adults', especially with respect to impulse control and self-regulation. These biological findings were a powerful corrective to folk theories of youth crime that relied on notions of street culture, poor rearing, or moral depravity, including political scientist John DiIulio's concept of a "super-predator," notions that have fueled draconian policies such as life sentences for children.[48] Science has helped reformers and criminal legal system actors see young people in a new light, and this has had profound implications for criminal justice theory and policy.

Target Norms Not Beliefs

Studies have shown that media interventions often have little impact on beliefs, but they do affect perceptions of social norms.[49] This suggests that narrative change campaigns could be more effective if they attempted to influence what people understood to be socially acceptable, rather than attempting to "change hearts and minds." This has implications for both the message and the medium. Robinson has stated that the rules of cultural production are "much less about ensuring or leveraging empathy as they are about capturing normativity, i.e., modeling in media the institution of inclusion that we want to see in society and changing the incentive structures of media makers to align with these practices."[50]

With respect to the message, presenting aspects of the criminal legal and immigration systems as especially cruel, inefficient, and outdated will likely resonate more deeply with audiences than presenting system-involved people in a sentimental light. This is because the former approach targets community norms ("We shouldn't do this anymore") while the latter approach targets individual behaviors ("A person can do better"). The system itself should be placed on the defensive.[51] Many of us do not seriously act on our values until we feel pressure or encouragement from our social network. For example, although a person might be deeply concerned about animal suffering, they may not change eating habits until their spouse does.[52] Moral reasoning, and particularly moral action, is a fundamentally social act. Reformers can draw on this fundamental insight, from citing polling data, to asking audiences to cosign on stances or policies, to empowering justice stories.

With respect to the medium, if social norms are the target of narrative campaigns, then executing those campaigns to promote "synchronized community attention" will likely be more effective than media consumed in a more individual or isolated way.[53] Studies have shown voters to be more persuaded by political speeches if they believe they are watching those speeches live with many other people, as opposed to watching a pre-recorded speech alone.[54] We should pay attention not only to the content of our messages but also to how those messages are consumed. An implication of this line of research is that communicating a narrative during a moment of collective watching (e.g., live sporting event, State of the Union address) is likely to have a more lasting impact on perceptions of social norms and behavior. This perspective affects all narrative change attempts at the community level, insisting that behavior is more responsive to perceptions of what is broadly tolerated than to underlying beliefs or ideologies.

Emblematic of synchronized community attention, public outrage at the Trump administration's separation of families at the border concentrated contentious political issues into a single media optic. As families were being detained, separated, and caged in squalid conditions, media attention homed in on how xenophobic policies were being implemented, documenting abuses and creating a moment of collective watching. The situation became even more urgent when COVID-19 began spreading through detention facilities. Detainees were trapped, and the broader public was quarantined, which only heightened the amount of attention trained on the crisis.

During this moment, the American public responded once again with outrage, making clear that such abuses would not be tolerated. In a way that typical immigration debates about jobs or legal process are rarely able to do, our collective watching of families incarcerated at the border and children separated from their caretakers mobilized public outcry and grassroots protests that likely affected election outcomes. But the outcry soon faded, and the American public moved on. Calls decrying dehumanizing migrant camps along the Southern border have been muted. The challenge, then, is to find a way to leverage momentum created by a specific event or crisis to a large enough degree that it brings about lasting change.

Collaborate on Reform Movements and Reform Narratives

In recent years, the boundary understood to separate immigration enforcement from crime enforcement has faded, and perhaps disappeared, with the increasing militarization of the border and the founding of U.S. Immigration and Customs Enforcement (ICE) and Customs and Border Protection (CBP). Collective fear leveraged to justify draconian immigration policy closely resembles the fearmongering used to fuel the prison boom.[55] And yet movements focused on immigration reform largely work separately from those focused on criminal justice policy.

New narratives will require new forms of collaboration and partnership. We believe those steered by "intersectional frameworks," which actively adopt the perspectives of others and elevate the voices of traditionally silenced groups, would be especially powerful.[56] Uniting criminal legal and immigrant rights movements would not only allow reformers to pool resources; it would also allow new narratives that tell a fuller story accounting for our shared humanity and collective aims.

Oftentimes new narratives require both repurposing previous efforts at advocacy and expanding the platform to new voices. One such example is the efforts of undocumented young people who have been advocating for the passage of the Development, Relief, and Education for Alien Minors, or DREAM, Act since the early 2010s. Rather than let their undocumented status keep them from advocating loudly and publicly, undocumented immigrant youth have proudly broadcasted their citizenship status at sit-ins, marches, and hunger strikes. In the same way that gay rights activists used their "coming out" to increase visibility of their cause, immigrant youth have defiantly declared their undocumented status in public, organizing around the chant of "Undocumented and unafraid!" a refrain resonant of "We're here, we're queer!" These efforts have been mobilized by organizations such as United We Dream, the largest immigrant-youth-led organization in the United States. United We Dream's network also takes on issues specific to racial justice and LGBTQ+ pride, demonstrating their pursuit of intersectional advocacy from multiple angles.[57]

The widespread embrace of undocumented status changed the course of dialogue in policy debates about granting citizenship. Although their undocumented status prevented immigrant youth from achieving some of their many goals—attending college, pursuing careers in public service, voting—their public acknowledgment that they were both undocumented and eager to contribute to society in meaningful, specific ways clearly demonstrated that the public welfare would increase with sensible immigration reform. Through these tactics, the public was confronted with multidimensional young people whose stories resisted flattening.

Base Civil Inclusion on Shared Values

We believe justice narratives should be grounded in a set of shared values. Doing so moves away from the individualizing tendency inherent to narratives of heroism and blame, and broadens the aperture to focus on the community.[58] Narratives about shared values are not about "them" but "us," the kind of nation we hope to create. When confronting recidivism, for example, instead of asking how someone failed, we might turn the question on ourselves to ask: How did we fail them? We need to develop narratives of failure as much as narratives of success. We need to be prepared for times when people harm each other in reprehensible ways. The opposition certainly is. More broadly, rather than only shaping our narratives in response to specific policies or debate points, we should also stretch ourselves in an aspirational way.

An example of policies driven by shared values involves the work of conservative reformers like Pat Nolan and Chuck Colson, both formerly incarcerated men. Nolan and Colson have helped to pass policy, including the Prison Rape Elimination Act and the Second Chance Act, by grounding arguments in the Christian principles of mercy and forgiveness. Liberal Judeo-Christian faith communities, meanwhile, have led on immigration reform by establishing sanctuaries against deportation based on the biblical injunction to "do no wrong or violence to the alien."[59]

The Committee on Causes and Consequences of High Rates of Incarceration, convened by the National Research Council of the National Academies, has articulated normative principles to which America's institutions of justice should aspire. "Questions regarding the appropriate use of prison in a democratic society cannot be resolved solely by reference to evidence," the Committee wrote in a 2014 report, "nor can a society decide whether prison rates are too high only by weighing narrowly quantifiable costs against benefits."[60] What was needed, then, was a formulation of "normative principles that have traditionally limited the penal power of the state." The Committee presented four:

- desert and proportionality (punishments should match the crime);
- parsimony (punishments should never be more severe than necessary);
- citizenship (punishments should never result in social or civic death); and
- social justice (the criminal legal system should promote equality and fairness).

Or consider the efforts of the Official Black Lives Matter Chapter in Memphis, Tennessee, which launched a campaign to pay the bail of incarcerated mothers by Mother's Day. In this case, the organizers did not address themselves to the conventional questions of guilt and innocence, responsibility and repair; nor did they present incarcerated mothers as heroes. Instead, they chose to root their campaign in widely shared family values. In so doing, they did not permit the criminal legal system to assign the primary identity to the caged women under its supervision. Those women were presented as mothers, and calls for their liberation were based on the importance of motherhood.[61]

Ask More of Each Other

Often, justice narratives respond to fear: the fear stoked by racial discord, moral panic, and violence, yes, but also the fear that the American public has an incredibly low tolerance for moral lapses. Yet the crime decline has lowered the public's fear of victimization, presenting an opportunity to promote narratives about mercy, second chances, safety, and full humanity. Although a significant minority of Americans consistently perceive crime to be increasing even when in fact the opposite is true, and although crime spikes through the COVID-19 pandemic may have shifted public opinion, overall the share of Americans who report being troubled by crime is decreasing. A 2001 Gallup poll reported that 62 percent of respondents worried "a great deal" about "crime and violence." In 2021, only 50 percent did. The share of respondents describing "the problem of crime in the United States" as "extremely serious" fell from 22 percent in 2000 to 18 percent in 2021.[62] Support for punitive politics has also fallen since the 1990s. In 1994, an estimated 80 percent of Americans supported the death penalty for a person convicted of murder; in 2021, only 55 percent did.[63]

Fearless narratives are what the American public deserves. There is perhaps no better place to find such narratives than youth-led progressive movements. In the wake of the September 11th terrorist attacks, an immense moment of collective pain, immigration reformers were reeling. While mainstream movement organizers pushed comprehensive reform measures in both houses of Congress, measures that eventually failed, younger movement organizers directed their attention at the DREAM Act, introduced in the Senate with bipartisan sponsorship.

Although the DREAM Act failed to pass by a slim margin, this legislation imagined a much more abolitionist path forward than older, more established reformers had urged. Young immigrant organizers were able to see the failures of the current day, and rather than let the contemporary constructs of the debate confine their sense of what was possible, they charted their own path and called for radical change, such as the abolition of ICE and CBP. Activist Mariame Kaba put the power of prophetic vision in plain terms: "I imagine a whole generation of young people being born in this moment who are going to grow up understanding that the world doesn't have to be this way."[64]

While antithetical to prophetic vision, tough-on-crime narratives, with their swaggering boasts of lock-them-up policies and death penalty support, are also incredibly fearless in their cruelty and misdirection. The same is true of border-security narratives, with their nativist tales of "the end of America as we know it" and their overwrought worries of job theft and crime spikes. Yet these stories persist because they offer a sense of solace in certainty—we know the results of the status quo of punishment and cyclical violence. We don't know what a future without reliance on these things looks like—movement leaders often admit they cannot predict the future—so crafting new narratives requires being comfortable with uncertainty.[65] Narratives of new criminal legal and immigration systems must be equally fearless in the pursuit of radical reimagining, even if the outcome is not yet known. Publics are not won over by apologies, nor by the half-truths of sentimentality, so honesty is necessary—hope, too. Perhaps it is time that our narratives of justice, citizenship, and dignity stop walking on eggshells, as movement building is persistent rather than perfect.

At the time of this writing, the United States is engaged in a moral reckoning with police violence. The killings of George Floyd, Breonna Taylor, and other unarmed Black people galvanized in the summer of 2020 what may have been the biggest social movement the country has ever witnessed.[66] Movement leaders adjusted their call from "abolish the police" to "defund the police," thinking the latter slogan more broadly palatable. Nonetheless, large sections of the American public recoiled from such language, even if they actually supported the specific policies movement leaders were demanding, such as the rerouting of funding from law enforcement to social services.

Imagining new justice and immigration systems will require telling new stories. We have attempted to raise some questions about how stories get told and the compromises we make in the telling. We have offered some suggestions about how collectively to build new narratives that influence public understanding and public policy having to do with safety, inequality, and new justice systems. We hope reformers will find our efforts useful as they work to bring about justice and immigration systems of which we can all be proud.

10

REDUCING RACIAL DISPARITIES: A CASE STUDY FROM OREGON

Abbey Stamp

Abbey Stamp serves as executive director of the Multnomah County Local Public Safety Coordinating Council in Oregon and is responsible for directing and coordinating interagency public safety policy discussions and intergovernmental projects to improve the effectiveness of the county's criminal justice system.

Quanice Hayes was seventeen years old when he was shot fatally in the chest and head by a Portland police officer.[1] The white officer who shot Quanice, who was African American, thought Quanice was attempting to rob a homeless person.

Early in 2018, a year after Quanice's death, I met with his grandmother, Donna Hayes, who had joined a local group of community members fighting to stop police violence against young Black and brown men. Ms. Hayes wanted to know what I was working on as a justice reformer in Multnomah County, Oregon. As we discussed reforms that we hoped would reduce incarceration and racial disparities in Portland, I described the criminal justice system as "broken." Ms. Hayes was clear the system is not broken. Like many in her community, she felt the system was doing exactly what it was built to do, which is to be especially harmful to young men of color like her grandson.

Ms. Hayes was right. When Oregon became a state in 1859, its constitution strictly prohibited any "negro or mulatto" from living, working, or owning property there—and this remained in effect until 1926.[2] In the 1980s and 1990s, Portland continued to be a hub of neo-Nazi and white power activity. Today, we see the consequences of our racist past alive and well. Multnomah County is about 6 percent African American and its neighborhoods are largely segregated and gentrified.[3] Communities of color have been pushed to the outer parts of the county, away from their longtime homes and communities. Traditional African American neighborhoods have turned into unaffordable areas full of skyrocketing real estate, farm-to-table restaurants, and hipster boutiques. The areas' historical residents are not the ones profiting from these changes.[4]

A 2014 report, *The African American Community in Multnomah County: An Unsettling Profile*, paints a disturbing picture of the lasting effects of Oregon's racist history.[5] African American families report approximately half the annual income and homeownership rates of that of their white counterparts. Half of the county's African American children experience poverty, they are three times more likely to be placed in foster care than white children, and they are also more likely to be expelled or suspended from school than white children, though they do not misbehave at higher rates. African American adults are unemployed at double the rate of white adults, and, thanks to gentrification, historically Black-owned businesses have shuttered as rising housing costs change the character of their neighborhoods.[6]

These tougher odds are also evident within the county's criminal justice system. The John D. and Catherine T. MacArthur Foundation Safety and Justice Challenge, an initiative to reduce over-incarceration and racial disparities, found that a person's race and ethnicity could affect their outcome throughout the legal process.[7] Its 2015 study confirmed that African American adults in the county are four times more likely than white adults to enter the criminal justice system, seven times more likely to be sentenced to prison, and seven times more likely to receive a parole violation resulting in additional jail time. America's long history of racial injustice is built into our criminal justice system. As many of the system's own leaders have acknowledged, our police, courts, and prisons have often deepened racial inequalities and undermined the trust of communities of color in public institutions.[8]

How can those of us who work within the criminal justice system— a system that has historically caused serious harm in Black and brown communities—approach our everyday work to reckon with, and reverse, those harms? I believe we must focus on reforms that acknowledge both current and historical racial injustice with the goal of eliminating racial inequities in the system.

As a consequence of the 2015 study and others like it, Multnomah County justice leaders are becoming more willing to look at and talk about racial disparities throughout society. But we have a lot of work to do. One key place this work is happening is in Criminal Justice Coordinating Councils, which provide a unique forum to promote policy-making that reckons with racial inequity.[9] These local councils, which emerged in the 1970s, include judges, police officials, defense attorneys, prosecutors, and other criminal justice leaders who have the power to change policies and programming in their community. They are facilitated by a dedicated—and ideally independent—staff, and charged with collaborating on meaningful justice reforms and turning these collaborations into action. Building relationships among these often adversarial agencies is essential to making real change throughout the system. Trust and mutuality among the membership increases the sense of unity, accountability, and success. Ultimately, a team must be strong to support the long-term political will for justice reform through trying times.

The Multnomah County Local Public Safety Coordinating Council works to reduce the jail population safely, lessen gun violence, overcome data-sharing obstacles, divert people from prisons and jails, and provide access to services outside of the justice system for people with behavioral health challenges.[10] Throughout all the Council's work, we aim to acknowledge racial and ethnic disparities and eliminate them.

I became the Council's executive director in 2013, after two decades working in the criminal justice field in many roles, from family therapist to internal investigator for community corrections. Unlike the district attorney or the chief probation officer, who sees only one stage of a person's interaction with the justice system, I have a role that gives me a bird's-eye view of the entire system, from initial police contact to reentry. This perspective, and what I learned as a social worker, put me in a unique position to spur collaborative relationships into policy action and mobilize the Council's efforts to reduce racial disparities in the criminal justice system.

The Council's executive committee is co-chaired by the Multnomah County chair and the mayor of Portland and includes traditional criminal justice leaders: the sheriff, district attorney, public defender, judges, police chiefs, and the community corrections director. In addition, our Council includes public health, behavioral health, child welfare, juvenile justice, and other key fields in the broader public safety continuum. The Council, as well as several topic-specific work groups, meets regularly. Whenever these stakeholders work together to develop justice policy, Council staff facilitate the collaboration and help identify other voices critical to the conversations.

In part because of the Council's presence, the criminal justice policymaking culture in Multnomah County is extremely collaborative and consensus-based. In 2013, Oregon passed legislation to reinvest some of the state Department of Corrections' budget into county-based community corrections approaches, in an effort to decrease the growing prison population. Council executives met every Friday morning at 7 a.m. to develop local justice reinvestment policies and programming. The conversations about who to divert from prison and who to incarcerate were both productive and challenging. Some became tense as we negotiated which types of crimes should be eligible, how to assess outcomes, and different interpretations of accountability. But the collaborative nature of the meetings, based on trust, camaraderie, and an agreed-upon voting structure, allowed us to reach consensus rather than get stuck in conflict. The group stayed at the table and hammered out agreements that resulted in the Multnomah County Justice Reinvestment Program. In fact, those 7 a.m. meetings continue today.

Through collaboration between the justice, medical, behavioral health, and housing sectors, the Council is uniquely situated to make real change. As the successful Reinvestment Program work showed, the Council can facilitate major reforms. Yet tackling institutionalized racism and the resulting racial disparities is a daunting task that pushes criminal justice policymaking conversations into new territory.

Policymakers face at least three major challenges to reducing racial and ethnic disparities in the criminal justice system. First, the heavy footprint of police, courts, and the penal system in communities of color has deep historical roots. Historians find that deep-seated ideas about Black criminality have infused everything we think we know about crime, from the definition and collection of data to the policy that results from it.[11] A modern history of economic marginalization, residential segregation, and collective violence has often fueled and concentrated crime in

communities of color.[12] Criminal justice policy has therefore been insep-
arable from racial control and punishment. Racial disparities in incarceration have endured and increased over the entire twentieth century.[13]
Over centuries, the links between crime, incarceration, and race were
not seen as the products of policy choice, but as naturally occurring connections. Policymakers and the public dismissed racial disparities as the
automatic consequence of disparities in crime. All need to be convinced
with hard evidence that the criminal justice system itself contributes to
the disproportionate arrests and incarceration of African Americans.

Second, because racial disparities are rooted in historical inequalities
and seen as the natural result of high crime rates in minority communities, authorities can be slow to recognize them as a problem. When they
are asked to see racial disparities as unjust or harmful, they can get defensive at the idea that they, and the system they represent, are failing to help
those who have been harmed. When they are charged with instead actually causing harm, they feel attacked. If the police, courts, and corrections are to be enlisted in these efforts to reduce disparities, the process
must feel practical and constructive.

Third, disparity is disempowering for communities of color. Living
with the stress and the consequences of disproportionately high levels
of policing and incarceration is a great burden on community residents,
fueling cynicism and estrangement from the political process.[14] It is a vicious cycle: reducing racial disparity requires community pressure, but
disparity itself tends to alienate a community, making it more difficult
for people to come together and apply that pressure. To work toward a
more equitable system, the voices of those most directly affected must be
elevated.

Each of these challenges makes racial disparity hard to eliminate. The
obstacles run too deep to be fixed by simply reforming the few points in
the system where the decision-maker has discretion. A policy process is
needed that can meet each of the obstacles to significant reform. It is here
that a coordinating council can exercise its leadership and effect change.
When council directors are trusted and independent, we can be provoca-
tive and ask hard questions that elected officials may not feel comfortable
asking. One of the most important parts of leading a Criminal Justice
Coordinating Council is to create political will for change. This takes
trust, time, and strategic thinking. My staff and I often ponder, "What

does [insert justice leader name] need in order to be able to accomplish [insert justice reform action]?"

Although Multnomah County has a unique history and group of actors, our experience offers some general lessons that can help many coordinating council directors effectively reduce racial and ethnic disparities in county criminal justice systems. Above all, we recommend focusing on three tactics.

First, use history and data to document, recognize, and collectively acknowledge the way that systems have created disparities. In 2015, Multnomah County worked to examine racial and ethnic disparities and how they are perceived at a variety of decision points in the criminal justice system. As our community of justice leaders read the report that resulted from that process, it galvanized them to address disparities more intentionally. To guide the work, Council staff completed a literature review to determine which, if any, jurisdictions across the country had successfully reduced racial and ethnic disparity in their criminal justice systems. In the area of adult criminal justice, there were none. We needed to figure out how to blaze a trail.

The literature pointed us in an important direction: when general criminal justice reforms are put into effect, not all communities benefit equally. Even when people of color benefit, white populations benefit more. This was true even of our own Multnomah County Justice Reinvestment Program—the prison diversion process that the Council spent so many 7 a.m. meetings discussing. The program had impressive reductions in prison sentences across the board, but white people benefited the most: prison sentences for white people were reduced by an average of 46 percent while sentences for Black people were reduced by only 26 percent.[15]

The data helped us to understand that it would not be possible to address the deep roots of institutionalized racism and implicit bias without intentionality. For example, most sentencing processes include criminal history as a major decision-making factor. Outcomes are therefore harsher for communities that are over-policed.[16] Programming and policies targeted toward the populations most impacted are necessary to eliminate the disparities woven throughout the criminal justice system. Preliminary results of the Multnomah County Justice Reinvestment Program confirm this.

The report and the literature review also gave the Council staff tools that justice leaders could use to communicate with their constituents about how the system harms communities of color. Council executives and staff pushed out the report in the media and held a community event to discuss the importance of equity in justice reform. The disparities the data revealed, along with these community conversations, motivated justice leaders to begin to think and act differently.

As discussions began about how the County would reduce jail use and support communities most disparately impacted by incarceration, leadership was open to conversations about race-specific policy interventions. Council staff and executives became willing to consider developing policies to decrease the harm caused by institutionally racist policies such as the entrenched disinvestment in communities of color and redlining practices. We discussed the negative impacts of the war on drugs on Black children, families, and communities. We acknowledged that structural and institutional racism and implicit bias resulted in over-policing, over-prosecution, and the placement of too many children in foster care; and that this perpetuated trauma and disconnection, resulting in more crime, more incarceration, more victimization, and more disparity.

Conversations about the deeply rooted, overlapping racial disparities in other systems including education, child welfare, and public health can make criminal justice executives feel overwhelmed. Some meetings result in frustration, as the Council has no power over adjacent systems that affect their adult justice system clients, and this feeling of helplessness can stymie creativity and optimism. In such moments, I remind participants of our criminal justice lane and the responsibility to make positive change where we have power. Then we can work with other system leaders to influence intentional policymaking that will decrease disparities in their systems, especially where such conversations are also starting to happen.[17] If implemented with racial justice as an affirmative goal, targeted policies in any system can start repairing the historical harm to communities of color, hopefully driving a virtuous cycle that will reduce disparities in all sectors.

The second tactic we recommend is to frame approaches and strategies that are familiar to criminal justice actors. Multnomah County began efforts to reduce racial and ethnic disparities over two decades ago. The Juvenile Services Division (Multnomah County's juvenile justice agency) has implemented the Juvenile Detention Alternatives Initiative (JDAI) since it began in the 1990s. This initiative follows a continual process that asks departments to pinpoint where disparities, and the decisions that lead to them, are occurring throughout the juvenile justice system.[18] The department must focus on a particular decision point (detention intake, for example) and change its policy accordingly. Then it must reassess to determine whether the change was a success or a failure in reducing racial and ethnic disparity, learn from that reassessment, and make further changes as needed.[19]

Juvenile justice professionals analyze decision points regularly and are accustomed to frequently updating their process. Council leaders with juvenile justice experience leaned on this approach to help move the adult system toward similar changes. Through the initiative's process, criminal justice workers come to see racial and ethnic disparity as a problem they can understand and address through targeted interventions and policy development. As the Council membership began to discuss disparity in the adult systems, I reminded them of the successes in our juvenile system for inspiration. Successes in this familiar area built understanding of and comfort with these otherwise new concepts.

The third tactic is to address race directly, both by amplifying, integrating, and empowering the voices of people with lived experiences and by choosing policies that intentionally seek to decrease disparities. As local justice leaders became more open to the idea of race-specific policy reforms, the question became how the Council could push this work forward. At the same time, successfully repairing some of the harm caused to communities of color meant involving in policy conversations those who have experienced these harms. People with lived experiences of structural racism in public health, education, welfare, and other systems have expertise that is essential to finding solutions that improve outcomes in their own lives, families, and communities. The stories of two programs illustrate what empowering people with lived experience can bring to the process, and the difficulty of introducing targeted policies.[20]

The Diane Wade House, an Afrocentric transitional housing program for women who are involved with the justice system, provides a successful example of targeted, race-based justice policy.[21] In 2017, policymakers in Multnomah County sought to prioritize reducing racial and ethnic disparities using non-jail programming, rather than implicit bias or officer training. We examined the data and identified that African American women on probation were ending up in jail more often and for longer than their white and male counterparts. This seemed to be partly caused by a lack of quality housing and program options for women of color. Policymakers and people with lived experience co-created a housing program to better support and serve justice-involved women of color: the Diane Wade House, named after a local parole and probation officer who was a leader both in the African American community and in advocating for justice-involved women.[22] The House had thirty-eight beds and provided services including mentoring and life-skills classes. Women came to it through referrals from the Multnomah County Department of Community Justice or Mental Health and Addiction Services.

Shared knowledge about disparity and research pushed policymakers to support culturally specific programming for African American women, as people of color are so often required to engage in dominant-culture programming. The Diane Wade House was designed as an alternative that would focus on Black women, but also would be open to women of all races. Achieving the political will to establish the program was easy because the program didn't change any current justice practices, such as filing charges or imposing sentences.

To help with the launch, we added two peers who were directly impacted by the criminal justice system to the planning team.[23] We also hosted a listening session, catering dinner for twelve current and formerly justice-involved African American women at a community-based agency. A Black woman who was a leader in her community and formerly incarcerated facilitated the event. The only white people in the room were two Council staff—the Wade House project manager and me. We took direction from the facilitator and sat in the back of the room to listen and take notes.

The facilitator created a space that allowed participants to be honest and tell their stories about what they needed in order to be successful on probation. Their truths told a narrative of exclusion, disenfranchisement, and systemic racism:

- "There are minimal places for African American women, period. There's nothing we can say is fully ours."

- "Don't try to come to me and try and tell me that you know or understand what I'm saying. If you learned it in a book then you can't even help me. If they don't know anything about oppression, what good is it gonna do anybody?"
- "[In] organizations that aren't culturally competent, Black women are seen as aggressive, 'resistant to treatment,' 'noncompliant' and kicked out because they are 'threatening' to white residents."
- "If you want it to work, you need us. It's not going to work without us. I don't want help from people who don't look like me."

These women's perspectives helped guide the rest of the program planning. The housing agency that would be running the program took the important step of hiring an equity consultant from The People's Institute for Survival and Beyond to lead anti-racism training and identify how the agency perpetuates structural racism. The voices of the women inspired the political will to ensure the Diane Wade House would have an Afrocentric approach. Their voices also made it clear that taking a risk and developing a policy intentionally focused on Black women, who are often overlooked in justice policymaking, was the right move.

With various definitions of "Afrocentric" in circulation, our planning involved many conversations on what "Afrocentric" would mean for this program. In Multnomah County's interpretation, the word meant centering the needs and wellness of Black women, and emphasizing African and African American culture. To these ends, the Diane Wade House was staffed by Black women with lived justice experience, and the interior was designed and decorated by staff. The programming focused on empowering and healing Black women, and the County worked with local providers to bring in culturally specific services, supports, hygiene products, and food.[24]

The Law Enforcement Assisted Diversion program in downtown Portland, commonly known as LEAD®, was based on a successful Seattle model in which people who would have been booked and prosecuted on drug possession charges are eligible for referral to services instead.[25] We could not get the same support for making the diversion program specifically targeted to a particular racial group, so instead it was applied universally without a focus on any one group.

As with the Diane Wade House, in the policy development sessions for LEAD® Multnomah County amplified the voices of those with lived experience in the criminal justice system and those with substance use disorders, seating two such people at the policy table. The County also hosted public events to help educate community members, faith leaders, and neighborhood associations about why we chose LEAD®'s harm reduction approach of referring people to case management and services instead of charging them. The program was voluntary and did not require engagement in treatment. The target neighborhood was downtown Portland and surrounding areas—a part of the city with significant social and public health challenges, including homelessness and behavioral health problems.

During the planning process for LEAD®, which predated the development of the Diane Wade House, the County was open to discussing approaches that targeted specific racial groups; however, while many policymakers were able comfortably to discuss racism and disparate outcomes, creating a program or policy for one specific population felt like withholding justice from others, creating another disparity.

I remember one of our first LEAD® policy meetings in 2016, when we discussed the goals of the program. One of the goals was to reduce disparity in prosecuting people of color for drug crimes. I remember feeling proud that leaders in my jurisdiction named racial disparity as a problem and wanted to find solutions. But I also had doubts that we could ultimately fulfill this goal.

At that time, I had been the Council executive director for a few years. I finally had my feet under me and it was time to use my voice and my influence. So I took a deep breath and asked, "If our goal is to reduce disparities in possession prosecution, why can't the program be for African Americans?" I introduced the concept of "targeted universalism," first developed by law and African American studies professor john a. powell, which entails "setting universal goals that can be achieved through targeted approaches." As powell explains, "This approach targets the varying needs of each group while reminding us that we are all part of the same social fabric."[26]

By prompting this discussion, I was afraid I was going to be seen as a rabble-rouser and that people would become angry. I knew the question would make people uncomfortable. And they were. Some policymakers in the room quivered in response. They said profiling one population would be unacceptable because it withholds diversion opportunities from others.

In Multnomah County, LEAD®, unlike the Wade House, did not become a targeted program. Instead, my win that day was discovering that I could successfully bring in a non-criminal-justice concept to facilitate challenging conversations about race and justice. The policymakers found resolution and corrected the goal: the program would reduce the number of people of color arrested and prosecuted for drug possession, though it might not reduce the racial disparity. The conversation was a step in the right direction, but it did not result in taking a political risk to decrease disparity.

Looking back on the LEAD® process, I should have pushed harder on policymakers to repair some of the harm done by laws and policies from the "war on drugs" era—which in retrospect we can all see clearly targeted a particular demographic. I wish I had asked the group to take a step toward reckoning with this injustice and centuries of white supremacy and said, "Let's recognize the damage caused by America's history of targeting communities of color with punitive policies and try to undo that harm by targeting them for deflections from booking and prosecution."

I could also have suggested the use of proxies to move the Council toward targeted policies. When analyzing data about criminal justice, we sometimes substitute one related type of data for another when the data we want to analyze is unavailable. Although not the most direct solution for improving equity, proxies can also provide cover for making progress in the right direction. Here, a proxy for targeted diversions for African Americans could have been a focus on either cocaine possession (where racial disparities were the worst) or a specific neighborhood. But as a jurisdiction, we were not ready to go down that path—some felt the political risk of any targeted diversion was too great.

In its work, the Diane Wade House successfully supported African American women. It also led elected officials and executives to speak publicly about the value of a targeted program and to acknowledge that the majority of justice programming is white-centric.[27] Talking openly about race and institutionalized racism in Oregon has enhanced County leadership's willingness to right past harms through policies and programming.

The lessons we learned in implementing these two programs clearly demonstrate the value of a trusted Criminal Justice Coordinating Council and skilled staff who are not embedded in specific criminal justice agencies. Council staff should be advocates for change when highly politicized environments make leaders cautious, and should make sure that the people most affected by criminal justice policy have a seat at the table. Council directors should be willing to name racism as an oppressive force that requires targeted intervention.

From a Council staff perspective, success means that by facilitating these processes, we have helped policymakers find direction and take action. The County is working with national partners to analyze the impact of the Diane Wade House. And while it's too soon to report on long-term outcomes, initial information showed that LEAD® participants were booked into jail less frequently. The biggest local win, however, has been the recognition from all leadership that reducing disparities takes intentional steps and political will.

The three tactics I've suggested are applicable beyond Multnomah County, and even beyond criminal justice policy. Using history and data to document and collectively acknowledge how systems have created disparities depersonalizes racism and increases willingness to make changes. Data also presents evidence of a problem, giving policymakers and lawmakers something tangible to respond and be held accountable to. In any field, change can be overwhelming and frustrating. By using past successes as blueprints for future change, we can decrease fear and anxiety and increase buy-in and success. Centering voices that are often ignored in structurally racist environments is key to gaining the insights to create meaningful and permanent change in any area of work. And as so many studies and our own experiences have shown, universal policies are not enough—we must pursue targeted reforms that acknowledge racial disparities to combat them.

I continue to carry Ms. Hayes's comments with me. The criminal justice system was built this way intentionally, and it is our responsibility to recreate it so that justice is not an exception, but the rule. My daily challenge is to capitalize on the acknowledgment of local leaders, across every sector, of institutionalized racism and the need for action. In my role, I do not make policy or law; that is in the hands of elected officials and agency executives. The approach I suggest here has moved Multnomah County's work forward, but there are limits. While some policy changes have been positive, people of color are still overrepresented in each stage of the justice system. Dismantling generations of racism and harm is slow work.

Yet, as change agents, Council directors should push policymakers and elected officials to have hard conversations about how a fair and equitable justice system should function. We are facilitators of change, and our challenge is to adhere to our values of repairing harm and advancing equity amid the chaos of local government. We will be challenged by colleagues who are concerned about what they perceive as withholding justice from one racial group but not another. We will be challenged by politics and shrinking budgets. No matter the chaos, it is critical for Council leadership to help shape the future of justice policy and begin to dismantle the racist carceral state.

Policymakers face deep challenges in their efforts to bend criminal justice in the direction of racial equity. When communities of color that are directly impacted by criminal justice bring their concerns to these agencies, they are often distrusted, faced with defensiveness, and reminded of generations of trauma. Most justice policymakers today see and understand the deep-rooted oppression and intentional incarceration of communities of color. The struggle is figuring out how to help fix it. Acknowledging this history and how it shapes the present can be the first step on a path forward toward reckoning. This acknowledgment can also be a model for how we as a society approach the broader conversation—about how we can create racial justice not only in the criminal justice system, but in all systems and institutions that have perpetuated oppression.

PART III

HUMAN DIGNITY AND HEALING

11

HOLISTIC SAFETY AT THE CENTER OF INCARCERATION

Nneka Jones Tapia

Nneka Jones Tapia is a clinical psychologist and the managing director of Justice Initiatives at Chicago Beyond, an impact investor working to ensure all young people have the opportunity to live free and full lives by investing in organizations, ideas, and individuals in Chicago and nationally.

The American correctional system is not a system that rehabilitates people, as it so often claims to be. Instead, it is a system of pain and punishment that continues to have a reverberating impact on the people confined there, the people who work there, and the families and communities of both.

This pain extends beyond its barbed-wire fences, making its way into our homes, our schools, our churches, and our communities. It's in the soul of the eight-year-old girl who sits in her classroom, wondering if her father will make it home safely from prison. It's in the touch of the mother pumping breast milk into the sink of her cell and longing to hold her newborn son. It's in the heart of the correctional officer who coaches the neighborhood soccer league, but can't shake his feelings of doom and fear. It's in the thoughts of the officer's wife as she kisses him goodbye and hopes that he returns home alive. The trauma generated by correctional institutions is real and felt by tens of millions of people every day. For this reason, I believe we must all make transformational changes in the here and now to reduce the harms caused by these systems.

For more than ten years, I worked for and eventually led the Cook

County Jail in Chicago, Illinois—one of the largest jails in the country, with a population that ranged from approximately 10,000 people when I started in 2006 to approximately 6,000 people when I retired in 2018, plus a staff of approximately 2,300 people. During that time, I experienced dozens of encounters that cumulatively inform my perspective on the scope of trauma in correctional facilities and the opportunities for harm reduction. I retraced the final moments of numerous men and women confined in the facility who died by suicide; I attended the funerals of staff members who died too soon as a result of being constantly overtaxed, both physically and emotionally; I visited the hospital beds of staff who had been assaulted; I looked in the eyes of men and women who were being disciplined, fired, and laid off; and I looked in the faces of tens of thousands of young children with tears in their eyes as they were leaving their loved ones at the massive jail complex.

Nothing prepared me for the trauma that existed within correctional facilities. There was no playbook on how to defeat the feelings that kept me awake at night in anticipation of the next incident—a massive fight, a fire, a suicide, a hostage situation, a murder, an escape, a death, a rape—and others that I encountered several times during my tenure in corrections.

The traditional perspective of trauma views people who are incarcerated, staff, and communities as three distinct entities. With this framing, we can neither fully understand the mechanisms of trauma at work, nor the opportunities available to us for harm reduction. My personal perspective as a former jail warden, a family member of a person who was incarcerated, and a family member of a current correctional professional demonstrates the shortcomings of this framing; and allows me to redefine the scope of trauma in the context of incarceration, explain where opportunities to reduce harm are missed, and propose a new framework for action and change.

Trauma is commonly understood as a harmful or life-threatening event that is experienced or witnessed by a person, and that has lasting consequences on their mental, emotional, spiritual, physical, and social well-being.[1] This experience is individualized and thus doesn't fully capture the depth and range of the impact of trauma. Even when the reality of trauma in correctional institutions is appreciated, policies often focus only on programs for people who are incarcerated, as if they are

the problem, instead of on the system itself. In doing so, they miss opportunities to support people who work in these institutions and carry the weight of things seen and unseen.

Neither people who are incarcerated nor an institution's correctional staff live in isolation. They all have families who are directly and indirectly exposed to their own traumatic experiences and who feel the impact of the trauma on their loved ones. The prevalence of trauma among people touched by correctional institutions far surpasses the prevalence within the general population. Because of the connections that exist among us, and the large number of people who are confined in and work in correctional institutions, the scope of this trauma is substantial. Approximately 1.9 million people are confined in our nation's jails and prisons at any one time. Every year, people are placed in jails 10.6 million times, and more than 600,000 people enter our nation's prisons.[2] On any given day, approximately 2.7 million U.S. children have a parent who is incarcerated, and more than 5 million children have experienced parental incarceration in their lifetime.[3] Perhaps even more striking is the fact that 113 million, or 1 in 2, U.S. adults have experienced the incarceration of an immediate family member (for example, a parent, sibling, spouse, romantic partner, or a co-parent).[4] Additionally, jails and prisons are staffed with approximately 415,000 correctional officers and a significant number of civilians.[5] Each of these people is connected to larger communities, extending the reach of trauma beyond what has been measured.

Nearly every person confined in our nation's jails and prisons has been exposed to trauma either prior to—or during—their period of detention.[6] One study of 592 adult men confined in a high-security prison found that virtually all of the respondents (99 percent) reported experiencing at least one traumatic event in their lifetime that involved violence directed toward them, and consequently resulted in injury or shock.[7] Almost 71 percent reported experiencing a traumatic event before age eighteen; more than half reported being hit with an object that caused bleeding or left marks, and more than 30 percent reported being threatened or harmed with a gun or a knife.

Another study found that 98 percent of women who were incarcerated had at least one traumatic experience prior to incarceration, with intimate partner violence being the most common experience.[8] And 86 percent of women confined in jail reported experiencing sexual violence in their lifetime, 77 percent reported physical or sexual violence from a partner, and 60 percent reported experiencing violence from a caregiver prior to age eighteen.[9]

During incarceration, the experience of trauma is multiplied. A study of approximately 7,500 men and women confined in thirteen U.S. prisons illuminated how harmful the prison environment is for people who are incarcerated.[10] More than 35 percent of the men and 24 percent of the women reported being physically victimized by either a staff member or another person who was incarcerated in their previous six months in the prison. More than 10 percent of the men who were incarcerated and more than 24 percent of the women who were incarcerated reported experiencing sexual victimization in their previous six months in the prison. Men who experienced sexual victimization were more likely to have been victimized by a staff member (8 percent) than by another person who was incarcerated (4 percent).

The effects of trauma exist on a continuum. Most people are able to recover shortly after a traumatic event. For some people, though, exposure to traumatic events happens with such frequency, duration, or intensity that they are at increased risk of developing posttraumatic stress disorder. PTSD is a mental health condition with symptoms that are serious, persist for more than one month, and create significant distress or impairment to daily functioning.[11] Symptoms include intrusive memories of the traumatic event; avoidance of conversation, places, people, or activities that remind the person of the traumatic event; negative thoughts and emotions; and changes in the person's physical and emotional reactions.[12] In the general population, an estimated 3 to 6 percent of men who experience a traumatic event go on to meet criteria for PTSD at some point in their lifetime.[13] Yet out of the 95 percent of incarcerated men who have experienced direct physical violence in their lifetime, 60 percent have experienced moderate to severe symptoms of PTSD, while 29 percent have experienced severe symptoms.[14]

The increased prevalence of trauma and PTSD in corrections is not limited to the people incarcerated in these institutions, although no other group's experience of trauma is as dehumanizing. Trauma in correctional institutions also affects correctional staff. In 2013, a study of 3,599 correctional professionals from forty-nine states and three U.S. territories examined the prevalence of PTSD and depression in this group.[15] It found that 27 percent met the criteria for a diagnosis of PTSD and approximately

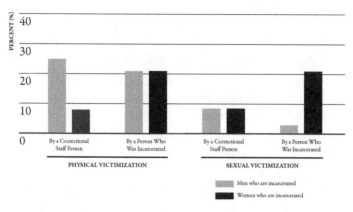

FIGURE 1: Prevalence of physical and sexual victimization of people incarcerated[16]

26 percent met the criteria for depression, with a high rate of comorbidity between the two. Prevalence rates were even higher among security staff—with more than 34 percent meeting the criteria for PTSD and 31 percent meeting the criteria for depression, again with high comorbidity between the two. These percentages stand in contrast to that of the general public, where approximately 7 percent of all U.S. adults have reported experiencing a major depressive episode or PTSD in their lifetime.[17] Correctional professionals also experience direct and indirect traumatic events at significantly higher rates than other professionals.[18] Direct exposure can occur when correctional professionals are assaulted (physically and sexually) by persons detained in the institution. Indirect exposure occurs when correctional professionals have experiences such as witnessing, responding to, or hearing about a violent incident; reading or hearing about the reported crimes of people who are incarcerated; or listening to the traumatic experiences of staff and people who are incarcerated.

Additionally, the nature of the work requires correctional staff to consider "what if" scenarios at all times to remain vigilant and prepared to respond appropriately. During my time as a jail warden, it was common for me to stand at the front of the tier and talk with a correctional officer for a few minutes to assess his or her ability to respond quickly and appropriately if something occurred. I would scan all of the people detained in the unit to see if there was tension. If I saw several people standing against the wall with sneakers on and shoelaces tied tight, I would not go further, recognizing the signs of increased tensions and higher probability of a fight.

On the contrary, if people were either sitting at tables and playing cards, or standing in flip-flops and laughing with each other, I could safely walk through the unit and sit down to play cards because the risk—though still present—was less salient. Ironically enough, in the more than ten years that I worked in corrections, I was never threatened nor physically harmed by any person who was incarcerated—only by a sworn officer.

Family members of correctional staff are often concerned about the physical safety of their loved ones every time they go to work. As the wife of a correctional professional, I am no exception. And when I worked in the jail, my husband worried just the same. Trauma not only affects the people who are detained in the institution and the people who work there, but also their families. As a child of a parent who was formerly incarcerated, and the wife of a correctional professional, I'm still dealing with the traumatic effects of both.

For children, having a parent incarcerated not only disrupts the family dynamic but also the financial stability of their home and larger community. Approximately 13 percent of children living in poverty have experienced parental incarceration, compared with only 4 percent of children whose household income is at least twice the federal poverty level.[19] While most studies have focused on the number of parents in prison, considerably less is known about the number of parents in jails.[20] To better understand the prevalence of parental incarceration in jails, I

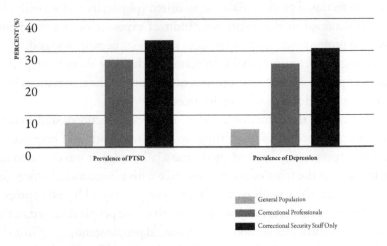

FIGURE 2: Prevalence of PTSD and depression among correctional professionals, correctional security staff, and the general population[21]

partnered with the Cook County Sheriff's Office in Chicago to gather one year of self-reported data from people remanded to the custody of the jail from approximately March 2019 to February 2020. Considering those newly admitted to the jail, as well as those who were already confined there, we recorded that close to eighty thousand youth under the age of eighteen had a parent in the Cook County Jail at some point during the year, accounting for approximately 7 percent of all youth under the age of eighteen living in Cook County.[22]

Parental incarceration affects children differently than other forms of parental separation because of the uncertainty of the duration, the threat of harm to their loved one, and the shame and stigma that is often linked to the experience. When children are too young to fully understand why they are separated from a parent who is incarcerated, feelings of abandonment and rejection can be magnified.[23] While not a universal experience, youth without positive adult support, or youth with an unhealthy relationship with a parent who is incarcerated, are often at increased risk of traumatic stress, emotional distress, and social problems. These include, but are not limited to, rule- and law-breaking behavior, engagement with the criminal justice system, poor school performance, high-risk behaviors, and chronic health conditions.[24] Youth who have positive supports and a healthy relationship with their parent who is incarcerated are better able to actualize their innate strengths, thereby increasing their likelihood for positive life outcomes.

Everyone within a correctional facility is exposed to traumatic events at a significantly higher rate than the general population. In this sense, the institution itself is traumatic.

In considering how to respond to and prevent the trauma of contact with incarceration, it is important to understand its impact. During normal human development, the brain undergoes many changes throughout its lifespan; thus the specific impact of exposure to trauma differs depending on a person's age at the time. Three primary areas within the brain are generally impacted by traumatic stress: the prefrontal cortex, responsible for rational thinking, planning, problem-solving, empathy, and awareness of other people; the anterior cingulate cortex, partly responsible for regulating our emotions; and the amygdala, responsible for identifying threats and producing fear, which results in our fight, flight, or freeze response.[25] When traumatic stress is experienced, the body experiences dramatic changes in cortisol levels, a hormone that facilitates

CHICAGO
BEYOND→

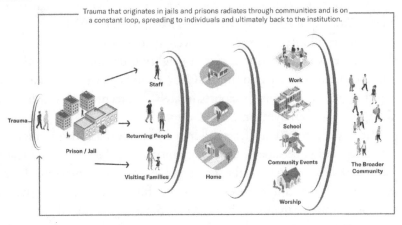

FIGURE 3: The spread of trauma from correctional institutions through community[26]

survival responses. As a result of trauma, the areas that regulate think-ing and emotions become underactive, while the area that regulates fear becomes overactive.[27] Exposure to frequent, prolonged, or intense trau-matic stress makes people more likely to experience chronic fear and dif-ficulty regulating their thoughts and feelings.

When a person who has a history of trauma experiences continued de-humanization during their incarceration, or when a correctional profes-sional experiences job-related traumatic stress, they are at increased risk of significant personality change, including more negative perceptions of the world; difficulty experiencing joy, hope, meaning, and other spiritual sentiments; difficulty regulating their emotions; "acting out" behavior; and conflict in interpersonal relationships.[28]

The negative impact of trauma also extends beyond the person who has directly experienced it. When a traumatic event occurs at a correctional fa-cility, everyone who has experienced, witnessed, or heard about it remains at risk. Staff and people who are incarcerated then make contact with their own family members, and the traumatic event may either be described in conversation or felt through the person's interactions. Each of those family members interacts in turn with hundreds of people at work, school, places of worship, community events, and other places, all of whom can be af-fected by what they have experienced, witnessed, or heard.

Fortunately, the neurological changes that occur following traumatic stressors can be minimized with intervention and healing supports.[29] This is true for everyone, including people who are incarcerated, correctional staff, and families. One of the most important things that can be done to help people correct the neurological impacts of trauma is to deactivate the amygdala, or fear center, by creating environments where people feel safe.[30] When people feel physically and psychologically safe, they are better able to activate and strengthen the rational and emotional centers of their brains, thereby making better decisions and becoming less likely to act out negatively. How can we put this knowledge into action in correctional institutions?

One of the most widely used models to create trauma-informed institutions was developed by the federal Substance Abuse and Mental Health Services Administration. According to the administration's model, a trauma-informed institution is one that not only recognizes the prevalence, signs, and impact of trauma, but also integrates this knowledge into policies and procedures to avoid re-traumatizing people.[31]

If correctional facilities used this model, I believe we would see some improvements to today's correctional systems. Some staff would feel valued and have a positive outlook on their jobs, which would improve some of the conditions for the people detained in the institution. Nevertheless, knowledge about trauma and its negative impacts alone has no clear pathway to safety, nor does it address the harm caused to children and families impacted by incarceration. It is necessary to move beyond understanding trauma to actively reduce harms inflicted by our correctional system, and this process requires more than the avoidance of re-traumatization; it requires action. We must acknowledge the harm that is inherent in these institutions and ground a more holistic concept of safety in every facet of our criminal justice operation.

Unfortunately, the models that exist do not fully encompass what, in my experience, is necessary to do this, especially with regard to families. Because families are natural extensions of people and almost immediately experience the impact of trauma, correctional facilities must focus on supporting positive family engagement. A 2016 study of a thousand men from across five states who were reentering the community from correctional facilities found that men who had more contact with their families during their period of incarceration were more likely to become employed, to financially support their children, and to have a positive relationship with the co-parent upon release; and were less likely to be re-incarcerated.[32]

As a correctional administrator, I often considered what I could do to help transform the institution from one focused on punishment and trauma to one primarily guided more by holistic safety. However, there were countless challenges to consider. I was responsible for the lives of more than eight thousand people who were incarcerated in a facility with high gang tensions, tense relationships among staff, a significant number of people with complex emotional and behavioral health needs, and a budget that would not allow for costly tools and programs.

Given all of the challenges and day-to-day activities that correctional administrators contend with, there is often very little time left to think through the best approach to holistic safety. Perhaps the most significant challenge I faced, though, was myself. About halfway through my tenure as a correctional administrator, I started to feel the impact of the job. I wasn't sleeping. I was eating poorly. I was slowly losing parts of myself to the institution, but I did not see it. On the surface, I thought I was relatively comfortable interacting with the men and women confined in the institution. What I later realized was that I was not only on high alert inside of the jail, but I was easily triggered at home and in the community.

Ultimately, it was a conversation with my husband that helped me realize that I was hurting as a result of how I approached the job, and I needed to start my own healing process. Specifically, I needed to create enough space between me and the job so that I could take better care of my physical and emotional health, and be better prepared to take care of other people. By acknowledging my own need for healing, I realized I could also acknowledge the needs of others. The steps I took to get back to a healthier version of myself improved my understanding of what could help the people detained in the facility, the staff, their families, and the larger community.

I started by creating a safe space for myself. To create that space, I set aside specific times in the day when I would close my office door or go for a walk outside the facility. As a result, I recognized that it was difficult for staff to find space for themselves outside of their breakroom, so we created a relaxation room for them to take fifteen minutes to relax during their lunch break.

The reality is that safe spaces do not exist for people when they are incarcerated, and "acting out" behavior may be the only tool at their disposal to increase their sense of safety. It was not uncommon for a young man or woman to threaten or to attack a person housed in their cell for fear of being attacked when sleeping. For this reason, we recognized the necessity of increasing programming in the facility. As we tracked incidents, we realized that people who participated in enrichment programming at the facility were less likely to act out. And we found that staff who were interested in facilitating some of these programs were more likely to have positive interactions with people who were incarcerated.

When staff and the people detained at the facility shared their concerns with me, I began being more transparent with them about the complexities of the problems they identified, and invited them to help me find solutions that would work for all. Typically, staff and people detained in the institution are required to direct their communications to their immediate supervisors. However, it was my experience that both groups were harmed by things that the executive staff knew nothing about, creating a greater divide. I made it a practice to walk through the institution multiple times throughout the week and connect directly with both the staff and the people detained there. At first, each walk ended with a list of problem areas. As we tackled some of the problems they identified, my interactions became more conversational. Through those interactions, I started to see similarities between the traumatic ways that I experienced the jail and the ways that staff and the people detained there did.

Recognizing the value of interpersonal connection, we created more opportunities for staff and the people detained in the institution to see value and similarities in each other. We instituted dozens of programs for the people detained in the facility, including mental wellness, employment skills training, education, and spiritual groups. We also championed a staff-led movement to create positive work environments that encouraged fellowship and healthy lifestyle practices. During its first year, our radically different approach to trauma garnered the support of a quarter of the staff. Ultimately, when we treat people with humanity and compassion, investing in their innate strengths, we take steps to reduce the many harms that these institutions cause.

The Holistic Safety Framework

To acknowledge the common humanity shared by people who are incarcerated, the staff, and their families, I created the Holistic Safety framework. This framework outlines necessary shifts in correctional system policy, procedure, and training through five core components that create the conditions for all community members—inside and outside correctional walls—to be and feel protected, resilient, and whole. At the core of this framework is the importance of empowering people with lived experience to drive these shifts. That is holistic safety. The Holistic Safety framework supports the notion that even in a system that is inherently traumatic, we must shift the values of the institution, so it is rooted in humanity and compassion.

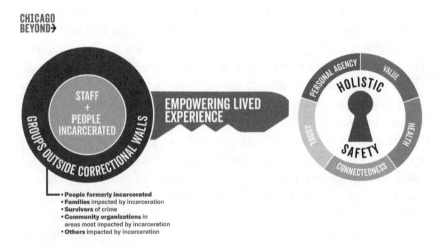

FIGURE 4: The Holistic Safety framework

Health: Health is more than the absence of injury. It is the ability for the key stakeholder groups—people detained in the facility, correctional staff, and their families and communities—to have the physical, mental, and emotional well-being needed to thrive. People incarcerated and correctional staff are healthy when they have access to wellness supports, programming, and resources that promote their ability to thrive.

Trust: Trust is our earned—not blind—belief in people to not only fulfill their responsibilities but also act in a manner beneficial to themselves and others. People who are incarcerated and correctional staff feel trust when they believe their physical and mental well-being is supported by the actions of those inside and outside the institution, including administrators. The community outside correctional walls feel trust when they believe that correctional institutions are returning their neighbors to the community with the tools they need to thrive and be well.

Personal Agency: The key stakeholder groups must have the tools and resources to support their own healing and that of their peers. Although incarceration historically inhibits personal agency among people who are detained and their families, these institutions must actively increase the ability of these groups to actualize their own healing.

Value: The facility administrators and policymakers must believe and invest in the strengths of the key stakeholder groups. They must build upon these strengths to promote voice, build resilience, and help ensure holistic safety through well-considered language, programs, policies, procedures, and training. The stakeholder groups must also believe in the strengths of themselves and each other and build upon those strengths.

Connectedness: We are all intrinsically bound, and we are best when our ties are positive and strong. The facility must actively promote positive interpersonal connectivity, seeking to minimize power dynamics among stakeholder groups as a reflection of their collective responsibility for holistic safety.

Holistic safety must be centered for everyone touched by the institution so that no group experiences injury as a result of institutional policy, practice, and training. While the shift toward holistic safety is a multi-year journey, there are many tangible ways that the framework can be implemented. The following are a series of recommendations for each key stakeholder group.

For People Detained in the Institution

- Acknowledge the magnitude of the trauma that people detained in the institution experience, and raise their awareness of the importance of self-care techniques.
- Engage them in discussions about the policies and procedures that affect them, and incorporate feedback when applicable.
- Use person-first language in policies, procedures, post orders, and in communications when talking with or about people detained in the institution, referring to them as people instead of "inmate," "detainee," or "offender."
- Engage them in discussions about the supports they believe would be beneficial to them, and incorporate the feedback they provide.
- Facilitate onsite programming for mental wellness, substance use services, education, life skills (e.g., computer skills, banking and budgeting, résumé writing), parenting skills, peer support, and job training skills.
- Ensure that disciplinary practices within the facility are humane and focused on accountability instead of punishment.
- Make the correctional environment as aesthetically pleasing and relaxing as possible, including using calming paint, soft music, plants and flowers, and more.
- Provide reentry services, such as a network of support services, to support and expand the institutional programs being offered.

For Families of People Detained in the Institution

- Acknowledge the trauma that families of people detained in the institution experience and actively work to reduce harm.

- Develop a family engagement program where families are able to offer feedback about institutional policies and procedures. Administrators should be prepared to explain the purpose of the policies and procedures, particularly with regard to safety, and to incorporate feedback when applicable.
- Engage families in ongoing discussions about the supports they believe would be beneficial to their healing, and provide access to these supports; also, actively seek out partnerships with community organizations focused on supporting the well-being of the family unit.
- Inform families of the potential stressors their loved ones could face and how to effectively engage with them in visits, phone calls, letters, and upon release from the facility.
- Provide family-friendly opportunities for visitation that allow for physical contact and child-centered activities. Families should have access to free telephone communication with their loved ones who are incarcerated. Video visitation should only be used as an adjunct to in-person visitation or in emergency situations.
- Provide correctional staff with pre-employment and annual training on effective engagement with children and families. Training should include information on the impact of parental incarceration on children and effective ways to engage with children and families. Additionally, the training should allow staff opportunities to practice, ask questions, and reflect on experiences.
- Make the correctional spaces that families experience—such as visitation spaces, bonding rooms, and pick-up locations—as aesthetically pleasing and relaxing as possible. This could include calming colors, soft music, plants and flowers, and child-friendly signage and play areas.

For Staff
- Acknowledge the experiences of trauma for staff and raise their awareness about the importance of self-care techniques.
- Engage staff in ongoing discussions about policies and procedures and what they believe would help them feel safer.

Administrators should be prepared to explain how positive interactions reduce the likelihood of violence; explain the purpose of policies and procedures as it relates to the safety of staff, the people detained in the facility, and the larger community; and increase transparency with all groups when violence occurs.

- Engage staff in ongoing discussions about the healing supports they believe would benefit them, and incorporate their feedback.
- Train all staff, including administrators, on effective ways to engage with others.
- Incorporate comprehensive staff wellness seminars into the pre-employment and annual trainings. These trainings should include a staff resource guide for services within and outside of the department.
- Make the work environment for staff as aesthetically pleasing and relaxing as possible, such as using calming paint colors, soft music, plants, flowers, and more.

For Families of Staff
- Acknowledge the impact of trauma on the families of employees, and raise their awareness about the importance of self-care techniques. Administrators must be prepared to provide access to the resources necessary for self-care.
- Offer seminars to families about the stressful nature of the job, signs of partner stress, and wellness resources available to the staff and their partners.
- Engage families in discussions about the supports they believe would be beneficial to them, and incorporate their feedback when applicable.

A Case Study of Holistic Safety in a Correctional Institution: Family-Friendly Visitation Pilot at Cook County Jail

I retired as the warden of Cook County Jail in 2018 and started working for Chicago Beyond, an impact investor that works to ensure all young people have the opportunity to live a free and full life. In my role as the managing director of Justice Initiatives, I am championing for justice from the community outside correctional walls. In 2019, I partnered with the sheriff of Cook County Jail in Chicago, Illinois, to design a program to support children who were visiting loved ones incarcerated at the institution. The program sought to revise the jail's policies, procedures, training, and visitation experience in order to reduce harms for the people detained in the facility, their children and families, and correctional staff. Chicago Beyond developed a model for family-friendly visitation that would allow for widespread use, increase family engagement, and garner staff buy-in.

Partnering with the local children's museum and a trauma-focused mental health organization, we piloted two visitation experiences to demonstrate the positive impact of this model. One visitation was organized outside of the correctional facility in a children's museum, and the other was organized in an area of the correctional facility that had been temporarily repurposed for child-friendly visitation with exhibit structures from the children's museum. Both visitation experiences had key elements rooted in ideas about holistic safety, including the elimination of uniforms for people detained in the facility and for the staff, humane security practices, positive engagement between the staff and others, the use of given names as opposed to terms like "offender" or "inmate," family activities, and case management services for families to access community resources.

The five tenets of holistic safety were emphasized throughout the development and implementation of the piloted visitation experiences. Fathers who participated in the visits were selected from an in-custody wellness program that fostered deep engagement among them (addressing the tenets of health and connectedness). To build upon their established relationships with each other, they were placed into a "cohort" so that familiar faces could help make the visit more comfortable (connectedness). They were also encouraged to attend parenting classes together. Correctional staff, correctional administrators, program staff, and program administrators were brought together to receive trauma training that focused on the impact of incarceration to staff, people incarcerated, and their families (health and connectedness). All of these groups were provided with strategies to reduce the impact of the trauma they experienced as well as strategies for effective engagement with other people who were exposed to trauma (health).

Both visits were deemed successful by the people incarcerated at the institution, the staff, and their families. When the doors of the visitation room opened and children ran to their fathers to embrace them, everyone in the room was overcome with emotion. Everyone, including the incarcerated fathers and the correctional staff, wore their personal clothing instead of their uniforms (value). For two hours, the room was filled with fathers, children, and staff from each partner organization who helped to facilitate play instead of fulfilling the conventional roles of people in their position (value). There were a wide range of age-appropriate activities for the youth to engage with freely with their fathers, and the staff were allowed to freely engage with the fathers and their families without feeling judged (personal agency). Bilingual mental health clinicians were made available as well as calming rooms in case there was any need for de-escalation (health).

The piloted visitation experiences were rooted in trust. Administrators and staff had to trust that by removing the barriers keeping families from being able to touch their incarcerated loved ones (barriers that were historically present in the jail and other correctional facilities), they could reduce the risk of incidents and promote healthy relationships. Participants shared their positive experiences in post-visit meetings and staff debriefings, with one father sharing, "Seeing my kid and being able to have this opportunity motivates me to be a better dad." A four-year-old daughter said, "I feel better knowing that my daddy has friends in here." Similarly, one staff member stated, "The visit helped change how law enforcement relates to the community and combat the stigma and bias associated with law enforcement."

Because the facility is in the process of expanding this visitation model throughout the jail, quantitative outcome data is not yet available. We anticipate that more families will be able to maintain positive relationships with their loved ones who are incarcerated, people who are incarcerated will have greater reentry success, and that the facility will experience a decrease in incidents.

Incarceration is traumatic. Prisons and jails operate in a way that is traumatic for the people who are incarcerated, the staff who work in them, their families, and the broader community. But if addressing trauma were adopted as a first priority, we could reconceive how prisons and jails might function to reduce their inherent harm. By promoting human interaction that is respectful, warm, and supportive in contexts of safety and mutual trust, we could place holistic safety at the center of incarceration.

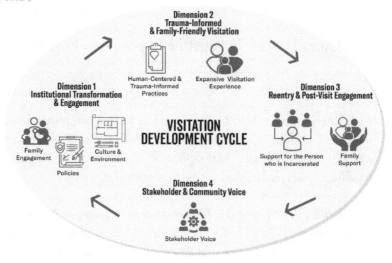

FIGURE 5: Jail visitation development cycle[33]

12

DECARCERATION THROUGH INVESTMENT: REDUCING RELIANCE ON PRISONS AND JAILS

Laura Hawks, Evangeline Lopoo, Lisa Puglisi, and Emily Wang

Laura Hawks, MD, MPH, is a primary care physician, public health researcher, and assistant professor at the Medical College of Wisconsin. Her research focuses on the effects of incarceration on long-term health outcomes for individuals and communities.

Evangeline (Evie) Lopoo is a PhD student in sociology at Northwestern University. Prior to her academic career, she was project coordinator and manager of research and writing for The Square One Project.

Lisa Puglisi, MD, is an assistant professor of medicine at Yale University, where she practices primary care and addiction medicine. She is the director of Transitions Clinic–New Haven, a multidisciplinary clinic that is part of a national network of programs that focus on care of individuals who are returning to the community from incarceration.

Emily Wang, MD, is a professor in the Yale School of Medicine and the School of Public Health and directs the SEICHE Center for Health and Justice. The SEICHE Center is a collaborative effort between Yale School of Medicine and Yale Law School focused on improving the health of individuals and communities who are impacted by mass incarceration through decarceration.

In a display of rare bipartisan agreement, policymakers and public figures from Kim Kardashian to Mariame Kaba to Charles Koch agree that America's criminal legal policies are a failure. Public interest in the topic has recently surged, as racial inequities throughout the legal system ignited nationwide organizing and demonstrating. Community leaders, public health experts, and physicians are among those calling to rebuild an inhumane and costly system. And, as a result of the COVID-19 pandemic, by fall 2020 prisons, jails, and detention centers comprised over ninety of the country's one hundred largest outbreaks, further bolstering calls for dramatic reductions in population density within prisons and jails—also known as "decarceration"—to prevent further public health crises.[1]

Calls to decarcerate will endure far beyond the pandemic and require both legal reform and comprehensive community investment. Yet research has yet to identify which investments will best support current and future efforts to reduce prison populations. In medicine, we have built a vast evidence base for how to decrease the negative impacts of disease. For example, researchers have conducted over 5,600 randomized control trials and nearly 1,000 systematic reviews of breakthrough cholesterol medications called "statins," and optimized prescribing guidelines accordingly.[2] This, among other experimental evaluations, caused national cardiovascular disease mortality to plummet by over 50 percent from 1980 to 2019.[3] Decarceration deserves a research approach as careful as that employed to study the prevention of cardiovascular disease. We now need to apply similar resources and rigor to efforts to improve the health of individuals, families, and communities impacted by the criminal legal system—an urgent need as efforts to decarcerate intensify.

Lowering the prison and jail population involves rethinking what we criminalize and how people navigate the criminal legal system. But just as importantly, decarceration, as described by leading scholars, involves "rebuilding the human resources and physical infrastructure—schools, healthcare facilities, parks, and public areas—of neighborhoods devastated by high levels of incarceration."[4] Addressing the communities hardest hit by mass incarceration through investment in the domains of education, housing, employment, health care, and social support has been shown to achieve decarceration, both by reducing "incident incarceration" (first contact with the criminal legal system) and by reducing recidivism (repeat involvement with the system, inclusive of arrests, new convictions, or repeated imprisonment).

Our goal was to review the literature and studies available and make prescriptions based on the strategies and "treatments" that have been shown to be most effective for decarceration through randomized trials, the same high quality of evidence that exists for treatments that work to reduce heart disease.[5] Here, we outline interventions of education, housing, healthcare, employment, and social supports provided in community settings aiming to reduce criminal legal system involvement and highlight their findings.

Decarcerating via Education

Research clearly demonstrates that early interventions that consistently and effectively provide intensive resources to both children and their parents reduce criminal legal system involvement, particularly among low-income children.[6] Three of four interventions that provided services to low-income youth from infancy through the age of four showed significant reduction in later criminal legal involvement.

The randomized High/Scope Perry Preschool Project offered children of low socioeconomic status three hours of "high-quality, active learning" preschool five days a week, plus a 1.5-hour home visit weekly.[7] At age twenty-seven, only 7 percent of intervention participants had been arrested five times or more, compared with 35 percent of control participants.[8] The Fast Track program—which offered social skills training, peer coaching for parents, and a social-emotional curriculum for children screened for aggressive disruptive behavior—found a 30 percent decrease in violent crime conviction and 35 percent decrease in drug conviction at eighteen years old for the treatment group compared with the control group.[9] The Children-Parent Center provided wraparound services to preschool-age Black boys and their parents in Chicago.[10] It reported an 8 percent reduction in arrest rates at eighteen years old compared with the control group.

All three effective interventions included support for parents, such as home visits. The fourth study we analyzed, the Abecedarian Project, which offered intensive educational activities to children under five but included no support for parents, found no significant improvement in criminal legal–related outcomes among youth in the treatment group.[11]

Our review also found that high-quality public schooling is a crime-reducing investment. Studies of randomized lotteries for school choice in the public education system found lower rates of arrest and criminal activity among those who "won" the lottery, especially among students deemed "high risk."[12] This may be a result of peer influence; having peers with lower levels of criminal behavior (or who are less likely to be criminalized) may protect students from system involvement. This finding clarifies the importance of studying community-wide—and not merely individual-level—interventions.

To prevent recidivism, research consistently shows that providing postsecondary degrees in prison makes people more likely to be employed and less likely to be reincarcerated. Receiving a postsecondary degree during incarceration reduces rates of rearrest (by 14 percent), reconviction (by 16 percent), and reincarceration for a new offense (by 24 percent).[13] People receiving a secondary degree also report significantly higher total wages during a three-year follow-up period.

However, receiving a GED while in prison, without access to higher education, does not lower the likelihood of recidivism. A study of people released from the New Jersey correctional system in 1999–2000 found that among those who received a GED while incarcerated and those who did not, there was no difference in the number of rearrests or in the length of time to rearrest.[14] A GED alone seems insufficient to overcome the stigma of a criminal record or help secure a job with a living wage. Another study found that the economic benefit from receiving a GED is modest, about $200 per financial quarter, and completely attenuated by the second year after release.[15] This underscores the need for strong labor policy (including frequent renewal of the minimum wage to keep up with inflation) alongside a well-resourced education system—both in penal facilities and in the community.

Decarcerating via Housing

While access to housing has been identified as key to economic stability, little research has focused on its effects on criminal legal system involvement. Several studies suggest that housing relocation may reduce a child's risk of future criminal legal involvement, but fail to achieve long-term effects or address structural disparity. The large Moving to Opportunity study ran in five cities nationwide starting in 1994. Low-income families with young children were randomly allocated to three groups: (1) those given a housing voucher that could be used only within a low-poverty neighborhood for the first year and then could be used anywhere; (2) those given a housing voucher that could be used anywhere; and (3) a control group that received no housing voucher.

The follow-up evaluation found short-term reductions in violent arrests for young men and women aged fifteen to twenty-five who received a housing voucher to move to a low-poverty neighborhood; in the long term, however, effects weakened as more participants returned to their original communities. Men who received vouchers to move to higher income neighborhoods experienced an increase in property crime arrests, which attenuated with time. Follow-up evaluation suggested that families with younger children (under thirteen at the time of move) saw the greatest and longest-lasting impact across domains.[16] The Moving to Opportunity study, however, fails to address crucial structural questions about racial residential segregation, including how structural racism creates high-crime neighborhoods composed of predominantly minority populations.[17] Other studies find that forced serial displacement—the essence of Moving to Opportunity's intervention—in fact contributes to the racially segregated, chaotic, and economically depressed urban environments that laid the foundation of mass incarceration.[18]

While two studies evaluating housing vouchers found no difference in recidivism rates between treatment and control groups, we note that both had caveats.[19] The first evaluated a Washington State policy that distributed three-month rent vouchers to incarcerated people whose release would have been delayed by lack of housing.[20] The treatment group showed no difference in recidivism rates, but members of the control group—who did not receive vouchers—incurred significantly more overall expense to society ($5,200 per participant) due to longer incarceration periods, both initially and at one-year follow-up. This suggests that a binary "recidivism" measure (i.e., did a person get re-incarcerated, yes/no) missed important difference in the length of reincarceration and indicates that providing housing upon release could decrease future length of time people spend behind bars. Further, participants in the Washington State house voucher natural experiment had higher rates of probation and parole violations, possibly because the intervention required "check-ins" with community supervision officers for voucher recipients. This requirement may have undermined the intervention's effect by creating additional revocations as those in the intervention group had more interactions with their community supervision officers as a result of the vouchers.[21]

The second study, a small pilot including men returning from the Maryland prison system, aimed to demonstrate the feasibility of giving people released from prison housing vouchers rather than testing the efficacy of whether providing housing vouchers to people upon release from prison was effective in improving criminal justice outcomes.[22] Among the participants who received a voucher, there were two arrests over the year-long follow-up period, compared with nine arrests among the participants who did not. While the study had too few participants to draw firm conclusions, it suggests housing could be an effective decarceration tool.

Decarcerating via Health Care

Nurse-Family Partnership, a network of national programs that provide pre- and post-natal support from a health care professional, yields impressive decarceration results. One study grouped women from mixed economic backgrounds who received one of the following treatments: (1) transportation and screening but no home visitation (the control group); (2) a home nurse visit through pregnancy; or (3) a home nurse visit through pregnancy and the first two years of the child's life.[23] At fifteen-year follow-up, low-income mothers who received either home visitation treatment experienced fewer arrests and convictions and spent fewer days incarcerated than the control group. Their children reported fewer arrests, convictions, and probation violations, and decreased alcohol and drug use. Findings were strongest among mothers and children randomized into the third group. Subsequent researchers replicated the study, recruiting a more diverse participant pool including low-income, predominantly Black women in the first or second trimester of their first pregnancy with no previous live births.[24] Following children through eighteen years of age, researchers found fewer criminal convictions, but only among females, for reasons which remain unclear.

Another intervention, a hospital-based violence prevention model, studied whether intensive case management among victims of interpersonal violence affects criminal justice outcomes.[25] Researchers recruited young (ten- to twenty-four-year-old) participants seeking emergency care in Chicago after a violent assault. The randomly assigned participants in the treatment group received five months of intensive case management which provided local resource referrals, while those in the control group were handed a brochure with listings of the same local resources. While the study showed no difference between groups for self-reported arrests or state-reported incarcerations, criminal legal involvement in both groups was low.

Timely and immediate health care can help stabilize people who have been involved in the legal system, potentially reducing recidivism. Both hospital-based violence prevention and the Transitions Clinic Network, a primary care–based model employing a peer community health worker with a past history of incarceration, provide promising examples.

An emergency department–based intervention in Baltimore recruited patients treated for a violent assault while on probation or parole.[26] It provided an intensive social worker and an individualized treatment plan, which could include addiction treatment, employment or education referrals, conflict resolution training, and family outreach. After participants were discharged from the hospital, social workers and probation officers conducted home visits and participated in an interdisciplinary meeting resembling a "tumor board"—a model of oncologic treatment where multiple practitioners (medical doctors, surgeons, radiation oncologists, as well as nurses, social workers, and others) jointly determine the best treatment approach. While the intervention did not reduce overall arrests, it significantly reduced arrests for violent crime, as well as convictions. The study authors calculated that "after the study period, the nonintervention group was sentenced to spend 50 more years in jail than the intervention group."[27]

The Transitions Clinic Network (TCN) is a group of primary care clinics providing care tailored to people returning to the community from incarceration. A previously incarcerated community health worker serves as a patient advocate and liaison. A study in San Francisco that recruited two hundred participants at weekly parole meetings found that for people treated by a TCN clinic, there was no difference in jail stays, but they did have significantly fewer emergency department visits than others who were referred to a traditional safety-net primary care center.[28] A second study, in New Haven, Connecticut, found that people treated by a TCN clinic spent fewer days reincarcerated and had fewer violations of probation and parole.[29]

Data from a study examining the impact of Medicaid coverage among people with serious mental illness indicates that such coverage may increase exposure to the criminal legal system. A Washington State policy expedited Medicaid referrals for people with serious mental illness preparing to leave incarceration; gave them a scheduled mental health appointment; and pre-filled their anti-psychotropic medication.[30] Yet, while expedited referral increased the amount of mental health treatment, after three years it led to no reduction in total reincarceration rates, and there was an increase in total days incarcerated. A follow-up study confirmed that the receipt of services was leading to increased risk of incarceration for a technical violation, demonstrating that well-meaning interventions can spur unintended harmful effects.[31]

Decarcerating via Employment

Summer employment for young people offers economic opportunity during the most violent season of the year, suggesting the intervention's decarcerative potential.[32] An eight-week summer program—One Summer Plus—enrolled teenagers from thirteen high-violence Chicago schools.[33] The program placed all the students in part-time, minimum-wage jobs with local community organizations and provided soft skills training founded upon cognitive behavioral therapy principles. Over a sixteen-month follow-up period, participants experienced 43 percent fewer arrests for violent crime than members of the control group, with no significant difference recorded between participants who received the soft skills training and those who did not. These reductions outlasted the participants' enrollment in One Summer Plus.

People leaving incarceration benefit from intensive job support and vocational training that begins before release and lasts through reentry. Two interventions that reduced recidivism gave participants rigorous career training and guidance through the job application process.[34] Minnesota's EMPLOY program paired participants—incarcerated people within five years of completing their sentence who had six or more months of successful work history while incarcerated—with a job development specialist. Post-release, EMPLOY gave participants bus fare, interview clothing, and paper copies of résumés and certifications. Over a two- to four-year follow-up, participants had lower rates of rearrest, reconviction, reincarceration, and revocation of parole.

Similarly, Florida's Workplace and Community Transition Training for Incarcerated Individuals program offered three hundred hours of vocational training in fields including construction, plumbing, landscape irrigation, culinary arts, and web design through community or technical schools.[35] After completing this program and a separate requirement of one hundred hours of employability training, participants received a vocational certificate. They also attended reentry seminars with employers looking to recruit. Participants in the program were much less likely to be rearrested, reconvicted, or reimprisoned after three years than a similar sample not offered the training. A similar, older study evaluating a program that provided minimum-wage jobs in the construction industry (minimum wage at that time being closer to a living wage) showed that the program significantly reduced rearrest rates at three years for older participants only.[36] Several further studies evaluating employment interventions to reduce recidivism were negative or inconclusive.[37]

Employment-focused interventions that do not come with tangible supports and a living wage appear to be ineffective. Successful reentry initiatives require rigorous vocational training and post-incarceration job search assistance, and need to provide meaningful career development opportunities. Training and support should start well before release from incarceration, and people should be connected, during reentry, to community resources and social support. Perhaps most importantly, interventions must provide pathways to living wage work.

Decarcerating via Social Support Programs

Few studies examine whether social support programs beyond strictly mental health or substance abuse treatment prevent contact with the criminal justice system. One, however, explored intensive wraparound support for people with serious mental illness requiring guardianship.[38] When program staff assisted appointed guardians in social service navigation, patients experienced less frequent psychiatric hospitalization, fewer arrests, and lower incarceration costs, but no reduction in total days incarcerated.

While we generally excluded behavioral health models from our review, we included multisystemic therapy—a family- and community-based intervention for young people under eighteen years old involved in the criminal legal system—as it includes extensive social support. Among various groups of young people with prior legal system involvement, multisystemic therapy effectively reduces further legal and criminal justice system contact;[39] for non-system-involved youth, this therapy has not been sufficiently tested to draw broad conclusions.[40] A single study for secondary prevention did not find a significant decline in recidivism for the treatment group; however, the treatment group self-reported less criminal behavior than the control group.[41]

Broadly speaking, intensive case management during the transition from incarceration into the community helps young people and adults. Federally funded interventions, including the Boston Reentry Initiative—which pairs reentering participants with mentors and caseworkers who help them access social services and vocational treatment—support people who have committed serious violent crimes as they reenter society.[42] Participants had 30 percent lower rates of recidivism. A similar study in Minnesota also reduced rearrest, reconviction, and reincarceration for its participants.[43]

Conversely, withholding key forms of monetary support, such as restricting access to income and food supports for people with drug felonies, does not reduce future encounters with the criminal legal system. The 1996 Personal Responsibility and Work Opportunity Reconciliation Act banned income supports and food stamp benefits for those convicted of a drug felony. A study of the bill's impact found no difference in recidivism, suggesting the ban did not disincentivize criminal behavior.[44]

As a nation, we have collectively struggled to imagine solutions to crime or harm other than correctional punishment.[45] As prison populations continue to decline, we hope this review supports efforts to repair the damage caused by mass incarceration and to fund effective community investments. As with the successful collaboration between the public health and medical community to transform the prevention and treatment of heart disease, new social programs must be interdisciplinary and well researched. Sustainable decarceration, the evidence suggests, should be informed by the following findings about what is most effective:

- **Interventions with intergenerational impact.** Community investments that span generations make long-term contributions to a safe and thriving community. The Nurse-Family Partnership, for example, benefited children almost two decades after the end of the intervention. These findings underline the importance of bolstering support for parents as well as children.
- **Interventions that promote income stability.** Interventions that promote income stability help people thrive and can be cost-saving. Studies of postsecondary education and vocational training show that successful interventions in these arenas offer pathways to financial stability and gainful employment.
- **Higher-touch interventions.** "Dose" matters: successful programs consistently provide a high level of material well-being. For employment interventions, minimum-wage programs are generally ineffective, while those leading to career jobs, good health care, and lifestyle stability are substantially more successful. While interventions such as these are more costly than simple transitional employment, we need to study and

implement larger, more sophisticated, and perhaps costlier interventions to rival the national $50 billion annual budget for
incarceration.

Yet our review's findings reveal that we still know very little about decar-
ceral policy. Specifically:

- **Too few studies focus on decarceration.** We identified only
  forty-three experiments focused on decarceration outcomes—
  in contrast, say, to the tens of thousands of trials on cardiovascular disease. The lack of well-researched pathways to
  decarceration may owe, in part, to the political difficulty of
  conducting experimental trials—while a treatment group
  could benefit, the control group receives the status quo, which
  provides fodder for political pushback or opens the door to
  unethical research. However, we should not rush to implement unstudied policies. While we do not need a clinical trial
  to reduce the size of the prison population, it may take one (or
  many) to understand how best to provide necessary supports
  to individuals, families, and communities impacted by mass
  incarceration.
- **Interventions that increase contact with community
  corrections, namely parole and probation, may perpetuate recidivism.** When interventions—even inadvertently—
  increase exposure to community corrections, participants face
  higher visibility and, thus, a higher potential for their probation
  or parole to be revoked. Our review supports activists' warnings
  about the risks of involving correctional agencies in providing
  decarceration supports that could otherwise be provided by
  community organizations.
- **No effective interventions have been implemented at scale.**
  Our review identified several superior "treatments" that have
  not been broadly implemented. There have been no efforts to
  make even those interventions with demonstrated, long-lasting
  benefits—and those that could save costs—the standard of care.
  To truly judge decarcerative potential, efficacious treatments
  should be implemented at scale.

- **Stakeholders, particularly system-impacted people, have not been included in research design, limiting potential for finding solutions and sustaining successful interventions.** People who have been incarcerated and their families have too often been omitted from research at every stage, from developing questions to conducting studies and disseminating findings. More must be done to elevate the perspectives of people with lived experience, as their perspective can offer insight into what works and what does not; create opportunities among system-impacted people for meaningful work; and may build trust in communities where generations of state neglect and harm have undermined trust in research.[46]

To achieve permanent decarceration, we must ask the right questions and seek evidence-based answers. Effective interventions can inform policy reform and help the United States shrink its carceral population if accompanied by sufficient funding and political organizing. Research can lay the scaffolding for decarceration, but only careful attention and investment can complete its structure.

13

HUMANIZING JUSTICE: SUPPORTING POSITIVE DEVELOPMENT IN CRIMINALIZED YOUTH

Elizabeth Trejos-Castillo, Evangeline Lopoo,
and Anamika Dwivedi

Elizabeth Trejos-Castillo is the C.R. Hutcheson Professor in Human Development and Family Sciences, Vice Provost for International Affairs, and Fulbright liaison at Texas Tech University. For more than twenty-five years, she has worked closely with several local community partners, statewide partners, and national and international collaborators to support the well-being and positive development of vulnerable youth.

Evangeline (Evie) Lopoo is a current PhD student in sociology at Northwestern University. Prior to her academic career, she was project coordinator and manager of research and writing for The Square One Project at the Columbia Justice Lab.

Anamika Dwivedi is the senior manager of research and partnerships for The Square One Project at the Columbia Justice Lab. Previously, she served as manager of The Square One Executive Session on the Future of Justice Policy.

A common misconception holds that crime has a face, a name, an age, a skin color, and a gender, and that it lives in a certain neighborhood. However, "deviance" does not lie in individuals. Instead, it is usually a condition forced upon people by difficult contexts and circumstances, by a lack of opportunities and resources, and by historical oppression and prejudice. Traumatic circumstances can make anyone feel hungry, angry, cold, unsafe, frustrated, sad, abandoned, confused, afraid, shameful, anxious, distrustful, resentful, despairing, and helpless—and lead them to act accordingly. A humanizing approach to justice acknowledges that under extreme strain, people will resort to survival skills. It also acknowledges that with supportive opportunities and resources, people can change, grow, and thrive. This insight should guide school personnel, community leaders, police officers, lawyers, judges, and the public alike, as we strive to meet our social responsibility to support vulnerable youth.

The field of developmental psychology offers helpful tools to understand the life trajectories of vulnerable young people. First is "process"— the way people respond internally to external factors, affecting their well-being, motivation, self-esteem, feelings of belonging, and more. Second is "context": factors beyond a person's control that directly or indirectly drive their decision-making and affect their overall mental and behavioral well-being. Together, process and context work to create a person's response mechanisms. When someone develops "competence," they acquire the skills to adapt and thrive, and the ability to direct their behaviors and decision-making to resolve life events. Yet the opposite process, "dysfunction," makes people ill-equipped to cope with and control their circumstances, causing difficulty in engaging appropriate behaviors to deal with situations. Both competence and dysfunction are— unsurprisingly—affected by the contexts to which a person is exposed and by any behavioral reinforcement they receive.

These concepts help explain why many youth who are exposed to harmful and traumatic contexts subsequently experience criminalization or confinement. Experiences including but not limited to abuse (emotional, physical, sexual), neglect, forced labor, sexual exploitation, human trafficking, forced displacement due to armed conflict or political instability, extreme poverty, parental death, natural disasters, and parental migration to other countries can cause youth to develop "maladaptive" processes, such as acting destructively or hurting others. Harmful contexts, not an innate sense of malice, produce these processes, which are often an attempt to cope with distressing experiences.

Adolescents, in general, tend to underestimate the risks and consequences of their actions—what researchers call "optimistic bias"—due to socio-emotional, cognitive, neurological, and physiological changes and levels of maturity that limit their decision-making and impulse control.[1] Yet, while vulnerable youth have no greater propensity to engage in riskier behaviors (i.e., "misbehave") than youth in general, they might do so at an earlier age, at a greater frequency, and with more intensity because of life contexts that deny them the opportunity to develop positive coping and life skills.[2]

Thus, before rushing to criminalize young people, we must understand the contexts in which they live. Vulnerable youth—who experience a lack of stability, direction, safety, relatedness, and continuity, leaving them feeling helpless—may develop a sense of inner "nowhereness." This phenomenon, called "learned helplessness," describes the internalized perception of powerlessness caused by exposure to uncontrollable, continuous negative events.[3] Learned helplessness can have short- and long-term detrimental effects on brain development; on cognitive, learning, and emotional processes; on physical and mental health; and on social adaptation and the development of healthy relationships. The vicious cycle might propel youth experiencing learned helplessness—who believe they are worthless, will not live long, and lack control over their futures—toward negative outcomes. Over time, learned helplessness affects not only individuals but also groups. It becomes a mechanism for the intergenerational transmission of inequalities, helping preserve an unjust status quo.

In interviews, young people in systems of care such as youth facilities have recognized and described the effect of outside forces on their choices:

> I've been on my own on the streets since I was twelve. Every time they put me somewhere I ran away. . . . There [in the street] I'm free and can take care of myself. . . . I've had foster parents who fed me dog food, who've beat me.
>
> —JOSEPH, THIRTEEN YEARS OLD (three-month detention)[4]

> I'm not ashamed of what I did. I am a "man of values" you see, I'm the man of the house and I need to feed my younger siblings every day. My only regret is that I got caught today and there is no[t] gonna be food on their plates tonight, tomorrow, and . . . (begins to cry)
>
> —RAUL, ELEVEN YEARS OLD (child-welfare/
> undetermined detention)[5]

I ran away from home. My parents can barely feed and clothe my brothers and I'm old enough to survive on the streets and work. . . . I was hiding from my family but the police caught me, I'm so far away I cannot go back now.

—SHANA, FIFTEEN YEARS OLD (six-month detention)[6]

In describing their lives, youth have also verbalized their experiences of learned helplessness:

Cuz I didn't have no, uh, teachings from Dad about the basic essentials about what a person's supposed to do in life, like human quality traits, stuff like that. I had to figure that out on my own. And me being without my mother I uh saw that, like it was hard for me to love somebody, cuz a father teaches his son how to be a man, and a mother teaches her son how to love and I didn't have none of that.

—ANONYMOUS[7]

Me, personally, I grew up around a lot of violence and my mom she had always been abused and I went to foster care and I always got abused and I always ran away. I always had to fight. Me fighting always landed me in being incarcerated which always ended up in me fighting again, so being abused and in foster care and all that I landed here.

—ANONYMOUS[8]

Social policies and justice systems typically take a "universalist" approach that pays little attention to people's unique life contexts and individual trajectories. Consequently, they are ill-equipped to address historical and complex interactions between race, ethnicity, class, and gender or sexual identity. They fail to acknowledge generations of harm and trauma that are unequally distributed in society. And, by ignoring intergenerational violence and its psychosocial effects, they perpetuate inequality when interacting with vulnerable youth.

An example of the disparate impact of "universalist" policymaking is the increase in disciplinary actions and school offenses through which young people of color have been referred to the youth justice system, even as rates of violent crime in schools have declined.[9] Starting in preschool, students of color are disciplined at higher rates than their white counterparts; Black preschoolers are about 3.5 times more likely to receive one or more school suspensions or be denied access to Head Start programs. In the 2011–12 school year, Black and Hispanic youth were four to six times more likely than white students to be suspended or expelled from middle and/or high schools.[10] School-based racial profiling also leads to the punishment and criminalization of young people of color for "defiant behaviors," "disrespect," and "ungovernability." Yet poverty strongly predicts behavioral problems in early adolescence, and "universalist" approaches to school discipline ignore the fact that Black people are twice as likely to be poor as white people.[11] The toll of poverty disadvantages poor Black students and other youth of color in school settings, leading, in many cases, to their incarceration and institutionalization.

Overall, system-impacted youth are disproportionately young people of color. Though total rates of youth arrests decreased from 49 percent in 2003 to 31 percent in 2013, racial disparities in the arrest rates between white youth and Black, Hispanic, and Native American youth increased during the same period.[12] Relatedly, in 2017, young people of color represented 49 percent of the entire youth population but accounted for approximately 67 percent of incarcerated young people. Also in 2017, young Black people accounted for approximately 42 percent of incarcerated boys and 35 percent of incarcerated girls. Hispanic youth account for 22 percent of all youth incarcerations, and Native American boys and girls—though comprising less than 1 percent of youth of color nationwide—represent, respectively, 1.5 percent and 3 percent of the incarcerated youth of color.[13]

School discipline policies contribute to these figures. Yet "zero tolerance" policies do not make school campuses or streets safer. Nor do the increasing number of school resource officers; the high rate of school suspensions, expulsions, and arrests; or referrals to the justice system from schools and the child welfare system. Instead, these policies mean that young people (particularly vulnerable youth of color) dealing with victimization—in the form of abuse and neglect; exposure to violence; separation and loss of family members; poverty; learning, physical, or mental disabilities; segregation; or racial and sexual discrimination—cannot count on schools and protective care services to provide safety or stability.

Systems-impacted youth might experience multiple relocations, finding little support no matter where they turn. Yet settings of "care" for vulnerable young people—including foster care and mental health care—sometimes employ restraining and disciplining practices that further criminalize and victimize vulnerable youth in the name of their "protection." These "protective measures" inflict further trauma on those who need healing. For example, Safe Harbor laws—which protect trafficked young people from prostitution and provide them with shelter and treatment—are enforced in just twenty-one states, and in some cases apply only to youth under fourteen years old.[14] While the commercial sexual exploitation of children is legally prohibited, prostituted children do not automatically receive a "victim" status and often face criminal charges in the United States. Relatedly, girls placed in the youth justice system for illicit sexual activities report experiencing sexual and emotional victimization while in youth correctional facilities.[15]

Systems also fail to protect the mental health of young people. National statistics show that 50 to 75 percent of incarcerated youth are diagnosed with a mental or behavioral health condition.[16] Exposure to trauma is ubiquitous; in a Cook County, Illinois, youth detention center, for example, almost 93 percent of detainees had experienced at least one form of trauma in their lifetime as reported by a study in 2004.[17] Justice-involved youth are disproportionately at risk for developing a mental or behavioral health condition or trauma disorder compared with youth in general, suggesting that the justice system functions as a germination chamber for mental illness.

The following report from a parole officer offers an unfortunately common example of the ways that some vulnerable youth encounter multiple social systems ill-equipped to effectively improve their circumstances or outcomes:

> Sonya (15 years old) had a long history of sexual abuse back home. Child Protective Services [CPS] placed her in a great facility where she was getting trauma-informed treatment for Domestic Minors Sex Trafficking [DMST] youth. She was getting all those services there, well, then she did really great for a month and then her "risk" level dropped. So, CPS got her out of there because her risk level did not qualify her anymore and even though we had emails from the therapist saying she was not ready to go anywhere else. So, she got out and ended up with the same gang

members who were trafficking her before and having her sell drugs for protection and survival. . . . She picked up prostitution and drug charges along the way and then she did not qualify for the DMST program anymore because she exceeded the "risk" level. She is now at this facility because she cannot [sic] longer go back to CPS. . . . It's a vicious cycle and we have to break it.[18]

We propose a set of approaches to address learned helplessness that can help to break this cycle. The first step is to embrace restorative justice practices and policies. Historically, many civilizations and societies have viewed youth crime as a consequence—not a cause—of social problems, and Indigenous justice practices have been adopted in contemporary justice systems through restorative justice. Restorative justice can be understood as both a structure and a set of values: the process "brings together all the parties affected by an incident of wrongdoing, to decide collectively on a consensual basis how to deal with the aftermath of the incident." [19] Restorative justice acknowledges that crime, fundamentally, is a violation of people and interpersonal relationships; relationships must be healed and wrongdoings made right.[20] Some Indigenous communities even have alternative legal systems entrenched in restorative justice principles, as evidenced by the Rangatahi and Matariki courts run by Māori New Zealanders.[21] Since 1980, forms of restorative justice have been adopted and implemented with increasing popularity in forty countries across Africa, Asia, Europe, Latin America, the Caribbean, the Middle East, and the Pacific region.

In the United States, however, restorative justice policies often face institutional resistance. In the youth system, they are typically implemented in conjunction with some elements of conventional retributive justice policies. State legislative codes variably cite restorative justice: only eleven states emphasize solely restorative justice principles in their youth justice statutes and codes; seven states use a "balanced approach" that combines regular youth justice policies with traditional accountability practices, community work, treatment and care, and rehabilitation services; and twenty states use the language of both "balance and restorative justice." [22] Yet despite the continued resistance to the widespread adoption of restorative justice, such an approach would help ameliorate the harms of the school-to-prison and care-to-prison pipelines. It would allow practitioners, professionals, and caregivers to examine the factors leading to youth offending, and prevent the unnecessary escalation of disciplinary actions for preventable and modifiable behaviors. It would also interrupt the cycle of victimization, learned helplessness, and criminalization.

Studies find that schools might be ideal settings for restorative justice practices. Schools can help develop young people's life skills, accountability, and civic responsibility while simultaneously promoting their dignity.[23]

Yet unless and until the U.S. legal system fundamentally shifts its focus from punishment to accountability and rehabilitation, the promise of restorative justice will remain unrealized. Restorative justice should be understood not as a "program," but as a reconceptualization of our moral imperatives—both in terms of sentencing and, more generally, our mutual obligations.

In addition to restorative justice, we must make community-based reintegration programs and welfare services an immediate and universal priority for justice-involved youth. Youth recidivism rates and the stigma of criminal activity could both be reduced by more meaningfully reintegrating justice-involved young people into society. This would involve offering welfare services (e.g., housing, food, health), educational or vocational training programs, and family therapy programs; utilizing open custody and halfway centers; and developing partnerships with industries and businesses to build social and human capital and enhance labor market opportunities. Countries with such model programs include Australia, Belgium, Brazil, Canada, Finland, France, Germany, New Zealand, Turkey, and the United Kingdom. These countries, which have stronger social service systems than the United States, respond to youth offending in more effective and productive ways, including by providing health care, pedagogical and psychiatric referrals, and life and soft vocational skills development. Instead of delivering punishment, these systems support young people's socio-emotional well-being and promote their positive growth.[24]

Yet *sustainability* and *scalability* are important challenges facing the implementation of such youth justice reentry models. Funds would need to be reallocated from traditional justice programs to community-led initiatives to enable the development, testing, implementation, evaluation, and—if successful—the maintenance of new efforts. Partnerships between community advocates, industry actors, organizations, nonprofits, and private foundations could support the scalability of evidence-based interventions, helping deliver their benefits to a broader population of youth.

Finally, we must fortify social service systems to prevent learned helplessness and diminish youth criminalization. To tackle learned helplessness among vulnerable young people who offend, we cannot rely solely on restorative justice and reintegration programs. Instead, we must also employ key preventive strategies. We need, for example, a social service model that supports the holistic development of long-lasting life skills, healthy habits, prosocial behaviors, positive character traits, and work skills across various welfare systems. Such a framework should be developed with the same urgency brought to restorative justice and reintegration practices. From schools to communities to care services, preventive practice frameworks should be contextually and culturally appropriate; be informed by human development; and emphasize young people's rights as active agents of their own resilience and growth. Strong partnerships across systems (such as health and education) and community-led advocacy could help effectively manage resources, avoid duplications, and prioritize interventions that would most efficiently repurpose funds. For example, the Center for Court Innovation, a New York City–based nonprofit organization, implemented a restorative justice project in five Brooklyn high schools. By facilitating conflict resolution in a safe, monitored space, the initiative significantly reduced schools' use of suspensions and the interference of school resource officers, in turn minimizing young people's potential exposure to criminalization.[25]

Yet robust social services need sufficient resources. Over the past ten years, social service–centered programs developed, piloted, and implemented nationwide vary widely by state and region. Evidence-based community outreach and engagement programs receive funding from federal, state, and private grants; work in different settings (e.g., schools, community centers); and exist in varying locations (e.g., urban, rural, suburban, online). Among these, the National Institute of Justice's Crime Solutions database lists twelve "effective" and thirty-five "promising" evidence-based youth programs, and three "effective" and five "promising" evidence-based practices (or general procedures or strategies) for youth.[26] To fund such programs, the U.S. Congress allocated $320 million for youth justice programs in 2020, representing the largest appropriation of such funding since the previous high of $424 million in 2010.[27] Funds have been allocated to new grants, such as those preventing the trafficking of girls, and to continuing grants studying opioid-affected youth and children exposed to violence. This work is promising and supports the unique needs of youth populations.

Along with developing a stronger social service net, we must create policies and offer training to social and health service providers to enhance young people's experiences across institutions. For example, in youth justice centers, we must prioritize trauma-informed services that include universal screenings for trauma and psychological and psychiatric conditions, and offer developmentally appropriate interventions, treatment, and follow-ups.[28] States including Massachusetts, Connecticut, Alaska, and California have developed a best-practice protocol for trauma-informed care of young people in multiple settings and implemented this protocol in judicial proceedings.[29] We also need continued training and education for all practitioners and staff to implement de-escalation techniques; support the development of adaptive behaviors, life skills, positive coping strategies, self-efficacy, and self-restraint; and help manage secondary traumatization and stress.[30]

It has been nearly a century since the Geneva Declaration of the Rights of the Child, over sixty years since its wide adoption by the United Nations, and over thirty years since its ratification as the Convention on the Rights of the Child. Yet the United States in particular has fallen short when it comes to defending young people's human rights. The Declaration compels us to protect young people's mental and physical development and shield them from abuse and exploitation; to safeguard their rights to life and survival; and to ensure their full participation in family, cultural, and social life.[31] We have yet to honor this obligation.

Despite recent efforts to undo some of the damage caused by punitive excess, the United States still overuses arrest, detention, and imprisonment for young people; still persecutes minors for petty crimes; still sentences young offenders to life in prison without parole; still confines youth in adult detention and corrections facilities; and still disrupts families and separates children from their caregivers. These ineffective and harmful practices owe, in part, to policymakers' failure to grasp the specialized needs of youth who are vulnerable to maladaptive coping mechanisms including learned helplessness.

To progress toward justice, we must listen to systems-impacted youth. Listening is the first step in acknowledging young people's inherent power to overcome their circumstances and, in doing so, to overcome learned helplessness. Only through centering young people's strengths and resilience can we effectively ensure their rights to safe, healthy, and thriving lives.

14

COORDINATED CARE: LESS SUPERVISION, MORE TREATMENT

Lynda Zeller and Jackie Prokop

Lynda Zeller is the senior fellow at the Michigan Endowment Fund. Previously she served eight years as the deputy director for the Behavioral Health and Developmental Disabilities at the Michigan Department of Health and Human Services, functioning as the state authority for behavioral health and developmental disabilities policy and service systems, as well as two years as health administrator for the state of Michigan Department of Corrections.

Jackie Prokop, a longtime state leader in Medicaid policy, has nearly three decades of experience serving the State of Michigan, including eleven years as director of the Medicaid Policy Division.

As policymakers grapple with the failures of mass incarceration, many are reevaluating how justice system dollars are spent. State and local justice reform initiatives demonstrate that coordinated changes to health and justice spending could reduce mass incarceration and build safer communities. Substantive reforms to probation and parole, coupled with targeted reforms in health spending, would achieve better outcomes.

To reduce mass incarceration, we call for two urgent changes. First, we need to strengthen social service programs (i.e., housing and education) and community-based health care programs for all people leaving incarceration. Second, probation and parole should be abolished. Such changes would particularly benefit groups who are currently overrepresented in jails and prisons, including people with mental illness.

People with chronic behavioral health conditions—such as serious mental illnesses and substance use disorders—are disproportionately incarcerated and re-incarcerated.[1] Yet probation and parole agencies are often unequipped to support these groups' unique needs, contributing to their over-incarceration. Attempts to divert people with behavioral health conditions into community-based treatment are often hindered by a lack of funding. Given this situation, targeted health care reform efforts could also promote critical justice reform. In particular, state Medicaid programs could tailor and fund specialty community-based behavioral health care for vulnerable populations. This investment of funds would not only reduce costs related to incarceration, but also improve health outcomes and lower incarceration rates, especially among people with mental illness and substance use disorders.

Community supervision—including probation and parole—was originally conceived as a progressive alternative to incarceration, allowing people to remain in their communities (probation) or reintegrate after incarceration (parole). However, during the 1980s and '90s, community supervision shifted from a casework model focused on rehabilitation toward a crime control model that relied on surveillance and punishment ("Trail 'em, nail 'em, and jail 'em").[2] The system incentivizes and often requires officers to return people to prison, rather than address their behavioral health needs or tackle the social conditions from which noncompliance with the conditions of supervision may emerge.

This shift in focus has helped sustain mass incarceration in the twenty-first century. It has increased not only the number of people supervised, but also the punishment of noncriminal conduct (e.g., staying out past curfew or missing parole appointments).[3] Practitioners lament that probation and parole officers no longer serve as rehabilitative agents, but are immersed, instead, in a bureaucratic process focused on compliance.

In the United States, a staggering 4.5 million people are under community supervision. This large population—twice the number of people incapacitated through incarceration—entails sizable caseloads for probation and parole officers. Increasing caseloads, paired with punitive correctional policy, means that probation and parole officers can rarely meet the needs of people with complex physical and behavioral health issues—a population overrepresented in jails and prisons.

An estimated 80 percent of people released from incarceration in the

United States have a substance use disorder, mental illness, or physical health condition. People in these populations are significantly more likely to fatally overdose after release.[4] In addition, the prevalence of hepatitis C is ten times higher in these groups than in the general population, and the prevalence of HIV is eight to nine times higher.[5] These health problems hinder successful reintegration into community life. Relatedly, a lack of access to health care undermines people's efforts to find or maintain employment and housing, to (re)build family relationships, and to maintain sobriety.[6]

The supervision system not only fails to provide people with resources, including transitional housing, vocational training, and physical and behavioral health care. It also imposes unrealistic expectations for correctional compliance. Symptoms of mental illness and addiction can negatively affect people's ability to comply with the terms of their probation and parole, leading to violations. Navigating the demands of community corrections, while also battling a chronic health condition, searching for employment and housing, and meeting basic material needs, is essentially impossible.[7] Community corrections officials recognize that while people with behavioral health conditions need support, the system overall neither provides such support nor accommodates people's mistakes, whether illness-related or not.

Scholars and practitioners alike have described the detrimental effects of probation and parole and identified the need for fundamental reform.[8] They have called for a dramatic reduction in the number of people under community supervision, and an increased focus on giving people the resources they need to thrive in their communities (e.g., the Executives Transforming Probation and Parole initiative).[9] Reformers propose a new model for community supervision, one that provides people with necessary care outside of parole and probation.[10] Reinventing community supervision by drawing from Medicaid-funded care coordination models could significantly reduce incarceration rates, especially among people with physical and behavioral health conditions.

The expansion of Medicaid is a key mechanism for the provision of targeted health and social services that could reduce the scope of the community supervision system. As of April 2022, thirty-nine states and the District of Columbia have expanded Medicaid under the Affordable Care Act. In Medicaid expansion states like Colorado and New York, 80 to 90 percent of people exiting incarceration are eligible for Medicaid and can receive critical behavioral health care; returning people with income at or below 133 percent of the federal poverty level and who meet other federal citizenship requirements are eligible for these services.[11] In states that have not expanded Medicaid, however, under 10 percent of people leaving incarceration are eligible for medical coverage and programs. In these non-Medicaid-expansion states, Medicaid typically covers only low-income children, the elderly, pregnant women, and people with disabilities; this leaves most people living at or near poverty without health care after incarceration.

Medicaid programs can help establish care coordination services for people under supervision, and ensure continuous treatment from prison into the community. With Medicaid expansion, these programs can be made available to most people leaving incarceration. Many people with chronic conditions receive consistent treatment in prison, but face the challenge of securing care once they return to the community. Continuity of care not only promotes well-being, particularly for people with chronic conditions, but also provides a point of access to other social services. As such, it both bridges gaps in health care provision and increases reentering people's ability to manage life challenges.

To provide care coordination, many expansion states are enrolling people in Medicaid before they are released from prison. Since mental illness and addiction are potent risk factors for re-incarceration, care coordination facilitated by Medicaid coverage can reduce high-risk patients' likelihood of returning to jail or prison. A well-designed system of care can improve health and increase the likelihood of successful reentry.

Yet while Medicaid helps expand the availability of resources, access to health care is not synonymous with receipt of care. The most effective treatment is offered through partnerships between state Medicaid agencies and the justice system, community-based health providers, and people with direct experience. Collaboratively designed and administered programs are best able to improve the health and well-being of reentering people.[12]

Most probation and parole systems do not address community and personal hardships that associate with a higher likelihood of incarceration and revocation of probation. These include economic instability, lack of access to housing and educational opportunities, food insecurity, and other social determinants of health. Additionally, inadequate management of behavioral health needs by probation and parole officers may also contribute to recidivism. A five-year study of communities implementing jail diversion programs, pre- and post-justice involvement, reports that people in Michigan with substance use disorders that co-occurred with mental illness were twice as likely to return to jail as people with mental illness but no addiction.[13] Yet connecting reentering populations with appropriate post-release health care to manage chronic conditions is challenging; managing health may be a low, or unattainable, priority for people dealing with various survival needs and health issues. To better support this population, researchers should consider the experiences of the people they hope to reach. Reentering people's perceptions of health and health care remain insufficiently understood.[14]

Collaboration between health and social service networks can help establish care coordination for people with chronic conditions and justice system involvement. Yet one challenging barrier to care coordination is the secure sharing of personal health information between the justice system and community-based health care staff, consistent with state and federal privacy laws. For example, a five-year Michigan-based pilot diversion program found that only four of the ten communities in which the program operated reported a close working relationship between parole, probation, and community behavioral health programs; only 30 percent of jail discharges incorporated a behavioral health–related service.[15]

While many challenges remain, Michigan's Departments of Corrections and Health and Human Services offer a good example of effectively working to promote people's success after incarceration, including by enabling them to manage chronic conditions and by securing stable income and housing. Michigan administers promising specialty reentry programs for people with mental illness and substance use disorders. It also offers bold employment efforts including "Vocational Village," which helps people exit incarceration not just with training, but with confirmed employment.

Medicaid enables states to expand care coordination among targeted population groups. Each state can choose and design Medicaid-funded care management programs for populations with complex needs. By opting to expand care coordination for people reentering the community after incarceration, states can reduce both incarceration and its related costs. Eighty percent of people exiting incarceration have chronic conditions, including mental illness and addiction. For this target population, intensive case management programs are good investments. States can select from two particular Medicaid tools to achieve intensive case management. Both programs—Medicaid Health Home and Targeted Case Management—share the costs of strengthened state services with the federal Medicaid system. Both programs assess and identify individuals' health and social needs. Both not only help provide people access to physical, behavioral, and mental health care, but also address their social determinants of health.

States vary significantly in whether they choose to implement such care coordination models, which populations they target, and which Medicaid policy path they pursue. Each program has pros and cons. For example, Medicaid Health Home offers state Medicaid programs a 90/10 federal/state match for health home services for the first eight quarters of implementation, while Targeted Case Management programs receive the state's regular federal Medicaid assistance percentage.[16] The Medicaid federal match rate for program services has a statutory minimum of 50 percent and a statutory maximum of 83 percent, which is determined annually based on the Medicaid Federal Medical Assistance Percentage formula.[17] But Medicaid Health Homes tend to have more administrative requirements than Targeted Case Management programs. Medicaid Health Homes entail more complex billing for providers—sometimes requiring significant technological changes—as well as specific quality monitoring and reporting requirements.[18] Targeted Case Management programs, by contrast, can have more flexibility.

Still, both programs have demonstrated reductions in emergency department visits and inpatient hospital admissions. Medical homes do so by better coordinating care for people with chronic diseases.[19] One study found that programs that combine targeted case management with health homes reduce the proportion of participants' emergency room visits not resulting in admissions; members are more likely to visit when medically necessary instead of for preventive care.[20] In New York, inpatient service costs decreased by approximately 30 percent for people enrolled in a Medicaid Health Home. And Missouri's Health Home program generated a 13 percent reduction in hospital admissions and an 8 percent reduction in emergency department use for the study population.[21]

Similarly, over an eighteen-month period beginning with Michigan's introduction of a Medicaid Health Home model in 2016, emergency department use and inpatient hospital admissions decreased steadily. These reductions were statistically significant when measured at 6-month, 7- to 12-month, and 13- to 18-month time frames. Health care service spending decreased over the same period.[22]

Managing chronic health conditions in the primary care setting is especially difficult for people recently released from incarceration; they may lack access to health care or other social services.[23] Yet barriers to care can cause poor health outcomes and also complicate people's ability to reintegrate into the community. A community-based model that integrates physical and behavioral health can help meet people's needs.

Tailored health home and targeted case management models show positive results for people exiting jail or prison in states including Arizona, New York, New Mexico, and Ohio.[24] These models use the principle of "integrated health care management," where health care provision is paired with social supports for people exiting incarceration. This combination helps people address health care and social needs, improves care management, and prevents costly emergency room or inpatient hospital stays. Coordinated care can also improve access to appropriate outpatient treatment, provide behavioral health services, and promote health equality.[25] Moreover, by building trust, providing patient-centered care, and addressing social determinants of health, pilot initiatives have significantly reduced recidivism rates; some decreased the rate of re-incarceration over a three-year period from 57 percent to 16 percent.[26]

One successful model is the Transitions Clinic Network, which coordinates care for people under supervision or exiting incarceration. Co-founded by Dr. Emily Wang and Dr. Shira Shavit in 2006, Transitions Clinic Network is a national network of medical homes for people leaving incarceration who are experiencing chronic disease. With a focus on community and a public health approach to serving reentering people with intensive health needs, the network helps vulnerable people successfully reintegrate into their lives and neighborhoods.

The first Transitions Clinic, based at Southeast Health Center, was opened by the San Francisco Department of Public Health to provide reentering people who have chronic illness with transitional and primary care as well as case management. In 2010, a formal analysis of the San Francisco clinic measured rates of participants' attendance at initial appointments and six-month follow-up appointments post-incarceration. Of 185 Transitions Clinic participants observed between 2006 and 2007, 55 percent attended initial appointments and 77 percent attended six-month follow-ups, compared with 40 percent and 46 percent, respectively, for non–Transitions Clinic patients seen at Southeast Health Center.[27] Clinics that employed community health workers with personal histories of incarceration helped increase the average of new patients seen per month from seven to eleven.[28]

A model piloted in Michigan in 2017 has seen similar success. Several Federally Qualified Health Centers partnered with the Department of Corrections to implement a care coordination program for people on parole. The program, Connection to Care, ensures that justice-involved people's behavioral and physical health needs are addressed after prison release. The model deploys a peer support specialist, or "health coach," and allows incarcerated people to form relationships with staff from the centers prior to their release. In the first year of operation, 100 percent of Connection to Care patients had an appointment scheduled and were seen by their primary care provider within seven days from discharge. Center staff successfully connected with paroled patients; peer support specialists contacted each patient an average of twice per month.[29] In a patient satisfaction survey, people under supervision were receptive to the model and their health coach. All respondents indicated that it was not hard to get to the appointment; 91 percent indicated they received help accessing health care; and 98 percent indicated it was easy to share health problems with the doctors and the Connections to Care staff. Respondents, on average, rated their first visit highly (4.7 on a 5.0 scale).[30]

Efforts to reduce mass incarceration will not succeed without providing health care and social supports to people with chronic health conditions, especially those with mental illness or substance use problems. Models such as those described above—and not traditional community supervision—help meet the unique needs of these groups. Until proba-tion and parole are replaced with a system that can address serious health needs, people with behavioral health conditions will continue to be over-represented in the penal system, suffer high rates of re-incarceration, and remain incarcerated for longer periods of time.

Data show that health system reform using Medicaid programs can help people with medical conditions successfully return to and remain in their communities. For states that expand Medicaid, such services can be offered to most people released from jails and prisons. Care coordi-nation models provided through Medicaid are effective and can finance the provision of health services in a socially supportive environment. As such, more states should seek federal approval to amend their Medicaid programs to include reimbursement for health home or targeted case management models. Through either mechanism, states could help re-entering people manage their chronic conditions and integrate into the community.

State Medicaid leaders can offer specialized community-based care management programs to people returning home from incarceration. With federal approval for specialty care coordination, financing is shared between state and federal governments, increasing the resources avail-able for these impactful and cost-effective strategies. When Medicaid is unavailable, however, financing of community supervision models is not shared. As such, states that do not expand Medicaid will be limited in their ability to substantially reform and reduce punitive community supervision.

While we focus, here, on tools to reduce the mass incarceration of people with chronic health needs, these reform tools could also help ad-dress the unique needs of other groups overrepresented in jails and pris-ons. Given the disproportionate incarceration of people in poverty and in racial and ethnic minority populations, researchers should consider how these tools could help mitigate racial health and justice disparities. Further study should explore whether specialty care coordination models need refinement to address the needs of specific racial, cultural, and local communities.

Replacing punitive supervision with health care reflects the spirit of rehabilitation that motivated community corrections as it was first en-visioned. Specialty care management models built upon state Medicaid programs can reduce and ultimately end the use of contemporary parole and probation models, leading to better results. This opportunity is much greater in states that expand Medicaid. Medicaid care coordination models can improve access to health care, raise the quality of available care, and help prevent future incarceration. When used jointly by state Medicaid and correctional system leadership, these tools—at the intersection of health and justice reform—can powerfully improve public health and help end mass incarceration.

PART IV

ENVISIONING AND
POWER SHARING

15

WEAVING THE SOCIAL FABRIC: A NEW MODEL FOR PUBLIC SAFETY AND VITAL NEIGHBORHOODS

Elizabeth Glazer and Patrick Sharkey

Elizabeth Glazer is the founder of Vital City, a policy venture dedicated to finding practical and fair solutions to public safety problems. Previously, she served as the director of the New York City Mayor's Office of Criminal Justice, where she led the strategy to produce a dramatic reduction in the jail population and to create community-led safety strategies.

Patrick Sharkey is William S. Tod Professor of Sociology and Public Affairs at Princeton University and the founder of AmericanViolence. org. Formerly, he was chair of the Department of Sociology at New York University and served as scientific director at Crime Lab New York.

It's hard to remember what New York City was like back in February of 2020, before a virus tore through its neighborhoods, demonstrations took over city streets, riot-geared police officers confronted New Yorkers in encounters streamed to the world, and a surge of shootings led to a summer of violence unlike any other in recent years. But it's important to think back.

In the years before the COVID-19 pandemic, New York City had been taking gradual steps toward a new model for public safety. After decades of relying on aggressive, zero-tolerance policing, the city was moving away from criminal justice enforcement as its exclusive response to violent crime, and toward a "lighter touch" approach guided by evidence-based strategies. Embracing strategies ranging from vibrant public spaces to summer youth employment, it began to recognize—and empower—community-oriented institutions and residents as central actors in the effort to build safe neighborhoods. Those strategies were part of a new approach to increase public safety while decreasing the unequal impact of the justice system, particularly within communities of color.

During this transition, conditions in New York City did not deteriorate as some had predicted. Crime kept falling to levels not seen in the modern history of the city. Among New York City's population of more than 8.5 million people, 319 were murdered in 2019, a fraction of the rate of other large American cities, and a fraction of the city's own murder rate decades before. As crime declined, the incarcerated population fell to a rate resembling less that of large U.S. cities and more that of a Western European nation. Arrests had also dropped significantly, and the New York Police Department had mostly ended its controversial use of stop, question, and frisk. Prosecutors had started to exercise their discretion to focus more on serious crime, and judges began to use different approaches to ensure accountability.

While the ongoing pandemic has revealed how fragile and limited the city's progress was—as well as how flawed the justice system is as the central approach to achieving safety—the pandemic also provides a critical opportunity to reshape how cities achieve safe and thriving neighborhoods. A new model for public safety identifies residents and local organizations—rather than law enforcement—as the primary means to achieving vital, safe neighborhoods. This model weaves together a social fabric composed of residents and community institutions and supported by government services.

New York was one of many major cities that went through a period of crisis at the end of the twentieth century, confronting issues including widespread joblessness, the outmigration of its middle class, concentrated poverty, retrenchment of social services, and rising violent crime. From the early 1960s to the late 1980s, the national murder rate rose from just over four murders for every one hundred thousand residents to over ten murders for every one hundred thousand residents (see figure 1).[1] During the first few years of the 1990s, this number skyrocketed to over thirty murders for every one hundred thousand residents in New York City (see figure 2).

These deteriorating conditions were met by a new, fundamentally punitive approach to violence.[2] Prosecutors pursued the harshest sentences possible, leading to rapidly rising rates of incarceration. While the national imprisonment rate had historically hovered around a hundred state and federal prisoners per one hundred thousand Americans, it skyrocketed to over five hundred per one hundred thousand in 1970 and continued to rise through the 2010s.[3] Federal, state, and local resources bolstered police forces, and political leaders gave police the authority to take over city streets with brute force.[4]

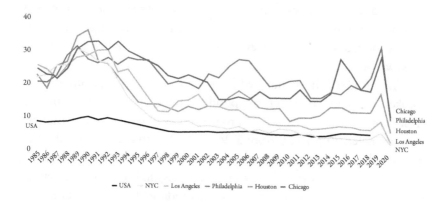

FIGURE 1: Change in murder rates in the five largest U.S. cities, 1985–2020[5]

This old, punitive model was refined under William Bratton, who became head of New York City's transit police in 1990, at the high-water mark for murders in the city. Bratton was advised by criminologist George L. Kelling, who with co-author James Q. Wilson introduced what is now known as the "broken windows" theory in an article published by the *Atlantic Monthly* in 1982. Wilson and Kelling argued that visible cues of disorder—for example, a broken window—signaled that a space was out of control, therefore inviting more violations of social norms. This cycle, if not stopped in its earliest stages, would escalate into larger problems: a broken window invited squatters, who gave way to crack dealers, who then resorted to violence to defend their territory. Wilson and Kelling argued that the policing of "deviant behavior," often prompted by calls from private residents, was the best antidote to disorder. Bratton took these lessons to heart and applied them both to the physical conditions of the subways (e.g., graffiti) and to the activity that he believed contributed to the breakdown in social controls (e.g., turnstile jumping).[6]

In 1994, Mayor Rudy Giuliani made Bratton head of the New York Police Department, and Bratton brought with him this new style of aggressive policing. His approach gradually expanded beyond its initial focus on physical conditions—the "broken windows"—and morphed into a zero-tolerance approach of stopping or arresting every possible "troublemaker" on the street and below ground. This style of policing institutionalized an idea of apparent simplicity, if disputed veracity: not only is crime controllable, but police actions are central to that control. As crime dropped year after year, every other measure of police activity rose in New York City.[7]

While it is still hotly debated how much to credit Bratton's style of "broken windows" policing, the pundits dubbed the stunning drop in crime as a "New York Miracle."[8] From 1990 to 1998, the annual number of murders fell 70 percent, from 2,245 to 649, with the sharpest drop in murders that the city has ever experienced (see figure 2). Bratton was featured twice on the cover of *Time* magazine, highlighting a police-centric model of crime control that was ultimately adopted by cities around the country and the world.[9]

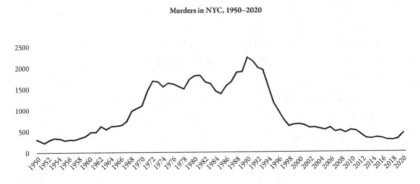

Murders in NYC, 1950–2020

FIGURE 2: New York City murders[10]

This conceptual breakthrough—that police can control crime—provided a powerful reason for New York City to rely on the police for more than reducing crime. Police began performing functions that might have otherwise been considered the province of city agencies, from controlling the presence of unhoused people on the streets to addressing addiction and mental illness issues, further blurring the line between police and civic power.[11]

Over the next thirty years, this approach to policing—and the larger deference to the criminal justice system—became the country's default approach to public safety. While murders declined in New York City by 86 percent between 1990 and 2019 (see figure 3), the number of uniformed police officers on the street increased from 26,000 to almost 40,000.[12] Meanwhile, felony and misdemeanor arrests hit a recent high of 312,399 in 2010, and the growing presence of police enforcement was reflected in the rise of stops to almost 700,000 in 2011 and summonses to 540,000 in 2010 (see figure 3).[13]

This style of intrusive policing was largely concentrated in communities of color, and had a significant and deleterious effect on residents' views of cops and the larger criminal justice system.[14] Young men of color were disproportionately stopped and frisked, and made to feel like suspects whenever they walked down the street. Thousands became enmeshed in the criminal justice system, many for minor offenses.[15] The widespread mistrust of law enforcement, especially in communities of color, is a central part of the legacy of the old model of violence prevention in New York City.[16]

Promising to address urban inequalities, including those within the criminal justice system, Bill de Blasio was elected mayor of New York City in January 2014. His opposition to the NYPD's stop, question, and frisk practices—and their pernicious effect on the lives of families and communities of color—had been a centerpiece of his campaign.

From police unions to the city's elites, critics expressed concern that the newly elected mayor would be unable to keep the city safe with what they perceived as a "soft" approach to crime.[17] Perhaps in response to these political pressures, de Blasio appointed Bill Bratton, the father of stop and frisk, as his first police commissioner.

The new administration moved to reframe New York City's approach to public safety as not just about "how to reduce crime" but "how to create safety" for its residents.[18] This new model focused on the creation

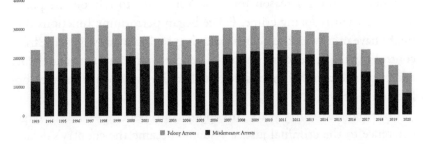

FIGURE 3: Felony and misdemeanor arrests in New York City, 1993–2020[19]

of well-being and opportunity rather than just the absence of crime—a strategy that would be "owned" by the community and not just the police. This wasn't just semantics: it was a shift away from policies of negation (arrest and incarcerate) and toward policies of creation (strengthen families, nurture neighborhood connections and networks, transform public spaces, and open up jobs).

The criminal justice system—police, prosecutors, courts, jails, and prisons—plays a role in creating public safety. But it is just one piece—done right, an ever-shrinking piece—of a larger civic enterprise necessary to build a thriving city. Both of these ideas—creating safety through coordinated civic goods and reshaping the uses of the criminal justice system to limit its disparities—were central to building this new model for public safety.[20]

This new approach had a dramatic impact: from 2013 to 2019, the city experienced a massive reduction in arrests and jail population, and crime continued to decline.[21] These changes were the result of a confluence of factors. With crime at the lowest it had been since the 1960s, decision-makers were able to look more closely at solutions that did not rely exclusively on the harshest measures of the criminal justice system.[22] At the same time, the overuse of police powers had resulted in an almost universal acknowledgment that the policies of the last thirty years had come at too great a cost. Owing to growing mistrust in the efficacy and fairness of the criminal justice system, victims of crime often did not report crimes or testify, and jurors and grand jurors were more skeptical of law enforcement witnesses.[23] Formerly incarcerated people sharply questioned whether the criminal justice system was fair or effective.

Between 2014 and 2020, a broad array of reforms, developed with the advice of hundreds of people from judges, to formerly incarcerated people, and others, resulted in a drop of 70 percent in the jail population (see figure 4).[24] These included programs that judges could offer instead of jail; "crisis intervention" training for cops who encountered people with behavioral health issues; and supportive housing to interrupt the cycle of those shifting from shelters to emergency rooms to jail. Additionally, de Blasio pledged to close Rikers Island, New York City's largest jail, and build humane facilities that would be physically closer to courts, communities, and services for those incarcerated.[25]

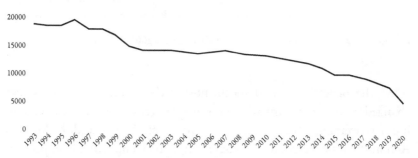

FIGURE 4: New York City jail population, 1993–2020[26]

Dramatic changes in policing were accelerated not just by the mayor's campaign commitments, but also by the deaths of Eric Garner in New York City and Michael Brown in Ferguson, Missouri, in 2014. These tragedies added even more urgency to a set of reforms underway to retrench the reach of police into the lives of people of color.

Stop and frisks, which had dropped significantly in the two years before de Blasio took office, now dropped even more precipitously, and by 2020, there were 93 percent fewer stops than there had been at the height of the controversial practice (see figure 5).[27] Marijuana arrests—a bellwether for racially disparate policing in light of evidence of similar use patterns for white and Black Americans—dropped 90 percent.[28] Providing police with the option to issue a civil ticket, instead of a criminal summons, for similar low-level violations led to a 94 percent reduction in criminal summonses.[29] Additionally, the approximately eight hundred thousand warrants issued over the past decade for these same low-level offenses were eliminated.[30]

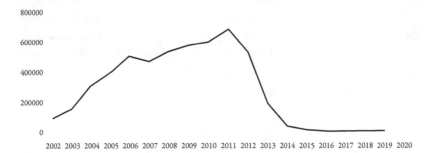

FIGURE 5: New York City stop-and-frisk annual encounters, 2002–19[31]

As the operations—and footprint—of the criminal justice system changed, a new, community-based strategy to reduce violence was emerging. Two examples, the city's Crisis Management System and the Mayor's Action Plan for Neighborhood Safety, have had a measurable impact on public safety through empowering neighborhoods and residents. Both build upon decades of research showing that social bonds can stop harmful behavior from occurring in the first place; and that people obey the law when they are respected and have voice, and believe decision-makers are fair, transparent, and legitimate.[32]

The Crisis Management System is a federation of approximately sixty organizations operating in the twenty-five neighborhoods that account for 60 percent of New York City's shootings.[33] From Brownsville to Mott Haven, these neighborhoods confront not only gun violence but high unemployment, low educational achievement, low birth rates, and high rates of asthma and diabetes.[34] During the COVID-19 pandemic, disproportionately high rates of Covid only added to this suffering.[35]

Nonprofits closely associated with the neighborhoods they serve employ violence interrupters and mental health workers to deliver services to heal the multiple effects of violence. The "interrupters" develop deep connections with people who may be on the path to violence and, supported by neighborhood information about when disputes are developing and where retaliations will take place, are able to "interrupt" the trajectory before it becomes violent.

The Crisis Management System also underscores the community's condemnation of violence. Every time there is a shooting, residents organize a vigil attended by the bereaved, neighbors, representatives from nonprofits, elected officials, and others. These vigils provide a moment of support and reflection, a physical expression of the peace that the neighborhood expects among its residents. These neighborhood norms are further reinforced as residents also occupy corners and walk along streets most plagued by gun violence. According to independent evaluations, gun violence drops by 30 percent in the twenty-four months following implementation in the neighborhoods where the Crisis Management System has been implemented, in comparison to similar neighborhoods without it.[36]

The Mayor's Action Plan for Neighborhood Safety operates within public housing developments, focusing on the few developments that drive 20 percent of violent crime. Focusing on the conditions that create violence, it organizes meetings with a group composed of residents, cops, and a range of representatives from city agencies, nonprofits, and community-based organizations. At these meetings, part of a process referred to as "NeighborhoodStat," the group identifies both problems and solutions. Key strategies have included the expansion of summer employment opportunities for youth and a community-led process to redesign public spaces to encourage positive activities and connections.[37]

The connections, networks, and supports resulting from NeighborhoodStat have proven not only adaptable but durable. During the pandemic, these networks were nimbly deployed, providing frontline services such as wellness checks and essential items such as food and personal protective equipment. And the approach of using physical space as an intentional connector and making the street and the stoop a communal "front yard" proved another avenue for enhancing well-being during a stressful and traumatic time.[38]

Encouraging results from an independent evaluation of the Mayor's Action Plan show a significant drop in crime and an increase in social cohesion, providing some evidence of its efficacy when residents have strong ties to one another, access to government resources, a voice in matters of importance, and trust in the fairness of government decisions.[39]

Along with these community-driven programs, the New York Police Department offered a change in outlook. Bratton, both a savvy politician and experienced police commander, understood the damage that decades of over-policing had inflicted on communities of color.[40] He understood that trust had to be the foundation of any policing strategy he would introduce: without it, people would not come forward as witnesses, serve as jurors, or vote to convict on the evidence. Consequently, he organized a strategy to deploy an additional 1,600 cops to walk the beat, interact and build relationships with residents under the slogan "Safe and Fair—Everywhere."[41]

By the beginning of 2020, the footprint of the criminal justice system had shrunk. The jails held half as many people as they had seven years before (see figure 4). Police arrested half as many people, and summonsed and stopped about 90 percent fewer people, than in 2013 (see figure 5). Index and violent crime fell 14 percent between 2013 and 2020 (see table 1). Elected officials demanded Crisis Management System sites in their districts when violence increased, and the Mayor's Action Plan was noticed—and praised—as a national model.[42] If not yet fully formed, there was a palpable turn from a police- and force-centric model of safety toward a model in which safety is secured through the opportunities that civil society can offer, guided by community aspirations.

When the COVID-19 pandemic tore through New York City, public life shut down. This was true in the criminal justice system as well: police made arrests for only the most serious offenses, prosecutors accepted only cases worth their time in court, and courts scaled back to the essentials.[43] Multiple city and state agencies worked to reduce the number of people in jail in order to make space for social distancing and quarantine. Within three weeks, the number of people in jail dropped from over 5,400—already the lowest population since 1953—to 3,800, the lowest since 1946.[44]

	Violent crime (subset of index)	Index crime	Homicides	Shooting incidents	Jail population
2020 vs 1993	−77%	−78%	−76%	−71%	−76%
2020 vs 2011 (2011 had similar shooting numbers to 2020)	−12%	−10%	−10%	1%	−64%
2020 vs 2013	−14%	−14%	38%	39%	−61%
2020 vs 2019	−2%	0%	45%	97%	−39%

TABLE 1: Change criminal justice system key indicators, 1993–2020[45]

Even as criminal justice operations slowed, tensions between the police and community members of color began to rise. Deployed to enforce social distancing, videos of police officers began cropping up on mobile phones displaying a casual and brutal use of force against people of color. One officer punched a man in the face while breaking up an evening cookout in a predominantly Black neighborhood. Another man in the same neighborhood was knocked unconscious in a dispute between officers and residents over the lockdown guidelines.[46]

By May 2020, 81 percent of summonses for noncompliance with COVID-19 social distancing protocols had been issued to Black and brown people. Advocates and others strengthened their calls for "education not enforcement," while videos documenting police officers' lax attitude toward wearing masks themselves further undermined the legitimacy of the police in a time of crisis.[47]

Within days of the death of George Floyd, large-scale demonstrations throughout the city called for defunding the police, with scattered scenes of looting and damage in commercial districts. Police responded with brute force, confronting mostly peaceful protesters in full riot gear. Videos showed officers slamming protesters to the ground, driving patrol cars straight through crowds gathered on the street, and kettling peaceful protesters into dangerously crowded areas.[48]

Gun violence—which had already begun to tick up by mid-May—rose sharply. From mid-June to the end of July, shootings increased by

192 percent compared with the previous year.[49] This phenomenon was not unique to New York, with almost all major cities experiencing a similar rise in gun violence, including Chicago, Detroit, Milwaukee, St. Louis, and Minneapolis.[50] These numbers are consistent with research linking high-profile incidents of police brutality and protests to increased violence; during these events, the local social order is disrupted and neighborhoods are consequently destabilized, creating the conditions for violence to emerge.

The disruption of local social order can happen for multiple reasons. Police, who have been asked to control violence by dominating public space, often step back and reduce their activity in the aftermath of widespread protests.[51] This was certainly the case in New York City. After the New York Police Department pulled back on enforcement, gun arrests decreased by 56 percent from May to June even while the number of shootings doubled (see figure 6). While the "solve" rate for shootings had hovered at about 50–60 percent the previous year, it sank to around 20 percent during the pandemic and rose very modestly in the months afterward.[52]

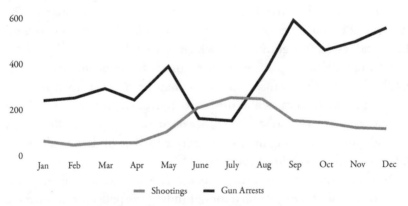

FIGURE 6: Shootings and arrests for gun violence in 2020[53]

Residents may also "check out" if they feel that they are not valued members of the city, becoming unwilling to work with city government or the police. Evidence suggests that this, too, happened in New York City. Establishing lines of communication between residents and the police on serious crimes like shootings had always been a challenge, and was one of the police department's motivations for improving community-police relations.

At the time, Police Commissioner Dermot F. Shea placed blame on those released from jail during the pandemic, on bail reform, on the closing of city courts, and on "outside agitators." Each claim was emphatically and conclusively refuted by published facts, further eroding the department's credibility, even among its staunchest tabloid supporters.[54] By the end of 2020, the citywide statistics were sobering, with murders up 44 percent and shootings up 97 percent (see figure 7).[55]

Before the COVID-19 pandemic, New York City had been gradually taking steps toward a new model of safety. While 2020 revealed how limited and incomplete these changes were, the structures that

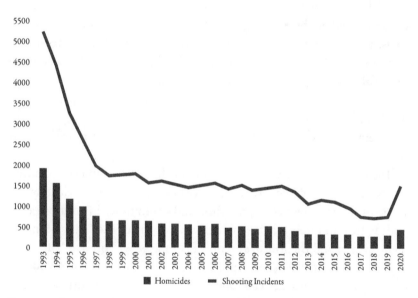

FIGURE 7: Shootings and homicides in New York City, 1993–2020[56]

had been put in place and the dynamics that produced the lowest crime and incarceration rates in the city's history from 2017 to 2019 provide some reason for optimism about a different approach to public safety. Instead of defaulting to police and the criminal justice system as the central institutions responsible for safety, strong evidence supports the wisdom of a shift toward a primary focus on community and government structures and services, of which policing is one. This shift should target two intertwined goals: the reduction of violence in New York City and the creation of strong neighborhoods that promote the well-being of all residents.

Everyone wants to be safe from small nuisances and significant threats—from the everyday annoyances of public urination to the wrecking ball of gun violence. For decades, our default response to this range of activity has been the police and the criminal justice system. This approach, especially during times of crisis, is appealing because police are easily deployed, readily visible, and present twenty-four hours a day.

But people also want to be safe from government overreach and abuse, which has been most vividly captured in instances of over-policing and violence carried out by police against the people.[57] Giving police the power to use up to deadly force, although necessary, corrodes the very trust that is essential to the operation of the criminal justice system. We need to be mindful of when police presence deters crime and when it deters cooperation.[58] We do not argue that these tools should be abandoned, but that we should question when, and under what circumstances, they promote well-being, and when they instead further fuel the cynicism with which many view the state.

The moderated role that we propose for the police—and the criminal justice system as a whole—is possible because we have another, largely untapped resource: the people, families, and community institutions that already play an important role in defusing violence. The Crisis Management System and the Mayor's Action Plan for Neighborhood Safety are two examples of the more organized efforts.[59] However, we are capable of building a much broader coalition that—if properly supported—could be the primary bulwark of public safety.

We have an opportunity to rethink significantly how the city's budget is allocated, particularly as the size of the criminal justice system shrinks and the role of other civic services in producing safety increases. Currently, the misalignment between the budget and activity of the system is striking. Between 2014 and 2020, the budgets of justice operations (jails, police, prosecutors, defenders, and probation) rose over 17 percent when adjusted for inflation. Meanwhile, actual justice operations—for example, arrests, arraignments, jail population, and probation caseloads—fell by about half (see table 2).

However, without a rigorous examination of how much public safety each dollar is buying, we end up stuck with budgets increasingly out of step with effective practice. We use arrest and jail less frequently than before and fewer people are committing crimes overall. Nevertheless, the "per unit" cost of running the justice agencies has more than doubled as the system itself has shrunk by half (see table 2). Rigorous examination of the agencies' functions and efficacy would yield better organization of resources to increase the safety and well-being of residents.

| | FY2014 | FY2020 | change | change% | Cost/work metric (constant $) | | |
					FY2014	FY2020	change%
NYPD arrests	396,460	175,809	−220,651	−56%	$11,998	$31,335	161%
DOC population	11,408	5,841	5,567	−49%	$93,365	$203,170	118%
Probation (adult)	23,805	14,504	−9,301	−39%	$3,499	$7,596	117%
DA arraignments	174,313	120,045	−54,268	−31%	$1,699	$3,513	107%

TABLE 2: Cost of NYC justice agencies by unit of work, FY2014 and FY2020[60]

New York City already funds an array of programs—and could fund others—that could considerably shrink the footprint of the criminal justice system while increasing safety. For example, the city could double the number of youths with access to summer employment, aiming at full enrollment from neighborhoods most affected by poverty and violence. Reaching this goal would require doubling the city's investment of $134 million to $236 million. According to results from a rigorous, randomized study, this investment would reduce deaths by 18 percent and the incarceration of people nineteen years and older by 54 percent.[61] Put another way, the city would pay $236 million to support the program but ultimately avoid $492 million in costs.[62]

Examining how New York City spends its annual budget will also reveal where it should be invested. Specific neighborhoods have disproportionately experienced worse health, education, and employment outcomes for decades.[63] These neighborhoods are overwhelmingly Black and brown. Focusing resources in these neighborhoods would have an outsized positive impact on the intersecting issues they face.

However, none of this will work unless someone with authority is driving the strategy. In New York City, we have deputy mayors to oversee housing, health, and human service agencies. Following this model, we propose a "Deputy Mayor for Justice Policy and Operations" who would supervise agency operations and resources, analyze and sort the options, and interweave the multiple agency budgets and functions as they relate to safety. The deputy mayor's function would also include the day-to-day operational and policy oversight of the police and other parts of the criminal justice system, as well as their intersection with both government and community.

The enterprise of creating concrete goals for neighborhoods, and fusing together resources toward a common objective of well-being and safety, could be further strengthened by the establishment of an "assistant mayor" for each borough: a position with direct ties to the mayoralty and the panoramic view of neighborhood conditions and needs. Neighborhood cabinets, along the lines of the current "NeighborhoodStat," could be created to provide regular feedback to city agencies and ensure accountability and appropriate alignment of resources.

For such a structure to succeed, the city government must commit to radical transparency in reporting what its agencies are doing and in engaging residents as paid partners to set the priorities. While residents experience issues firsthand, community problems are also often shared across the city. Providing information on a real-time basis about what, exactly, is driving particular issues—from shootings to homelessness—is a key step in identifying and implementing practical solutions.

If supported with sufficient resources and public commitment, community actors and institutions can generate safe, strong neighborhoods that promote public safety and community well-being. This idea—that those most closely connected to their own communities can most effectively confront violence—is supported by a large body of rigorous evidence. For example, when a local organization led an effort to clean up, redesign, and maintain abandoned lots in Philadelphia, violence fell by 17 percent and residents' perceptions of safety improved by a much larger margin.[64] Similarly, a large literature base shows that redesigning vacant buildings and empty lots, cleaning alleyways and overgrown weeds, and improving lighting are all effective ways to reduce violence and improve residents' perceptions of safety.[65] When people and institutions care for public spaces, they become vibrant places where collective life can happen, rather than abandoned places where violence is possible.

Programs that are run by nonprofits, community-led organizations, and city agencies to engage young people—both after school and during the summer months—are similarly successful. For example, the "Becoming a Man" program, run by a Chicago nonprofit, randomly selected students and provided an after-school sports program that featured cognitive behavioral therapy; it reduced arrests for violent crime by 45 to 50 percent among participants.[66] This program is one of many that have been rigorously and independently evaluated, demonstrating that providing activities, mentorship, job training, and summer employment for youth can have an enormous impact on violence while also generating long-term improvement in academic outcomes.[67]

Community groups have also provided other interventions, including short-term financial assistance, cognitive behavioral therapy, job training, and social services, with much evidence of success. These have been shown to be effective in reducing participants' involvement with violence—either as perpetrators or victims—and re-integrating them into their families and communities.[68] These examples reflect an insight that has been expressed by urban theorists for decades, yet has rarely been considered in debates about how to reduce violence: streets remain safe, and communities remain strong, when an intricate network of people and institutions are watching over them, making sure that no dangerous activity is taking place.[69]

To put this idea into practice, we propose a demonstration project designed around a new coalition, composed of residents and local community-oriented organizations, as the primary institution responsible for public safety and community well-being. This coalition should be led by a single organization but include other nonprofits, community leaders from religious congregations and schools, residents, and public and private partners. Beginning with a planning process, it should consider the goals and desires of residents, the relationship between itself and law enforcement, procedures for different types of events and situations, and its own organizational structure. As a long-term commitment, it should be funded at a level that reflects the value it brings to the community and to the city as a whole.

We anticipate the development of this coalition in several steps. First, we must select a set of communities or precincts to implement the project. Because some residents in a neighborhood will inevitably oppose these changes, a plan must be developed to determine how to handle public input and opposition. It will be key to select a well-respected leader for the interim planning process who understands the neighborhood and political dynamics, and can work with community groups and analytic teams to shape the coalition.

Funding should support the creation of a planning committee, as well as focus groups of residents and leaders. Their goal should be to develop procedures for dealing with incidents and scenarios that have traditionally been handled by the police, including traffic violations, public order violations, all calls by the public to the police for service, criminal investigations, and arrests and prosecution. Promising models from cities both within and outside the U.S. would need to be identified and studied, along with their plans with regard to coordination, communication, hiring, and training. Ideally, the planning committee should be able to hire consultants who can describe and create training guides with best practices for methods of de-escalation, conflict mediation, domestic violence, mental health crises, physical health crises, youth outreach, and more.

Developing a plan for long-term funding is essential for the success of the coalition. Funding should be roughly equivalent to the budget for New York Police Department operations in the area, including costs incurred during the planning stage. Ideally, a long-term commitment for at least ten years would be in place so that residents could be confident in the coalition's longevity, adaptability, and commitments. An oversight committee should be created to gather feedback from residents, as well as collect information about new challenges and opportunities. This committee could follow the model of NeighborhoodStat, where community leaders and public officials come together to identify problems and, ultimately, implement solutions.

Meanwhile, law enforcement should continue to play a central role in responding to all forms of gun violence. Police should work with this new coalition to solve problems in locations where shootings are common, focusing their attention on the tiny fraction of community members who account for a disproportionate share of serious violence. Beyond this role, we envision a community where police officers serve as backup to outreach workers, counselors, mediators, social service providers, unarmed traffic safety agents, and EMTs, becoming involved only if assistance is requested or if there is an arrest to be made.[70]

This blueprint relies on the assumption that most conflicts and altercations can be defused with street outreach workers, violence interrupters, and professionals trained in methods of mediation and de-escalation. Physical and mental health crises can be handled by paramedics and medical professionals; and public order violations can be handled by homeless assistance providers, counselors, and other social service providers. This assumption is not naive; this is in fact already happening. Data from the National Crime Victimization Survey reveal that roughly half of serious violent victimizations—sexual assaults, robberies, and aggravated assaults—are not reported to the police.[71] The best models of restorative justice indicate that prosecution is not always the right response to violence: when given multiple options, a large majority of those who have survived violence do not want the people who harmed them to go to prison; most seek a reckoning, driven by the goals of accountability and healing.[72]

Around the country, residents in many neighborhoods have stopped relying on the police for public safety. They have developed their own methods to mediate and de-escalate conflict; to help neighbors experiencing a health crisis; to support those suffering from poverty or addiction; to provide appropriate responses for people with mental illness; and to seek healing and reconciliation in the aftermath of victimization. From Reclaim the Block to the Black Visions Collective in Minneapolis, advocacy for new public safety mechanisms has long existed, well before the more recent killings of George Floyd and so many other Black Americans at the hands of police.[73] Despite these available models, the United States has never made a sustained public safety commitment to any institution other than the police and the criminal justice system in its current form.

If the police are no longer given the task of dominating public space and regulating violence, we must ensure that someone is watching over every community and taking responsibility for the safety and well-being of everyone within it. With fewer warriors on the street, we need to invest in more guardians. The evidence available suggests that community organizations and residents are qualified to play this role. We must invest in giving them the opportunity to do so.

16

WHO GOVERNS? SAFETY, GOVERNANCE, AND THE FUTURE OF JUSTICE

Katharine Huffman and Robert Rooks

Katharine Huffman serves as the executive director of The Square One Project at the Columbia Justice Lab. She is a founding principal at The Raben Group, a national advocacy, strategy, and communications firm based in Washington, DC.

Robert Rooks is the executive director for Reform Alliance. Formerly, he co-founded and was vice president of the Alliance for Safety and Justice, where he oversaw state-based advocacy strategies and campaigns.

Over the past several decades, justice reformers have devoted tremendous energy to policy change. They have gathered signatures for initiatives to end three-strikes laws, lobbied for sentencing and bail reforms, called for increased access to diversion programs, and testified in support of marijuana decriminalization. In our advocacy for these policy changes, our arguments refer to saving lives, saving resources, increasing fairness, and giving people second chances. Sometimes, our arguments also talk about safety. We assure our audiences that the policy changes we propose will create—or at least not decrease—safety. Too often, however, we use traditional definitions of safety generated by our current law enforcement–centered approach. In doing so, we accept that safety can be measured entirely by things like reductions in arrest numbers, recidivism rates, and interpersonal violence.

Such advocacy and arguments have helped begin the dismantling of laws that drive mass incarceration in this country. Ultimately, however, they are insufficient. They fail to address two core aspects of sustained, foundational justice: the creation of robust, equitable, and enduring safety for all; and the establishment of civically accountable governance to implement this safety. We must look beyond policy change to create a new, comprehensive governance system that acknowledges human dignity and meets community needs. We must claim the political and moral authority to redefine "safety," seizing that authority from the punitive and criminalizing actors who have co-opted the concept to keep power for centuries.

Essentially, safety is protection from harm and the opportunity to thrive. Since protection and opportunity are necessarily achieved in relation to others, nobody can achieve safety alone. Formal and informal agreements, which govern how we help and relate to each other, define the shapes that protection and opportunity take. In turn, these agreements depend on values. They depend on who has a seat at the table when policies are developed, and who has the authority to define and secure safety. Historically, people with the most political power have both set and sat at the table. However, we believe that the group of people at the policy-setting and governance table should be much broader. The group should involve not just those whose power comes from traditional structures—such as government and economic resources—but also those with moral authority, namely, those most affected by historic lack of protection and opportunity. Together, these actors can redefine safety and propose holistic policies to ensure it for everyone.

To chart a path forward, we must look back over our journey thus far. Fifty years ago, the American incarceration rate was only marginally higher than that of most other countries. Then as now, the country—and particularly Black and brown communities—faced a set of real issues. These included violence, wealth disparities, lack of treatment for addiction, and insufficient and inequitably available tools to allow people to thrive. Then as now, the stories told about these problems tapped into powerful narratives of racism and fear; they framed Black and brown people, young people, immigrants, and others as a threat to so-called law-abiding citizens. And then as now, mainstream political voices, amplified by the media, used these social problems to conjure an omnipresent sense of danger. This generalized threat was used to justify a large-scale increase in punishment. At the same time, health-focused and community-strengthening responses—including education and affordable housing—were neglected.

Bipartisan state and federal policy responses to crime and related social problems fueled the exponential growth of the justice system. Politicians defined safety as "freedom from violence at the hands of a dangerous stranger," and insisted it could be achieved through multi-billion-dollar investments in police, prisons, and jails.[1] This narrative, which intentionally tapped into the American public's fear of danger, not to mention its racism, supported the War on Crime launched by President Johnson, the War on Drugs launched by President Nixon (and expanded by Presidents Reagan and Bush), and the 1994 crime bill initiated by President Clinton. As a result, this narrative—and this definition of safety—dominated decades of policy conversations about the government's duty to protect its citizens and keep people safe.

Throughout this time and in the decades since, "departments of public safety" grew significantly. Tiny agencies grew into enormous government bureaucracies that in many states and localities are now the largest budget item.[2] Yet these agencies, which leave the biggest state footprint in many communities, have continued to rely on a definition of "safety" that reflects the narrative of the violent stranger, and on narrow measures of "success" such as reductions in reported crime, increased arrests, lowered recidivism rates, and the like. Media coverage perpetuated the "dangerous stranger" narrative; the common wisdom, "if it bleeds, it leads," granted extensive coverage to carjackings, mass shootings, and serious acts of violence.[3] As a result, the definition of safety remained limited, and law enforcement was positioned at the center of social responses to violence. This bolstered the policy consensus that safety should be measured only using the metrics of the justice system.

Alongside this investment in policing and prisons was mass divestment from systems of community thriving. As governments scaled up the War on Drugs in the 1970s, they closed mental health centers; today, the repercussions of these decisions endure in the vast scale of homelessness, and in people with mental health challenges cycling in and out of jail.[4] In the 1980s and 1990s, when crack emerged as a pervasive public threat, states and localities failed to build treatment centers or increase health services; today, those failures persist in the struggle to address the challenges of the opioid crisis. Over and over again, we failed to take opportunities or find political will to build true public health systems, in part because such systems did not fall under our common definition of safety.

Moreover, the belief that "only the justice system can make us safer" cut across communities and the political spectrum. Large and influential African American leadership organizations, including the Congressional Black Caucus and many major civil rights groups, were among those calling for investments in safety that relied on increased police presence and longer sentences.[5] While such groups also often called for more health-focused responses—mental health treatment, affordable housing, the removal of lead paint from walls—only the justice system requests were fulfilled. Community voices calling for a broader safety agenda were often subsumed into the narrative that safety is exclusively a law enforcement responsibility. Even non-punitive and preventive responses, when they did exist, were typically channeled through the justice system: a child might receive mental health services, but through the juvenile justice system, not from a school counselor or community clinic. A teenager looking for access to the arts or a sports team could find it through the police department's after-school program, not one run by a school or neighborhood group.

In all these ways, law enforcement received the resources and sole legitimacy to define safety, to determine which policies would secure safety, and to distribute resources. This led directly to our situation today: a country that has the world's largest prison system yet cannot deliver health and healing to protect people—not only from "dangerous strangers," but also from more intimate physical violence or the manifestations of poor physical and mental health, substance abuse, lack of access to housing and education, and so much more.[6] True safety cannot be guaranteed by prisons and police. As people—including members of law enforcement—are increasingly recognizing, "we can't arrest our way out of this."[7] We need, therefore, an urgent change in who leads and participates in our discussions and actions about safety.

A justice reform movement has emerged in recent years, as community members, advocates, and policymakers have all begun to see the negative impacts of over-incarceration. Initially, however, such advocacy did not challenge the core definition of safety. Instead, it often focused on cost containment, or on whether people arrested for "nonviolent crimes" or "low-level drug offenses" should be sent to prison.[8] While these arguments helped protect some people from the dehumanizing label of "dangerous," they did not fundamentally challenge the notion of who or what makes us safer or acknowledge a basic human dignity for all. They did not call for investment in a new kind of social infrastructure, or hold accountable the large health, education, and human services systems that can truly contribute to safety. And they did not question whether the growing reach of the justice system was really making us safe at all.

Gradually, however, a different narrative about safety has started to gain power, thanks to the efforts of people themselves impacted by the over-built justice system (and the under-built social support systems). Nationwide, people across the political spectrum are questioning the status quo, pointing to its harms and costs, and demanding change. They are realizing the need to reckon with our past—with the history of dehumanization, racism, classism, and more—to finally approach true safety for all.

This narrative change reflects the increasing power of people who have long been denied political power but who have the moral authority to change our conversations about safety and justice. Moral authority belongs to those most affected—whether through state action or inaction—by the lack of protection and opportunity to thrive. Who has moral authority by this measure? One group is crime survivors, who have not received from the justice system bureaucracy what they need to heal. Another is people who have been arrested, convicted, and sentenced for crimes, but denied the robust supports and services needed to thrive.

Safety has never been evenly distributed, even by traditional measures. When reported crime rose in the 1980s and 1990s, criminologists found that despite the media image of omnipresent violence, crime trends did not change much outside of big cities. In addition, study after study showed that those most affected by changing rates of violence were poor communities of color.[9] Today, whether rates of crime and violence rise or fall, the fact remains that people who have higher incomes, are white, and are over twenty-four are less likely to be victimized than those who are not white, have lower incomes, and are young.[10]

Under the status quo, our definition of "safety" is failing to meet the needs of crime survivors. Survey research shows that while one in four people has been a victim of crime in the past ten years (half of whom experienced a violent crime), two out of three victims did not receive help of any kind following the incident. Moreover, the minority who do receive help are more likely to get it from family and friends than the criminal justice system. Nor do the billions spent on the justice system provide victims with more general support; even when mainstream measures of danger (reported crime rates) were at all-time lows, only three in ten victims of crime report feeling very safe in their community.[11]

Incarcerated people are another large group whose safety needs are not met by the status quo. Incarcerated people face high levels of violence, illness, and chronic health conditions. Many continue to struggle after release owing to a lack of reentry assistance and to nonsensical rules making them ineligible for many jobs, services, and other social supports. This dearth of support puts at risk not only the people returning from incarceration, but also the families and communities that they rejoin.

Importantly, neat boxes cannot be drawn around those impacted by crime and violence, dividing them into separate monolithic groups; many people who have been arrested and convicted of crime are themselves survivors of violence and other harms.[12] This underscores the need to eliminate barriers that prevent people with past convictions from fully participating in our civic life, and to build systems that promote safety by helping people break cycles of crime. To create this supportive social infrastructure, both crime survivors and those convicted of crimes must be at the table to direct meaningful change.

A revitalized future that ensures health and safety for everyone must engage all segments of society. We must center voices that have been historically marginalized. Yet we must also attend to the dignity and healing of those who have been part of the status quo, including law enforcement and corrections officers. Only by addressing the need for stability and recovery from past trauma and harm for everyone—wherever they have stood in relation to the past—can we guarantee true and lasting safety in the future.

When people with moral authority lead in a way that centers human dignity, they can build an agenda for safety that provides everyone with protection and the opportunity to thrive. This work, however, cannot be accomplished only by identifying new solutions or by changing laws or policies. Instead, the power of new voices must extend to the creation of new systems of governance, accountability, and civic involvement. Only such structural change will bring about a more just form of safety that can withstand backlash from traditionally powerful actors.

Over the past ten to twenty years, many laws and policies governing justice systems have changed. At the same time, overall levels of violence have dropped in many localities. Yet this has not resulted in a general sense of robust and resilient safety. Why? The answer lies in the fact that real safety depends on systems of governance and accountability that turn "on paper" initiatives into enduring social change.

Communities are tied together by shared agreements. Yet these have never meaningfully existed for all members of our society. Moreover, many such agreements appear to be falling apart all around us. For example, what we call "civil rights"—a set of agreements about what we share as community members—are disintegrating because of ongoing efforts to disenfranchise certain voters. And during the COVID-19 pandemic, the basic notion that we—as a community—should prioritize our collective health and well-being buckled under the expectation that we should sacrifice people to sickness and even death to hasten the reopening of businesses.

Ultimately, we need a new set of agreements based on our shared values, and a new social contract to hold our institutions accountable to a holistic redefinition of safety. A new social contract must center new agreements about what it means to be part of the community of our nation and clarify how our representative government can secure values such as equity, protection, safety, and thriving. This new social contract depends on the inextricable connection between accountability and human dignity. An unyielding emphasis on human dignity has a huge operational impact in the agreements and policies we enact. Without a shared concept of dignity, we cannot hold our large institutions responsible for meaningful protection.

When dignity frays, people can no longer rely for their protection and well-being on the social institutions responsible for health and safety. When certain groups—including racial minorities or people with criminal convictions—are systemically dehumanized, they cannot hold to account the public institutions charged with acting on their behalf. Similarly, when other people participate in—or benefit from—this dehumanization, they, too, are denied membership in an equitable society. This explains why large public institutions often operate without accountability, even in metropolitan areas that otherwise seem "progressive." Dehumanization leads to the "othering" that blocks accountability. It leads to a situation where thousands of laws exist that have no objective relationship to safety yet prevent people with past convictions from getting jobs, securing housing, and participating in civic life. It leads to a situation where people facing unaddressed trauma and mental health challenges do not receive treatment but instead cycle through our homeless shelters and jails.

Currently, even hard-won and significant policy changes usually depend on existing criminal justice institutions and bureaucracies for their implementation. This limits their transformative power. It is one thing for advocates and elected officials to agree on reforms; it is another to see those reforms carried out on the ground. Our nation's criminal justice system, while very large, is decentralized. In every town and county, practice is shaped by tradition and inertia—"how we've always done things"—and is thus passively resistant to change. In addition, reforms often face active opposition to change from those who most benefit from the status quo. To help bypass these obstacles, advocates and organizers must be well resourced and supported; community-based organizations (outside of government structures) must be elevated; and people with direct justice system experience must be represented within government structures.

An agenda of real safety will be implemented by a mixture of government leaders, government workers, activists, and the public. Our broader definitions of safety must be met by the people and institutions that support people's physical and mental health; provide housing, education, or employment; and promote economic security. Moreover, as government, philanthropy, and civic institutions reallocate resources according to these new definitions of safety, they must follow the example of community leaders who have already found ways to disrupt cycles of violence, even with limited resources.

Successful implementation will need government leaders who seek to address the root causes of crime, substance abuse, and mental health issues, and to expand restorative justice at scale. Those elected officials should include people who have direct experience with crime and who have personally experienced the shortcomings of our old, limited definition of safety through incarceration. In this way, they will have the moral authority to guide policy efforts through legislative processes and to navigate bureaucracies invested in the old status quo.

Relatedly, successful implementation will also require building a new workforce. People with direct experience of violence, incarceration, or both, as well as those who have suffered the impacts of inadequate social investments, bring a wealth of experience and capacity to jobs that support the new safety paradigm. Additionally, as resources shift away from traditional justice structures over time, people employed in the current criminal justice system must have the opportunity to shift into jobs within the new structure of safety and thriving.

A community of activists, constituents, and the public will need to make their voices heard. This constituency will support elected officials striving to push for this new safety agenda and will ensure its implementation. Some of these activists are already leading efforts through the small, under-resourced network of nonprofits and community organizations that research shows are best equipped to address community challenges. In order to sustain change over the long term, investments in their efforts should match those dedicated to local enforcement mechanisms in the past.

Finally, along with this newly accountable public sector and engaged public, we need an increasingly responsive private sector. Businesses, philanthropy, private civic organizations, nonprofits, and many other entities can support the development and implementation of robust policies and practices. As employers, service providers, advocates, and more, the private sector can respond to and fuel the building of a new public health and safety infrastructure.

We can look to California for an example of positive change largely driven by, and accountable to, leaders with the moral authority to redefine safety. As some states have worked to reduce their incarcerated populations, California has proven to be a leader: over a little more than a decade, half the total prison population decline across all states took place in California. Several policy changes contributed to this: in 2009, California passed legislation to reduce the number of people entering the state prison system (AB 109, known as "Realignment"), addressing dangerous overcrowding in state prisons; and in 2016, voters approved a ballot initiative to expand rehabilitation services and the use of parole (Proposition 57). The largest driver of change, California's Proposition

47 (also known as the Safe Neighborhoods and Schools Act), passed in 2014 and significantly reduced incarceration in the state. Importantly, it arose out of advocacy built on a new safety agenda, and it instituted changes in the structures of governance and accountability to support and implement that new understanding of safety.

Proposition 47 intentionally adhered to a new definition of safety through its design, enactment, and implementation. It elevated new leaders with the moral authority to change policy, and ultimately built an enduring movement capable of resisting efforts to return to the status quo. Crime survivors drove the passage of Proposition 47, served as the initiative's lead advocates, and actively challenged prevailing notions of who had the right to define "safety." In passing Proposition 47, California voters changed sentencing for low-level crimes, leading to significantly reduced prison and jail populations. In addition, it allocated the funds that were recovered as savings to local community programs, trauma recovery services for crime survivors, and programs for vulnerable youth.[13]

In the eight years since the initiative passed, Proposition 47 has led to a significant drop in incarceration, with prison and jail populations falling by about twenty thousand. As part of his fiscal year 2022–23 budget proposal, California governor Gavin Newsom announced an additional $150 million in prison savings attributable to Proposition 47 and available for reallocation.[14] This would bring to almost $600 million the total funding reallocated to local public safety programs as a result of Proposition 47—services including mental health support, substance abuse treatment, diversion from jail, and housing programs for people who have been arrested, charged, or convicted of crimes.[15] Diverted prison funding has also gone to education programs designed to reduce truancy and support children deemed at risk of dropping out of school or committing crimes.[16] And finally, Proposition 47 has fueled a dramatic expansion in trauma recovery services. Ten percent of prison savings are directed to trauma recovery centers statewide,[17] and eighteen dedicated centers now provide crime survivors with mental health and other services, up from just one prior to the initiative's passage.[18]

Yet these positive changes were not simply caused by voters changing a law. They came about because the coalition of voices that helped pass Proposition 47 continued its determined work even after passage of the measure. Members of this coalition worked to secure not only policy change, but governance change. They built sustainable, impactful community power and advocacy to ensure that bureaucracies followed and effectively implemented the new law. They also became active partners and participants in that implementation.

The leadership of crime survivors was particularly key throughout this process. A new organization, Crime Survivors for Safety and Justice, had formed in 2012 and played a large role in the development, passage, and implementation of Proposition 47. Crime Survivors for Safety and Justice is now leading a nationwide effort to refocus a safety agenda focused on what research demonstrates crime survivors most want: healing, supportive resources, and rehabilitation to break cycles of crime.[19]

Crime Survivors for Safety and Justice and its many partners worked to hold bureaucracies and government actors accountable after the passage of Proposition 47. To do this, they pushed lawmakers and those responsible for accurate budgeting to calculate the savings from reduced prison and jail spending, and to appropriately redistribute those funds. Trained, talented advocates demanded that the governor's office, the state Department of Finance, and the Department of Corrections followed the new law. At the same time, small, agile, and culturally competent community-based organizations worked with survivors to push government bureaucracies to reallocate resources to programs that effectively reduce recidivism and promote healing.

A key feature of successful implementation was representation: governmental decision-making bodies were pressed to include input from and representation of crime survivors, people with past convictions, and reentry service providers. Advocacy from these voices ensured that half of all dollars reinvested by the state through Proposition 47 went to community-based organizations. It also ensured that counties and cities were obligated to subcontract with at least one community-based organization through the grant awards.[20]

These significant changes—which upended decades of rhetoric, spending, and power distribution—met resistance. Some stakeholders saw the initiative as a threat to the status quo and sought to undo its effects. Opponents even organized an effort to repeal Proposition 47 and other state criminal justice reform laws, placing an initiative on the November 2020 ballot to this effect. Reform opponents—including a small number of police, some elected officials, and a crime victims' group historically funded by the prison guards' union—sought to reclaim their historic role as the exclusive definers of safety. They drew on old narratives of fear and dehumanization. They made false statements, including inaccurate assertions about what the reforms did and false claims that community crime sprees were being fueled by people who would be in prison but for Proposition 47.

All too often, such resistance results in the reversal of progress made through policy change. But thanks to the ongoing work to build a new vision of safety, this opposition did not prevail. Before the repeal vote, state lawmakers convened an informational hearing on Proposition 47 and the repeal effort.[21] They heard from dozens of people who supported keeping Proposition 47 in place: crime survivors, treatment providers whose services would dry up without the new funding for trauma recovery centers, formerly incarcerated youth and adults who were able to resolve a past conviction because of the law, and community-based providers that worked with people who would be incarcerated without Proposition 47. In contrast to this new, diverse, and vocal safety constituency, nobody at the hearing made the case for repeal.[22]

Californians soundly defeated the repeal effort at the polls, by a margin of 62 percent to 38 percent.[23] This demonstrated that meaningful, durable reforms can take place when a new vision for safety is laid out by a constituency with moral authority, and then effectively implemented with that constituency's input. While challenges will continue to arise, over the long term such reforms can even resist the opposition of those who do not want to give up the power assigned to them by the traditional definition of safety. The leadership of crime survivors and others with moral authority helped redefine safety, reallocate resources, and defeat efforts to maintain the status quo. Proposition 47 was a step toward a new vision of safety that centers investment in treatment, interventions, and programs serving people outside of a prison or jail. This new vision of safety also seeks to hold governance institutions accountable for providing true protection for all.

People with moral authority—those who have the most to gain or lose by the government's action or inaction—must lead efforts to redefine safety. They must also be able to hold the government accountable for the implementation of this new approach to protection and social support.

Building power and changing structures can enable reforms to withstand resistance from the status quo, whether that resistance comes from actors seeking to preserve their own power or by a lack of imagination to understand new forms of safety. Going beyond policy change to true governance change will lead to a future of resilient safety, justice, and dignity for all.

17

REIMAGINING JUDGING

Nancy Gertner

Nancy Gertner joined the faculty at Harvard Law School as a professor of practice after she retired as a judge in 2011. At Harvard, she teaches various courses on criminal justice. Appointed to the bench in 1994 by President Clinton, Nancy served on the U.S. District Court for the District of Massachusetts for seventeen years.

As we come to grips with our country's long history of racial injustice, many of us who have worked within the criminal justice system have discussed the need to address the legacy of mass incarceration, including the impact of over-policing, over-prosecuting, and over-punishing. Judges, though, rarely participate in these conversations—and if they do, their first question is: "What does this have to do with me?" The answer is, on reflection, a great deal.

Judges can effect change in many ways, but their role is arguably most important at sentencing. Over the past forty years, sentencing practices have changed dramatically, particularly following the imposition of strict federal guidelines and controversial mandatory minimums. Today, it has shifted again, paving the way for judges to exercise more discretion in sentencing. Why, though, have judges hesitated not only to support but to enact these institutional reforms? And how can judges who have participated in an extraordinarily punitive system—one that produced mass incarceration—begin to transition to a fundamentally different approach?

Judicial Resistance to Reform

For decades, federal judges have resisted even the most modest criminal justice reforms. Despite recent legislation, such as the 2007 Second Chance Act, the 2010 Fair Sentencing Act, and the 2019 First Step Act, many federal judges hesitate to exercise judicial discretion in sentencing, even when given the option. This resistance is especially surprising given their high-profile opposition—through testimony, articles, and opinions—to mandatory sentencing laws.[1]

Following the passage of the Federal Sentencing Reform Act in 1984, two hundred federal judges made their opposition public, declaring the newly established Federal Sentencing Guidelines unconstitutional.[2] However, once the Supreme Court rejected these constitutional challenges—signaling to the lower courts that these "guidelines" were, in fact, mandatory—sentencing practices dramatically changed. Most federal judges—especially those serving after the Guidelines were established—began to enforce federal sentencing rules with a rigor that none had anticipated. Scholars argued that judges had become "passive," allowing themselves to be "marginalized" in the sentencing process by ceding all authority to the Sentencing Commission.[3] The job of sentencing became mechanical—nothing more than mastering the eight-hundred-page Guidelines Manual.

As a result, many judges increasingly came to believe in the Sentencing Commission and the rationality of the Guidelines it had enacted.[4] This was especially true among judges who had never been criminal defense lawyers, with no framework from which to evaluate, much less criticize the Guidelines they were given. And it was important to critically evaluate these Guidelines. They were not a rational, carefully conceived set of rules; they were unmoored from reality and evidence, often representing nothing more than what criminologist Michael Tonry characterized as "back-of-an-envelope calculations and collective intuitive judgments."[5]

Today, judges' commitment to punitive sentencing is nowhere clearer than in their opposition to the policies of progressive prosecutors. Historically, judges have deferred to the decisions of prosecutors—no matter how problematic those decisions have been—because the constitutional separation of powers has demanded that deference: judges are in the judicial branch, and prosecutors are in the executive branch. However, in recent years, there has been pushback. Judges have second-guessed the decisions of prosecutors who have, for example, declined to prosecute minor crimes that are more a product of aggressive policing in communities of color than threats to public safety, or those who have rejected the death penalty.[6]

To be sure, there are obvious exceptions to judicial resistance to change. Judges have led the movement toward problem-solving courts, restorative justice, pretrial diversion, and reentry programs.[7] These programs are important, but they exist in the interstices of an otherwise punitive system. They have not led to a fundamental reexamination of ordinary sentencing for the majority of people not lucky enough to be included in these specialized programs.

This is especially clear with respect to people accused of violent crimes. Pre- and post-trial diversion programs cherry-pick defendants, excluding those convicted of violent crimes, a category that is often too broadly defined.[8] This leaves the so-called "nonviolent drug offenders," a label that seems to mirror earlier—even racist—efforts to separate the "deserving" from the "undeserving" poor that date from Tudor England.[9] The vast majority of the men I sentenced were at once victims, witnesses, or perpetrators of violence. Reducing imprisonment for "nonviolent offenders," or eliminating it entirely, is good—but not good enough.

We can recognize the judicial habits that enable mass incarceration in the follow-up to the Supreme Court's 2012 decision in *Miller v. Alabama*, which held that the imposition of a mandatory life without parole sentence on a juvenile violated the Constitution's prohibition against cruel and unusual punishment.[10] Rather than effecting a sea change in the treatment of juveniles, the decision led to the resentencing of juveniles around the country—this time to "virtual" life sentences, such as thirty or forty years.[11] Given the chance to reconsider the culpability of defendants who were under eighteen at the time of the crimes, some state courts hardly budged. Nine years later, in *Jones v. Mississippi*, the Supreme Court added fuel to the fire, gutting *Miller*'s presumption against life without parole for juveniles and its core conclusion that the vast majority of adolescents do not deserve life even if their crime reflects "unfortunate yet transient immaturity."[12] As long as the judge knew he had discretion to reject a life sentence, Justice Brett Kavanaugh found, that was all that mattered. Kavanaugh's idea of discretion, in short, is all about form and not remotely about substance.

While the COVID-19 pandemic has accelerated the pace of decarceration, it is striking how many judges remain resistant to releasing defendants at risk for the life-threatening illness.[13] Some have even punished defendants who did not physically appear in court because they feared infection.[14] Much of this resistance is grounded in judicial risk aversion after thirty years of mass incarceration—of not wanting to be that judge whose release decision, however well-grounded, leads to a violent crime.[15] This is even the case for judges with life tenure.

As a result, the lessons that might have been learned from releases under COVID-19, drug programs, and reentry courts—that it was not remotely necessary for public safety to imprison at the rates we have—are not getting through. Narratives persist that the recent increase in violent crime is attributable to those releases and even to bail reform, rather than to the deterioration of whatever social supports existed in the communities hardest hit by the pandemic; and that the only answer to the uptick is to flood the streets with police and imprison our way out of the problem again.

Barriers to Reimagining Judging

Why are judges so opposed to criminal justice reform, particularly with regards to sentencing?[16] I'm reminded of a quote in *Just Mercy*, in which Bryan Stevenson shares his grandmother's advice to him, long before Stevenson first embarked on his storied civil rights career: "You can't understand most of the important things from a distance. You have to get close."[17] He describes this as "getting proximate"—to the condemned and unfairly judged.

Judges are socialized not to be proximate in the way that Stevenson recommends. They are supposed to be on a pedestal, removed from the parties and the lawyers involved. Reverend, advocate, and scholar Vivian Nixon has spoken of the rage she has felt about the criminal justice system, and the importance of not describing it in neutral terms. But judges are taught to use neutral terms—words that distance, that are emotionless. One scholar referred to this as "the cultural script of judicial dispassion," the idea that judging must be as "insulated from human life and emotion as possible."[18] Disciplinary rules and judicial training encourage judges to avoid social situations in which their neutrality can be compromised, or interpreted as such.

I felt that distance the moment I became a federal judge. As a civil rights and criminal defense lawyer, I had represented people accused of crimes from all of Boston's communities; I had visited homes, spoken at churches and schools, and bailed out defendants in police stations across the city, often in the middle of the night. As a federal judge, however, I drove to the courthouse from a Boston suburb, on the Turnpike, and arrived in the federal court garage. If I had not purposely reached out, I would have missed all the communities that my route bypassed and my decisions impacted.

The distance—and resulting sense of "otherness"—derives in part from the ideology of judging. This ideology is largely rejected by the legal academy and most judges, but still alive and well in the media and the judicial selection process. It was reflected in Chief Justice John G. Roberts's confirmation hearing before the Judiciary Committee in 2005, when he said, "It's my job to call balls and strikes."[19] And similarly, in Justice Clarence Thomas's remarks, as he was anticipating his role on the Supreme Court, that he would be "stripped down like a runner," and would ultimately "shed the baggage of ideology."[20] Judicial selection—at least up until recently—mirrored this view.[21] Federal judges were often chosen based on how little they had publicly said about controversial issues.[22] Most were white and male, either from large law firms, or with prosecutorial experience, or both.[23] And those who disagreed with the "balls and strikes" mantra, who believed that judging was more complex, were labeled "activist."

When I was on the bench, I refused to consider traffic convictions in sentencing a Black man because they amounted to "driving while Black." The convictions were for driving an unregistered car on multiple occasions, which if considered, would have increased the Sentencing Guideline calculation and potentially the length of his sentence. No other traffic violations (such as driving too fast, or failure to stop) were charged, just the unregistered car charge; worse, in every case, the location was a white suburb of Boston. A colleague asked whether I was afraid that I would be labeled an "activist" because of this decision.[24] I was not. The decision was a fair interpretation—and application—of the law to the facts at hand. It looked at the rules not as abstractions, but as having real consequences and reflecting real biases. More recently, a scholar commented on a story I related about one of the men I did sentence, a young Black man with a bullet in his brain, whose trauma was largely ignored by the prosecutors. I stated that I had done what I could to mitigate the harsh effects of the law, giving him a sentence as low as I could lawfully go. Wrong, this scholar suggested. I was being "results-oriented."[25]

It was an extraordinary comment. Sentencing, after all, is about results—what outcomes make sense, and what alternatives exist that might do the least harm.[26] Even under mandatory guidelines, judging is an interpretive process, informed by considerations of justice and equity, empathy and compassion, a view far more complex than Roberts or Thomas would suggest. As Judge Denny Chin of the U.S. Court of Appeals for the Second Circuit made clear, although empathy "should play no role in a judge's determination of what the law is," empathy is "essential . . . in the real-world, day-to-day administration of justice."[27] Judge Ketanji Brown Jackson, now a Supreme Court Justice, used her empathy and her sense of equity to make distinctions among defendants accused of possessing child pornography, from the less culpable to the more culpable. In doing so, she did what judges across the country had done, and what even the U.S. Sentencing Commission acknowledged was appropriate.

Judges' experiences necessarily figure into the equation. For many judges, the failure to acknowledge how their own experiences affect their judging could well mean ignoring their own biases. A judge's experience affects judging in a number of ways, from how complicated they see the case as being, to how much time they spend on it, and how they evaluate a witness's credibility on the stand, to name a few. For example, one judge told me that if he handled sentencing the way I did, it would require him to spend the same amount of time for a criminal sentencing as he spends on complex patent cases. He did not think sentencing required that, privileging efficiency over all—except in his commercial cases. Judicial shortcuts affect not just the speed of justice, but the quality. Efficiency is not neutral—you choose it over access to justice and a more complete understanding of the case.

Similarly, if you have never seen a police officer lie on the stand, you may well believe—as a judicial colleague once told me—that an officer witness is not likely to do so. That colleague's threshold for evaluating a police officer's credibility was different—higher—than the threshold of someone who had had the experience of seeing a police officer lie. If you have never been in communities of color when a policeman stops a Black teenager, you may believe that the teenager must be guilty of a crime when he runs, rather than fearful of arbitrary violence at the hands of the police. If you have never selected jurors when a Black defendant is on trial, you might not have rejected the elderly white woman from one of Boston's suburbs who said that she was "afraid" to come into Boston when asked if there was any reason why she should not serve. While I excused her, a judge in another courtroom might believe that her comments were not problematic—or worse, that they were valid. While we screen jurors for their biases, we assume judges' neutrality once they are confirmed and on the bench.

Experience also determines the issues—and people—that judges identify as problematic. Judges do not have to learn much about the groups to which they already belong; given the makeup of the bench, they are more than familiar with middle-class or upper-class white male defendants. This is not the case with Black or Latinx defendants, who make up the bulk of most urban dockets. When thirty Black defendants were brought into my courtroom and described as members of a violent street gang, I was doubtful. As someone who knew the communities in which the defendants lived, I was concerned that the "Castlegate gang" was simply a group of men who lived on one street and grew up together, or, as one mother described a similar group, were in Pampers together. I wondered whether what the government described as their "aliases" were just nicknames they gave each other as children. They may have been dealing drugs, but to caricature them as if they were members of MS-13—or worse, the "super-predators" of the Clinton era—was absurd to me.[28]

Apart from the experiences judges bring to the bench, additional influences derive simply from their judicial service. The longer one is on the bench, the more likely embedded assumptions about the criminal legal system remain unexamined: judges believe that they have "no choice" but to follow them. Robert Cover, speaking of the antislavery judges who enforced the Fugitive Slave Act more rigorously than they had to, described this as the "judicial can't."[29] The habits of mass incarceration have framed sentencing for over thirty years. As one scholar described it:

> Tough on crime policies have dominated the country for decades, and judges have been at the frontline of enforcing these policies. As public sentiment changes and legislatures pursue reforms, judges are likely to lag behind. For a judge, being less punitive means reversing course on a career of judicial decision-making. Ideologically motivated or not, many judges have grown comfortable in their practices, trust the wisdom and experience they have gathered from years on the bench, and will not be eager to change how they collect fines and fees or impose bail.[30]

Caseload pressures—real or imagined—have their own impact, particularly with regard to writing opinions. Judicial trainers have sometimes discouraged judges from writing opinions unless they had to; it slowed down case management. Writing opinions is important, though, not simply for its impact on the public, but also because it changes the decision-making process, or the way a judge sees the case. As the legal literature suggests, "writing opinions could induce deliberation that otherwise would not occur," while using "scripts, checklists, and multifactor tests" decreases judges' reliance on their own experiences.[31]

There is no more pernicious checklist than the Federal Sentencing Guidelines, which—though now advisory—still exert a gravitational pull on what judges do, and necessarily lead to higher sentences. Judges feel anchored to the Guideline ranges, even when they have discretion to reject them, imposing harsher sentences than they would otherwise give.[32] The power of precedent has normalized harsh Guideline sentences, and even mandatory minimum sentences, that would have been obscene years before. Judges—indeed all of the participants in the criminal legal system—have come to view imprisonment as the default punishment for most crimes.[33]

Legal doctrine, or precedent, whatever its initial rationale, has also taken on a life of its own. Judicial precedent too often excuses police misconduct through the doctrine of qualified immunity, or justifies illegal searches through good-faith defenses. While these precedents may have made sense initially, their meaning is lost in their application to contexts far afield from the original case. They also have cognitive consequences that are hidden from view. The habit of excusing police errors, case after case, may well prevent a judge from seeing police or prosecutor errors even when they are clear. As a result, judges lose the ability to envision what error even looks like.[34] And if they never had any personal experience in the criminal legal system—especially as a defense lawyer—they may never have had that ability in the first place.

What does it take to make this system, with these pressures and influences, fairer for everyone? Given judicial resistance to changing the habits of mass incarceration, there are a number of realistic possibilities for how we can provide institutional support for meaningful change.

Institutional Changes

Judicial Selection

An important first step is to change whom we select for the bench. It is not simply a question of racial, ethnic, or even gender diversity, but one of personal experience. A bench can be diverse in terms of race, gender, or sexual orientation, and still display a lack of sociocultural diversity. The vast majority of judges are former prosecutors and government civil attorneys rather than defense or civil rights attorneys.[35] And if they are not prosecutors, they are corporate lawyers. Eighty-five percent of former president Obama's appointees fell into either category.[36] Recent selections have also done little to change the gender or racial makeup of the bench. While these judges may be extraordinary legal thinkers with the appropriate temperament, they represent a narrow swath of attitudes and experiences.

Judicial Training

Judicial training, at least in the federal courts, is largely about rules, as if the only measure of a fair sentence is whether it is lawful or within statutory limits. While the Federal Sentencing Guidelines are now supposed to be advisory, judges are primarily taught about how to apply them. The U.S. Sentencing Commission continues to focus on the application and interpretation of the Guidelines, with little or no analysis about how to deal with sentencing discretion, or what programs and considerations might be relevant as alternatives. It is no small wonder federal judges continue to default to the Guideline analysis; there is no framework for anything else.

There should be required training about the impact of trauma, exposure to violence, poverty, and lack of access to schools, health care, employment, and so on. Judges should hear from scientists about the neuroscience of trauma, addiction, and adolescent neurodevelopment; from sociologists about the social and cultural contexts of individuals they are sentencing; from health professionals about the social determinants of health. This information—with which many judges may not be familiar—shapes how judges see a case, how carefully they will question the parties involved, how deeply they will delve into the issues at hand, and how much time they will give to the case, as well as what they may do in their final decision.

One of the many factors that ushered in mandatory sentencing was an article by sociologist Robert Martinson that seemed to suggest that nothing worked to rehabilitate people who committed harm.[37] Today, we know that the "nothing works" argument is wrong in many contexts related to crime, violence, and harm.[38] Additionally, we need training programs that include information about other countries' criminal justice systems in order to enable judges to envision approaches other than the usual ones. Judges often believe that what they are doing is the only way criminal legal work can be done, as if U.S. penal practices reflect the natural order of things. They do not. And all of these discussions need to be paired with a sophisticated understanding of the risk of pathologizing defendants from Black and Latinx communities.

Sentinel Event Audits

In medicine, doctors hold "sentinel event" reviews whenever there is a death or serious physical or psychological injury to a patient or patients. Too often, though, the only outcome that matters to judges is a reversal by a higher court or press criticism. For the police, we have discussed changing incentives from arrests and convictions to more substantial measures of a community's health and safety.[39] Likewise, we need to change the incentives for judges, and in so doing change their deliberative processes. Judges could hold a retrospective review when there is a wrongful conviction, a pattern of recidivism, or an unexpected tragic event. For example, they could discuss what happened, what could be changed, what was missed, and what program worked or did not work. Judges could even review case studies of what has happened to the defendants sentenced to lengthy retributive sentences, reexamining them, critiquing them, and considering alternatives. In a given case, did a thirty-, or twenty-, or ten-year sentence make sense in a humane, or even rational, sentencing system? How much did it disrupt the defendant's life course? Was it justified? What else could have—or should have—been done?

Statistical Reviews

One way to address racial bias in policing is an after-the-fact statistical analysis of arrests to examine the extent to which they correlate with the race of the defendant. To be sure, this requires a commitment to accurate data collection and periodic reviews. Judicial decisions are rarely subject to that kind of analysis, except by scholars; even then, the analysis happens on a group, not an individual, level. Fearful of public criticism, judges are reluctant to allow scrutiny of their sentencing decisions. The fear is well founded in a world in which press coverage of criminal cases is often more parody than fact. Still, there is no other way to address unexamined bias.

For example, I am working to analyze my seventeen-year record to identify racial bias in my decisions. When I proposed such a program while I was still on the bench, there was considerable resistance; judges feared that the analyses would become public, that they would be criticized in the media, and that Congress would swoop in with additional mandatory minimums. But without a statistical examination of sentencing, even if only for the internal review of the courts and individual judges, there is a risk that a judge will see racial bias as an abstraction applying to other judges' decisions, not their own. For the public, such reports could enhance the court's legitimacy, suggesting "we have nothing to hide" and that "we are trying."

Community Engagement

Federal judges are too often removed from the communities they serve. The community's "voice" is filtered through the prosecutor and occasionally the victims, who typically pass on the information that is most supportive of seeking harsh sentences. Before the perils of mass incarceration became clear, the Black community had broadly supported police-driven efforts to deal with crime in their communities, but their attitudes began to change as more and more young men were sentenced to extraordinarily long sentences and as abusive police practices in the stop-and-frisk of young Black men were exposed. The support for aggressive policing dissipated, and the community sharply criticized the government, as when the U.S. Attorney in the District of Massachusetts chose to seek the death penalty in one of my cases involving the murder of one alleged gang member by another.

Judges are rarely held accountable in a meaningful way for their criminal legal decisions. They may be appealed to a higher court, but that is not real accountability. Appellate review is only about conforming with rules and procedures, not necessarily justice. Judges may be criticized in the press, but this is rarely a dispassionate review and is often discounted. In fact, judges are likely to be criticized for sentencing too little, never too much—held responsible when someone they sentenced commits another crime, and not when someone they sentenced succeeds in creating a good life. It results in a one-way ratchet, in which judges are rewarded for overpunishing or for adopting whatever sentence the prosecutor requests, but rarely for the humanity and compassion they display.

Narrative Change

How can we create a new narrative about crime, justice, and equity, which can then be reflected in the work of judging? One way to achieve this is opinion writing, in which judges can shine a light on the humanity of the defendants and the inhumanity of the criminal legal system. In "Do Judges Cry? An Essay on Empathy and Fellow-Feeling," the authors highlight the dissent of Justice John Harlan in *Plessy v. Ferguson*, which they describe as "lamenting the sterile formalism by which the majority found nothing wrong with a railroad ordinance that required separate seating for white and black passengers." They also discuss the opinion of Judge David Bazelon of the DC Circuit in *United States v. Alexander*, who explored the ways in which a "rotten social background," including child abuse, violence, and maltreatment, should figure into the court's understanding of a defendant; and my opinion in *United States v. Leviner*, which rejected the consideration of prior convictions that resulted from "driving while Black."[40] Another example might include Judge Jack Weinstein's decision in *United States v. Bannister*, which warned that mandatory minimum sentencing "impose[s] grave costs not only on the punished but on the moral credibility upon which our system of criminal justice depends."[41]

Even in situations in which a judge must impose a mandatory sentence—when the opinion is nothing but a *cri de coeur*—a judge should write the opinion if only to decry the unfairness of the result. In *United States v. Vasquez*, Judge John Gleeson began:

> When people think about miscarriages of justice, they generally think big, especially in this era of DNA exonerations, in which wholly innocent people have been released from jail in significant numbers after long periods in prison. As disturbing as those cases are, the truth is that most of the time miscarriages of justice occur in small doses, in cases involving guilty defendants. This makes them easier to overlook. But when they are multiplied by the thousands of cases in which they occur, they have a greater impact on our criminal justice system than the cases you read about in the newspapers or hear about on *60 Minutes*.[42]

The goal of writing opinions is explicit: to speak not simply to the litigants and possibly the appellate courts, but to the public. Chief Justice Warren was clear that the majority decision in *Brown v. Board of Education* reversing *Plessy* should have the public in mind: "[The opinion outlawing separate but equal education] should be short, readable by the lay public, non-rhetorical, unemotional, and above all, non-accusatory."[43] During my time on the bench, I tried to make the first three or four pages of any opinion the functional equivalent of a press release.

Judges speak through their opinions—to the lawyers, to other judges, to the media, to the people before them. They can speak in the sanitized language of the law, guidelines, and rules. They can pretend that what they are doing is fair when it is not. Or they can change the narrative.

The habits of mass incarceration die hard, helped by the insularity of the courts, the system's composition, and other factors I have only begun to address. But these habits are not impenetrable. The goal is to engage the courts in the wider discussion about the unfairness of the system, particularly its impact on communities of color. The goal is to invite judges to reimagine what community safety really looks like outside of police, prosecutors, and exorbitant mandatory minimums—and the role that judges can play in facilitating it. James Forman put it best, describing the criminal justice system as so disaggregated and uncoordinated that no single actor can take responsibility.

> Nobody has to take responsibility for the outcome, because nobody is responsible—at least not fully. This lack of responsibility is crucial to understanding why even reluctant or conflicted crime warriors . . . become part of the machinery of mass incarceration and why the system continues to churn even to this day, when its human toll has become increasingly apparent.[44]

The way to pave a path to change is to hold all of the players in the criminal justice system—including judges—accountable.

18

CLOSING THE WORKHOUSE: SUPPORTING RADICAL CAMPAIGNS AT NATIONAL NONPROFITS

Thomas Harvey

Thomas Harvey is the executive director of the Children's Defense Fund, California, and CDF's national litigation strategist. Formerly, he was the justice program director and senior attorney at the Advancement Project.

Although poor people and Black people are deeply familiar with the racism and neglect at the root of the criminal legal system, recent uprisings following the police murders of Black people have sparked critical conversations about its inherent injustice. No such inquiry is complete without exploring the role that foundations and nonprofits play in preventing radical campaigns—campaigns that target the root of injustice—from transforming our criminal legal system. These radical campaigns expose the inherent racism and predation of the legal system, envision a more just future, and articulate a plan to achieve that vision. Drawing upon an abolitionist framework, as well as a nuanced understanding of race, class, and gender, they ultimately aim to build a community with shared values and a supportive infrastructure. Their work may take years and sometimes even have to pause and restart depending on their members' material needs, such as housing, food, transportation, jobs, and health care. The campaigns' long-term goals—including to develop real power—far outstrip their immediate targets.

To achieve these goals, these campaigns require money and resources from large, private foundations whose culture, history, and expectations are often antithetical to radical change. Often, these very foundations derive their money from exploitation, distribute only 5 percent of their assets, and have historically been vehicles through which the extremely wealthy avoid taxes.[1] Given this history, it is unsurprising that foundations have historically funded national nonprofits with campaigns that pose no threat to the status quo, distributing money in ways that tame radical work, subvert radicals, and shrink the scope of campaign goals, downgrading them from transformative to incremental.[2]

The 2007 book *The Revolution Will Not Be Funded* comprehensively analyzed these dynamics and popularized the term the "nonprofit industrial complex."[3] One of the book's contributors, Dylan Rodríguez, describes the nonprofit industrial complex as "the set of symbiotic relationships that link together political and financial technologies of state and owning-class proctorship and surveillance over public political intercourse, including and especially emergent progressive and leftist social movements, since about the mid-1970s."[4] Consequently, nonprofits—and the foundations that fund them—have a deradicalizing effect on campaigns, even when they support them. They often take people doing radical work and subsume them in an organizational structure that reproduces rigid and violent capitalist hierarchies.

I share this critique as someone who is subject to this structure and has grappled with it for the past thirteen years. I am not an outsider criticizing these institutions or dynamics. I am a part of them, in more than just my institutional role. I am a cisgender, heterosexual, white man and a lawyer who now has easy access to foundations and other national nonprofits. As a lawyer, I must swear an oath of loyalty to the United States Constitution and to the very state I oppose in most of my actions. Regardless of identity, however, no one can stand fully outside of the racist systems inherent to our capitalist society—even those working every day to challenge them and build a new vision.

Considering the enormous power nonprofits wield over the distribution of resources—and the massive needs of radical campaigns—it's important to think through how nonprofits can mitigate harm and share resources. Nonprofits must commit to cultivating relationships with campaign members and leaders undertaking radical local work. They must take the time to deeply understand a campaign's history; develop long-term, trusting relationships; move at the pace of local organizers;

share resources, relationships, and credit; and leverage their resources to build local power. When the relationship between a national nonprofit and local organizations is authentic and successful, radical work can be catalyzed and pushed further than it may have gone on its own.

Drawing on my experiences with Close the Workhouse, a campaign to close a St. Louis jail, in this chapter I share what I have learned in order to guide people in supporting radical work, particularly leaders at national nonprofits. My involvement with Close the Workhouse began with ArchCity Defenders, one of the campaign's core local nonprofit partners, which I co-founded and ran from 2009 to 2017. Subsequently, I worked for two national nonprofits that supported the campaign between 2018 and 2021: The Bail Project, the nation's largest revolving bail fund, and the Advancement Project, a national racial justice nonprofit offering legal, communications, and campaign strategy to support organizers.

Close the Workhouse: An Overview[5]

The Close the Workhouse campaign began as a collaboration to close the Medium Security Institute in St. Louis, Missouri, colloquially known as "the Workhouse." The campaign is led by people who were locked in the jail and supported by four core partners: Action St. Louis, ArchCity Defenders, The Bail Project, and Missourians Organizing for Reform and Empowerment (MORE).[6]

Together, members of the campaign developed an expansive vision not only of closing the jail, but also of divesting from St. Louis's larger criminal legal system by establishing a new ecosystem of programs and services for the people most impacted by the jail's racist and predatory history.[7] This included a plan to retrain and hire correctional employees in new jobs; a Neighborhood Crime Reduction Fund, which would allocate $7.6 million in anti-poverty resources to neighborhoods disproportionately affected by serious harm;[8] and a Division of Recidivism Reduction, which would focus on social workers working with people facing mental health crises.[9]

Radical work is never done alone. It takes generations of people and a multitude of strategic interventions to even get close to achieving radical outcomes in the real world. This is demonstrated by the history of the

Close the Workhouse campaign, which seems simple at first glance: it grew out of the Ferguson Uprising following the murder of Mike Brown. Yet it is also a more complex story, involving dozens of people and organizations working independently and in coalition, over the course of years. While each individual victory was important, they originated from the history—and deepening relationships—between numerous organizers who combined forces to close the jail.

The Close the Workhouse campaign did not begin with the physical jail. Rather, it emerged from the outcry after Ferguson cop Darren Wilson shot and killed an eighteen-year-old unarmed Black man, Michael Brown Jr. Over the course of the subsequent four hundred days—the longest sustained direct action in U.S. history—people went to the streets to protest not only Brown's murder, but also the apartheid-like legal regime that produced physical, economic, and psychological violence.[10]

During the protests, cops beat, tear gassed, falsely arrested, jailed, and threatened protesters in an overwhelmingly militarized response. The courage and commitment of protesters forced a renewed national debate on the racist violence inherent to policing; the related illegal and immoral practices of arresting, charging, fining, and jailing poor and Black people to generate municipal revenue; and the complicity ingrained in anti-Black racist systems created by our society's elite power structure.

But that is not the full story of the Ferguson Uprising's enduring power. There was also a feeling of community created and led by Black people responding to a tragedy. Even just in brief moments, it felt as if a very different world was possible. Local resident Dwayne Wickerson described the atmosphere ten days after Brown's murder: "Everybody coming together, everybody is family, everybody is looking out for one another."[11] As Tef Poe, St. Louisan rapper, protester, and scholar, put it, "We all knew what time it was—what happened, and it didn't need any explanation."[12]

Protesters faced down the police, led nightly direct actions in Ferguson and throughout the region, shared meals, fell in love, fought, drew lines, and broke down barriers. They developed a political lens and power that endures to this day. As in any successful movement, there wasn't one leader, there were many, a dynamic that still exists in St. Louis. People who tried to claim leadership inauthentically, especially those who were not from St. Louis and hadn't been protesting in the streets, were rejected.

Figures including Jesse Jackson, Al Sharpton, and various leaders from legacy civil rights organizations were run out of town or asked to leave. Tef Poe said, "None of us can take credit for organizing that response from the community. [Mike Brown's] blood organized the response—his blood pouring out onto the pavement was what brought people out." [13]

The Workhouse is part of the backdrop of the Ferguson Uprising. The Workhouse is such a part of St. Louis, especially for poor and Black residents, that it seems always to have existed. As Inez Bordeaux, a leader of the Close the Workhouse campaign who was formerly incarcerated there, said, "I had heard about the Workhouse over the years—if you're Black in St. Louis, you either know somebody who's been in the Workhouse or you've been in the Workhouse." [14] It began as a debtors' prison, where poor and mostly Black people paid off their debts by breaking down giant chunks of limestone to make the stones that paved the streets of St. Louis. [15] St. Louis–area newspapers have chronicled the incarceration of poor people and Black people at the Workhouse, recounting 1,100 women who "picked up their hammers and headed to the rockyards" while jailed there in 1875. In 1905, the *Post-Dispatch* wrote, "There would be no more chance of a man with money having chains put on him in the Workhouse than there would be of a camel passing through the eye of a needle. Has it come to this—that poverty itself has become a crime?" [16]

In 1966, the physical location of the jail changed, moving from downtown to the outskirts of the City of St. Louis, but the story remained the same. In 1974, the City was sued because of "inoperative toilets, inadequate ventilation, inadequate lighting, and infestations of rats and insects" in its other jail. [17] That investigation was later expanded to include the Workhouse in 1982. In an eerie precursor to the current lawsuit against the City for its bail practices, a federal judge in 1990 said that "certain neighborhoods in St. Louis have become the target of intensive police activity. . . . These intrusive tactics, coupled with detention because of poverty, lead to a destruction of confidence in the criminal justice system." [18] More recently, a 2009 report detailed "the rampant abuses, policy violations, overcrowding, negligence, staff assaults on individuals, systematic cover-up of incidents by staff and higher-ups, and squalid conditions inside of the Workhouse." [19] And in 2013, the Workhouse made headlines again because guards were routinely raping people locked inside and forcing people into "gladiator"-style fights and recording them.[20]

In 2015, an organizer from Missourians Organizing for Reform and Empowerment (MORE) emailed me at ArchCity Defenders to inquire about a possible lawsuit against the Workhouse. MORE had collected harrowing stories from people who recounted abuse, neglect, and awful conditions in the Workhouse. As they considered a campaign to close the jail, they thought class action litigation might be a useful tool.[21] While the litigation did not proceed, I worked with MORE to draft the demands for a campaign, "Decarcerate STL," to shut down the Workhouse and end mass incarceration in St. Louis.[22] This campaign, staffed primarily by organizers Julia Ho, Kennard Williams, and Nabeehah Azeez, set up a Facebook page, a website, and a blog to inform people about the jail and call for its closure.[23]

As a result of this partnership, ArchCity worked with MORE to sketch out a work plan that included outreach to people inside the jail; a survey of its conditions; a plan to leverage these stories to shift the narrative; and, potentially, litigation.[24] Ultimately, MORE was unable to continue leading the campaign because of leadership changes and funding challenges. Yet the groundwork laid by the Decarcerate STL campaign paid dividends for years to come. It helped form a narrative about shutting down the workhouse, which critically shaped what would become the Close the Workhouse campaign.

In 2016, ArchCity Defenders, Organization for Black Struggle (OBS), MORE, and the Ferguson Collaborative held a series of town hall meetings in the City of St. Louis, Pine Lawn, and Ferguson.[25] These town halls focused on divesting from jails, courts, and police, and were another precursor to the Close the Workhouse campaign.[26] They included workshops encouraging people living in areas impacted by serious harm to imagine their own definitions of public safety, ways to improve their lives with their own tax money, and how to create a better future for their children. This five-month series deepened relationships between key organizers.

That same year, two further milestones shaped the official campaign to close the Workhouse: the election of Kim Gardner as the circuit attorney, and City Treasurer Tishaura Jones's call to close the Workhouse in the *St. Louis American*, which made her the first city official to support the idea.[27] Mayoral and circuit attorney debates co-hosted by Action St. Louis, ArchCity Defenders, Decarcerate STL, and OBS built on the issues raised in the town halls and asked questions about the criminalization of poverty and race.[28] These debates were enormously well attended; and activists Blake Strode and Kayla Reed co-moderated the event to great success. While Tishaura Jones didn't win the mayoral race that year (she was elected mayor in 2020), her positions on the Workhouse—and her commitment to the coalition's underlying principles—brought her to within eight hundred votes in the election.[29]

Perhaps most importantly, these forums paved the way for Kayla and Blake to organize more closely together. Blake, who was from St. Louis, joined ArchCity in 2015 after graduating from Harvard Law School with a prestigious two-year Skadden Fellowship. Even though this fellowship project centered on tenant organizing in Canfield Green Apartments (the same complex where Mike Brown was murdered), Blake quickly got up to speed and guided our civil rights litigation and pitched in wherever he was needed. His humility stood in contrast to stereotypes about graduates of elite institutions; and his ability to nimbly adapt to the needs of our organization as well as to the organizing ecosystem is among his many strengths as a leader. Blake stayed on after the fellowship ended and eventually replaced me as executive director of ArchCity Defenders, growing it into the powerhouse it is today. Kayla, also from St. Louis, went into the streets after the murder of Mike Brown, trained as an organizer, and eventually founded her own organization, Action St. Louis. Kayla and Blake's close friendship has fundamentally transformed the region. It's at the heart of the campaign to close the workhouse, and every major change that has occurred in the past six years in St. Louis.

Action St. Louis, co-founded by Kayla Reed and Michelle Higgins, became ArchCity's most frequent organizing partner. As my relationship with Kayla grew, I invited her to join the board of ArchCity Defenders, bringing our organizations even closer. Our partnership made two future bailout campaigns possible, in addition to a follow-up campaign called Beyond Bail to support people after they left jail. Our first campaign, the Black Mama's Bail Out Day, was inspired by Mary Hooks, executive director of the abolitionist LGBTQ organization Southerners on New Ground. Her work and that of countless other organizers has freed thousands and inspired legal and policy change across the country; it inspired us to do the same in St. Louis.[30] Ultimately, our Black Mama's Bail Out Day raised $13,000 in twenty-four hours, enabling countless people to spend Mother's Day with their kids.[31] This was made possible by the support of activists Mike Milton and Michelle Higgins, who took on the transport of tens of thousands of dollars in cash from the bank. I had gotten to know Mike through his work supporting formerly incarcerated men in the reentry process as well as his work with Action St. Louis. He is from St. Louis, has a deep commitment to racial justice, and has been incarcerated in the workhouse. Mike began offering friendship and support to five young men going through the reentry process, a volunteer effort that eventually led him to work with 120 men a year at a local non-profit organization, Mission St. Louis, and then found his own organization, the Freedom Community Center.[32] Michelle, the co-founder of Action St. Louis, persuaded public officials and volunteers alike to support this groundbreaking effort.

Mike and Michelle bailed people out and coordinated volunteers to support the moms we bailed out, getting them to court appearances and doctor's appointments or finding childcare. Our second bailout was prompted by a record-high temperature of 108 degrees Fahrenheit in July 2017, which left people inside the Workhouse screaming through the jail's windows, pleading for their lives.[33] Together, ArchCity and Action St. Louis raised $25,000 and bailed out as many people as we could. ArchCity also agreed to help those who were bailed out resolve any municipal legal issues and connect them with social services. In response to activists' calls to close the Workhouse, the mayor offered air-conditioning and promised upgrades.[34]

As Action St. Louis and ArchCity worked together, we heard story after story about the horrific conditions in the jail and the unconstitutional procedures through which people were detained. Bail hearings that took ninety seconds, often without counsel, led to pretrial detention lasting more than 290 days.[35] This disproportionately impacted Black people, who because of racial discrimination and poverty were forced to pay excessive cash bonds. ArchCity filed a lawsuit against the city in November 2017, another milestone in the history of the Close the Workhouse campaign.[36]

In 2018, I had the opportunity to help start The Bail Project—the nation's largest revolving bail fund—shaping the work, choosing the sites, hiring the people who posted bail in local communities, and connecting the work to local organizing. To support The Bail Project's work in St. Louis, I hired Action St. Louis organizers Mike and Michelle to actually post bail for people and connect them to housing, transportation, health care, and employment awaiting their cases.[37] Their deep connections with organizing in St. Louis and relationships with Action St. Louis were crucial to the work's success. That model in St. Louis led to the largest number of people being bailed out among all Bail Project sites. After I joined the Advancement Project, Mike expanded The Bail Project's reach throughout the entire St. Louis region; doubled the size of the team; bailed out thousands of people; and made the St. Louis Bail Project site one of the anchor partners in the Close the Workhouse campaign.

When I joined the Advancement Project to run its criminal justice work (organized as the Justice Project), we deepened an existing relationship with Action St. Louis, supporting them with organizing training at a retreat facilitated by the Justice Project team. The retreat covered theories of change, basic organizing tenets, and how to build campaigns. For many Action members, this was the first formal organizing training they'd received. The retreat led Action St. Louis to launch the "Bye Bob" campaign, devoted to removing the notorious St. Louis County prosecutor Robert McCulloch, who relished his announcement that Darren Wilson would not be indicted for the murder of Mike Brown.[38] Lawyers from the Justice Project provided research and education about the role prosecutors played in the criminal legal system. In turn, Action St. Louis hosted regular "Woke Voter" brunches, events to educate the public on topics including cash bail, electronic monitoring, fines and fees, prosecutorial discretion, grand juries, and people's voting rights in the upcoming election. After McCulloch was handily defeated, the Justice Project continued supporting Action St. Louis's Close the Workhouse campaign.

From narrative change and litigation to electoral advocacy and direct-action protests, the Close the Workhouse campaign deployed multiple strategies with remarkable success. So far, its efforts have led to a massive reduction in the jail's population from 1,138 to 0;[39] the elimination of its budget;[40] two federal class action lawsuits;[41] a 28–0 vote by the local board of aldermen to close the jail;[42] the election, for the first time, of a

Black women as St. Louis's prosecuting attorney and mayor;[43] and finally, a commitment to permanently close the jail.

For National Nonprofits: Lessons from the Campaign

Find the Right Funders

Nonprofits must be aware of how foundations shape them in subtle—but critical—ways. For example, foundations require applicants to overcome administrative hurdles to access limited funding for narrowly defined work—funding that can be reclaimed for any number of minor transgressions. In response, nonprofits shift organizational structures, hiring people who may excel at oral and written presentations, budget construction, and grant reporting, but have little to no connection to local partners.

During my time at ArchCity Defenders, two funders stood out as positive examples. The Rockefeller Family Fund stepped up in a short time frame to support a series of town halls we organized. There was sufficient money, very little paperwork, and enough latitude for us to move quickly, easily, and effectively. Similarly, the Deaconess Foundation played the most important role of any foundation in the Ferguson Uprising and its aftermath. Deaconess was responsive, moved fast, and provided enough money both to fund every base-building organization ArchCity collaborated with and, eventually, to build a whole center for organizers and activists to call their own. While funders have come and gone, none of them has had Deaconess's enduring impact.[44]

To mitigate the restrictions imposed by foundation grants, nonprofits must find creative ways to receive money, support radical work, and not ignore their political principles. Without this, nonprofits will never be able fully to support radical work, and the future of justice will look a lot like its past. For example, the Advancement Project avoided politically problematic foundations who contradicted programmatic goals. This required careful and principled coordination on the organization's part, as certain funders could, on the one hand, support voting rights protections but, on the other, oppose removing cops from schools. Consequently, the Advancement Project favored receiving general operating support funding, which gave it the flexibility to support the Close the Workhouse campaign in ever-changing ways.

Don't Let Form Dominate Content

Many of the problems nonprofits face in supporting radical work stem from their reliance on foundations for revenue. Foundations ask nonprofits to focus on research, policy, and legal wins, emphasizing individual—rather than collective—achievements. These dynamics not only stand in stark contrast to the underlying principles of movements, but also require professionalized staff exclusively dedicated to responding to foundation goals. Often the product of elite institutions, these staffers increase the disconnect between the national nonprofit and the radical, local campaigns it seeks to support.

Nonprofits must not de-emphasize their primary work in service of foundation-specific needs. For example, the Justice Project—another partner of Close the Workhouse and a division of the Advancement Project—created an environment where success was not measured in legal victories, lawsuits filed, or briefs drafted. The Advancement Project's executive director, Judith Browne Dianis, understood that the definition of a win was not based just on a judge's decision, but could be measured in many different ways. Because of the culture she created and fostered, the Justice Project had the latitude to create political education materials, canvass with organizers, and draft op-eds in response to Close the Workhouse's needs. This dedication and willingness to push boundaries are what national nonprofits need to meet the evolving demands of a radical, local campaign.

Hire People with Direct Relationships to the Campaign,
and Build Your Own

Knowing the campaign's history is critical to supporting it. Staff can learn it from the campaign, or the nonprofit can hire people who have been involved. But without a genuine, authentic connection to the campaign, it is extremely difficult to support it successfully. The success of the Close the Workhouse campaign owed to long-term, deeply held personal and professional relationships between key organizers that predated the campaign. Judith Browne Dianis, Shuya "Shu" Ohno, and Denise Lieberman were all core members of the Advancement Project's national team, and Derecka Purnell joined the Justice Project team in 2017 as a Skadden Fellow and staff attorney. Shu and Judith had cultivated relationships in St. Louis during the Uprising, assembling a team to support local organizers, providing on-the-ground organizing training, amplifying the Uprising's message in the media, moving money to where it needed to go, and connecting local organizers with elected officials. Derecka and Denise, originally from St. Louis, had the deepest connections to the region. Denise's history of civil rights work in St. Louis helped establish strong credibility among organizers. Derecka was born and raised in St. Louis, protested during the Uprising, and was a protest leader during the Belinda Hall occupation at Harvard Law School in 2016.

My own history of work in St. Louis helped deepen trust with local organizers and also increased the Advancement Project's collective knowledge of the ecosystem there. ArchCity Defenders provided direct legal representation in civil and criminal cases for people experiencing homelessness, and helped them obtain the housing, health care, transportation, and employment critical to remaining housed. That commitment to supporting people's legal and non-legal needs shaped my systemic analysis and commitment to racial justice, including working with organizers and activists in St. Louis.

During the Ferguson Uprising, I worked closely with organizers at MORE and OBS, where I first met Montague Simmons, Kennard, Jamala Rogers, and Kayla. ArchCity issued a report on the systemic racism in municipal courts and for-profit policing in the region, including in Ferguson, collaborating with MORE to support its campaign against these courts. When we sued thirty cities and the police for their racist, predatory practices, we again worked with MORE and OBS to find plaintiffs and get out the word when we won $4.75 million from the city of Jennings, pointing out that that settlement was awarded to the residents of just one city alone.

Other Advancement Project staff also had existing local relationships. For example, Shu and Judith had cultivated relationships in St. Louis during the Uprising. After being invited by organizers to come to Ferguson, they assembled a team to support them. They provided on-the-ground organizing training, helped amplify the Uprising's message in the media, moved money to where it needed to go, and connected local organizers with elected officials. Shu also offered organizing support to OBS, helping train two of their members—Montague Simmons and Kayla Reed—who would later become key figures in the Close the Workhouse campaign. At the time of the Uprising, there were few more important organizations than OBS, led by Jamala and then Montague. Kayla, who had first been introduced to formal organizing through OBS, participated in trainings that Shu offered, interning at the Advancement Project before co-founding Action St. Louis with Michelle.

All this underscores the importance of national nonprofits building relationships with local organizers. In supporting the work in St. Louis, the Advancement Project's politics, staff, and vision centered on the shared experience and lessons learned from the Uprising. Connection to that history and the principled support for organizers in 2014 helped ensure our credibility. These deep relationships and our role in the history and understanding of the campaign's context let us move quickly and nimbly in response to their needs.

Be Nimble and Responsive to Campaign Needs

Nonprofits are not the crucial element in campaigns; the radical work at the center is. However, national nonprofits can take on valuable supporting roles as intermediaries or connectors. Being in community with campaign organizers is key to any possible successful collaboration and allows national nonprofit organizations to respond to local needs quickly.

The Justice Project team members sought to fill gaps identified at the local level: for example, Derecka and I taught a political education session on the history of policing, the prison industrial complex, and abolitionist principles. Shu offered organizing training. Drew Ambrogi, from our communications team, helped develop Action St. Louis's website. Justice Project staff edited and wrote portions of the "Plan to Close the Workhouse," helping to develop an abolitionist framework and fleshing out their invest/divest strategy; and helped cover graphic design and printing costs.[45]

Being physically present and available was also important. We went to St. Louis as much as we could and filled whatever role people needed at that juncture of their campaign. For example, when the BET series *Finding Justice* featured the Close the Workhouse campaign, Justice Project flew to St. Louis to organize a watch party with Montague from OBS.[46] To increase attendance, we arranged for Ben & Jerry's to provide free ice cream, live-tweeted the event, and revamped the Close the Workhouse website before the party. Following the watch party, I worked with Sima

Atri from ArchCity and Mike Milton from The Bail Project to train new volunteers to observe bail hearings and record data, amplifying awareness of the role judges and prosecutors play in bail hearings. At other points in the campaign, we canvassed with organizers Inez, Rodney Brown, and Montague, knocking on doors and asking people to call their alderperson about voting to close the jail; or worked with Montague to coordinate volunteers providing rides to bail hearings, text and phone call updates, and wraparound support in the form of housing and treatment.

Give Money and Access to More
To appropriately share resources, nonprofits must have a deep relationship with radical campaigns. Without this, efforts to share resources may permanently characterize the nonprofit as a funder, creating a transactional relationship. This kind of relationship cannot survive difficulties. However, once trust is established, nonprofits should share resources as much as possible, whether in the form of meals, drinks, stipends, printing, website assistance, videography, transcription, filing fees, or anything else. There is simply no better use of foundation money than to make sure it reaches the people harmed by the very inequities that created the wealth that the foundation distributes. This also includes connecting local organizations directly to national foundations so that money flows with no intermediary.

Leverage Creative In-kind Resources for the Campaign
Nonprofits can support radical work by focusing on shifting power. They should conscientiously and intentionally leverage their credibility to bring in resources and cultivate supportive connections. For the Close the Workhouse campaign, this included resources for litigation and for media and communication.

The Close the Workhouse campaign hoped that federal civil rights litigation challenging St. Louis's cash bail system would complement organizing and communications efforts to reduce the state's capacity to incarcerate people. In response to this campaign need, national nonprofits made their litigation resources available: this bail case, built on litigation brought by ArchCity, Saint Louis University Law Legal Clinics, and civil rights lawyer Alec Karakatsanis in 2015, became essential leverage for

Close the Workhouse. The theory was that, because more than 90 percent of people in the Workhouse were held on unaffordable cash bail, successful litigation would effectively close the front door to the jail.

With ArchCity in the lead, Civil Rights Corps, the Advancement Project, and Georgetown Law's Institute for Constitutional Advocacy and Protection filed a federal civil rights case in January 2019.[47] It aimed to change policies, shrink the jail population to help close the Workhouse, and reshape media narratives about public safety. The day we filed, St. Louis's major newspapers, radio stations, and television networks all ran stories on the litigation; campaign members were interviewed for every piece.[48]

Simply filing the litigation led to change. Our named clients—who had waited weeks for a bail hearing that should have happened within forty-eight hours—had bail hearings within a day.[49] Two were released but two others were not, their bond amounts remaining intact.[50] I coordinated with Wade McMullen at Robert F. Kennedy Human Rights to post bond for these remaining two plaintiffs, allowing us to leverage the organization's involvement to get more press for the campaign and help reshape the public narrative around bail.[51]

Additionally, we connected the campaign to Ben & Jerry's and Borealis Philanthropy, both of whom made grants to Close the Workhouse. Ben & Jerry's sent staff to St. Louis to support Close the Workhouse and created signs, banners, posters, stickers, and buttons for the campaign. They drove an ice cream truck through neighborhoods, offered free ice cream, and talked to residents about the campaign, serving 13,420 scoops of ice cream at twenty-seven separate events.[52] We worked with Ben & Jerry's to place an op-ed in the local Black newspaper, the *St. Louis American*; a full-page ad in both the *American* and the *St. Louis Post-Dispatch*; and a letter to the editor from its CEO in support of the campaign.[53] Ben & Jerry's co-founder Ben Cohen traveled to St. Louis for radio and TV interviews with Close the Workhouse's Inez Bordeaux, and participated in a press conference on the day of our win in federal court.[54]

Have Fun Together
Every trip should include a meal, drinks, or some other shared activity. During my time at the Advancement Project, the last three trips I took to St. Louis included breakfast, lunch, dinner, and drinks for our team

and our organizing partners. It's good for your team to know that radical work almost always includes play, and it's great for organizers to be celebrated for the generally unrewarded daily grind. Judith wanted the team she hired and the partners we worked with to have fun. She went out of her way to find unrestricted funding to make this possible. Not everyone does this, but everyone should. It is a sign of love and care for people to be treated well and celebrated while they are doing hard work.

Tend to Internal Institutional Relationships

National nonprofits are large organizations, sometimes with more than a hundred staff across multiple departments and program areas. The communications, development, and finance team all work with the campaign, even though they may not have direct relationships with local people on the ground. Their actions, both internally and externally, may influence the organization's relationship with the radical campaign. Nonprofits must be careful about managing these relationships and ensuring that their bureaucratic processes and procedures don't undermine established trust with a radical campaign.

Despite the support the Justice Project team provided to Close the Workhouse, we were not always on the same page internally with the rest of the Advancement Project's staff. As a result, the organization made mistakes that hurt our relationship with Close the Workhouse. For example, our website listed Close the Workhouse as an Advancement Project campaign, which was obviously wrong; for a national organization to claim this kind of ownership reflected carelessness at best, and at worst, an attempt to claim other people's work as its own. Similarly, in emails to supporters our development team erroneously listed the Close the Workhouse report as an Advancement Project publication; we had contributed to the report but were not the primary author. The Close the Workhouse campaign saw this as an attempt to raise money off its work. We issued a correction, but the damage was done.

Finally, our finance policies created massive hurdles when our local partners sought reimbursement for expenses Justice Project was covering. The intent was to ensure the Advancement Project met its fiscal responsibilities, but the perception was that we were slow to pay local printing presses, videographers, and other support for the campaign. By our policies, the process wasn't "slow"; but long, complicated paperwork processes are not compatible with fast-moving, quick-acting, nimble local campaigns. Such missteps—although seemingly small—diminish the trust that has been established over many years.

Step Back, and Pivot to a New Role

While the Justice Project continued to play a central role in writing and supporting the publication of the second Close the Workhouse report released in January 2020, our role changed over time. We still regularly checked in, continued our bail litigation, and helped amplify the campaign's work on social media. But as Michelle and Montague moved on to other work, the leaders of ArchCity Defenders, Action St. Louis, and The Bail Project (St. Louis) took on a more active role. With Blake, Kayla, and Mike devoting more time, and Inez and Jae Shepherd, two Action St. Louis members hired to support Close the Workhouse, the campaign no longer needed the type of support the Justice Project once provided. We continued to seek litigation, media, and funding opportunities for the campaign, handing over the relationship with Ben & Jerry's to enable direct communication without our involvement. We also collaborated on litigation during the COVID-19 pandemic; and, during the George Floyd Rebellion, I was able to connect Blake and Kayla with a funder making large-scale emergency grants, which led to substantial funding for their organizations.

Though the Justice Project team was no longer as active in the daily or weekly aspects of Close the Workhouse, we continued to provide support as needed. In addition, we worked with Defund. Re-envision. Transform., Freedom Community Center, and Fatal State Violence—all of which grew out of the work described above—and Close the Workhouse to help them create political education training modules on the prison industrial complex for their staff and membership.

A long-term commitment to radical work, predicated on deep relationships, is the goal for national nonprofits. Campaigns come and go; organizational priorities change. But the relationships endure, paving the way for the organization not only to quickly resume work that has been halted or on pause, but also to leverage that hard-earned reputation to support work in places where connections are not as strong. Ultimately, even though the Justice Project team has reduced its role in the Close the Workhouse campaign, that work has translated to other work in St. Louis, Detroit, Miami, Washington, DC, and East Baton Rouge. That massive change, the shift from one campaign to another, and from litigation to political education, is a victory. Simply being asked to fill those roles with other groups is a victory.

These victories in support of radical campaigns don't lend themselves to the typical metrics of advocacy and reform. They may not look like victories to your big funders, or even to your boss. It may be difficult to explain that your work started out supporting a campaign to close a jail, but now works with families who have lost loved ones to state violence. Funding doesn't easily shift from litigation to training people on the history of policing, prisons, and the prison industrial complex. In the end, however, this is what these radical campaigns need most from national nonprofit partners: strong relationships; humility; a deep understanding of the campaigns and their history, flexibility, funding, and other resources; and a long-term commitment to supporting their goals.

19

WHAT MAKES A CITY SAFE? STRATEGIES THAT DON'T RELY ON POLICE OR PRISONS

Amanda Alexander and Danielle Sered

Amanda Alexander is the founding executive director of the Detroit Justice Center, a nonprofit law firm working alongside communities to create economic opportunities, transform the justice system, and promote equitable and just cities. She is a senior research scholar at University of Michigan Law School.

Danielle Sered is the executive director of Common Justice, which develops and advances solutions to violence that meet the needs of those harmed, advance racial equity, and do not rely on incarceration. She is the author of Until We Reckon: Violence, Mass Incarceration, and a Road to Repair.

In the months after police officer Derek Chauvin murdered George Floyd in Minneapolis, the streets in cities and towns across the United States rang out with calls to "defund the police." Since then, as people have worked to turn those outcries into policy, major urban centers have seen an uptick in violence that has underscored the urgency of demands for neighborhood safety. These trends are often framed as being in opposition to each other, as though defunding the police might be viable but for the fact of pressing safety challenges that, many people assume, require more police. Yet reducing interpersonal violence in communities is not only compatible with divestment from law enforcement; it depends on it. To understand why, we must understand what causes violence in the first place.

The law enforcement perspective on violence assumes that individuals must be deterred from enacting their desires to cause harm, or contained if that strategy of intimidation fails. It suggests a person-by-person, block-by-block state pursuit of "individual wrongdoers," a dynamic that makes for good TV drama but terrible public policy. An individualistic focus generates solutions that control, punish, isolate, and even kill those regarded as dangerous. These "solutions"—including policing and incarceration—fail, in part, because they rest on inaccurate assumptions about the causes of interpersonal violence.

Interpersonal violence is not caused by people's characters. It is systematically produced by institutions, laws, and practices that harm groups of people and shape the conditions of their lives. Interpersonal violence emerges as a nearly inevitable result of barriers to living wages, clean water, and nourishing food; underfunded schools; and poor physical and mental health infrastructure.[1] This set of conditions—formed by policies that reflect a society's explicit or implicit choices—is called structural violence, because deprivation and poor health cause grave harm. Also, in a more literal sense, such inequity creates the conditions known to generate interpersonal violence.

As a structural problem, violence requires structural solutions. Until we as a society invest in structural solutions, inequity will continue fueling the fire of violence. And as we seek to make these long-term structural changes, we must still work to solve the problem of interpersonal violence; people's survival depends on it.

As we consider structural conditions in the United States, defined for centuries by precisely the choices that generate violence, we should ask not only, *Why is there so much violence in certain neighborhoods?* but also, *Why isn't there more?* This question directs us to the widespread, underrecognized work that people across the country are undertaking to limit violence and fight for the society everyone deserves.

Structural violence has never been equally distributed. Since the United States' founding, Black, Indigenous, and other communities of color have been the primary targets of divestment from community wellbeing and investment in criminalization and premature death. They have also been the targets of state and state-sanctioned violence including slavery, lynching, and police brutality.[2] This generations-long violence has defined the character of the United States and generated its wealth (for some) since its inception.

Policing is among the greatest contributors to this structural violence. In the United States, policing has long been entwined with racist, colonialist, and sexist violence and control. Police have never provided meaningful protection to Black, Indigenous, and Latinx communities and other communities of color, migrant people, disabled people, and queer, trans, or gender non-conforming people. Moreover, police have harmed these communities in ways that are not incidental to their roles, but definitive of them.

The behaviors and aims of police departments trace to "slave patrols," where plantation owners enjoined local governments to ensure that enslaved people who escaped were returned and punished brutally, in the name of both the state and white "property" owners. Continuing their mission of protecting white wealth and preserving the racial hierarchy, these same law enforcement organizations—and the government agencies that established and empowered them—arrested people and forced them into systems of convict leasing, upheld Jim Crow legislation, carried out and abetted lynchings, and enforced segregation. Today, they continue to enact widespread and often fatal brutality against those they are purportedly tasked with protecting and serving. Simultaneously, they use force to suppress resistance that would challenge and seek an end to these abuses and change these harms.

The United States is founded and built upon this violence. Going forward, any attempt to create a society characterized by justice and democracy must acknowledge and repair this harm. The argument for doing so is not simply moral. It is pragmatic. The narrative upheld by cop show propaganda, police unions, and legislators riding "tough on crime" campaigns to victory was interrupted in the summer of 2020, when the movement for racial justice pressured the country to contend with our brutal present and past. Now, we have a chance to break with the myth that police promote public safety, a myth that has enabled them to monopolize conversations about violence prevention. We have a chance to seat others at the head of the public safety table, including those who have long produced safety: community residents; health care workers; people impacted by gun violence; educators; and people providing housing, community development, and economic development across the country.

The movements fighting to defund police are right to recognize policing as an obstacle to safety and stability. Sometimes, a short-term, localized increase in police presence can decrease rates of reported violent crime. But empirical evidence establishing policing's effect on interpersonal violence leaves many questions unanswered, including about the durability of these impacts, and whether targeted, place-based enforcement strategies merely displace violence to other blocks or neighborhoods.

Moreover, these limited and often impermanent gains come with vast and permanent losses. As we consider policing's impact, we must consider the immediate and lasting harms caused by increased enforcement. These include near-term, medium-term, and intergenerational effects on people arrested and incarcerated and their families. People with a loved one incarcerated can suffer emotional loss and associated mental health effects, economic destabilization, displacement from permanent housing, disruption to neighborhood relationships and support systems, disruption of caregiving relationships, and more. People themselves incarcerated experience the negative effects of incarceration, including the loss of freedom, loved ones, and connection; exposure to violence; limited access to physical and mental health care; and lifelong restrictions on access to education, employment, and other pathways to a sustainable, legal living wage.

Even for people not arrested or incarcerated, the presence of a militarized police force in one's neighborhood is traumatizing. It conveys to residents that they are viewed as dangerous, incapable of civil coexistence and conflict resolution, and so far outside the social contract that their neighborhood must be occupied to be secured. Moreover, residents who know that police have killed people may fear that any officer interaction could lead to the loss of their life or that of someone they love; the presence of police everywhere implies the presence of death everywhere. These effects of police presence on people's psyches and bodies long outlast the time a neighborhood maintains a "hot spot" status. Police presence also corrodes the shared sense of dignity, efficacy, power, and belonging that are not only human entitlements, but also prerequisites for the long-term production of safe neighborhoods.

If policing does not produce safety, what does? Ultimately, the answers will be structural, systematic, and just as far-reaching as the harm and divestment that generated interpersonal violence in the first place. To end violence, we must ask, *What is currently producing safety?* and, *How can we expand and support these efforts?* Effective solutions are located in thousands of local community endeavors to foster the safety, healing, and well-being of people most impacted by violence.[3] Some solutions are housed at nonprofits. Others are more informal, including neighbors who rush to crime scenes as soon as—if not before—police arrive, helping minimize retaliatory violence and support people in the first crushing moments of grief. They include elders who hold circle processes in their homes to address harms that the police, courts, and prisons cannot or will not reach. They include those who empower survivors when the justice system fails to do so. Such neighbors—or "solutionaries"—are everywhere and long have been.[4] Communities—especially those of color historically subjected to violence and inequity—would not survive without these contributors to safety.

Society has conditioned us to associate safety with policing and prisons. Addressing interpersonal violence as a structural, economic, or public health concern can seem discordant with prevailing views about the issue. Yet many researchers, practitioners, and local leaders are moving toward public health-based approaches to violence, which focus on preventing injury or death by addressing underlying social determinants of health, defined by the Centers for Disease Control as "conditions in the places where people live, learn, work, and play that affect a wide range of health and quality-of-life risks and outcomes."[5] Examples include transportation options, employment and education opportunities, safe housing, and access to healthy food, air, and water. Of course, these conditions are shaped by the distribution of resources and power at local and national levels. Poor, majority-Black and people of color communities across the country have been subjected to severe retractions in public investment in health-promoting fields, such as education, housing, and public transportation. At the same time, these communities have borne the brunt of state investment in criminalization, policing, and incarceration.

Medical and public health researchers first recognized violence as a public health crisis in the early 1980s. Violence behaves like a chronic, recurrent, but preventable disease, as described by the National Network of Hospital-based Violence Intervention Programs. Interpersonal violence is an epidemic that disproportionately harms Black and Latino men and boys as well as young adults aged fifteen to thirty-four years, for whom it is the leading cause of death.[6] Black men and boys in this age group, who make up 2 percent of the U.S. population, comprised 38 percent of people who died from gunshot injuries in 2016.

Moreover, violent victimization is considered a "recurrent disease"; in cities, up to 41 percent of patients treated for violent injury are re-injured within five years. Further, being a victim of violence "also significantly increases the likelihood of engaging in violent behaviors against others, oftentimes as retaliation for the initial injury."[7] Violent injury also affects mental health, with many individuals experiencing PTSD, depression, and substance use disorders after the violence—which may add to the PTSD caused by living in environments that produce chronic stress.[8] The epidemic of interpersonal violence causes premature death and disability among young people, in turn leading to further violence, along with community destabilization, poverty, and incarceration.

Still, while public health frameworks help illuminate factors driving interpersonal violence, they are not free of racism. For instance, a disease-based model justifies the identification and removal of those deemed most "sick" or "contagious." This has been used to isolate, coerce, and punish those most likely to experience violence—that is, Black and Latino boys and men—even as it has emphasized healing, trauma-informed care, community ties, material support, and dignity. We focus on the latter interventions here, acknowledging that the field of public health has helped to create and uphold racist systems and to justify oppression and punishment.

Public health approaches to addressing violence include "credible messenger" and violence interruption programs to prevent violence, hospital-based programs to interrupt cycles of violence, and other strategies. Save Our Streets (S.O.S.) in New York City helps people who have experienced violence use their credibility and relationships to mediate conflicts before they escalate to gun violence, and to respond immediately after shootings to prevent further violence. Hundreds of violence prevention organizations perform similar work in neighborhoods nationwide, including Communities Partnering 4 Peace in Chicago; Advance Peace in Richmond, California; the Jersey City Anti-Violence Coalition Movement; the Newark Anti-Violence Coalition; and others. Many of these programs center economic stability—helping meet people's basic needs—as a key component of violence intervention.

The first hospital-based violence intervention programs—created in the mid-1990s, when community organizations in Oakland and Milwaukee teamed up with hospital staff—applied this "credible messenger" model in a new, high-impact setting.[9] Too often, medical teams treat violence and harm in the same way that the criminal punishment system does: as consequences of individual behavior. By contrast, hospital-based violence intervention programs enable staff and their community partners to do more than treat physical injuries before sending patients home, knowing that they may well end up injured, dead, or incarcerated, or harm someone else.[10] Instead, these programs—of which there are now more than thirty-five across the United States, many part of a network called Health Alliance for Violence Intervention (HAVI)—address interpersonal violence within a broader context of structural violence. Policing, criminalization, and incarceration exacerbate poverty and worsen other social determinants of health. To break this cycle, interventions must center the needs of the most vulnerable community members and focus on trauma-informed healing, not incarceration.

One notable hospital-based violence intervention program is Detroit Life Is Valuable Everyday (DLIVE) at Detroit Medical Center Sinai-Grace Hospital.[11] The DLIVE team connects with young adult patients who have sustained an injury, and initiates a therapeutic relationship to support a healing transformative journey. DLIVE offers integrated mental health therapy, transportation, housing, employment opportunities, and other trauma-informed supports addressing critical social determinants of health. It delivers this support in a trauma-informed way to mitigate barriers and prevent re-traumatization. DLIVE may provide resources directly (e.g., transportation, mental health support) or facilitate support through community partners (e.g., legal advocacy and community lawyering). Consistent with a structural approach to understanding violence, programs like DLIVE are guided by questions including, *How can we ensure that this does not happen again? What supports will promote this young person's health and well-being?* Amid a widespread lack of trauma-informed support for survivors of violence, DLIVE has created a model for holistic care and healing.

In 2018, DLIVE formed a medical-legal partnership with the Detroit

Justice Center to holistically support youth and young adults who have sustained forms of acute violent trauma such as gunshot wounds. The partnership offers DLIVE members assistance to remove legal barriers including suspended licenses, outstanding warrants, tickets and fines, and criminal records. This helps minimize the criminal punishment system's power to undercut DLIVE's success. DLIVE and the Detroit Justice Center have already helped more than twenty-five clients—mostly Black men in their twenties and thirties—avoid re-injury, resolve court obligations, obtain employment, reconnect with their children, avoid incarceration, and build pathways toward success and prosperity.

Studies demonstrate the profound promise and success of hospital-based programs in several areas including decreasing PTSD and preventing reinjury, violent harm, and criminal legal system involvement.[12] Five randomized control trials have offered encouraging results about the link between participating in a hospital-based violence intervention program and future risk of reinjury. In one trial in Baltimore, for example, 36 percent of the control group was re-hospitalized, compared with just 5 percent of people who participated in the hospital-based violence intervention program.[13]

The takeaway is clear: to interrupt cycles of violence, we must invest in programs that center credible messengers and promote public health and safety. We must invest in improving social determinants of health to create the conditions where people can be safe.

When people who experience violence, policing, and incarceration are asked how they would create safe, healthy, livable neighborhoods, their answers are remarkably consistent. Their answers also reflect the social determinants of health. As the Durham Beyond Policing coalition found, "When we surveyed Durham residents in 2016 and 2017 about how they would spend the $71M allocated to build the new [Durham Police Department] headquarters to keep their communities safe, they said they wanted affordable housing, healthcare access, good jobs, and better public transportation. They wanted to address structural problems." People want to address the underlying structural factors that create, in the words of Durham organizers, "criminally unlivable contexts."[14]

Similarly, when the Detroit Justice Center asked Detroit teenagers how they would spend the $533 million allocated to a new jail complex, none said that the city needed more police or jails. Instead, they asked for mental health support, restorative justice mediation centers, public transit, affordable and accessible public housing, investments in quality schools, and well-paid teachers.[15]

And researchers heard similar responses in yet another study, this one conducted in 2015 and led by the Ella Baker Center for Human Rights, in which over twenty organizations in fourteen states surveyed 1,080 people who had either been incarcerated or were related to someone who had been.[16] Two-thirds of families struggled to meet their basic needs owing to a loved one's incarceration. When asked how they would reinvest the $80 billion spent annually in the United States on "corrections," respondents prioritized education; job training, creation, and placement; and affordable housing. People know what drives instability and violence, and they know what types of investments and resources promote safety and well-being.

Risk factors that contribute to high levels of interpersonal violence include neighborhood poverty, lack of economic opportunities, a high density of retail alcohol outlets, residential segregation, lack of public transportation, and high rates of reentry from prison without adequate supports. Factors that prevent community violence include employment and economic opportunities, parks and recreation facilities where people can socialize and build strong networks, quality schools, accessible community centers, and opportunities for cultural and artistic expression.[17] Communities that experience high levels of violence do not simply lack these resources; they have also been subjected to investments in institutions that make communities unsafe. High incarceration rates *undermine* community social and economic well-being. Jails *produce* poverty, job loss, evictions, lack of housing, neighborhood instability, violence, trauma, debility, and death, making communities less safe and healthy.[18]

As part of a coordinated strategy to reduce violence, many violence prevention programs help meet people's basic needs for economic well-being, social supports, and housing. In Chicago, for instance, Heartland Alliance's Rapid Employment and Development Initiative (READI) connects men impacted by gun violence to crucial supports.[19] The one-year program includes cognitive behavioral therapy, paid transitional jobs, and wraparound support services. Recognizing the importance of safe, stable housing (an essential social determinant of health), it helps participants locate suitable housing, offers a rental subsidy, and provides ongoing landlord mediation.[20]

Advance Peace in Richmond also improves the health and economic well-being of people involved in gun violence. Like other violence interruption programs, Advance Peace connects people (mostly Black men between ages fourteen to twenty-seven) with mentorship, internships, job training, and support services. Participants receive a stipend to help meet economic needs and travel together to places such as Washington, DC, South Africa, and Mexico. Unlike other initiatives (such as CeaseFire, a multi-city focused deterrence strategy), Advance Peace does not share information from participants with the police or threaten punishment for noncompliance with the program. As one participant put it, "When I knew they weren't the police, that's when they gained my trust."[21] Between 2010, the year Advance Peace was launched, and 2017, firearm assaults causing injury or death in Richmond fell by two-thirds. Programs that meet people's basic needs exist. They work, and they do not require police or threats of punishment.

Organizers across the country provide models for how we can shift resources away from policing and incarceration and toward institutions, infrastructure, and programs that make communities safer. Addressing structural violence comes down to deciding how resources are allocated—which means it comes down to power. A number of organizations are building community-level initiatives to prevent and address violence, and shifting public resources through organizing campaigns.

In an effort led by the Colorado Criminal Justice Reform Coalition, formerly incarcerated people and their allies have won millions in reinvestment for housing, jobs, reentry supports, and health care, helping prevent violence and create communities where people can thrive. Colorado's Transforming Safety Initiative, launched after the state legislature passed the Justice Reinvestment Crime Prevention Initiative bill with bipartisan support in 2017, invests in the economic and community development of neighborhoods most impacted by crime and incarceration. Community members themselves identify safety priorities and solutions, and direct investments toward organizations that provide supports, such as housing for formerly incarcerated people. For example, the Second Chance Center's Providence at the Heights (PATH) housing project, which opened in 2020, provides fifty supportive low-income housing units, as well as a common area with views of nature, trauma-informed relaxation rooms, a kitchen for cooking classes, and a barbershop. It also employs counselors and connects residents to community-based health care, treatment, and employment services.[22]

In Atlanta in 2019, after pressure from formerly incarcerated women and their allies, the City Council moved to shut down the City Detention Center and repurpose the building as the Center for Equity, Wellness, and Freedom. Through this center, residents would be able to access health care, housing, childcare, and more. As activists fought to reduce pretrial incarceration, end cash bail, eliminate city ordinances that criminalize poverty, and cut city contracts with Immigration and Customs Enforcement, the jail population shrank from over one thousand to less than a hundred. Organizers articulated a vision for the reallocation of the $32.5 million spent annually on the jail, including funding the repurposed center to help meet communities' needs.

In Chicago, youth organizers with the #NoCopAcademy campaign helped ensure that calls to defund the police gain traction in the city. In fall 2020, 87 percent of the over 38,000 residents who participated in the city's budget survey supported redirecting funds from policing to community services and public health.[23] Relatedly, Chicago organizers are building sustainable local economies that do not rely on extraction and criminalization. On the South Side, for example, the coalition Just Chicago is building a non-exploitative "solidarity" economy and supporting safe, inviting public spaces using community land trusts, worker-owned cooperative businesses, participatory budgets, and public banks.[24] Another Chicago organization, Equity and Transformation, founded by and for formerly incarcerated and marginalized Black people, empowers those working in the informal economy. Equity and Transformation's work includes a guaranteed income pilot, helping Black and Latinx people navigate the cannabis dispensary licensure process, advocating for the Illinois BREATHE Act, and more.[25]

In Detroit, after the killing of George Floyd in the spring of 2020, youth organizers with 482Forward campaigned to remove police from Detroit schools, and called for the complete defunding of the Detroit Public Schools Community District Police Department. In addition, young people proposed the formation of a committee made up of parents, students, union leaders, youth development experts, administrators, and community leaders to oversee the defunding of police; create a holistic safety plan for schools including restorative justice training, peer-to-peer de-escalation training, and school safety initiatives; and evaluate the school district's educator training to ensure the process is anti-racist, anti-adultist, and trauma-informed.[26]

Organizers recognize that it is not merely the absence of police, but the presence of other protective factors that will make policing, criminalization, and incarceration obsolete. Durham Beyond Policing, which has provided a model for organizers in other cities to reallocate public funds toward true public safety, summarizes what is at stake:

> Cities and counties represent a local social contract to pool collective resources for the public good. We create cities like Durham based on a principle that we can live safer, more joyful lives by relying on the collective rather than the individual. Public safety thus entails an ongoing commitment to sustaining community through relationship building and accountability, not by severing people's ties to community and disposing of them. Our public resources are best used in the service of bolstering the integrity of communities, rather than undermining them.[27]

We now face a choice. We can keep pouring money into institutions that police, prosecute, and cage people—institutions which have never produced safety—or we can follow local organizers and community builders who are helping meet people's needs and creating safer communities.

To address violence without centering punishment, we must consider and emphasize the needs of those harmed by it. Healing reduces future harm. It is also inherently valuable; people are entitled to healing simply because they were hurt. Investing in healing both affirms the value of the person who was harmed and reasserts the values of the community that were breached.

Yet this country's legal court system is neither designed nor equipped to offer healing to survivors of violent crime. Crime survivors are disproportionately low-income, young people of color, and many experience significant challenges in recovery and healing; eight in ten report at least one symptom of trauma.[28] Researchers and practitioners are coming to understand what people with firsthand knowledge of the criminal punishment system have long known: investigations, prosecutions, and court processes are designed to mete out punishment, not to facilitate holistic, trauma-informed healing for survivors of violence.

Since the criminal punishment system cannot and should not perform healing labor, groups across the country have taken up this work. For example, Detroit Heals Detroit fosters healing justice for youth in ways that transform their pain into power. With a goal of combating trauma, participants use healing-centered engagement to share their "greatest vulnerabilities with the rest of the world while simultaneously working to dismantle oppressive systems for marginalized Detroit youth."[29]

Some of the most powerful models for such healing have deep roots in Indigenous and other cultural traditions. The National Compadres Network, for instance, uses the Healing Generations Framework, which promotes familial and community healing and addresses persistent community strife through retreats, gatherings, and the incorporation of Indigenous cultural practices.[30] Core principles include centering culture and healing in all service development and implementation; an intergenerational focus on elders, fathers, and the extended kinship network—or Compadres—taking responsibility for young men in the community; the long-standing traditional *huehuetlatolli* (wisdom of the elders) and *circulos de palabra* (talking/healing circles) to reclaim people's dignity, health, character, and strength; and principles of Un Hombre Noble (Noble Men), where honorable men are true to their word, have a sense of responsibility for their well-being and that of others in their circulos and the greater community, and build on their positive cultural traditions. At the programmatic level, La Cultura Cura, or Transformational Healing, promotes healing and healthy development by emphasizing cultural identity as the foundation of well-being for individuals, families, communities, and society.

In Albany, New York, Urban Grief, founded by Lisa W. Good, responds to the trauma of community violence, death, and loss through education, crisis response, victim advocacy, and grief support.[31] The organization understands that cycles of violence cannot end if harm remains unhealed, and thus creates spaces for people to process their grief amid chronic loss and pain. Relatedly, mothers who have lost children to violence have organized groups to support one another in healing. They undertake the grueling labor of grief, and many also work collectively to prevent others from experiencing similar loss. Many groups (including small nonprofits, as well as individuals unfalteringly dedicated to the work) gather in the network Mothers in Charge. Led by Dr. Dorothy Johnson-Speight, Mothers in Charge is a violence prevention, education, and intervention-based organization that advocates for and supports youth, young adults, families, and communities affected by violence.[32] Unlike many of the more familiar advocacy configurations of crime victims, who call for more policing and incarceration, these groups recognize that the criminal punishment system not only failed to protect their children but also often contributed to their deaths. In the names of their children, these groups call for new responses to violence that center prevention and healing.

Our criminal punishment system responds to the pain caused by violence by inflicting more pain—this time on the person who caused harm. But those who have suffered unthinkable losses insist that pain demands not more pain, but rather relief and healing. Many survivors find the criminal legal system process fundamentally re-traumatizing, as it doubts their memories, forces them to relive their pain, blames them and their loved ones for the harm they endured, places them at heightened risk of retaliatory violence from which it cannot protect them, and neither answers their questions nor provides opportunities to shape outcomes. Survivors demand and create another way, not typically because they philosophically disbelieve in punishment, but because the punishment system deployed in their names—and paid for with resources that could have helped them—is so inadequate.

Although prevention work is critical, no approach can prevent all violence. Structural conditions continue to generate violence, and healing work currently in process will take generations to achieve the mutually life-affirming social relations it seeks to produce. Since people, at least for now, continue to harm each other, communities need methods to address this harm. Restorative justice and transformative justice, among the most effective methods, have recently gained traction and popularity. But their core tenets are durable and rooted in long-standing traditions.

In restorative justice processes, all parties impacted by harm— survivors, those who caused harm, and their support people—come together to acknowledge the harm's impact and agree on ways the responsible party can make things as right as possible. These processes, which have roots in Indigenous practices, have been passed down through generations and created anew in countless communities and formations. Restorative justice processes, also called "circles," identify actions that help repair harm and ensure that similar harm—both to the survivor(s) and to others—will not recur. Transformative justice models, while consistent with restorative approaches to instances of harm, also consider the social conditions that give rise to violence. As described by generationFive, a collaborative that addresses child sexual abuse through an integrated approach to personal, community, and social transformation, transformative justice "seeks safety and accountability without relying on alienation, punishment, or state or systemic violence, including incarceration or policing."[33] Both restorative and transformative approaches respond to violence in ways that are positioned to end it. They address interpersonal harm by transforming relationships and behavior, and address structural violence by freeing people from the conditions that create and perpetuate pain.

Restorative justice has long been practiced both formally and informally. Over the past several decades, it has been used systematically as an "alternative" to courts and prisons. While most applications involve cases of nonviolent crime, such as theft and vandalism, some long-standing organizations dedicated to these processes, including Restorative Response Baltimore, also work with cases of more serious harm. Countless interventions and community leaders—including Cheryl Graves and the Community Justice for Youth Institute; Mariame Kaba, founding leader of both Project Nia and TransformHarm.org; and Mimi Kim and Creative Interventions—are building transformative responses to violence outside the criminal punishment system. Political conditions have limited the expansion of such alternative approaches to violence. These political constraints, however, must not be misattributed as limitations of the interventions themselves.

Still, the application of restorative justice to violence has largely been limited to young people in juvenile or family courts. Impact Justice, drawing on its demonstrated success in the Bay Area, is working nationwide to support such diversion work with an aim of reaching into the adult criminal court system. One organization that works exclusively with violent crime among adults is Common Justice, based in Brooklyn, New York, and run by one of the authors of this chapter. Common Justice diverts serious and violent felonies including robberies and assaults from the adult criminal court system into a highly successful, restorative justice violence intervention model. The model offers an alternative to prison for those responsible, and an avenue to healing for those harmed.

Harm requires repair. Punishment is not repair. Punishment is passive—it is done to us—but accountability is active. Accountability requires that we (1) acknowledge what we have done, (2) acknowledge its impact, (3) express genuine remorse, (4) make things as right as possible, ideally in ways defined by those harmed, and (5) commit to never again causing similar harm. Accountability is some of the hardest work people can do, and, unlike the passivity of punishment, the labor it requires produces positive change.[34]

Similarly, punishment hinges on shame. However, shame is a core driver of violence, so its cultivation undermines public safety.[35] Accountability, by contrast, grants people dignity. That dignity entails an obligation to take responsibility and make right. With punishment, society seeks to diminish and disempower someone who has caused harm. Accountability assumes instead that people can use their power to correct past harms.

Moreover, since most incarcerated people return home and continue living in communities, we must consider the goals of our responses to violence. Do we wish people who have caused harm to be shaped by prison or by processes of restorative justice?[36] No safe neighborhood is populated by ashamed, isolated, injured, disenfranchised people. As such, we must respond to violence not with prison—characterized by shame, isolation, injury, and disenfranchisement—but with restorative justice. Restorative justice recognizes and develops the very human attributes—dignity, connectedness, healing, responsibility, and agency—that help avert violence. It offers a rational, pragmatic, coherent approach to violence that helps produce short- and long-term safety.

Society, when responding to violence, must not only account for the interests of the responsible party and the larger community; there is also an obligation to the survivor. This only strengthens the argument for restorative justice to displace incarceration as our primary response to violence. The popular image of survivors as mostly white and mostly vengeful is inaccurate. Not only are people of color far more likely to experience violence than white people, but, when given the choice, a vast majority of survivors across races prefer alternatives to incarceration.

At Common Justice, people responsible for violence are given the opportunity to participate in the program only if the survivors of their crimes agree. All these survivors participated in the criminal court system, placing them in the minority of victims who called the police, and the even smaller minority who continued their engagement through the grand jury process. They are people who suffered serious violence— wounds from knives and guns, lacerations to their livers, punctured lungs—and people who initially chose a path that could lead to prison. Even among these survivors, however, 90 percent chose restorative justice when it was offered.[37] Ninety percent is a stunning number, and it challenges common narratives that harsh punishments benefit survivors. Among this group that opts for restorative justice, some choose it for more philosophical reasons, motivated by compassion, forgiveness, the belief that people can change, an experience of causing harm themselves or loving someone who did, or a desire to support transformation. But most survivors choose restorative justice because they are pragmatic. They believe something other than incarceration will better meet their needs for safety and justice, and will more reliably prevent others from facing similar harm.

Evidence supports this view. Restorative justice processes substantially reduce recidivism. Moreover, survivors express greater satisfaction with these approaches than with the criminal court system.[38] This makes sense; restorative justice processes meet survivors' needs, including answers to their questions, an opportunity to be heard, acknowledgment of their pain, and a sense of power over the outcome of the harm. Survivors want to help shape repair. They want assurance that the person who harmed them will change their behavior and refrain from causing further harm. They want to form a coherent narrative that can act as scaffolding for their healing.

Survivors' experiences and needs vary. Yet nearly all survivors of violence want two things: to know that the person who hurt them will not hurt them again, and to know that the person will not hurt anyone else.[39] Restorative justice, particularly when informed by transformative justice processes aimed at changing the conditions that gave rise to violence, offers a promising path to meet those desires. Restorative and transformational justice processes do something policing and prisons cannot: deliver on the promise of true safety.

Ultimately, our current dominant approaches to violence—policing and incarceration—do not work. Policing and incarceration enact and exacerbate large-scale structural harm while simultaneously treating violence as though it depends on individual behavior. Violence is a public health issue, and, as we have learned too well through the COVID-19 pandemic, public health issues cannot be punished away. Violence results from inequity and a lack of opportunity; policing and incarceration exacerbate these things, both through their immediate application and through the collateral consequences attached to convictions. Violence is the product of pain, and policing and incarceration reproduce, rather than heal, pain. Violence requires accountability and repair; policing and incarceration systematically separate people from both things to the detriment of those responsible for harm and those who survive it. It is not surprising, then, that incarceration has been shown to be criminogenic— meaning that it is a measurable, statistically significant *driver* of crime and violence. After all, its defining features are things that generate violence.

The community safety strategies described above consistently and overwhelmingly reduce violence more effectively than criminal legal interventions. Still, they are vastly underutilized compared with surveillance, arrests, convictions, and incarceration. What prevents us from drawing on and growing solutions that are known to be effective?

One barrier is the notion that we must start from scratch, that the project requires a blank slate. Fortunately, this is not the case: solutions have long existed among us. The solutions answer the question, *Why isn't there more violence?* They explain why we have the safety we do have, why harm sometimes diminishes rather than escalates, how people become well individually and together. They are what have enabled Black, Indigenous, and other communities of color to persist, heal, and thrive despite centuries of white supremacist violence, both individual and structural. The solutions may not be known to some people with the authority to determine governmental responses to violence, but they are known to thousands, even millions of people, oftentimes informally and without the labels or categories offered here. They have been handed down across generations and reshaped and regenerated by young people countless times.

Certainly, a future without violence will require imagination. But the idea that we must start from scratch is inaccurate, ahistorical, and racist.

Another barrier to the expansion of community safety strategies is political. Many alternatives to the criminal punishment system are seen as "soft" on crime, and being soft on crime has often been a losing political position. Fearmongering is a tried and tested campaign strategy for elected prosecutors, sheriffs, mayors, and legislators; looming over criminal legal system reform agendas is the prospect of someone being released from incarceration and causing further harm. This approach is shifting, however. Over the past several years, prosecutors—in Chicago, St. Louis, San Francisco, Los Angeles, Baltimore, New Orleans, Brooklyn, and other communities—have run on proposals to reduce incarceration while increasing safety and racial equity. And they are winning. In a country where one in two people has had a loved one incarcerated, more and more people know that policing and incarceration do not ensure justice or safety.[40] Elected officials are increasingly embracing the views of their constituents, particularly constituents who will be directly impacted by criminal justice policy and who often make up majorities in their districts.

Indeed, the most significant barrier to the expansion of these solutions is power—political power, narrative power, and economic power. Political power includes the capacity of a group of people to ensure elected officials act in their interest and the interests of their loved ones. It also includes the capacity to develop and sustain solutions outside of and apart from the state apparatus. This connects to the power to define what constitutes safety and to choose how it will be achieved.

Narrative power is about which stories shape our culture and how. It includes not only broad visibility but the power to influence society and to render certain things possible and others impossible. As Color of Change explains, narrative power is "the ability to create leverage over those who set the incentives, rules, and norms that shape society and human behavior."[41] Too many popular stories demonize people who commit violence; conflate Blackness and dangerousness; center certain survivors at the expense of others; and foreclose options and imagination. Narrative power is not just about which stories get told, but the ability of those stories to determine our collective behavior.

In terms of economic power, the state has funded policing and prisons at the expense of schools, hospitals, public health systems, healthy food and clean water, mental health and substance use disorder treatment, and other solutions to interpersonal violence. We have systematically divested from the things that reduce violence while investing in the things that produce it. To promote public safety meaningfully and permanently, we must invert where the money goes.

Public debate has primarily asked: *Can we be safe while defunding the police*? Instead, we should ask: *Can we be safe* without *defunding the police*? There are two reasons why we cannot. The first is simple: resources are not unlimited. Budgets are moral documents that require trade-offs. As is, we spend virtually all our safety money on police instead of funding resources and social supports that actually reduce violence. Second, policing as we know it actively undermines both individual and structural approaches to producing safety. It generates racial inequity, a driver of violence. It responds to harm with separation, even though safety emerges through connection. Policing inflicts violence that exacerbates historic harm. And, it enforces collateral consequences that reduce economic and social well-being, even though the ability to meet one's basic needs and contribute to one's community protects against violence. Currently, interventions that are successfully producing safety are doing so not only without adequate resources, but also in spite of the interruption of their work by police and by the criminal punishment system.

Displacing police and prison is not primarily a project of doing less. As abolitionists including Dr. Angela Davis and Dr. Ruth Wilson Gilmore teach us, displacing these systems involves creation, not destruction. To end violence, we must ask, *What is currently producing safety? What barriers exist to the expansion of those strategies?* An honest and rigorous account reveals that policing and the enormous quantity of resources it consumes is one of the largest barriers to public safety. It is, as such, our duty to make urgent changes so that people can and will survive.

THE SQUARE ONE PROJECT

In the spring of 2018, the Justice Lab at Columbia University launched The Square One Project—a multi-year effort to imagine a new vision for the future of justice. The project brought together a range of perspectives to take on this challenge: abolitionists and reformers; optimists and skeptics; Republicans and Democrats; community organizers, academics, and government officials; formerly incarcerated leaders and law enforcement professionals. Square One asked a group of twenty-nine people to take part in a series of sustained, facilitated conversations. Together, they set out to excavate the interwoven roots of injustice—racism, economic injustice, and violence—learning from and leaning on each other for the ideas and solutions that are represented in the chapters of this book.

This process was neither comfortable nor easy. Each person brought specific life experiences that shaped their own perspectives on harm, healing, and safety. Members talked, argued, grieved, expressed anger, experienced awe, slumped their shoulders in shame, and lit up with hope. There were moments when an observation left everyone speechless. There were others when someone got up from the table—out of frustration, to clear their head, to provide comfort to another. Over three years, every person was asked to balance their personal and professional lives to teach and to learn from one another. Seeing the process all the way through took love, humility, grace, patience, courage, and a tremendous amount of hard work.

Through The Square One Project, this volume's contributing authors begin to reimagine justice. In doing so, they envision a society that responds to harm in ways that are less punishing, more healing, and socially integrative. Their writings seek to challenge conventional wisdom. They grapple with history to understand the present and consider a different future. They reflect radical ideas—some old, some new—that try to get to the root of what justice should be. The chapters do not present a consensus; the authors each speak for themselves. But taken together, they point a way forward, urging us to recommit to the pursuit of justice—not just for some, but for all.

This opportunity to work collaboratively, to engage in civil discourse, and to think radically about justice would not have been possible without the support of the John D. and Catherine T. MacArthur Foundation's Safety and Justice Challenge. The Square One Project is grateful for the foundation's belief in the power of intentional conversations to advance change, and for the deep engagement and partnership of Laurie Garduque, Director of Criminal Justice. We greatly appreciate the excellent editing work of Madison Dawkins, Shaina Evans, Rachel Krul, Evie Lopoo, Sarah McGavick, Jasmin Sandelson, and Sonia Tsuruoka; the support of Columbia University and our colleagues at the Columbia Justice Lab; and the vision and guidance of Diane Wachtell and the entire team at The New Press. Most of all, Square One is indebted to each contributor, and all the members of the group, for their willingness to bring such wisdom and experience to this emotional and intellectual process.

Katharine Huffman
Executive Director, The Square One Project

Anamika Dwivedi
Manager, Executive Session on the Future of Justice Policy

NOTES

Introduction: Reimagining Justice

1. Throughout this volume, some contributors use the term "criminal legal system," and others say "criminal justice system." The preference for "criminal legal system" is justified by the argument that criminal justice is descriptively inaccurate for a system whose outcomes are often unjust. However, the same criticism applies to the term "criminal legal system." Police and correctional officers, for example, often act outside the law, and, as the historian Khalil Muhammad has argued, the system itself was founded on lawlessness. While the system is certainly not just, neither is it particularly legal. Still, both terms have nominal but not substantive meaning, designating the institutions of police, criminal courts, jails, and penal supervision. "Criminal justice," being in more common usage, is used in this introduction. Khalil Gibran Muhammad, "The Foundational Lawlessness of the Law Itself: Racial Criminalization and the Punitive Roots of Punishment in America," *Daedalus* 2022; 151 (1): 107–120.

2. Jeremy Travis et al., "Punitive Excess," Brennan Center for Justice, April 13, 2021, www.brennancenter.org/series/punitive-excess.

3. Shannon Tracy, "Statement of Principles," Right On Crime, July 21, 2016, https://rightoncrime.com/statement-of-principles/.

4. "Vision for Black Lives," Movement for Black Lives, April 28, 2021, https://m4bl.org/policy-platforms/.

5. Angela Y. Davis, *Are Prisons Obsolete?* (Seven Stories Press, 2011).

1. The Power of Parsimony

1. We recognize that the state can limit individual liberty in many ways, such as requiring school attendance for young people, conscripting adults into military service, or imposing restrictions on travel in the name of public health. Here we analyze those limits on liberty imposed through enforcement of the criminal law.

2. Derecka Purnell, "How I Became a Police Abolitionist," *The Atlantic*, July 6, 2020, www.theatlantic.com/ideas/archive/2020/07/how-i-became-police-abolitionist/613540/.

3. Pierre Bourdieu, "The Left Hand and the Right Hand of the State," *Variant*, January 14, 1992, www.variant.org.uk/32texts/bourdieu32.html.

4. Cesare Bonesana and Marchese Beccaria, "Of Crimes and Punishments," 1764, criminologytoday.com/beccaria.pdf.

5. Jeremy Bentham, "An Introduction to the Principles of Morals and Legislation," n.d., www.earlymoderntexts.com/assets/pdfs/bentham1780.pdf.

6. Norval Morris, "The Future of Imprisonment: Toward a Punitive Philosophy," *Michigan Law Review* 72, no. 6 (1974): 1161, doi.org/10.2307/1287619. This article is a revised version of the third of three lectures given by the author in the Thomas M. Colley Lecture Series.

7. Morris, "The Future of Imprisonment: Toward a Punitive Philosophy."

8. Morris, "The Future of Imprisonment: Toward a Punitive Philosophy."

9. Michael Tonry, "Fairness, Equality, Proportionality, and Parsimony: Towards a Comprehensive Jurisprudence of Just Punishment," SSRN Scholarly Paper, Social Science Research Network, January 29, 2017, papers.ssrn.com/abstract=2912344.

10. American Law Institute, "Model Penal Code," www.ali.org/publications/show /model-penal-code/.

11. American Law Institute, "Model Penal Code."

12. Mary Bosworth, "Introduction: Reinventing Penal Parsimony," *Theoretical Criminology* 14, no. 3 (August 2010): 251–56, doi.org/10.1177/1362480610373219.

13. Jamie Fellner, "Lawmakers Should Be Parsimonious—Not Sanctimonious— on Drug Sentencing," *The Hill*, June 14, 2014, thehill.com/blogs/congress-blog /judicial/209325-lawmakers-should-be-parsimonious-not-sanctimonious-on-drug.

14. Jeremy Travis, Bruce Western, and Steve Redburn, eds., *The Growth of Incarceration in the United States: Exploring Causes and Consequences*, National Research Council (Washington, DC: National Academies Press, 2014), doi.org/10.17226/18613.

15. Travis, Western, and Redburn, *The Growth of Incarceration in the United States*.

16. Travis, Western, and Redburn, *The Growth of Incarceration in the United States*.

17. Morris, "The Future of Imprisonment."

18. Travis, Western, and Redburn, *The Growth of Incarceration in the United States*.

19. It's important to note that there are many other measures of success under the rehabilitation rationale—e.g., employment, improved health.

20. Travis, Western, and Redburn, *The Growth of Incarceration in the United States*.

21. Leigh Courtney et al., *A Matter of Time: Causes and Consequences of Rising Time Served in America's Prisons*, Urban Institute, July 2017, https://apps.urban.org/features /long-prison-terms/a_matter_of_time_print_version.pdf; Danielle Sered, *Until We Reckon: Violence, Mass Incarceration, and a Road to Repair* (New York: The New Press, 2021).

22. Laura M. Maruschak, Lauren E. Glaze, and Thomas Bonczar, "Adults on Parole, Federal and State-By-State, 1975–2012," Bureau of Justice Statistics, December 2013, https://bjs.ojp.gov/library/publications/adults-parole-federal-and-state-state-1975-2012.

23. Jeremy Travis, "Invisible Punishment: An Instrument of Social Exclusion," in *Invisible Punishment: The Collateral Consequences of Mass Imprisonment*, ed. Marc Mauer and Meda Chesney-Lind (New York: The New Press, 2002), 15–36.

24. "About CCRC," Collateral Consequences Resource Center, ccresourcecenter.org/about-the-collateral-consequences-resource-center/.

25. The Collateral Consequences Resource Center's Restoration of Rights project includes a fifty-state comparison on the restrictions on the lives of people convicted of sex offenses. "Restoration of Rights Project," Collateral Consequences Resource Center, https://ccresourcecenter.org/restoration-2/.

26. "Welcome to the NICCC," National Inventory of Collateral Consequences of Criminal Conviction, https://niccc.nationalreentryresourcecenter.org/.

27. American Bar Association, *Second Chances in the Criminal Justice System: Alternatives to Incarceration and Reentry Strategies*, American Bar Association, Commission on Effective Criminal Sanctions, Washington, DC, 2007.

28. U.S. Commission on Civil Rights, "Collateral Consequences: The Crossroads of Punishment, Redemption, and the Effects on Communities," U.S. Commission on Civil Rights, Washington, DC, June 2019, www.usccr.gov/files/pubs/2019/06-13-Collateral-Consequences.pdf?eType=EmailBlastContent&eId=d37030a2-bfe6-4784-866a-7db61d64f357.

29. Travis, Western, and Redburn, *The Growth of Incarceration in the United States*.

30. Travis, Western, and Redburn, *The Growth of Incarceration in the United States*.

31. Jeremy Travis, "But They All Come Back: Rethinking Prisoner Reentry," *Sentencing & Corrections* no. 7 (2000): 11, www.ojp.gov/pdffiles1/nij/181413.pdf.

32. Kirsten Weir, "Alone, in 'the Hole,'" *Monitor on Psychology* 43, no. 5 (May 2012): 54, www.apa.org/monitor/2012/05/solitary.

33. Craig Haney, "Mental Health Issues in Long-Term Solitary and 'Supermax' Confinement," *Crime & Delinquency* 49, no. 1 (January 2003): 124–56, doi.org/10.1177/0011128702239239.

34. The United Nations has adopted the "Nelson Mandela Rule," which if followed would impose restrictions on the use of solitary confinement. United Nations, Office on Drugs and Crime, "Nelson Mandela Rules," www.unodc.org/unodc/en/justice-and-prison-reform/NMRules.html.

35. Correctional Leaders Association and Arthur Liman Center for Public Interest Law, *Time-In-Cell 2019: A Snapshot of Restrictive Housing Based on a Nationwide Survey of U.S. Prison Systems*, Yale Law School, September 2020, law.yale.edu/sites/default/files/area/center/liman/document/time-in-cell_2019.pdf.

36. Solitary Watch, *Louisiana on Lockdown: A Report on the Use of Solitary Confinement in Louisiana State Prisons, with Testimony from the People Who Live It*, June 2019, American Civil Liberties Union of Louisiana, https://solitarywatch.org/wp-content/uploads/2019/06/Louisiana-on-Lockdown-Report-June-2019.pdf.

37. Haney, "Mental Health Issues in Long-Term Solitary and 'Supermax' Confinement"; Paul Gendreau et al., "Changes in EEG Alpha Frequency and Evoked Response

Latency During Solitary Confinement," *Journal of Abnormal Psychology* 79, no. 1 (1972): 54–59, doi.org/10.1037/h0032339; Stuart Grassian, "Psychiatric Effects of Solitary Confinement," *Washington University Journal of Law & Policy* 22, no. 325 (January 2006): 60, openscholarship.wustl.edu/law_journal_law_policy/vol22/iss1/24; Stuart Grassian, "Psychopathological Effects of Solitary Confinement," *American Journal of Psychiatry* 140, no. 11 (November 1983): 1450–54, doi.org/10.1176/ajp.140.11.1450.

38. Kaba Fatos et al., "Solitary Confinement and Risk of Self-Harm Among Jail Inmates," *American Journal of Public Health* 104, no. 3 (February 2014): 442–47, doi .org/10.2105/AJPH.2013.301742.

39. Hannah Pullen-Blasnik, Jessica T. Simes, and Bruce Western, "The Population Prevalence of Solitary Confinement," *Science Advances* 7, no. 48 (November 2011), doi .org/10.1126/sciadv.abj1928.

40. Alison Shames, Jessa Wilcox, and Ram Subramanian, *Solitary Confinement: Common Misconceptions and Emerging Safe Alternatives*, Vera Institute of Justice, May 2015, www.vera.org/publications/solitary-confinement-common-misconceptions-and-emerging -safe-alternatives.

41. Judith Resnik, "(Un)Constitutional Punishments: Eighth Amendment Silos, Penological Purposes, and People's 'Ruin,'" *Yale Law Journal* 129 (January 2020), www.yale lawjournal.org/forum/unconstitutional-punishments.

42. David Garland, "Criminal Justice and the Social Contract," Columbia University Justice Lab, August 2020, squareonejustice.org/wp-content/uploads/2020/08/David-Garland-Criminal-Justice-and-the-Social-Contract.pdf.

2. Presumption of Liberty: Reducing Pretrial Incarceration

1. Equal Justice Initiative, *Lynching in America: Confronting the Legacy of Racial Terror*, 3rd ed., 2017, lynchinginamerica.eji.org/report/.

2. "Understanding Trends in Jail Populations, 2014–2019: A Multi-Site Analysis," Data Collaborative for Justice, John Jay College of Criminal Justice, January 2022, https://datacollaborativeforjustice.org/work/confinement/understanding-trends-in-jail -populations-2014-2019-a-multi-site-analysis/.

3. Wendy Sawyer and Peter Wagner, "Mass Incarceration: The Whole Pie 2022," Prison Policy Initiative, March 14, 2022, https://www.prisonpolicy.org/reports/pie2022 .html.

4. Melissa Neal, "Bail Fail: Why the U.S. Should End the Practice of Using Money for Bail," Justice Policy Institute, September 2012, www.justicepolicy.org/uploads/justice policy/documents/bailfail.pdf; Spike Bradford, "For Better or For Profit: How the Bail Bond Industry Stands in the Way of Fair and Effective Pretrial Justice," Justice Policy Institute, September 2012, www.justicepolicy.org/wp-content/uploads/justicepolicy/docu ments/_for_better_or_for_profit.pdf.

5. Nick Peterson, "Low Level, but High Speed? Assessing Pretrial Detention Effects on the Timing and Content of Misdemeanor Versus Felony Guilty Pleas," *Justice Quarterly* 36, no. 7 (July 2019): 1314–35.

6. "Magna Carta," British Library, n.d., www.bl.uk/magna-carta.

7. Robert Gebelhoff, "The Right to a Fair Trial: A Primer," *Washington Post*, January 19, 2016.

8. Dattatreya Mandal, "The Code of Hammurabi: 10 Things You Should Know," The Realm of History: The Future Lies in the Past, September 6, 2019, www.realmofhistory .com/2019/09/06/10-incredible-facts-about-the-code-of-hammurabi/.

9. John Adams, "Adams' Argument for the Defense: 3–4 December 1770," National Archives and Records Administration, Founders Online, founders.archives.gov /documents/Adams/05-03-02-0001-0004-0016.

10. *Coffin v. United States*, 156 U.S. 432 (1895).

11. United States Congress, "H.R.5865 – 98th Congress (1983–1984): Bail Reform Act of 1984," www.congress.gov/bill/98th-congress/house-bill/5865.

12. *United States v. Salerno*, 481 U.S. 739 (1987).

13. Matthew G. Rowland, "The Rising Federal Pretrial Detention Rate, in Context," *Federal Probation* 82, no. 2 (September 2018), www.uscourts.gov/sites/default/files /82_2_2_0.pdf.

14. Michael Louis Corrado, "Punishment and the Wild Beast of Prey: The Problem of Preventive Detention," *Journal of Criminal Law and Criminology* 86, no. 3 (1996): 778–814.

15. Connecticut General Assembly, Constitution of the State of Connecticut, § Article 1, Section 8, www.cga.ct.gov/asp/Content/constitutions/CTConstitution.htm.

16. National Conference of State Legislatures, "Pretrial Release Eligibility," March 13, 2013, www.ncsl.org/research/civil-and-criminal-justice/pretrial-release-eligibility.aspx.

17. Connecticut Sentencing Commission, *Report to the Governor and the General Assembly on Pretrial Release and Detention in Connecticut*, February 2017, www.ct.gov/ctsc /lib/ctsc/Pretrial_Release_and_Detention_in_CT_2.14.2017.pdf.

18. Alysia Santo, "Kentucky's Protracted Struggle to Get Rid of Bail," The Marshall Project, November 12, 2015, www.themarshallproject.org/2015/11/12/kentucky-s -protracted-struggle-to-get-rid-of-bail.

19. Glenn Grant, *Jan. 1–Dec. 31, 2018 Criminal Justice Reform Report to the Governor and the Legislature*, New Jersey Judiciary, April 2019, njcourts.gov/courts/assets /criminal/2018cjrannual.pdf?c=taP.

20. Grant, *Jan. 1–Dec. 31, 2018 Criminal Justice Reform Report*, 8.

21. Grant, *Jan. 1–Dec. 31, 2018 Criminal Justice Reform Report*, 45.

22. Alexander Volokh, "N Guilty Men," *University of Pennsylvania Law Review* 146, no. 173 (1997): 173–216, scholarship.law.upenn.edu/cgi/viewcontent.cgi?article=3427&con text=penn_law_review; Adams, "Adams' Argument for the Defense."

23. Michael J. Klarman, "The Racial Origins of Modern Criminal Procedure," *Michigan Law Review* 99, no. 1 (October 2000): 48–97.

24. William F. Fox Jr., "The 'Presumption of Innocence' as Constitutional Doctrine," *Catholic University Law Review* 28, no. 2 (1979): 253–69, scholarship.law.edu/lawreview/vol28/iss2/3.

25. *Taylor v. Kentucky*, 436 U.S. 478, 484 (1978).

26. Fox, "The 'Presumption of Innocence,'" 261.

27. Lars Trautman and SteVon Felton, "The Use of Lay Magistrates in the United States," R Street Institute, May 2019, www.rstreet.org/wp-content/uploads/2019/05/Final-No.-173.pdf.

28. Megan T. Stevenson, "The Distortion of Justice: How the Inability to Pay Bail Affects Case Outcomes," University of Pennsylvania Law School Working Paper, 26; Paul Heaton, Sandra Mayson, and Megan Stevenson, "The Downstream Consequences of Misdemeanor Pretrial Detention," *Stanford Law Review* 69, no. 3 (March 2017), 711; Insha Rahman and Chris Mai, *Empire State of Incarceration*, Vera Institute of Justice, 2017, https://www.vera.org/state-ofincarceration.

29. Pretrial Justice Institute, "The State of Pretrial Justice in America," November 2017, university.pretrial.org/HigherLogic/System/DownloadDocumentFile.ashx?DocumentFileKey=484affbc-d944-5abb-535f-b171d091a3c8&forceDialog=0.

30. Sandra Mayson, "Dangerous Defendants," *Yale Law Journal* 127 (2018): 490–568.

31. Yousur Al-Hlou et al., "How Coronavirus at Rikers Puts All of N.Y.C. at Risk," *New York Times*, April 8, 2020.

32. Peterson, "Low Level, but High Speed?"

33. Stephanos Bibas, "Plea Bargaining Outside the Shadow of Trial," *Harvard Law Review* 117, no. 8 (2004): 2463–547; Bowers, "Punishing the Innocent."

34. Peterson. "Low Level, but High Speed?"

35. Will Dobbie, Jacob Goldin, and Crystal Yang, "The Effects of Pre-trial Detention on Conviction, Future Crime, and Employment: Evidence from Randomly Assigned Judges," *American Economic Review* 108, no. 2 (February 2018): 201–40; Arpit Gupta, Christopher Hansman, and Ethan Frenchman, "The Heavy Costs of High Bail: Evidence from Judge Randomization," *Journal of Legal Studies* 45, no. 2 (June 2016): 471–505.

36. Bibas, "Plea Bargaining Outside the Shadow of Trial."

37. Peterson, "Low Level, but High Speed?"

38. Peterson, "Low Level, but High Speed?"

39. The Center for Evidence-Based Crime Policy, "Michael Wilson – Pretrial Cost-Benefit Analysis," YouTube, April 5, 2014, www.youtube.com/watch?v=e549oEJ7ULw.

40. Heaton, Mayson, and Stevenson, "The Downstream Consequences of Misdemeanor Pretrial Detention."

41. *Stack et al. v. Boyle*, 342 U.S. 1 (1951).

42. Brian Palmer, "Can States Exile People?," *Slate*, January 24, 2013.

43. Office of the Chief Clerk of the Senate, Constitution of the State of Tennessee (2014), www.capitol.tn.gov/about/docs/tn-constitution.pdf; Delegates of Maryland, Constitution of Maryland, 1776, www.nhinet.org/ccs/docs/md-1776.htm; Palmer, "Can States Exile People?"; Nancy Gertner, "A Short History of American Sentencing: Too Little Law, Too Much Law, or Just Right," *Journal of Criminal Law and Criminology* 100, no. 3 (2010): 691–708.

44. Harry Elmer Barnes, "Historical Origin of the Prison System in America," *Journal of Criminal Law and Criminology* 12, no. 1 (1921): 35–60, scholarlycommons.law.north western.edu/cgi/viewcontent.cgi?article=1772&context=jclc.

45. Mary Freeman, "Time and Punishment: Parents Whose Kids Break Curfew Face Stockade," *Sunday Telegraph* (Nashua, NH), August 13, 1989, news.google.com/newspapers?nid=2209&dat=19890813&id=CvYlAAAAIBAJ&sjid=R_wFAAAAIBAJ&pg=6975,3114559.

46. Reinforcing this idea was the fact that enslaved peoples were not incarcerated in the antebellum South.

47. Laura I. Appleman, "Justice in the Shadowlands: Pretrial Detention, Punishment, & the Sixth Amendment," *Washington and Lee Law Review* 69, no. 3 (June 2012): 1297–1369.

48. *Stack et al. v. Boyle.*

49. Christopher T. Lowenkamp, Marie VanNostrand, and Alexander Holsinger, "The Hidden Costs of Pretrial Detention," Laura and John Arnold Foundation, November 2013, craftmediabucket.s3.amazonaws.com/uploads/PDFs/LJAF_Report_hidden-costs_FNL .pdf.

50. Lowenkamp, VanNostrand, and Holsinger, "The Hidden Costs of Pretrial Detention," 11.

51. Lowenkamp, VanNostrand, and Holsinger, "The Hidden Costs of Pretrial Detention," 10.

52. Centers for Disease Control, "Legal Authorities for Isolation and Quarantine," February 24, 2020, www.cdc.gov/quarantine/aboutlawsregulationsquarantineisolation.html.

53. Ann E. Marimow, "When It Comes to Pretrial Release, Few Other Jurisdictions Do It D.C.'s Way," *Washington Post*, July 4, 2016.

54. Serge F. Kovaleski, "Justice Delayed: 10 Years in Jail, but Still Awaiting Trial," *New York Times*, September 19, 2017.

55. Grant, *Jan. 1–Dec. 31 2018 Criminal Justice Reform Report.*

56. Adams, "Adams' Argument for the Defense."

3. Least Restrictive Environment: The Case for Closing Youth Prisons

1. W.J. Bennett, J. DiIulio, and J.P. Walters, *Body Count: Moral Poverty and How to Win America's War Against Crime and Drugs* (New York: Simon and Schuster, 1996),

26; Fox Butterfield, "Serious Crimes Fall for Third Year, but Experts Warn Against Seeing Trend," *New York Times*, May 23, 1995.

2. Lori Dorfman and Vincent Schiraldi, *Off Balance: Youth, Race & Crime in the News*, Justice Policy Institute, April 1, 2001, p. 40.

3. Melissa Sickmund and Charles Puzzanchera, *Juvenile Offenders and Victims: 2014 National Report*, National Center for Juvenile Justice, 2014, p. 86.

4. Barry Feld, "Criminalizing the American Juvenile Court," *Crime & Justice* 17 (1993): 264, doi.org/10.1086/449214; Coalition for Juvenile Justice, *A Celebration or a Wake? The Juvenile Court After 100 Years*, 1998, www.juvjustice.org/sites/default/files /resource-files/resource_125_0.pdf.

5. Vincent Schiraldi, "Will the Real John DiIulio Please Stand Up," *Washington Post*, February 5, 2001.

6. Eleanor Hinton Hoytt et al., *Reducing Racial Disparities in Juvenile Detention: Pathways to Juvenile Detention Reform*, Annie E. Casey Foundation, 2002, eric.ed .gov/?id=ED467685, 10.

7. Wendy Sawyer, "Youth Confinement: The Whole Pie 2019," Prison Policy Initiative, December 19, 2019, www.prisonpolicy.org/reports/youth2019.html.

8. Jason Ziedenberg, *You're an Adult Now: Youth in Adult Criminal Justice Systems*, U.S. Department of Justice, National Institute of Corrections, 2011, s3.amazonaws.com /static.nicic.gov/Library/025555.pdf, 2; Allen J. Beck and Jennifer C. Karberg, *Prison and Jail Inmates at Midyear 2000*, U.S. Department of Justice, Bureau of Justice Statistics, March 2001, bjs.ojp.gov/library/publications/prison-and-jail-inmates-midyear-2000, 5–6.

9. Office of Juvenile Justice and Delinquency Prevention (OJJDP), "Statistical Briefing Book," 2022, www.ojjdp.gov/ojstatbb; Melissa Sickmund et al., "Easy Access to the Census of Juveniles in Residential Placement. Bureau of Justice Statistics," Washington, DC: U.S. Department of Justice, 2019.

10. Vincent Schiraldi, Marc Schindler, and Sean J. Goliday, "The End of the Reform School?," in *Juvenile Justice: Advancing Research, Policy, and Practice*, ed. Francine T. Sherman and Francine H. Jacobs, 1st ed. (Hoboken, NJ: Wiley, 2011), 409–32.

11. Jill Tucker and Joaquin Palomino, "Vanishing Violence: Examining the Fall of Youth Crime in California," *San Francisco Chronicle*, March 21, 2019.

12. Office of California Governor Gavin Newsom, "Revised Budget Summary: Public Safety," California State Government, 2020, www.ebudget.ca.gov/2020-21/pdf/Revised /BudgetSummary/PublicSafety.pdf.

13. OJJDP, "Statistical Briefing Book."

14. Marcy Mistrett, "15 Years of Impact: How We Won," Campaign for Youth Justice, 2020, www.campaignforyouthjustice.org/15-years-of-impact-how-we-won.

15. Federal Bureau of Investigation, "Crime in the U.S. 2000, Section IV: Persons Arrested," 2000, ucr.fbi.gov/crime-in-the-u.s/2000/00sec4.pdf, 226; Federal Bureau of Investigation, Uniform Crime Reporting, "Crime in the U.S. 2018, Table 38: Arrests, by Age,"

ucr.fbi.gov/crime-in-the-u.s/2018/crime-in-the-u.s.-2018/tables/table-38/table-38.xls; U.S. Census Bureau, "U.S. Summary: 2000," 2002, www2.census.gov/library/publications /decennial/2000/c2kprof00-us/c2kprof00-us.pdf; U.S. Census Bureau, "National Population by Characteristics: 2010–2019," www.census.gov/data/tables/time-series/demo/pop est/2010s-national-detail.html.

16. From 1997 to 2017, there has been an 87 percent decline in the number of youths held in facilities of more than two hundred people. See OJJDP, "Statistical Briefing Book."

17. Schiraldi, Schindler, and Goliday, "The End of the Reform School?"

18. National Research Council, *Reforming Juvenile Justice: A Developmental Approach*, ed. Richard J. Bonnie et al. (Washington, DC: National Academies Press, 2013), doi.org/10.17226/14685.

19. Richard Mendel, *No Place for Kids: The Case for Reducing Juvenile Incarceration*, Annie E. Casey Foundation, 2011, www.aecf.org/resources/no-place-for-kids-full-report, 10.

20. Anna Aizer and Joseph J. Doyle Jr., "Juvenile Incarceration, Human Capital and Future Crime: Evidence from Randomly-Assigned Judges," Working Paper 19102, National Bureau of Economic Research, June 2013, doi.org/10.3386/w19102.

21. OJJDP, "Statistical Briefing Book."

22. Starting in 2017, OJJDP stopped including the race "Latino" in its sampling criteria. Instead, survey data included the ethnicity "Hispanic" or "Non-Hispanic"; thus, after 2015, Latino-white racial disparities cannot be determined. See OJJDP, "Statistical Briefing Book"; The Sentencing Project, "Latinx Disparities in Youth Incarceration," 2017, www .sentencingproject.org/wp-content/uploads/2017/10/Latinx-Disparities-in-Youth-Incar ceration.pdf.

23. Christopher Harney and Fabiana Silva, *And Justice for Some: Differential Treatment of Youth of Color in the Justice System*, National Council on Crime and Delinquency, January 2007, evidentchange.org/sites/default/files/publication_pdf/justice-for-some.pdf, 1–3.

24. Carl E. Pope, Rick Lovell, and Heidi M. Hsia, "Disproportionate Minority Confinement: A Review of the Research Literature from 1989 Through 2001," U.S. Department of Justice, Office of Justice Programs, www.ojp.gov/ncjrs/virtual-library/abstracts /disproportionate-minority-confinement-review-research-literature, 5.

25. Christopher Harney and Fabiana Silva, *And Justice for Some: Differential Treatment of Youth of Color in the Justice System*, National Council on Crime and Delinquency, January 2007.

26. George S. Bridges and Sara Steen, "Racial Disparities in Official Assessments of Juvenile Offenders: Attributional Stereotypes as Mediating Mechanisms," *American Sociological Review* 63, no. 4 (1998): 554–70, doi.org/10.2307/2657267, 564.

27. Bridges and Steen, "Racial Disparities in Official Assessments of Juvenile Offenders," 564.

28. Marsha Weissman, Vidhya Ananthakrishnan, and Vincent Schiraldi, "Moving Beyond Youth Prisons," Columbia University Justice Lab, February 2019, justicelab

.columbia.edu/sites/default/files/content/Moving%20Beyond%20Youth%20Prisons%20
-%20C2H_0.pdf, 38.

29. Vincent Schiraldi, "What Mass Incarceration Looks Like for Juveniles," *New York Times*, November 10, 2015.

30. Mie Lewis, *Custody and Control: Conditions of Confinement in New York's Juvenile Prisons for Girls*, American Civil Liberties Union and Human Rights Watch, September 2006, www.aclu.org/report/custody-and-control-conditions-confinement-new-yorks -juvenile-prisons-girls.

31. Cassi Feldman, "State Facilities' Use of Force Is Scrutinized After a Death," *New York Times*, March 4, 2007.

32. Loretta King, "Re: Investigation of the Lansing Residential Center, Louis Gossett, Jr. Residential Center, Tryon Residential Center, and Tryon Girls Center," August 14, 2009, www.justice.gov/sites/default/files/crt/legacy/2010/12/15/NY_juvenile_facilities _findlet_08-14-2009.pdf, 5.

33. Elizabeth Dwoskin, "Shutting Upstate Jails for City Kids Has Made a Fiery Bronx Bureaucrat a Host of Enemies," *Village Voice*, August 4, 2010; Task Force on Transforming Juvenile Justice, Office of Governor David Paterson, *Charting a New Course: A Blueprint for Transforming Juvenile Justice in New York State*, Vera Institute of Justice, December 2009, www.vera.org/publications/charting-a-new-course-a-blueprint -for-transforming-juvenile-justice-in-new-york-state.

34. New York State Office of Children and Family Services, *2010 Annual Report, Youth Placed in OCFS Custody*, 2010, ocfs.ny.gov/reports/jj-yic/Youth-In-Care-Report -2010.pdf, 9; New York State Division for Youth, *Youth in Care: 1995 Annual Report*, 6.

35. Nell Bernstein, *Burning Down the House: The End of Juvenile Prison* (New York: The New Press, 2016), 481.

36. Thomas Kaplan, "Cuomo Administration Closing 7 Prisons, 2 in New York City," *New York Times*, July 1, 2011; "New York State of the State Address," C-SPAN, January 5, 2011, www.c-span.org/video/?297338-1/york-state-state-address.

37. Russ Buettner, "Bloomberg Makes a Proposal on Youth Prisons," *New York Times*, December 22, 2010.

38. Weissman, Ananthakrishnan, and Schiraldi, "Beyond Youth Prisons."

39. Newsweek Staff, "The Orphanage," *Newsweek*, December 11, 1994.

40. James K. Whittaker, review of *Diversity in a Youth Correctional System: Handling Delinquents in Massachusetts*, by Robert B. Coates, Alden D. Miller, and Lloyd Ohlin, *Social Service Review* 53, no. 3 (1979): 504–10, www.jstor.org/stable/30015770; Barry Krisberg and James Austin, "What Works with Juvenile Offenders: The Massachusetts Experiment," in *Reforming Juvenile Justice: Reasons and Strategies for the 21st Century*, ed. Dan Macallair and Vincent Schiraldi (Dubuque, IA: Kendall/Hunt, 1998).

41. Jerome G. Miller, *Last One over the Wall: The Massachusetts Experiment in Closing Reform Schools* (Columbus: Ohio State University Press, 1991), 18.

42. Holbrook Mohr, "13,000 Abuse Claims in Juvie Centers," Associated Press, March 2, 2008.

43. Erica L. Smith and Jessica Stroop, *Sexual Victimization Reported by Youth in Juvenile Facilities, 2018*, U.S. Department of Justice, Bureau of Justice Statistics, December 2019, bjs.ojp.gov/content/pub/pdf/svryjf18.pdf, 1.

44. Richard Mendel, *The Missouri Model: Reinventing the Practice of Rehabilitating Youthful Offenders*, Annie E. Casey Foundation, January 1, 2011, www.aecf.org/resources /the-missouri-model/.

45. Doug Simpson, "Louisiana Shuts Down Youth Prison After a Decade of Abuse Allegations," *Journal Times* (Racine, WI), May 28, 2004, journaltimes.com/news/national /louisiana-shuts-down-youth-prison-after-a-decade-of-abuse-allegations/article_7c472aae -c000-5aae-a566-ffee3c65641a.html.

46. Annie E. Casey Foundation, "Casey Foundation Forms Advisory Council of Youth for Juvenile Justice Work," *Annie E. Casey Foundation* (blog), September 29, 2015, www.aecf.org/blog/casey-foundation-forms-advisory-council-of-youth-for-juve nile-justice-work.

47. Jeffrey Butts, Gordon Bazemore, and Aundra Saa Meroe, *Positive Youth Justice: Framing Justice Interventions Using the Concepts of Positive Youth Development*, John Jay College of Criminal Justice, April 2010, academicworks.cuny.edu/jj_pubs/380.

48. Chief Justice Earl Warren Institute on Law and Social Policy staff, *An Evaluation of the Juvenile Detention Alternatives Initiative: JDAI Sites Compared to Home State Totals*, University of California, Berkeley Law, November 2012, www.law.berkeley.edu/wp -content/uploads/2015/04/JDAI-Rep-1-FINAL.pdf.

49. Patrick McCarthy, Vincent Schiraldi, and Miriam Shark, "The Future of Youth Justice: A Community-Based Alternative to the Youth Prison Model," Cambridge, MA: Harvard Kennedy School, Executive Session on Community Corrections, 2016; "Research Network on Adolescent Development & Juvenile Justice," MacArthur Foundation, www .macfound.org/networks/research-network-on-adolescent-development-juvenil.

50. "Youth First State Advocacy Fund," Art for Justice, artforjusticefund.org/grantee /youth-first-state-advocacy-fund/.

51. Youth Correctional Leaders for Justice, "Statement on Ending Youth Prisons," yclj.org/statement.

52. "Washington State Institute for Public Policy," http://www.wsipp.wa.gov/.

53. GBAO Strategies, "New Poll Results on Youth Justice Reform," Youth First Initiative, March 18, 2019, backend.nokidsinprison.org/wp-content/uploads/2019/03/Youth -First-National-Poll-Memo-March-2019-Final-Version-V2.pdf, 1–2.

54. Bernstein, *Burning Down the House.*

55. Miller, *Last One over the Wall.*

56. Vincent Schiraldi, "In D.C., a Promise Kept in Juvenile Justice," *Washington Post*, January 31, 2010.

57. New York Correction Law Section 79-A - Closure of Correctional Facilities; Notice (2016), COR 43(4) Section 79-A §, newyork.public.law/laws/n.y._correction _law_section_79-a.

58. Tucker and Palomino, "Vanishing Violence."

59. Press Office of New York Mayor Andrew Cuomo, "Governor Cuomo Outlines Transformational Plan for a New NY," readMedia, January 5, 2011, readme.readmedia .com/Governor-Cuomo-Outlines-Transformational-Plan-for-a-New-NY/1818773.

60. "Capital Guardian Youth ChalleNGe Academy," District of Columbia National Guard, dc.ng.mil/Youth-Challenge/Capital-Guardian-Youth-ChalleNGe-Program/.

61. Bruce Western, *Homeward: Life in the Year After Prison* (New York: Russell Sage Foundation, 2018).

62. Schiraldi, Schindler, and Goliday, "The End of the Reform School?"; Dana Schoenberg, Casey Pheiffer, and Ruth Rosenthal, "Kansas Sees 63% Decline in Youth Confinement," *PEW Charitable Trusts* (blog), April 24, 2019, pew.org/2PrDVtv; Virginia Association of Counties, "Status Update on Juvenile Justice Transformation," January 18, 2018, www.vaco.org/status-update-juvenile-justice-transformation/; Josh Kovner, "State Begins Search for New Juvenile Jail Location," *Hartford Courant*, June 16, 2016.

63. McCarthy et al., "Future of Youth Justice," 19.

64. Jeffrey Butts, "Are We Too Quick to Claim Credit for Falling Juvenile Incarceration Rates?," *Juvenile Justice Information Exchange*, March 7, 2013, jjie.org/2013/03/07/are -we-too-quick-to-claim-credit-for-falling-juvenile-incarceration-rates/; Nate Balis and Tom Woods, "Reform Matters: A Reply to Jeffrey Butts," *Juvenile Justice Information Exchange*, March 17, 2013, jjie.org/2013/03/17/reform-matters-a-reply-to-jeffrey-butts/.

65. Travis, Western, and Redburn,, *The Growth of Incarceration in the United States*; McCarthy et al., "Future of Youth Justice"; James Austin et al., *Unlocking America: Why and How to Reduce America's Prison Population*, U.S. Department of Justice, Office of Justice Programs, November 2007, www.ojp.gov/ncjrs/virtual-library/abstracts/unlocking -america-why-and-how-reduce-americas-prison-population.

66. National Research Council, *Reforming Juvenile Justice*; Patrick Sharkey, *Uneasy Peace: The Great Crime Decline, the Renewal of City Life, and the Next War on Violence*, 1st ed. (New York: W.W. Norton, 2018).

67. William A. Gamson, "Commitment and Agency in Social Movements," *Sociological Forum* 6, no. 1 (1991): 27–50, www.jstor.org/stable/684380; Robert J. Sampson et al., "Civil Society Reconsidered: The Durable Nature and Community Structure of Collective Civic Action," *American Journal of Sociology* 111, no. 3 (November 2005): 673–714, doi.org/10.1086/497351; Robert Sampson, Stephen W. Raudenbush, and Felton Earls, "Neighborhoods and Violent Crime: A Multilevel Study of Collective Efficacy," *Science* 277, no. 5328 (1997): 918–24, doi.org/10.1126/science.277.5328.918.

68. Patrick Sharkey, Gerard Torrats-Espinosa, and Delaram Takyar, "Community and the Crime Decline: The Causal Effect of Local Nonprofits on Violent Crime,"

American Sociological Review 82, no. 6 (December 2017): 1214–40, doi.org/10.1177/0003
122417736289.

69. Quote obtained through correspondence with Candice Jones's administrative office at the Public Welfare Foundation.

70. Jennifer Trone, "Mapping the Connection Between Stronger and Safer Neighborhoods: A Report on the Mayor's Action Plan for Neighborhood Safety," New York City
Mayor's Office of Criminal Justice, 2019, criminaljustice.cityofnewyork.us/wp-content
/uploads/2019/07/1-MAP-Case-Study_Final.pdf, 5.

71. Matthew Lynch et al., *Arches Transformative Mentoring Program: An Implementation and Impact Evaluation in New York City*, Urban Institute, February 2018, www
.urban.org/sites/default/files/publication/96601/arches_transformative_mentoring_pro
gram_0.pdf.

72. Western, *Homeward*.

73. Derek Gilna, "When Halfway Houses Pose Full-Time Problems," *Prison Legal News* (blog), January 10, 2015, www.prisonlegalnews.org/news/2015/jan/10/when
-halfway-houses-pose-full-time-problems/.

74. Criminal Justice Investment Initiative, "DA Vance Announces $7.2 Million In-
vestment in New Yorkers Reentering Their Communities After Incarceration," April 9,
2018, cjii.org/da-vance-announces-7-2-million-investment-new-yorkers-reentering-commu
nities-incarceration/.

75. "The Homecoming Project," Impact Justice, impactjustice.org/impact/home
coming-project/.

76. Information obtained through personal correspondence between author and
Burns Institute representatives.

77. Vincent Schiraldi, "Community Justice, Maori-Style," *The Crime Report* (blog),
September 24, 2019, thecrimereport.org/2019/09/24/community-justice-maori-style/.

4. Mercy and Forbearance:
A Parsimonious Approach to Violent Crime

1. BJS Corrections Reporting Program, "The Impact of Covid-19 on Crime, Arrests,
and Jail Populations," Safety + Justice Challenge, John D. and Catherine T. MacArthur
Foundation, June 22, 2021.

2. "Obama at Federal Prison," C-SPAN, July 16, 2015, www.c-span.org/video/.?c4
544894/obama-federal-prison.

3. Newt Gingrich and Pat Nolan, "How to Fix the Federal Prison System," *Washington Times*, June 25, 2015, www.washingtontimes.com/news/2015/jun/25/newt-ging
rich-pat-nolan-how-to-fix-the-federal-pri/.

4. Branko Marcetic, "The Two Faces of Kamala Harris," *Jacobin Magazine*, August 10, 2017, www.jacobinmag.com/2017/08/kamala-harris-trump-obama-california-att
orney-general.

5. Jennifer Bronson and E. Ann Carson, "Prisoners in 2017," U.S. Department of Justice, Bureau of Justice Statistics, April 2019, www.bjs.gov/content/pub/pdf/p17.pdf.

6. Jeremy Travis, Bruce Western, and Steve Redburn, eds., *The Growth of Incarceration in the United States: Exploring Causes and Consequences*, National Research Council (Washington, DC: National Academies Press, 2014).

7. Anthony Bottoms, "Interpersonal Violence and Social Order in Prisons," *Crime and Justice* 26 (1999): 205–81.

8. Nancy Wolff, Jing Shi, and Jane A. Siegel, "Patterns of Victimization Among Male and Female Inmates: Evidence of an Enduring Legacy," *Violence and Victims* 24, no. 4 (2009): 469–84; Danielle Sered, *Until We Reckon: Violence, Mass Incarceration, and a Road to Repair* (New York: The New Press, 2019).

9. Andrea J. Sedlack and Karla McPherson, "Survey of Youth in Residential Placement: Youth's Needs and Services," in *SYRP Report* (Rockville, MD: Westat, 2010).

10. J.F.A. Institute and Arkansas Department Corrections, "Unpublished Inmate Data," 2018.

11. Bruce Western, *Homeward: Life in the Year After Prison* (New York: Russell Sage Foundation, 2018).

12. Western, *Homeward: Life in the Year After Prison*.

13. See *Sessions v. Dimaya*, 138 S. Ct. 1204 (2018), deeming the "residual clause" unconstitutionally vague, which reads, "any other offense that is a felony and that, by its nature, involves a substantial risk that physical force against the person or property of another may be used in the course of committing the offense." 18 U.S.C. § 16.

14. *United States v. Delgado-Enriquez*, 188 F.3d 592 § (5th Cir. 1999) (199AD); "Texas Penal Code - Burglary of Vehicles," 30.04(a) § (2021); Under § 237(a)(2)(A)(iii) of the Immigration and Nationality Act (8 U.S.C.A. § 1227(a)(2)(A)(iii)), aliens are subject to deportation based on the commission of an "aggravated felony." An "aggravated felony" under 8 U.S.C.A. § 1101(a)(43)(F) is defined as a crime of violence—as defined in 18 U.S.C.A. § 16.

15. See, e.g., N.M. Stat., § 30-2-1 (1978).

16. *Hickman v. Commonwealth*, 11 Va. App. 369, 398 S.E.2d 698 (Va. Ct. App. 1990), n.d.

17. Jordan Smith, "Landmark California Law Bars Prosecutors from Pursuing Murder Charges Against People Who Didn't Commit Murder," *The Intercept*, November 23, 2018, theintercept.com/2018/11/23/california-felony-murder-rule; Fla. Admin. Code R. 33-601.210 (2014).

18. Data received on February 8, 2019, from a communication with Brooke McCarthy, Esq., of the Juvenile Law Center.

19. Travis, Western, and Redburn, *The Growth of Incarceration in the United States*.

20. "Truth-in-Sentencing Incentive Grants 34 U.S. Code § 12104," n.d.

21. Derek Neal and Armin Rick, "The Prison Boom and the Lack of Black Progress After Smith and Welch," Working Paper 20283, National Bureau of Economic Research, 2014.

22. Leigh Courtney et al., "A Matter of Time: The Causes and Consequence of Rising Time Served in America's Prisons," Urban Institute, 2017, apps.urban.org/features/long-prison-terms/intro.html.

23. BJS Corrections Reporting Program. The BJS does not break out the Negligent Homicide Manslaughter and "Other Sexual Assault" offenders in its prison population reports. It does report them for its prison release reports.

24. Danielle Kaeble, "Time Served in State Prison, 2018," U.S. Department of Justice, Bureau of Justice Statistics, March 2021.

25. DeAnna R. Hoskins, "Is This Really the Best We Can Do for Criminal Justice Reform?," *Washington Post*, December 20, 2018; James Austin et al., *Unlocking America: Why and How to Reduce America's Prison Population*, JFA Institute, November 2007, www.jfa-associates.com/publications/srs/UnlockingAmerica.pdf.

26. California Department of Corrections and Rehabilitation, "Proposition 57: Credit-Earning for Inmates Frequently Asked Questions (FAQ)," www.cdcr.ca.gov/proposition57/docs/FAQ-General-Pro-57-Final-Regs-Dec-2018.pdf.

27. Families Against Mandatory Minimums, "Frequently Asked Questions about the Residential Drug Abuse Program," 2012, famm.org/wp-content/uploads/FAQ-Residential-Drug-Abuse-Program-5.3.pdf.

28. South Carolina Department of Corrections, "Frequently Asked Questions," 2019, www.doc.sc.gov/faqs.html.

29. Marvin E. Wolfgang, Robert M. Figlio, and Thorsten Sellin, *Delinquency in a Birth Cohort* (Chicago: University of Chicago Press, 1972); Robert Bursik, "The Dynamics of Specialization in Juvenile Offenses," *Social Forces* 58, no. 3 (1980): 851–64; David P. Farrington, Howard N. Snyder, and Terrence A. Finnegan, "Specialization in Juvenile Court Careers," *Criminology* 26, no. 3 (1988): 461–88.

30. Stephen D. Gottfredson and Don M. Gottfredson, *Classification, Prediction, and Criminal Justice Policy* (Rockville, MD: NCJRS, 1992).

31. Mariel Alper, Matthew R. Durose, and Joshua Markman, "2018 Update on Prisoner Recidivism: A 9-Year Follow-Up Period 2005–2014," U.S. Department of Justice, Bureau of Justice Statistics, May 2018, www.bjs.gov/content/pub/pdf/18upr9yfup0514.pdf.

32. Delbert S. Elliott, David Huizinga, and Barbara Morse, "Self-Reported Violent Offending: A Descriptive Analysis of Juvenile Violent Offenders and Their Offending Careers," *Journal of Interpersonal Violence* 1, no. 4 (1986): 472–514.

33. Terrie E. Moffitt, "Adolescence-Limited and Life-Course-Persistent Anti-Social Behavior: A Developmental Taxonomy," *Psychological Review* 100 (1993): 674–70; Wolfgang, Figlio, and Sellin, *Delinquency in a Birth Cohort*.

34. John H. Laub and Robert J. Sampson, *Shared Beginnings, Divergent Lives: Delinquent Boys to Age 70* (Cambridge, MA: Harvard University Press, 2003).

35. William D. Bales and Alex R. Piquero, "Assessing the Impact of Imprisonment on Recidivism," *Journal of Experimental Criminology* 8, no. 1 (2012): 177.

36. Allen J. Beck and Bernard E. Shipley, "Recidivism of Prisoners Released in 1983," Table 8, 1990; Patrick A. Langan and Daniel J. Levin, "Recidivism of Prisoners Released in 1994," Tables 8 and 9, 2002; Matthew R. Durose, Alexia D. Cooper, and Howard N. Snyder, "Recidivism of Prisoners Released in 30 States in 2005: Patterns from 2005–2010," Tables 8 and 16, 2014.

37. Durose, Cooper, and Snyder, "Recidivism of Prisoners Released in 30 States in 2005: Patterns from 2005–2010."

38. Marie Gottschalk, *Caught: The Prison State and the Lockdown of American Politics* (Princeton, NJ: Princeton University Press, 2015).

39. Alper, Durose, and Markman, "2018 Update on Prisoner Recidivism: A 9-Year Follow-up Period 2005–2014."

40. Durose, Cooper, and Snyder, "Recidivism of Prisoners Released in 30 States in 2005: Patterns from 2005–2010."

41. Brian Reaves, "Pretrial Release of Federal Felony Defendants," U.S. Department of Justice, Bureau of Justice Statistics, 1994; Sonya Tafoya et al., *Pretrial Release in California* (Sacramento, CA: Public Policy Institute of California, 2017), www.ppic.org/content/pubs/report/R_0517STR.pdf).

42. James Austin, *The Nevada Pretrial Risk Assessment: Final Report*, JFA Institute, OJP Diagnostics Center, 2018; Matthew DeMichele et al., "The Public Safety Assessment: A Re-Validation and Assessment of Predictive Utility and Differential Prediction by Race and Gender in Kentucky," 2018, doi.org/10.2139/ssrn.3168452.

43. Richard A. Berk, Susan B. Sorenson, and Geoffrey Barnes, "Forecasting Domestic Violence: A Machine Learning Approach to Help Inform Arraignment Decisions," *Journal of Empirical Legal Studies* 13, no. 1 (2016): 94–115.

44. Cindy Redcross et al., "New York City's Pretrial Supervised Release Program: An Alternative to Bail," MDRC and Vera Institute of Justice, April 2017, bit.ly/2V5iFLm.

45. Curtis Karnow, "Setting Bail for Public Safety," *Berkeley Journal of Criminal Law* 13, no. 1 (2008): 1–30.

46. Columbia University Justice Lab, "Too Big to Succeed: The Impact of the Growth of Community Corrections and What Should Be Done About It," January 2018, justicelab.columbia.edu/sites/default/files/content/Too_Big_to_Succeed_Report_FINAL.pdf.

47. Alex R. Piquero, Wesley G. Jennings, and J.C. Barnes, "Violence in Criminal Careers: A Review of the Literature from a Developmental Life-Course Perspective," *Aggression and Violent Behavior* 17, no. 3 (2012): 171–79.

48. "Alvin Bragg: Day 1 Memo," Alvin Bragg Manhattan DA-Elect, n.d., www.alvinbragg.com/day-one.

49. Marc Mauer and Ashley Nellis, *The Meaning of Life: The Case for Abolishing Life Sentences* (New York: The New Press, 2018).

50. "Domestic Violence Survivors Justice Act," S1077 § (n.d).

51. Sered, *Until We Reckon*.

52. Patrick Sharkey, Gerard Torrats-Espinosa, and Delaram Takyar, "Community and the Crime Decline: The Causal Effect of Local Nonprofits on Violent Crime," *American Sociological Review* 82, no. 6 (2017): 1214–40.

53. Sharkey, Torrats-Espinosa, and Takyar, "Community and the Crime Decline"; Patrick Sharkey, Thomas Laetsch, and Chelsea Daniels, "American Violence," Marron Institute of Urban Management, New York University, 2018.

5. A Call for New Criminal Justice Values

1. Nancy Gertner, "A Short History of American Sentencing: Too Little Law, Too Much Law, or Just Right," *Journal of Criminal Law and Criminology* 100, no. 3 (2010): 691.

2. Associated Press, "Sessions Calls on Congress to Get Tough on Crime," *USA Today*, August 1, 2018; Mia Love, "Criminal Justice Reform: A Women's Issue 2017," *The Hill*, March 13, 2017.

3. Craig Henderson and Faye Taxman, "Competing Values Among Criminal Justice Administrators: The Importance of Substance Abuse Treatment," *Drug and Alcohol Dependence* 103, no. S1 (2009): S11.

4. Gertner, "A Short History of American Sentencing," 692–93.

5. Gertner, "A Short History of American Sentencing," 695.

6. Francis Allen, "Criminal Justice, Legal Values and the Rehabilitative Ideal," *Journal of Criminal Law and Criminology* 50, no. 226 (1959): 226; Gertner, "A Short History of American Sentencing," 696.

7. Gertner, "A Short History of American Sentencing," 695–96.

8. Doris L. Mackenzie, *Sentencing and Corrections in the 21st Century: Setting the Stage for the Future*, University of Maryland, Department of Criminology and Criminal Justice, July 2001, www.ncjrs.gov/pdffiles1/nij/189106-2.pdf, 7–8.

9. Francis Allen, *The Decline of the Rehabilitative Ideal: Penal Policy and Social Purpose* (New Haven, CT: Yale University Press, 1981).

10. Andrew von Hirsch, "The 'Desert' Model for Sentencing: Its Influence, Prospects, and Alternatives," *Social Research: An International Quarterly* 74, no. 2 (2007): 414–15.

11. Raymond Paternoster, "How Much Do We Really Know About Criminal Deterrence," *Journal of Law and Criminology* 100, no. 30 (2010): 782.

12. Paternoster, "How Much Do We Really Know About Criminal Deterrence," 766; Jeremy Travis, Bruce Western, and Steve Redburn, eds., *The Growth of Incarceration in the United States: Exploring Causes and Consequences* (Washington, DC: National Academies Press, 2014), 322.

13. Travis, Western, and Redburn, *The Growth of Incarceration in the United States*, 325.

14. Paternoster, "How Much Do We Really Know About Criminal Deterrence," 802–3; Alfred Blumstein and Richard Rosenfeld, "Factors Contributing to U.S. Crime Trends," in *Understand Crime Trends: Workshop Report*, ed. Arthur S. Goldberger and Richard Rosenfeld (Washington, DC: National Academies Press, 2008), 22.

15. Paternoster, "How Much Do We Really Know About Criminal Deterrence"; Blumstein and Rosenfeld, "Factors Contributing to U.S. Crime Trends," 22, 34; Richard Rosenfeld and Steven Messner, "The Crime Drop in Comparative Perspective: The Impact of the Economy and Imprisonment on American and European Burglary Rates," *British Journal of Sociology* 60, no. 3 (2009): 447.

16. Daryl Atkinson, "A Revolution of Values in the U.S. Criminal Justice System," Center for American Progress, February 27, 2018, www.americanprogress.org/issues/criminal-justice/news/2018/02/27/447225/revolution-values-u-s-criminal-justice-system/; Arthur Rizer and Lars Trautman, "Where the Right Went Wrong on Criminal Justice," *American Conservative*, July 6, 2018, www.theamericanconservative.com/articles/where-the-right-went-wrong-on-criminal-justice/.

17. John Locke, "Second Treatise of Government," 1689, www.earlymoderntexts.com/assets/pdfs/locke1689a.pdf.

18. Edwin Meese III, "Too Many Laws Turn Innocents into Criminals," Heritage Foundation, May 26, 2010, www.heritage.org/crime-and-justice/commentary/too-many-laws-turn-innocents-criminals.

19. Meese, "Too Many Laws Turn Innocents into Criminals"

20. Meese, "Too Many Laws Turn Innocents into Criminals."

21. Ginette G. Ferszt, Michelle Palmer, and Christine McGrane, "Where Does Your State Stand on Shackling of Pregnant Incarcerated Women?," *Nursing for Women's Health* 22, no. 1 (2018): 19.

22. Ferszt, Palmer, and McGrane, "Where Does Your State Stand on Shackling of Pregnant Incarcerated Women?," 20.

23. Craig Haney, "Restricting the Use of Solitary Confinement," *Annual Review of Criminology* 1 (2018): 285–310; Nathaniel Penn, "Buried Alive: Stories from Inside Solitary Confinement," *GQ*, March 2, 2017, www.gq.com/story/buried-alive-solitary-confinement.

6. Telling the Truth: Confronting White Supremacy, Period

1. David Hoffman, "The Most Intense Heartfelt Description of Racism I Ever Filmed," YouTube, June 17, 2020, 16:40:00–17:40:00, https://youtube.com/clip/UgkxAuILnhDUFaNUEH1-ktDrif9p8x9OkETq.

2. Hoffman, "The Most Intense Heartfelt Description of Racism I Ever Filmed," YouTube, 17:45:00–18:45:00, https://youtube.com/clip/UgkxxDgrsxc08aVgI3vnyr5ODrCqo68djYM-.

3. Adele Perry, "Vocabularies of Slavery and Anti-Slavery: The North American Fur-Trade and the Imperial World," *Australian Historical Studies* 45, no. 1 (2014): 34–45, https://doi.org/10.1080/1031461X.2013.877504.

4. Robin D.G. Kelley, *Freedom Dreams: The Black Radical Imagination* (Boston: Beacon Press, 2002)

5. Kelley, *Freedom Dreams*.

6. W.E.B. Du Bois, *Darkwater: Voices from Within the Veil* (New York: Harcourt, Brace and Howe, 1920), chap. 2.

7. João H. Costa Vargas, "The Liberation Imperative of Black Genocide: Blueprints from the African Diaspora in the Americas," *Souls* 10, no. 3 (2008): 256–78, https://doi.org/10.1080/10999940802347756.

8. Hoffman, "The Most Intense Heartfelt Description of Racism I Ever Filmed," YouTube, 10:36:00–10:37:00, https://youtube.com/clip/Ugkx2XC2WpllsKodeuf6pNDm23ffFg-CXh6X.

9. Hoffman, "The Most Intense Heartfelt Description of Racism I Ever Filmed," YouTube, 24:30:00-26:00:00, https://youtube.com/clip/UgkxvmOcvh5BL852F6ufSRWCJ_IV39JDLHZt.

7. The Challenge of Criminal Justice Reform

1. Patrick Sharkey, *Uneasy Peace: The Great Crime Decline, the Renewal of City Life, and the Next War on Violence* (New York: Norton, 2018).

2. Anne E. Carson, *Prisoners in 2016*, U.S. Department of Justice, Bureau of Justice Statistics, 2018; Anne E. Carson, *Prisoners in 2020*, U.S. Department of Justice, Bureau of Justice Statistics, 2021; Todd D. Minton and Zhen Zeng, "Jail Inmates in 2015," U.S. Department of Justice, Bureau of Justice Statistics, December 2016, https://bjs.ojp.gov/content/pub/pdf/ji15.pdf; Zhen Zeng and Todd D. Minton, "Jail Inmates in 2019," U.S. Department of Justice, Bureau of Justice Statistics, March 2021, https://bjs.ojp.gov/library/publications/jail-inmates-2019.

3. Dan Berger, Mariame Kaba, and David Stein, "What Abolitionists Do," *Jacobin*, August 24, 2017.

4. Bruce Western, *Homeward: Life in the Year After Prison* (New York: Russell Sage Foundation, 2018)

5. Elizabeth Hinton and DeAnza Cook, "The Mass Criminalization of Black Americans: A Historical Overview," *Annual Review of Criminology* 4 (2021): 261–86.

6. Robert J. Sampson, *Great American City: Chicago and the Enduring Neighborhood Effect* (Chicago: University of Chicago Press, 2012); Todd R. Clear, *Imprisoning Communities: How Mass Incarceration Makes Disadvantaged Neighborhoods Worse* (New York: Oxford University Press, 2007); Jessica T. Simes, *Punishing Places: The Geography of Mass Imprisonment* (Berkeley: University of California Press, 2021).

7. Monica C. Bell, "Essays on Police Relations in the Context of Inequality" (PhD thesis, Harvard University, 2016).

8. Sara Wakefield and Christopher Uggen, "Incarceration and Stratification," *Annual Review of Sociology* 36 (2010): 387–406; Christopher Wildeman and Christopher Muller, "Mass Imprisonment and Inequality in Health and Family Life," *Annual Review of Law and Social Science* 8 (2012): 11–30.

9. John DiIulio, "My Black Crime Problem, and Ours," *City Journal* 6 (1996): 14–28.

10. Bruce Western, *Punishment and Inequality in America* (New York: Russell Sage Foundation, 2006); Christopher Muller, "Exclusion and Exploitation: The Incarceration of Black Americans from Slavery to the Present," *Science* 374, no. 6565 (2021): 282–86.

11. Western, *Homeward: Life in the Year After Prison*.

12. Stephen Metraux, Caterina G. Roman, and Richard S. Cho, "Incarceration and Homelessness," National Symposium on Homelessness Research, 2007; Claire W. Herbert, Jeffrey D. Morenoff, and David J. Harding, "Homelessness and Housing Instability Among Former Prisoners," *Russell Sage Foundation Journal* 1 (2015): 45–79.

13. Mitchell Duneier, *Sidewalk* (New York: Farrar, Straus, and Giroux, 1999).

14. Hannah Pullen-Blasnik, Jessica T. Simes, and Bruce Western, "The Population Prevalence of Solitary Confinement," *Science Advances* 7, no. 48 (2021): 1928.

15. Bruce Western, "Inside the Box: Safety, Health, and Isolation in Prison," *Journal of Economic Perspectives* 35, no. 4 (2021): 97–122.

8. Reckoning with Racial Harm from the Bench: Learn, Acknowledge, and Repair

1. Danielle Sered articulates five actions that are necessary to account for the harm one has caused: "(1) acknowledging responsibility for one's actions; (2) acknowledging the impact of one's actions on others; (3) expressing genuine remorse; (4) taking actions to repair the harm to the degree possible, and guided when feasible by the people harmed . . . ; and (5) no longer committing similar harm." Danielle Sered, *Until We Reckon: Violence, Mass Incarceration, and a Road to Repair* (New York: The New Press, 2019), 96.

2. "Reimagining America Project," Center for World Religions, Diplomacy, & Conflict Resolution, George Mason University, February 26, 2021, https://crdc.gmu.edu/reimagining-america-project/.

3. Jeremy Travis, Bruce Western, and Steve Redburn, eds., *The Growth of Incarceration in the United States: Exploring Causes and Consequences* (Washington, DC: National Academies Press, 2014), 33.

4. Lauren-Brooke Eisen, *Charging Inmates Perpetuates Mass Incarceration*, Brennan Center for Justice, May 2015, https://www.brennancenter.org/our-work/research-reports/charging-inmates-perpetuates-mass-incarceration.

5. Saneta deVuona-Powell et al., *Who Pays? The True Cost of Incarceration on Families*, Ella Baker Center for Human Rights, Forward Together, and Research Action Design, September 2015, http://whopaysreport.org/who-pays-full-report/.

6. Michelle Alexander, *The New Jim Crow: Mass Incarceration in the Age of Colorblindness* (New York: The New Press, 2010); Kia Makarechi, "What the Data Really Says About Police and Racial Bias," *Vanity Fair*, July 14, 2016, https://www.vanityfair.com /news/2016/07/data-police-racial-bias.

7. Alexes Harris, Heather Evans, and Katherine Beckett, "Drawing Blood from Stones: Legal Debt and Social Inequality in the Contemporary United States," *American Journal of Sociology* 115, no. 6 (2010): 1753–99.

8. Dan Kopf, "The Fining of Black America," Priceonomics, June 24, 2016, https:// priceonomics.com/the-fining-of-black-america/.

9. Heather Hunt and Gene R. Nichol Jr., "Court Fines and Fees: Criminalizing Poverty in North Carolina," University of North Carolina School of Law, Carolina Law Scholarship Repository, 2017, https://scholarship.law.unc.edu/cgi/viewcontent.cgi?article=1443 &context=faculty_publications.

10. "Reimagining America Project."

9. Creating New Narratives for Criminal Justice and Immigration Reform

1. Tim O'Brien, *The Things They Carried* (New York: Mariner Books, 2009).

2. Sidney Madden, Sam Leeds, and Rodney Carmichael, "'I Want Us to Dream A Little Bigger': Noname and Mariame Kaba on Art and Abolition," NPR, December 19, 2020, www.npr.org/2020/12/19/948005131/i-want-us-to-dream-a-little-bigger-noname-and -mariame-kaba-on-art-and-abolition.

3. David Garland, "Capital Punishment and American Culture," *Punishment & Society* 7, no. 4 (2005): 347–76.

4. Walter Nicholls, *The DREAMers: How the Undocumented Youth Movement Transformed the Immigrant Rights Debate* (Redwood City, CA: Stanford University Press, 2013).

5. Lawrence Bobo and Devon Johnson, "A Taste for Punishment: Black and White Americans' Views on the Death Penalty and the War on Drugs," *Du Bois Review: Social Science Research on Race* 1, no. 1 (2004): 151–80.

6. Matthew Desmond, "Relational Ethnography," *Theory and Society* 43 (2014): 547–79.

7. Jennifer Gonnerman, "Before the Law," *New Yorker,* September 29, 2014; Rebecca Rosenberg, Tina Moore, and Aaron Feis, "Man Accused of Driving Drunk, Killing Pedestrian Freed Due to New Criminal Justice Reforms," *New York Post*, January 2, 2020, https://nypost.com/2020/01/02/man-accused-of-driving-drunk-killing-pedestrian-freed -due-to-new-criminal-justice-reforms.

8. Tali Mendelberg, *The Race Card: Campaign Strategy, Implicit Messages, and the Norm of Equality* (Princeton, NJ: Princeton University Press, 2017); Ann M. Oberhauser, Daniel Krier, and Abdi M. Kusow, "Political Moderation and Polarization in the Heartland: Economics, Rurality, and Social Identity in the 2016 U.S. Presidential Election," *Sociology Quarterly* 60, no. 2 (2019): 224–44.

9. John T. Jost et al., "The Politics of Fear: Is There an Ideological Asymmetry in Existential Motivation?," *Social Cognition* 35, no. 4 (2017): 324–53; Stuart Soroka, Patrick Fournier, and Lilach Nir, "Cross-National Evidence of a Negativity Bias in Psychophysiological Reactions to News," *Proceedings of the National Academy of Sciences* 116, no. 38 (2019): 18888–92; Pavlos Vasilopoulos et al., "Fear, Anger, and Voting for the Far Right: Evidence from the November 13, 2015 Paris Terror Attacks," *Political Psychology* 40, no. 4 (2019): 679–704.

10. Barry Glassner, *The Culture of Fear: Why Americans Are Afraid of the Wrong Things* (London: Hachette, 2010).

11. Carol T. Kulik, Elissa L. Perry, and Anne C. Bourhis, "Ironic Evaluation Processes: Effects of Thought Suppression on Evaluations of Older Job Applicants," *Journal of Organizational Behavior* 21 (2000): 689–711; Elizabeth Levy Paluck and Michael Suk-Young Chwe, "Confronting Hate Collectively," *PS: Political Science & Politics* 50, no. 4 (2017): 990–92.

12. James Baldwin, "Smaller Than Life," *The Nation*, July 14, 1947.

13. Baldwin, "Smaller Than Life."

14. Marie Gottschalk, *Caught: The Prison State and the Lockdown of American Politics* (Princeton, NJ: Princeton University Press, 2016).

15. Chad Alan Goldberg, *Citizens and Paupers: Relief, Rights, and Race, from the Freedmen's Bureau to Workfare* (Chicago: University of Chicago Press, 2007).

16. Gottschalk, *Caught*, 79.

17. Karla Cornejo Villavicencio, *The Undocumented Americans* (New York: One World, 2020), 9.

18. Robert J. Sampson and John H. Laub, "Crime and Deviance in the Life Course," *Annual Review of Criminology* 18 (1992): 63–84; Lisa Stolzenberg and Stewart J. D'Alessio, "Co-Offending and the Age-Crime Curve," *Journal of Research in Crime and Delinquency* 45, no. 1 (2008): 65–86.

19. Gottschalk, *Caught*, 240.

20. Gottschalk. *Caught*, 167–68, 183.

21. Eric Holder Jr., "Hearing on the Retroactive Application of the Proposed Amendment to the Federal Sentencing Guidelines Implementing the Fair Sentencing Act of 2010," United States Sentencing Commission, June 1, 2011, www.ussc.gov/sites/default/files /pdf/amendment-process/public-hearings-and-meetings/20110601/Testimony_AG _Eric_Holder.pdf.

22. Joan Petersilia, "Racial Disparities in the Criminal Justice System: A Summary," *Crime & Delinquency* 31, no. 1 (1985): 15–34; Ben Feldmeyer et al., "Racial, Ethnic, and Immigrant Threat: Is There a New Criminal Threat on State Sentencing?," *Journal of Research in Crime and Delinquency* 52, no. 1 (2014): 62–92.

23. Fanny Lauby, "Leaving the 'Perfect DREAMer' Behind? Narratives and Mobilization in Immigration Reform," *Social Movement Studies* 15, no. 4 (2016): 374–87.

24. The White House, Office of the Press Secretary, "Remarks by the President in Address to the Nation on Immigration," November 20, 2014, https://obamawhite house.archives.gov/the-press-office/2014/11/20/remarks-President-address-nation -immigration.

25. Gottschalk, *Caught*, 167.

26. Wendy Sawyer and Peter Wagner, *Mass Incarceration: The Whole Pie 2020*, Prison Policy Initiative, March 2020, www.prisonpolicy.org/reports/pie2020.html.

27. Migration Policy Institute, "MPI: As Many as 3.7 Million Unauthorized Immigrants Could Get Relief from Deportation Under Anticipated New Deferred Action Program," November 19, 2014, www.migrationpolicy.org/news/mpi-many-37-million-un authorized-immigrants-could-get-relief-deportation-under-anticipated-new.

28. Marisa Lagos, "Jerry Brown Will Leave Lasting Impact on Criminal Justice in California," KQED, December 29, 2018, www.kqed.org/news/11714104/jerry -brown-will-leave-lasting-impact-on-criminal-justice-in-california.

29. Marie Gottschalk, "Democracy and the Carceral State in America," *Annals of the American Academy of Political and Social Science* 651 (2014): 288–95; Patrick Sharkey, *Uneasy Peace: The Great Crime Decline, the Renewal of City Life, and the Next War on Violence* (New York: W.W. Norton, 2018).

30. Jeffrey Butts, "Are We Too Quick to Claim Credit for Falling Juvenile Incarceration Rates?," *Juvenile Justice Information Exchange*, March 7, 2013, jjie.org/2013/03/07/are -we-too-quick-to-claim-credit-for-falling-juvenile-incarceration-rates/.

31. Derek Thompson, "Why America's Great Crime Decline Is Over," *The Atlantic*, March 24, 2021, www.theatlantic.com/ideas/archive/2021/03/is-americas-great -crime-decline-over/618381.

32. john a. powell, "Bridging or Breaking? The Stories We Tell Will Create the Future We Inhabit," *Nonprofit Quarterly,* February 15, 2021, https://nonprofitquarterly.org /bridging-or-breaking-the-stories-we-tell-will-create-the-future-we-inhabit.

33. Jean-Paul Sartre, preface to *The Wretched of the Earth*, by Frantz Fanon (New York: Grove Press, 1969).

34. Sartre, preface to *The Wretched of the Earth*, xlv, li; Rachel Kaadzi Ghansah, "The Radical Vision of Toni Morrison," *New York Times Magazine*, April 8, 2015.

35. James Whitman, "Presumption of Innocence or Presumption of Mercy?: Weighing Two Western Modes of Justice," *Texas Law Review* 94 (2016): 933–94.

36. Lindsey Devers, "Plea and Charge Bargaining: Research Summary," U.S. Department of Justice, Bureau of Justice Statistics, 2011, bja.ojp.gov/sites/g/files/xyckuh186 /files/media/document/PleaBargainingResearchSummary.pdf; Issa Kohler-Hausmann, *Misdemeanorland: Criminal Courts and Social Control in an Age of Broken Windows Policing* (Princeton, NJ: Princeton University Press, 2018).

37. David Broockman and Joshua Kalla, "Durably Reducing Transphobia: A Field Experiment on Door-to-Door Canvassing," *Science* 352, no. 6282 (2016): 220–24.

38. Matthew Desmond, "Relational Ethnography"; Bruce Western, *Homeward: Life in the Year After Prison* (New York: Russell Sage Foundation Publishing, 2018).

39. Broockman and Kalla, "Durably Reducing Transphobia."

40. Rashad Robinson, "Changing Our Narrative About Narrative," University of California, Berkeley, Othering & Belonging Institute, 2018, https://belonging.berkeley .edu/changing-our-narrative-about-narrative.

41. Bryan Stevenson, *Just Mercy: A Story of Justice and Redemption* (New York: Spiegel & Grau, 2015).

42. Slavoj Žižek, *Violence: Six Sideways Reflections* (New York: Picador Press, 2008), 46.

43. Clifford Geertz, *Works and Lives: The Anthropologist as Author* (Redwood City, CA: Stanford University Press, 1998).

44. Danielle Sered, *Until We Reckon: Violence, Mass Incarceration, and a Road to Repair* (New York: The New Press, 2019), 41.

45. Alex Kotlowitz, *An American Summer: Love and Death in Chicago* (New York: Anchor Books, 2019).

46. Bessel van der Kolk, *The Body Keeps the Score: Brain, Mind, and Body in the Healing of Trauma* (New York: Penguin Books, 2015).

47. National Research Council, *Reforming Juvenile Justice: A Developmental Approach*, Richard J. Bonnie et al., eds. (Washington, DC: National Academies Press, 2013).

48. Equal Justice Initiative, "The Superpredator Myth, 25 Years Later," April 7, 2014, eji.org/news/superpredator-myth-20-years-later.

49. Elizbeth Levy Paluck and Donald P. Green, "Prejudice Reduction: What Works? A Review and Assessment of Research and Practice," *Annual Review of Psychology* 60 (2009): 339–67; Benjamin Justice and Tracy L. Meares, "The Wolf We Feed: Democracy, Caste, and Legitimacy," *Michigan Law Review* 119 (2021): 95–119.

50. Robinson, "Changing Our Narrative About Narrative."

51. Kevin Munger, "Tweetment Effects on the Tweeted: Experimentally Reducing Racist Harassment," *Political Behavior* 39 (2017): 629–49.

52. This example comes from Ezra Klein's conversation with Peter Singer on the former's podcast. "Pete Singer on the Lives You Can Save," *Vox Conversations*, December 6, 2019.

53. Paluck and Chwe, "Confronting Hate Collectively."

54. Benjamin Justice and Tracy L. Meares, "How the Criminal Justice System Educates Citizens," *Annals of the American Academy of Political and Social Science* 651, no. 1 (2013): 159–77; Garriy Shteynberg et al., "The Broadcast of Shared Attention and Its Impact on Political Persuasion," *Journal of Personality and Social Psychology* 111, no. 5 (2016): 665–73.

55. Teresa A. Miller, "Lessons Learned, Lessons Lost: Immigration Enforcement's Failed Experiment with Penal Severity," *Fordham Urban Law Journal* 38 (2010): 217–46; Katherine Beckett and Heather Evans, "Crimmigration at the Local Level: Criminal Justice Processes in the Shadow of Deportation," *Law & Society Review* 49, no. 1 (2015): 241–77; Walter Ewing, Daniel E. Martínez, and Rubén G. Rumbaut, *The Criminalization of Immigration in the United States*, American Immigration Council, July 2015, www.american immigrationcouncil.org/research/criminalization-immigration-united-states.

56. Sumi Cho, Kimberlé Williams Crenshaw, and Leslie McCall, "Toward a Field of Intersectionality Studies: Theory, Applications, and Praxis," *Signs: Journal of Women in Culture and Society* 38, no. 4 (2013): 785–810.

57. Julia Preston, "How the Dreamers Learned to Play Politics," *Politico*, September 9, 2017, www.politico.com/magazine/story/2017/09/09/dreamers-daca-learned-to -play-politics-215588; "About UWD," United We Dream, https://unitedwedream.org /about/#mission.

58. Anat Shenker-Osorio, *Messaging This Moment: A Handbook for Progressive Communicators*, Center for Community Change, 2017, https://communitychange.org/wp-con tent/uploads/2017/08/C3-Messaging-This-Moment-Handbook.pdf.

59. Jeremiah 22:3; Bill Keller, "How the Right Got Religion on Justice," The Marshall Project, June 22, 2015, www.themarshallproject.org/2015/06/22/how-the-right -got-religion-on-justice.

60. Jeremy Travis, Bruce Western, and Steve Redburn, eds. *The Growth of Incarceration in the United States: Exploring Causes and Consequences* (Washington, DC: National Academies Press, 2014): 321–23.

61. Shenker-Osorio, *Messaging This Moment*, 37.

62. John Gramlich, "What the Data Says (and Doesn't Say) About Crime in the United States," Pew Research Center, November 20, 2020, www.pewresearch.org/fact -tank/2020/11/20/facts-about-crime-in-the-u-s.; Gallup, "Crime," news.gallup.com/poll /1603/crime.aspx.

63. William R. Kelly, *Criminal Justice at the Crossroads* (New York: Columbia University Press, 2015); Gallup, "Death Penalty," news.gallup.com/poll/1606/death-penalty .aspx.

64. Madden, Leeds, and Carmichael, "'I Want Us to Dream a Little Bigger.'"

65. Marshall Ganz, "Why Stories Matter," *Sojourners* 38, no. 3 (2009): 16–18; Madden, Leeds, and Carmichael, "'I Want Us to Dream a Little Bigger.'"

66. Larry Buchanan, Quoctrung Bui, and Jugal K. Patel, "Black Lives Matter May Be the Largest Movement in U.S. History," *New York Times*, July 3, 2020.

10. Reducing Racial Disparities: A Case Study from Oregon

1. Leah Sottile, "A Teen and a Toy Gun," *Longreads* (blog), February 5, 2018, longreads.com/2018/02/05/a-teen-and-a-toy-gun/.

2. "The Oregon Constitution and Proceedings and Debates of the Constitutional Convention of 1857," Oregon State Archives, https://sos.oregon.gov/archives/exhibits/con stitution/Documents/transcribed-1857-oregon-constitution.pdf.

3. U.S. Census Bureau, "QuickFacts: Portland City, Oregon," www.census.gov /quickfacts/fact/table/portlandcityoregon/AGE295219; Greta Smith, "'Congenial Neighbors': Restrictive Covenants and Residential Segregation in Portland, Oregon," *Oregon Historical Quarterly* 119, no. 3 (2018): 358–64, doi.org/10.5403/oregonhistq.119.3.0358; K. Barber et al., "Invisible Walls Mapping Residential Segregation in Portland," *Oregon Historical Quarterly* 119, no. 3 (January 2018): 400–405, pdxscholar.library.pdx .edu/hist_fac/42; Alana Semuels, "The Racist History of Portland, the Whitest City in America," *The Atlantic*, July 22, 2016, www.theatlantic.com/business/archive/2016/07 /racist-history-portland/492035/.

4. Daniel Monroe Sullivan and Samuel C. Shaw, "Retail Gentrification and Race: The Case of Alberta Street in Portland, Oregon," *Urban Affairs Review* 47, no. 3 (May 2011): 413–32, doi.org/10.1177/1078087410393472; Karen Gibson, "Bleeding Albina: A History of Community Disinvestment, 1940–2000," *Transforming Anthropology* 15, no. 1 (January 2007): 3–25, doi.org/10.1525/tran.2007.15.1.03.

5. Lisa Bates, Ann Curry-Stevens, and Coalition of Communities of Color, *The African American Community in Multnomah County: An Unsettling Profile*, January 2014, pdxscholar.library.pdx.edu/socwork_fac/135.

6. Bates, Curry-Stevens, and Coalition of Communities of Color, *The African American Community in Multnomah County*; Gibson, "Bleeding Albina"; Michael Maciag, "Portland Gentrification Maps and Data," *Governing*, February 5, 2015, www.governing .com/archive/portland-gentrification-maps-demographic-data.html.

7. Jennifer Ferguson, "Racial and Ethnic Disparities and the Relative Rate Index (RRI) Summary of Data in Multnomah County," Multnomah County, Portland, OR, 2015, https://multco.us/file/48681/download. The Safety and Justice Challenge Initiative is supported by the John D. and Catherine T. MacArthur Foundation.

8. Bruce Western, *Punishment and Inequality in America* (New York: Russell Sage Foundation, 2006); Sara Wakefield and Christopher Wildeman, *Children of the Prison Boom: Mass Incarceration and the Future of American Inequality*, Studies in Crime and Public Policy (New York: Oxford University Press, 2013), doi.org/10.1093/acprof:oso /9780199989225.001.0001.

9. Aimee Wickman and Nastassia Walsh, "Resources on Criminal Justice Coordinating Councils (CJCCs)," NACo (blog), July 28, 2015, www.naco.org/blog /resources-criminal-justice-coordinating-councils-cjccs.

10. "Local Public Safety Coordinating Council," Multnomah County, June 24, 2010, www.multco.us/lpscc.

11. Khalil Gibran Muhammad, *The Condemnation of Blackness: Race, Crime, and the Making of Modern Urban America* (Cambridge, MA: Harvard University Press, 2010).

12. Robert Sampson, *Great American City: Chicago and the Enduring Neighborhood Effect* (Chicago: University of Chicago Press, 2012); Robert J. Sampson and William J. Wilson, "Toward a Theory of Race, Crime, and Urban Inequality," in *Crime and Inequality*, ed. John Hagan and Ruth D. Peterson (Stanford, CA: Stanford University Press, 1995), 37.

13. Christopher Muller, "Northward Migration and the Rise of Racial Disparity in American Incarceration, 1880–1950," *American Journal of Sociology* 118, no. 2 (September 2012), doi.org/10.1086/666384.

14. Monica C. Bell, "Essays on Policing, Legal Estrangement, and Urban Marginality," (PhD dissertation, Harvard University, Graduate School of Arts and Sciences, 2018), dash.harvard.edu/handle/1/41129143.

15. Kimberly Bernard, Amanda Lamb, and David Schwager, *"Examining the Implementation of Justice Reinvestments in Multnomah County: Measurement, Preliminary Analysis, and Future Evaluations*, Multnomah County Justice Reinvestment Program, Portland, OR, November 10, 2016, multco-web7-psh-files-usw2.s3-us-west-2.amazonaws.com/s3fs -public/Examining%20the%20Implementation%20of%20Justice%20Reinvestment%20 in%20Multnomah%20County.pdf, 45.

16. Jeremy Travis, Bruce Western, and Steve Redburn, eds., *The Growth of Incarceration in the United States: Exploring Causes and Consequences*, National Research Council (Washington, DC: National Academies Press, 2014).

17. David R. Williams and Lisa A. Cooper, "Reducing Racial Inequities in Health: Using What We Already Know to Take Action," *International Journal of Environmental Research and Public Health* 16, no. 4 (February 2019): 606, doi.org/10.3390/ijerph16040606.

18. The Juvenile Detention Alternatives Initiative was developed by the Annie E. Casey Foundation and the W. Haywood Burns Institute.

19. "Juvenile Detention Alternatives Initiative (JDAI)," Multnomah County, October 7, 2015, www.multco.us/dcj-juvenile/jdai.

20. This information was originally published in October 2019. Since that time, some of the names, positions, and programming have changed.

21. "The Diane Wade House," Multnomah County, August 7, 2018.

22. "'It's More than Just a House. It's a Home and a Safe Place to Heal . . .' Community Rallies for Grand Opening of the Diane Wade House," *Multnomah County* (blog), February 27, 2019, www.multco.us/multnomah-county/news/%E2%80%98its-more-just -house-it%E2%80%99s-home-and-safe-place-heal-%E2%80%99-community-rallies-grand.

23. The team members were added through support from staff at the County's Office of Consumer Engagement.

24. "Multnomah County Celebrates Opening of Diane Wade House with Ribbon-Cutting Ceremony," *Multnomah County* (blog), April 11, 2019.

25. "Law Enforcement Assisted Diversion (LEAD®)," Multnomah County, March 8, 2017, www.multco.us/law-enforcement-assisted-diversion.

26. "Targeted Universalism: Animated Video + Curriculum," Othering & Belonging Institute, February 8, 2017, belonging.berkeley.edu/targeted-universalism-animated -video-curriculum.

27. See the following articles on public support for the DWH: "Board Updated on Soon-to-Open Diane Wade House, 'It's Like a Rumble of Excitement in the Black Community,'" *Multnomah County* (blog), November 29, 2018, https://multco.us/multnomah-county /news/board-updated-soon-open-diane-wade-house-%E2%80%98it%E2%80%99s-rum ble-excitement-black; Lani Seelinger, "What Criminal Justice Reform Looks Like When Black Women's Needs Are Put First," *Bustle*, April 3, 2019, www.bustle.com/p/what -criminal-justice-reform-looks-like-when-black-womens-needs-are-put-first-16896437; Abbey Stamp and Ebony Clark, "Decreasing Harm to Communities Impacted by the Criminal Justice System," *The Skanner*, February 14, 2019, www.theskanner.com/opin ion/commentary/28118-harm-to-communities-impacted-by-the-criminal-justice-system; Shani Saxon, "Q&A: How These Oregon Leaders Are Empowering Black Women in the Criminal Justice System," *ColorLines*, April 10, 2019, www.colorlines.com/articles /qa-how-these-oregon-leaders-are-empowering-black-women-criminal-justice-system.

11. Holistic Safety at the Center of Incarceration

1. Substance Abuse and Mental Health Services Administration, "SAMHSA's Concept of Trauma and Guidance for a Trauma-Informed Approach," U.S. Department of Health and Human Services, 2014, https://ncsacw.samhsa.gov/userfiles/files/SAMHSA _Trauma.pdf.

2. Wendy Sawyer and Peter Wagner, "Mass Incarceration: The Whole Pie 2022," Prison Policy Initiative, March 14, 2022, https://www.prisonpolicy.org/reports/pie2022 .html.

3. Most studies on children with incarcerated parents only focus on prisons and not jails so this number may be much higher. Bryce Peterson, Lindsey Cramer, and Jocelyn Fontaine, "Policies and Practices for Children of Incarcerated Parents: Summarizing What We Know and What We Do Not Know," in *Handbook on Children with Incarcerated Parents: Research, Policy, and Practice*, ed. J. Mark Eddy and Julie Poehlmann-Tynan (Cham, Switzerland: Springer Nature, 2019), 331–43.

4. Peter K. Enns et al., "What Percentage of Americans Have Ever Had a Family Member Incarcerated?: Evidence from the Family History of Incarceration Survey (Fam-HIS)," *Socius: Sociological Research for a Dynamic World* 5 (2019): 1–45.

5. U.S. Bureau of Labor Statistics, "Occupational Employment Statistics: Correctional Officers and Jailers," 2017.

6. Nancy Wolff, Jing Shi, and Jane A. Siegel, "Patterns of Victimization Among Male and Female Inmates: Evidence of an Enduring Legacy," *Violence and Victims* 24, no. 4 (2009): 469–84; Nancy Wolff et al., "Trauma Exposure and Posttraumatic Stress Disorder Among Incarcerated Men," *Journal of Urban Health* 91, no. 4 (2014): 707–19; Sharyn Adams, Jaclyn Houston-Kolnik, and Jessica Reichert, "Trauma-Informed and Evidence-Based Practices and Programs to Address Trauma in Correctional Settings," Illinois Criminal Justice Information Authority Research Hub, 2017, https://icjia.illinois.gov/researchhub/articles/trauma-informed-and-evidence-based-practices-and-programs-to-address-trauma-in-correctional-settings.

7. Wolff et al., "Trauma Exposure and Posttraumatic Stress Disorder Among Incarcerated Men."

8. Bonnie L. Green et al., "Trauma Exposure, Mental Health Functioning, and Program Needs of Women in Jail," *Crime & Delinquency* 51, no. 1 (2005): 133–51, https://doi.org/10.1177/0011128704267477.

9. Shannon M. Lynch et al., *Women's Pathways to Jail: The Roles & Intersections of Serious Mental Illness & Trauma*, U.S. Department of Justice, Bureau of Justice Assistance, September 2012, https://www.ce-credit.com/articles/102134/Women_Pathways_to_Jail.pdf.

10. Wolff, Shi, and Siegel, "Patterns of Victimization Among Male and Female Inmates."

11. American Psychiatric Association, *Diagnostic and Statistical Manual of Mental Disorders*, 5th ed. (Arlington, VA: American Psychiatric Association, 2013), 271–72.

12. American Psychiatric Association, *Diagnostic and Statistical Manual of Mental Disorders*.

13. American Psychiatric Association, *Diagnostic and Statistical Manual of Mental Disorders*.

14. Wolff et al., "Trauma Exposure and Posttraumatic Stress Disorder Among Incarcerated Men."

15. Michael D. Denhof and Caterina G. Spinaris, "Depression, PTSD, and Comorbidity in United States Corrections Professionals: Prevalence and Impact on Health and Functioning," Desert Waters Correctional Outreach, 2013, https://desertwaters.com/wp-content/uploads/2021/03/Comorbidity_Study_09-03-131.pdf.

16. Wolff, Shi, and Siegel, "Patterns of Victimization Among Male and Female Inmates: Evidence of an Enduring Legacy."

17. National Institute of Mental Health, "Major Depression," www.nimh.nih.gov/health/statistics/major-depression.shtml; National Institute of Mental Health, "Post-Traumatic Stress Disorder," www.nimh.nih.gov/health/statistics/post-traumatic-stress-disorder-ptsd.shtml.

18. Caterina Spinaris, Michael Denhof, and Gregory Morton, "Impact of Traumatic Exposure on Corrections Professionals," National Institute of Corrections, 2013, https://info.nicic.gov/virt/sites/info.nicic.gov.virt/files/06Impact_of_Traumatic_Exposure.pdf.

19. Lindsey Cramer et al., *Parent-Child Visiting Practices in Jails and Prisons: A Synthesis of Research and Practice*, Urban Institute, 2017, www.urban.org/sites/default/files/publication/89601/parent-child_visiting_practices_in_prisons_and_jails.pdf.

20. Cramer et al., *Parent-Child Visiting Practices in Jails and Prisons*.

21. National Institute of Mental Health. "Major Depression"; National Institute of Mental Health, "Post-Traumatic Stress Disorder."

22. Census Viewer, "Population of Cook County Illinois: Census 2010 and 2000 Interactive Map, Demographics, Statistics, Graphs, Quick Facts," http://censusviewer.com/county/IL/Cook.

23. Cramer et al., *Parent-Child Visiting Practices in Jails and Prisons*.

24. Ross Parke and K. Alison Clarke-Stewart, "Effects of Parental Incarceration on Young Children," Urban Institute, 2002, https://www.urban.org/sites/default/files/publication/60691/410627-Effects-of-Parental-Incarceration-on-Young-Children.PDF.

25. J. Douglas Bremner, "Traumatic Stress: Effects on the Brain," *Dialogues in Clinical Neuroscience* 8, no. 4 (2006): 445–61; Jennifer Sweeton, "How to Heal the Traumatized Brain," *Psychology Today*, March 13, 2017, www.psychologytoday.com/us/blog/workings-well-being/201703/how-heal-the-traumatized-brain.

26. Chicago Beyond, "The Spread of Trauma from Correctional Institutions Through Community," 2021.

27. Bremner, "Traumatic Stress"; Sweeton, "How to Heal the Traumatized Brain."

28. Bremner, "Traumatic Stress"; Sweeton, "How to Heal the Traumatized Brain."

29. Bremner, "Traumatic Stress"; Sweeton, "How to Heal the Traumatized Brain."

30. Bremner, "Traumatic Stress: Effects on the Brain"; Sweeton, "How to Heal the Traumatized Brain."

31. Substance Abuse and Mental Health Services Administration, *SAMHSA's Concept of Trauma and Guidance for a Trauma-Informed Approach*, U.S. Department of Health and Human Services, July 2014, https://ncsacw.samhsa.gov/userfiles/files/SAMHSA_Trauma.pdf.

32. Christine Lindquist et al., "Predictors of Reentry Success," U.S. Department of Health and Human Services, Office of the Assistant Secretary for Planning and Evaluation, December 2016, https://aspe.hhs.gov/system/files/pdf/255886/reentrysuccessbrief.pdf.

33. Chicago Beyond, "Jail Visitation Development Cycle," 2021.

12. Decarceration Through Investment: Reducing Reliance on Prisons and Jails

1. Emily A. Wang, Bruce Western, and Donald M. Berwick, "COVID-19, Decarceration, and the Role of Clinicians, Health Systems, and Payers: A Report From the National Academy of Sciences, Engineering, and Medicine," *JAMA 324*, no. 22 (December 2020): 2257–58, doi.org/10.1001/jama.2020.22109.

2. Angelia M. Paschal et al., "Evaluating the Impact of a Hypertension Program for African Americans," *Journal of the National Medical Association* 98, no. 4 (April 2006): 607–15, www.ncbi.nlm.nih.gov/pmc/articles/PMC2569226/; Barbara Resnick et al., "Pilot Testing of the PRAISEDD Intervention Among African American and Low-Income Older Adults," *Journal of Cardiovascular Nursing* 24, no. 5 (October 2009): 352–61, doi .org/10.1097/JCN.0b013e3181ac0301.

3. National Center for Health Statistics, "Vital Statistics of the United States, 1980: Volume II – Mortality," U.S. Department of Health and Human Services, 1985, www.cdc .gov/nchs/data/vsus/mort80_2a.pdf; National Center for Health Statistics, "Mortality in the United States, 2019," U.S. Department of Health and Human Services, 2020, www.cdc .gov/nchs/data/databriefs/db395-H.pdf.

4. Natasha A. Frost, Todd Clear, and Carlos E. Monteiro, "Ending Mass Incarceration: Six Bold Reforms," in *Decarcerating America: From Mass Punishment to Public Health*, ed. Ernest Drucker (New York: The New Press, 2018).

5. For a detailed description of our scoping review methodology, see L. Hawks et al., "Community Investment Interventions as a Means for Decarceration: A Scoping Review," *Lancet Regional Health—Americas*, 8 (2022): 100150, doi.org/10.1016/j .lana.2021.100150.

6. Lawrence J. Schweinhart and David P. Weikart, "The High/Scope Preschool Curriculum Comparison Study Through Age 23," *Early Childhood Research Quarterly* 12, no. 2 (January 1997): 117–43, doi.org/10.1016/S0885-2006(97)90009-0; David P. Weikart, "Changing Early Childhood Development Through Educational Intervention," *Preventive Medicine* 27, no. 2 (April 1998): 233–37, doi.org/10.1006/pmed.1998.0280; Arthur J. Reynolds et al., "Long-Term Effects of an Early Childhood Intervention on Educational Achievement and Juvenile Arrest: A 15-Year Follow-Up of Low-Income Children in Public Schools," *JAMA* 285, no. 18 (May 2001): 2339–46, doi.org/10.1001/jama.285.18.2339; Kenneth A. Dodge et al., "Impact of Early Intervention on Psychopathology, Crime, and Well-Being at Age 25," *American Journal of Psychiatry* 172, no. 1 (January 2015): 59–70, doi.org/10.1176/appi.ajp.2014.13060786; Alison Giovanelli et al., "African-American Males in Chicago: Pathways from Early Childhood Intervention to Reduced Violence," *Journal of Adolescent Health* 62, no. 1 (January 2018): 80–86, doi.org/10.1016/j .jadohealth.2017.08.012.

7. Schweinhart and Weikart, "High/Scope Preschool."

8. Weikart, "Changing Early Childhood Development."

9. Dodge et al., "Impact of Early Intervention."

10. Reynolds et al., "Long-Term Effects of an Early Childhood Intervention on Educational Achievement"; Giovanelli et al., "African-American Males in Chicago."

11. Frances A. Campbell et al., "Adult Outcomes as a Function of an Early Childhood Educational Program: An Abecedarian Project Follow-Up," *Developmental Psychology* 48, no. 4 (July 2012): 1033–43, doi.org/10.1037/a0026644.

12. Julie Berry Cullen, Brian A. Jacob, and Steven Levitt, "The Effect of School Choice on Participants: Evidence from Randomized Lotteries," *Econometrica* 74, no. 5 (September 2006): 1191–230, doi.org/10.1111/j.1468-0262.2006.00702.x; David J. Deming, "Better Schools, Less Crime?," *Quarterly Journal of Economics* 126, no. 4 (November 2011): 2063–115, doi.org/10.1093/qje/qjr036.

13. Ryang Hui Kim and David Clark, "The Effect of Prison-Based College Education Programs on Recidivism: Propensity Score Matching Approach," *Journal of Criminal Justice* 41, no. 3 (May 2013): 196–204, doi.org/10.1016/j.jcrimjus.2013.03.001; Grant Duwe and Valerie Clark, "The Effects of Prison-Based Educational Programming on Recidivism and Employment," *Prison Journal* 94, no. 4 (December 2014): 454–78, doi .org/10.1177/0032885514548009.

14. Kristen M. Zgoba, Sabrina Haugebrook, and Krista Jenkins, "The Influence of GED Obtainment on Inmate Release Outcome," *Criminal Justice and Behavior* 35, no. 3 (March 2008): 375–87, doi.org/10.1177/0093854807311853.

15. John H. Tyler and Jeffrey R. Kling, "Prison-Based Education and Re-Entry into the Mainstream Labor Market," Working Paper 12114, National Bureau of Economic Research, March 2006, doi.org/10.3386/w12114.

16. Raj Chetty, Nathaniel Hendren, and Lawrence F. Katz. "The Effects of Exposure to Better Neighborhoods on Children: New Evidence from the Moving to Opportunity Experiment," *American Economic Review* 106, no. 4 (April 2016): 855–902, doi.org/10.1257 /aer.20150572.

17. Arline T. Geronimus and J. Phillip Thompson, "To Denigrate, Ignore, or Disrupt: Racial Inequality in Health and the Impact of a Policy-Induced Breakdown of African American Communities," *Du Bois Review* 1, no. 2 (September 2004): 247–79, http:// dx.doi.org.ezproxy.cul.columbia.edu/10.1017/S1742058X04042031.

18. Mindy Thompson Fullilove and Rodrick Wallace, "Serial Forced Displacement in American Cities, 1916–2010," *Journal of Urban Health?: Bulletin of the New York Academy of Medicine* 88, no. 3 (June 2011): 381–89, doi.org/10.1007/s11524-011-9585-2; Rob Sampson, *Great American City: Chicago and the Enduring Neighborhood Effect* (Chicago: University of Chicago Press, 2011).

19. Zachary Hamilton, Alex Kigerl, and Zachary Hays, "Removing Release Impediments and Reducing Correctional Costs: Evaluation of Washington State's Housing Voucher Program," *Justice Quarterly* 32, no. 2 (March 2015): 255–87, doi.org/10.1080/074 18825.2012.761720; David S. Kirk et al., "The Impact of Residential Change and Housing Stability on Recidivism: Pilot Results from the Maryland Opportunities Through Vouchers Experiment (MOVE)," *Journal of Experimental Criminology* 14, no. 2 (June 2018): 213–26, doi.org/10.1007/s11292-017-9317-z.

20. Hamilton, Kigerl, and Hays, "Removing Release Impediments."

21. Hamilton, Kigerl, and Hays, "Removing Release Impediments."

22. Kirk et al., "The Impact of Residential Change and Housing Stability."

23. D. L. Olds et al., "Long-Term Effects of Home Visitation on Maternal Life Course and Child Abuse and Neglect. Fifteen-Year Follow-Up of a Randomized Trial," *JAMA* 278, no. 8 (August 1997): 637–43; D. Olds et al., "Long-Term Effects of Nurse Home Visitation on Children's Criminal and Antisocial Behavior: 15-Year Follow-Up of a Randomized Controlled Trial," *JAMA* 280, no. 14 (October 1998): 1238–44, doi.org/10.1001/jama.280.14.1238; John Eckenrode et al., "Long-Term Effects of Prenatal and Infancy Nurse Home Visitation on the Life Course of Youths: 19-Year Follow-Up of a Randomized Trial," *Archives of Pediatrics & Adolescent Medicine* 164, no. 1 (January 2010): 9–15, doi.org/10.1001/archpediatrics.2009.240; John Eckenrode et al., "The Prevention of Child Maltreatment Through the Nurse Family Partnership Program: Mediating Effects in a Long-Term Follow-Up Study," *Child Maltreatment* 22, no. 2 (May 2017): 92–99, doi.org/10.1177/1077559516685185.

24. David L. Olds et al., "Prenatal and Infancy Nurse Home Visiting Effects on Mothers: 18-Year Follow-Up of a Randomized Trial," *Pediatrics* 144, no. 6 (December 2019): e20183889, doi.org/10.1542/peds.2018-3889.

25. Leslie S. Zun, Lavonne Downey, and Jodi Rosen, "The Effectiveness of an ED-Based Violence Prevention Program," *American Journal of Emergency Medicine* 24, no. 1 (January 2006): 8–13, doi.org/10.1016/j.ajem.2005.05.009.

26. Carnell Cooper, Dawn M. Eslinger, and Paul D. Stolley, "Hospital-Based Violence Intervention Programs Work," *Journal of Trauma* 61, no. 3 (September 2006): 534–37; discussion 537–40, doi.org/10.1097/01.ta.0000236576.81860.8c.

27. Cooper, Eslinger, and Stolley, "Hospital-Based Violence Intervention."

28. Emily A. Wang et al., "Engaging Individuals Recently Released from Prison into Primary Care: A Randomized Trial," *American Journal of Public Health* 102, no. 9 (September 2012): e22–e29, doi.org/10.2105/AJPH.2012.300894.

29. Emily A. Wang et al., "Propensity-Matched Study of Enhanced Primary Care on Contact with the Criminal Justice System Among Individuals Recently Released from Prison to New Haven," *BMJ Open* 9, no. 5 (May 2019): e028097, doi.org/10.1136/bmjopen-2018-028097.

30. Brigid K. Grabert et al., "Expedited Medicaid Enrollment, Service Use, and Recidivism at 36 Months Among Released Prisoners with Severe Mental Illness," *Psychiatric Services* 68, no. 10 (October 2017): 1079–82, doi.org/10.1176/appi.ps.201600482.

31. Marisa Elena Domino et al., "Do Timely Mental Health Services Reduce Reincarceration Among Prison Releasees with Severe Mental Illness?," *Health Services Research* 54, no. 3 (June 2019): 592–602, doi.org/10.1111/1475-6773.13128.

32. Janet L. Lauritsen and Nicole White, *Seasonal Patterns in Criminal Victimization Trends*, U.S. Department of Justice, Bureau of Justice Statistics, June 2014, https://bjs.ojp.gov/content/pub/pdf/spcvt.pdf.

33. Sara B. Heller, "Summer Jobs Reduce Violence Among Disadvantaged Youth," *Science* 346, no. 6214 (December 2014), 1219–33, doi.org/10.1126/science.1257809.

34. Grant Duwe, "An Outcome Evaluation of a Prison Work Release Program: Estimating Its Effects on Recidivism, Employment, and Cost Avoidance," *Criminal Justice Policy Review* 26, no. 6 (2015): 531–54, doi.org/10.1177/0887403414524590.

35. Leslie Hill, Samuel Scaggs, and William Bales, "Assessing the Statewide Impact of the Specter Vocational Program on Reentry Outcomes: A Propensity Score Matching Analysis," *Journal of Offender Rehabilitation* 56 (January 2017): 61–86, doi.org/10.1080/1 0509674.2016.1257535.

36. Christopher Uggen, "Work as a Turning Point in the Life Course of Criminals: A Duration Model of Age, Employment, and Recidivism," *American Sociological Review* 65, no. 4 (2000): 529–46, doi.org/10.2307/2657381.

37. See Miriam Northcutt Bohmert and Grant Duwe, "Minnesota's Affordable Homes Program: Evaluating the Effects of a Prison Work Program on Recidivism, Employment and Cost Avoidance," *Criminal Justice Policy Review* 23, no. 3 (September 2012): 327–51, doi.org/10.1177/0887403411411911; David Farabee, Sheldon Zhang, and Benjamin Wright, "An Experimental Evaluation of a Nationally Recognized Employment-Focused Offender Reentry Program," *Journal of Experimental Criminology* 10, no. 3 (September 2014): 309–22, doi.org/10.1007/s11292-014-9201-z; Cindy M. Schaeffer et al., "RCT of a Promising Vocational/Employment Program for High-Risk Juvenile Offenders," *Journal of Substance Abuse Treatment* 46, no. 2 (February 2014): 134–43, doi.org/10.1016/j .jsat.2013.06.012; Gary R. Bond et al., "A Controlled Trial of Supported Employment for People with Severe Mental Illness and Justice Involvement," *Psychiatric Services* 66, no. 10 (October 2015): 1027–34, doi.org/10.1176/appi.ps.201400510.

38. Eliot Levine et al., "Outcomes of a Care Coordination Guardianship Intervention for Adults with Severe Mental Illness: An Interrupted Time Series Analysis," *Administration and Policy in Mental Health* 47, no. 3 (May 2020): 468–74, doi.org/10.1007 /s10488-019-01005-1.

39. Aaron M. Sawyer and Charles M. Borduin, "Effects of Multisystemic Therapy Through Midlife: A 21.9-Year Follow-Up to a Randomized Clinical Trial with Serious and Violent Juvenile Offenders," *Journal of Consulting and Clinical Psychology* 79, no. 5 (October 2011): 643–52, doi.org/10.1037/a0024862; Charles M. Borduin et al., "Multisystemic Treatment of Serious Juvenile Offenders: Long-Term Prevention of Criminality and Violence," *Journal of Consulting and Clinical Psychology* 63, no. 4 (August 1995): 569–78, doi .org/10.1037//0022-006x.63.4.569; Charles M. Borduin, Cindy M. Schaeffer, and Naamith Heiblum, "A Randomized Clinical Trial of Multisystemic Therapy with Juvenile Sexual Offenders: Effects on Youth Social Ecology and Criminal Activity," *Journal of Consulting and Clinical Psychology* 77, no. 1 (February 2009): 26–37, doi.org/10.1037/a0013035; Jane Timmons-Mitchell et al., "An Independent Effectiveness Trial of Multisystemic Therapy with Juvenile Justice Youth," *Journal of Clinical Child and Adolescent Psychology* 35, no. 2 (June 2006): 227–36, doi.org/10.1207/s15374424jccp3502_6.

40. Bahr Weiss et al., "An Independent Randomized Clinical Trial of Multisystemic Therapy with Non-Court-Referred Adolescents with Serious Conduct Problems," *Journal of Consulting and Clinical Psychology* 81, no. 6 (December 2013): 1027–39, doi.org/10.1037/a0033928.

41. Elizabeth J. Letourneau et al., "Multisystemic Therapy for Juvenile Sexual Offenders: 1-Year Results from a Randomized Effectiveness Trial," *Journal of Family Psychology* 23, no. 1 (February 2009): 89–102, doi.org/10.1037/a0014352; Elizabeth J. Letourneau et al., "Two-Year Follow-Up of a Randomized Effectiveness Trial Evaluating MST for Juveniles Who Sexually Offend," *Journal of Family Psychology* 27, no. 6 (December 2013): 978–85, doi.org/10.1037/a0034710.

42. Anthony A. Braga, Anne M. Piehl, and David Hureau, "Controlling Violent Offenders Released to the Community: An Evaluation of the Boston Reentry Initiative," *Journal of Research in Crime and Delinquency* 46, no. 4 (November 2009): 411–36, doi.org/10.1177/0022427809341935.

43. Grant Duwe, "Evaluating the Minnesota Comprehensive Offender Reentry Plan (MCORP): Results from a Randomized Experiment," *Justice Quarterly* 29 (June 2012): 347–83, doi.org/10.1080/07418825.2011.555414.

44. Jeremy Luallen, Jared Edgerton, and Deirdre Rabideau, "A Quasi-Experimental Evaluation of the Impact of Public Assistance on Prisoner Recidivism," *Journal of Quantitative Criminology* 34 (September 2018): 1–33, doi.org/10.1007/s10940-017-9353-x.

45. Angela Davis, *Are Prisons Obsolete?* (New York: Seven Stories Press, 2005).

46. Barbara A. Israel et al., "Critical Issues in Developing and Following CBPR Principles," in *Community-Based Participatory Research for Health: Advancing Social and Health Equity*, ed. Nina Wallerstein et al. (San Francisco: Jossey-Bass, 2008), 31–46.

13. Humanizing Justice: Supporting Positive Development in Criminalized Youth

1. Valerie F. Reyna and Frank Farley, "Risk and Rationality in Adolescent Decision Making: Implications for Theory, Practice, and Public Policy," *Psychological Science in the Public Interest* 7 (2006): 1–44, doi.org/10.1111/j.1529-1006.2006.00026.x; Ethan M. McCormick, Yang Qu, and Eva H. Telzer, "Adolescent Neurodevelopment of Cognitive Control and Risk-Taking in Negative Family Contexts," *NeuroImage* 124 (2016): 989–96, doi.org/10.1016/j.neuroimage.2015.09.063; Linda Patia Spear, "Adolescent Neurodevelopment," *Journal of Adolescent Health* 52, no. 2 (2013): S7–S13, dx.doi.org/10.1016%2Fj.jadohealth.2012.05.006; Laurence Steinberg, "Risk Taking in Adolescence: New Perspectives from Brain and Behavioral Science," *Current Directions in Psychological Science* 16, no. 2 (2007): 55–59, doi.org/10.1111/j.1467-8721.2007.00475.x.

2. Centers for Disease Control and Prevention, "Youth Risk Behavior Surveillance 2015," June 10, 2016, www.cdc.gov/healthyyouth/data/yrbs/pdf/2015/ss6506_updated

.pdf; Eva Moore et al., "International Youth Justice Systems: Promoting Youth Develop-ment and Alternative Approaches: A Position Paper of the Society for Adolescent Health and Medicine," *Journal of Adolescent Health* 59, no. 4 (2016): 482–86, doi.org/10.1016/j .jadohealth.2016.08.003; Elizabeth Trejos-Castillo and Nancy Trevino-Schafer, eds., *Handbook of Foster Youth* (New York: Routledge, 2018).

3. Lyn Y. Abramson, Martin E.P. Seligman, and John D. Teasdale, "Learned Helplessness in Humans: Critique and Reformulation," *Journal of Abnormal Psychology* 87 (1978): 49–74.

4. Interviews conducted by Trejos-Castillo at a Texas youth facility; study partially funded by a U.S. Department of Health and Human Sciences, Administration on Children, Youth and Families grant.

5. Interviews conducted by Trejos-Castillo at a Brazilian youth detention facility; study funded by a Fulbright Scholar Grant, U.S. Department of State, Bureau of Educational and Cultural Affairs.

6. Interviews conducted by Trejos-Castillo in western India at a child welfare center; study partially funded by C.R. Hutcheson Endowed Professorship in Human Development & Family Studies, Texas Tech University.

7. Interviews conducted by Trejos-Castillo at a Texas youth facility; study partially funded by a U.S. Department of Health and Human Sciences, Administration on Children, Youth and Families grant.

8. Interviews conducted by Trejos-Castillo at a Texas youth facility; study partially funded by a U.S. Department of Health and Human Sciences, Administration on Children, Youth and Families grant.

9. Justice Policy Institute, "More Police—in Schools and Out—Not the Answer," news release, January 16, 2013, www.justicepolicy.org/news/4829; Jason. P. Nance, "Student Surveillance, Racial Inequalities, and Implicit Racial Bias," University of Florida Levin College of Law Research Paper No. 16–30 (2017), papers.ssrn.com/sol3/papers .cfm?abstract_id=2830885; Edward J. Smith and Shaun R. Harper, "Disproportion-ate Impact of K-12 School Suspension and Expulsion on Black Students in Southern States," University of Pennsylvania Center for the Study of Race and Equity in Educa-tion, 2015, web-app.usc.edu/web/rossier/publications/231/Smith%20and%20Harper%20 (2015)-573.pdf; Amanda Petteruti, *"Education Under Arrest": The Case Against Police in Schools*, Justice Policy Institute, November 2011, https://justicepolicy.org/research /education-under-arrest-the-case-against-police-in-schools/.

10. U.S. Department of Education, Office for Civil Rights, "2013–2014 Civil Rights Data Collection: Data Snapshot (School Discipline)," March 2014, www2.ed.gov/about /offices/list/ocr/docs/crdc-discipline-snapshot.pdf.

11. Pew Research Center, "On Views of Race and Inequality, Blacks and Whites Are Worlds Apart," June 27, 2016, www.pewsocialtrends.org/2016/06/27/1 -demographic-trends-and-economic-well-being; Julie Rachel Mazza et al., "Early Adolescence Behavior Problems and Timing of Poverty During Childhood: A Comparison of Lifecourse

Models," *Social Science & Medicine* 177 (2017): 35–42, https://assets.pewresearch.org/wp
-content/uploads/sites/3/2016/06/ST_2016.06.27_Race-Inequality-Final.pdf.

12. Joshua Rovner, *Racial Disparities in Youth Commitments and Arrests*, The Sentencing Project, April 2016, www.sentencingproject.org/publications/racial-disparities
-in-youth-commitments-and-arrests.

13. Annie E. Casey Foundation, "Child Population by Race in the United States," 2019, datacenter.kidscount.org/data/tables/103-child-population-by-race#detailed/1/any
/false/871,870,573,869,36,868,867,133,38,35/68,69,67,12,70,66,71,72/423,424; Office of Juvenile Justice and Delinquency Prevention, "OJJDP Statistical Briefing Book," 2020, www.ojjdp.gov/ojstatbb/corrections/qa08205.asp?qaDate=2017.

14. Rich Williams, "Safe Harbor: State Efforts to Combat Child Trafficking," National Conference of State Legislatures, April 2017, www.ncsl.org/Portals/1/Documents/cj
/SafeHarbor_v06.pdf.

15. Allen J. Beck and David Cantor, *Sexual Victimization in Juvenile Facilities Reported by Youth*, 2012, U.S. Department of Justice, Bureau of Justice Statistics, June 2013, www.bjs.gov/content/pub/pdf/svjfry12.pdf.

16. Lee A. Underwood and Aryssa Washington, "Mental Illness and Juvenile Offenders," *International Journal of Environmental Research and Public Health* 13, no. 2 (2016): 228–42, doi:10.1001/archpsyc.61.4.403.

17. Karen M. Abram et al., "Posttraumatic Stress Disorder and Trauma in Youth in Juvenile Detention," *Archives of General Psychiatry* 61 (2004): 403–10, doi.org/10.1001
/archpsyc.61.4.403.

18. Interviews conducted by Trejos-Castillo at a Texas youth facility; study partially funded by a U.S. Department of Health and Human Sciences, Administration on Children, Youth and Families grant.

19. Declan Roche, "Restorative Justice and the Regulatory State in South African Townships," *British Journal of Criminology* 42 no. 3 (2002): 514–33.

20. Howard Zehr and Harry Mika, "Fundamental Concepts of Restorative Justice," *Contemporary Justice Review* 1, no. 1 (1998): 47–56.

21. See The District Court of New Zealand, "Matariki Court," 2020, https://www
.districtcourts.govt.nz/criminal-court/criminal-jurisdiction/specialist-criminal-courts/ma
tariki-court/; Youth Court of New Zealand, "Rangatahi Courts & Pasifika Courts," 2020, https://youthcourt.govt.nz/about-youth-court/rangatahi-courts-and-pasifika-courts/.

22. Sandra Pavelka, "Restorative Justice in the States: An Analysis of Statutory Legislation and Policy," *Justice Policy Journal* 2, no. 13 (2016): 6–8, www.cjcj.org/uploads/cjcj
/documents/jpj_restorative_justice_in_the_states.pdf.

23. Trevor Fronius et al., *Restorative Justice in US Schools: An Updated Research Review*, WestEd Justice and Prevention Research Center, March 2019, www.wested.org
/wp-content/uploads/2019/04/resource-restorative-justice-in-u-s-schools-an-updated-re
search-review.pdf.

24. Fleur Souverein et al., "Overview of European Forensic Youth Care: Towards an Integrative Mission for Prevention and Intervention Strategies for Juvenile Offenders," *Child Adolescent Psychiatry and Mental Health* 13, no. 6 (2019), doi:/10.1186/s13034 -019-0265-4; Susan Young, Ben Greer, and Richard Church, "Juvenile Delinquency, Welfare, Justice and Therapeutic Interventions: A Global Perspective," *BJPsych Bulletin* 41, no. 1 (2017): 21-29, doi.org/10.1192/pb.bp.115.052274.

25. Center for Court Innovation, "Restorative Justice in Schools," January 2020, www.courtinnovation.org/restorative-justice-schools.

26. U.S. Department of Justice, National Institute of Justice, "Crime Solutions Database," 2020, https://crimesolutions.ojp.gov.

27. Congressional Research Service, "Juvenile Justice Funding Trends," January 22, 2020, fas.org/sgp/crs/misc/R44879.pdf.

28. Christopher Edward Branson et al., "Trauma-Informed Juvenile Justice Systems: A Systematic Review of Definitions and Core Components," *Psychological Trauma: Theory, Research, Practice and Policy* 9, no. 6 (2017): 635-46, doi.org/10.1037/tra0000255.

29. Sharon Fishel et al., *Transforming Schools: A Framework for Trauma-Engaged Practice in Alaska*, Association of Alaska School Boards, 2019, dps.alaska.gov/getme dia/a2fc763c-aba5-4b25-875e-b0f63c54c301/Transforming-Schools-A-Framework-for -Trauma-Engaged-Practice-Final.pdf; U.S. Department of Health and Human Services, Substance Abuse and Mental Health Administration, *SAMHSA's Concept of Trauma and Guidance for a Trauma-Informed Approach*, July 2014, https://ncsacw.samhsa.gov /userfiles/files/SAMHSA_Trauma.pdf; Sheryl H. Kataoka et al., "Applying a Trauma Informed School Systems Approach: Examples from School Community-Academic Partnerships," *Ethnicity & Disease* 28, Suppl 2 (2018): 417-26, doi.org/10.18865/ed.28 .S2.417.

30. Precious Skinner-Osei et al., "Justice-Involved Youth and Trauma-Informed Interventions," *Justice Policy Journal* 16, no. 2 (2019): 1-25, www.cjcj.org/uploads/cjcj/docu ments/justice-involved_youth_and_trauma-informed_interventions.pdf.

31. UNICEF, "The Convention on the Rights of the Child," 1990, www.unicef.org /child-rights-convention/convention-text.

14. Coordinated Care: Less Supervision, More Treatment

1. Jason Matejkowski and Michael Ostermann, "Serious Mental Illness, Criminal Risk, Parole Supervision, and Recidivism: Testing of Conditional Effects," *Journal of Law and Human Behavior* 39, no. 1 (2015): 75-86, https://doi.org/10.1037/lhb0000094.

2. Cecilia Klingele, "Rethinking the Use of Community Supervision," *Journal of Criminal Law and Criminology* 103, no. 4 (2013): 1015-70.

3. Fiona Doherty, "Obey All Laws and Be Good: Probation and the Meaning of Recidivism," *Georgetown Law Journal* 104, no. 2 (2016): 291-354.

4. Dan Mistak, "The Affordable Care Act and the Excellence Act: An Evolving Terrain to Meet the Needs of the Neediest," *Cornerstone* (magazine) 37, no. 1 (2016): 20–23.

5. Jocelyn Guyer et al., "State Strategies for Establishing Connections to Health Care for Justice-Involved Populations: The Central Role of Medicaid," The Commonwealth Fund, January 2019, www.commonwealthfund.org/publications/issue-briefs/2019/jan /state-strategies-health-care-justice-involved-role-medicaid.

6. Kamala Mallik-Kane, Ellen Paddock, and Jesse Jannetta, *Health Care After Incarceration*, The Urban Institute, 2018, www.urban.org/sites/default/files/publication/96386 /health_care_after_incarceration.pdf.

7. Michelle S. Phelps, "Ending Mass Probation: Sentencing, Supervision, and Revocation," *The Future of Children* 28, no. 1 (2018): 125–46.

8. Martin F. Horn, "Rethinking Sentencing," *Corrections Management Quarterly* 5, no. 3 (2001): 30–34; Doherty, "Obey All Laws and Be Good: Probation and the Meaning of Recidivism"; Phelps, "Ending Mass Probation."

9. David Muhammad and Vincent Schiraldi, "How to End the Era of Mass Supervision," *The Imprint*, September 30, 2019, imprintnews.org/justice/how-to-end-the -era-of-mass-supervision/37846.

10. Kendra Bradner, Jarred Williams, and Vincent Schiraldi, *The Wisconsin Community Corrections Story*, Columbia University Justice Lab, January 2019, https://justicelab.co lumbia.edu/sites/default/files/content/Wisconsin%20Community%20Corrections%20 Story%20final%20online%20copy.pdf.

11. Guyer et al., "State Strategies for Establishing Connections to Health Care for Justice-Involved Populations"; Embry Howell, Cybele Kotonias, and Jesse Jannetta, "Case Management for Justice-Involved Populations: Colorado," Urban Institute, Health Policy Center and Justice Policy Center, January 2017, https://www.urban.org/sites/default/files /publication/88061/final_clean_case_management_1_09_17.pdf.

12. U.S. Department of Health and Human Services, "Report to Congress on the Medicaid Health Home State Plan Option," May 2018, www.medicaid.gov/state-resource -center/medicaid-state-technical-assistance/health-home-information-resource-center /downloads/medicaidhomehealthstateplanoptionrtc.pdf.

13. Sheryl Kubiak et al., *Mental Health Across the Criminal Legal Continuum: A Summary of Five Years of Research in Ten Counties*, Wayne State School of Social Work, Center for Behavioral Health and Justice, April 2019, behaviorhealthjustice.wayne.edu/pdfs/diver sion_5_yr_summary.pdf.

14. Mallik-Kane, Paddock, and Jannetta, *Health Care After Incarceration*.

15. Kubiak et al., *Mental Health Across the Criminal Legal Continuum*.

16. "Stepping Up Initiative," Centers for Medicare and Medicaid Services, Council of State Governments Justice Center, 2013, stepuptogether.org.

17. Congressional Research Service, "Medicaid's Federal Medical Assistance Percentage," July 2020, https://sgp.fas.org/crs/misc/R43847.pdf.

18. Social Security Administration, "State Option to Provide Coordinated Care Through a Health Home for Individuals with Chronic Conditions," Pub. L. No. 42 U.S.C. 1396w-4, www.ssa.gov/OP_Home/ssact/title19/1945.htm.

19. Sara N. Bleich et al., "Systematic Review of Programs Treating High-Need and High-Cost People with Multiple Chronic Diseases or Disabilities in the United States, 2008–2014," *Preventing Chronic Disease* 12 (2015), doi.org/10.5888/pcd12.150275.

20. Herbert, C. Fillmore et al., "Health Care Savings with the Patient-Centered Medical Home: Community Care of North Carolina's Experience," *Population Health Management* 17, no. 3 (June 2014): 141–48, doi.org/10.1089/pop.2013.0055.

21. "Stepping Up Initiative."

22. Renuka Tipirneni et al., *MI Care Team Demonstration Evaluation Report*, Institute for Healthcare Policy and Innovation, University of Michigan, January 2020, https://deepblue.lib.umich.edu/handle/2027.42/171504.

23. Jackie Prokop, Danita Alfred, and Catherine Reid, "Nursing Impact on Chronic Disease Medicaid Health Home Patients: A Qualitative Study," *Nursing Forum 2020* 55, no. 2 (2019): 99–105, https://doi.org/10.1111/nuf.12403.

24. U.S. Department of Health and Human Services, "Report to Congress on the Medicaid Health Home State Plan Option"; Guyer et al., "State Strategies for Establishing Connections to Health Care for Justice-Involved Populations"; Prokop, Alfred, and Reid, "Nursing Impact on Chronic Disease Medicaid Health Home Patients."

25. Kathryn M. McDonald et al., *Closing the Quality Gap: A Critical Analysis of Quality Improvement Strategies*, vol. 7, U.S. Department of Health and Human Services, Agency for Healthcare Research and Quality, 2007, www.ncbi.nlm.nih.gov/books/NBK44015; Jackie Prokop, "Care Coordination Strategies in Reforming Health Care: A Concept Analysis," *Nursing Forum* 51, no. 4 (2016): 268–74, https://doi.org/10.1111/nuf.12157.

26. Prokop, Alfred, and Reid, "Nursing Impact on Chronic Disease Medicaid Health Home Patients"; Guyer et al., "State Strategies for Establishing Connections to Health Care for Justice-Involved Populations."

27. Emily A. Wang et al., "Transitions Clinic: Creating a Community-Based Model of Health Care for Recently Released California Prisoners," *Public Health Reports* 125, no. 2 (2010): 171–77, https://doi.org/10.1177/003335491012500205.

28. Wang et al., "Transitions Clinic."

29. Prashanti Boinapally, "Internal Michigan Primary Care Association Report to the State of Michigan" (unpublished, 2019).

30. Boinapally, "Internal Michigan Primary Care Association Report to the State of Michigan."

15. Weaving the Social Fabric: A New Model
for Public Safety and Vital Neighborhoods

1. Patrick Sharkey, *Uneasy Peace: The Great Crime Decline, the Renewal of City Life, and the Next War on Violence* (New York: W.W. Norton, 2018).

2. Kim Phillips-Fein, *Fear City: New York's Fiscal Crisis and the Rise of Austerity Politics* (New York: Metropolitan Books, 2017).

3. Bruce Western, *Punishment and Inequality in America* (New York: Russell Sage, 2006).

4. John Pfaff, *Locked in: The True Causes of Mass Incarceration and How to Achieve Real Reform* (New York: Basic Books, 2017).

5. "Breaking the Frame? Remaking the Criminal Justice System in New York City," City of New York Office of the Mayor, 2019; U.S. Department of Justice, "2019 Crime in the United States," Uniform Crime Reporting Program, 2019; Vincent Crivelli, "Houston Is Averaging More Than 1 Homicide a Day So Far in 2021," Click2Houston.com, February 11, 2021; Kevin Rector, "A Year Like No Other for L.A. Crime: Homicides Surge, Robberies and Rapes Drop," *Los Angeles Times*, January 3, 2021; "Crime Maps and Stats," Philadelphia Police Department, 2021; Jessica D'Onofrio and Craig Wall, "2020 Cook County Deaths Break Records Due to Gun Violence, Opioid Overdoses, COVID-19, ME Says," ABC7 Chicago, January 1, 2012.

6. Franklin E. Zimring, *The City That Became Safe: New York's Lessons for Urban Crime and Its Control* (New York: Oxford University Press, 2011).

7. "Dispositions of Adult Arrests," New York State Division of Criminal Justice Services, 2020, www.criminaljustice.ny.gov/crimnet/ojsa/dispos/nyc.pdf; "Adult Arrests 18 and Older by County: Beginning 1970," New York State Division of Criminal Justice Services, 2020, https://data.ny.gov/Public-Safety/Adult-Arrests-18-and-Older-by-County-Beginning-197/rikd-mt35); "Stop, Question and Frisk Data," City of New York, 2021, www1.nyc.gov/site/nypd/stats/reports-analysis/stopfrisk.page.

8. Zimring, *The City That Became Safe*; Tracey L. Meares, "The Law and Social Science of Stop and Frisk," *Annual Review of Law and Social Science* 10 (2014): 335–52.

9. Henry Goldman, "Bratton Seeks to Export New Crime-Fighting Miracle," *Bloomberg*, March 21, 2014, www.bloomberg.com/news/articles/2014-03-21/bratton-seeks-to-export-new-york-crime-fighting-miracle.

10. "Crime in New York City," Wikipedia, 2021, https://en.wikipedia.org/wiki/Crime_in_New_York_City#cite_note-NYC_murders_1939-59-190).

11. Ross MacDonald et al., "The Rikers Island Hot Spotters: Defining the Needs of the Most Frequently Incarcerated," *American Journal of Public Health* 105, no. 11 (2015): 2262–68.

12. In 2019, the total strength of the police department was 51,894, of which 36,643 were uniformed officers. New York City Independent Budget Office, "Police Staffing Levels

and Reported Crime Rates in America's Largest Cities: Results of Preliminary Analysis," 1998, https://ibo.nyc.ny.us/iboreports/crimerep.html; City of New York, "Mayor's Management Report: Fiscal 2020," 2020, www1.nyc.gov/assets/operations/downloads/pdf /mmr2020/2020_mmr.pdf.

13. New York City's Mayor's Office of Criminal Justice, "Breaking the Frame," 2019, https://criminaljustice.cityofnewyork.us/wp-content/uploads/2019/11/Breaking-the -Frame____.pdf.

14. Rod K. Brunson and Brian A. Wade, "'Oh Hell No, We Don't Talk to Police': Insights on the Lack of Cooperation in Police Investigations of Urban Gun Violence," *Criminal Public Policy* 18 (2019): 623–48; Tom Tyler, Jeffrey Fagan, and Amanda Geller, "Street Stops and Police Legitimacy: Teachable Moments in Young Urban Men's Legal Socialization," *Journal of Empirical Legal Studies* 11, no. 4 (2014): 751–85.

15. Issa Kohler-Hausmann, *Misdemeanorland: Criminal Courts and Social Control in an Age of Broken Windows Policing* (Princeton, NJ: Princeton University Press, 2018).

16. Amanda Geller and Jeffrey Fagan, "Police Contact and the Legal Socialization of Urban Teens," *RSF: The Russell Sage Foundation Journal of the Social Sciences* 5, no. 1 (2019): 26–49; Monica C. Bell, "Police Reform and the Dismantling of Legal Cynicism," *Yale Law Journal* 50, no. 2 (2016): 314–47; "How They Doing? NYPD's Use of 'Sentiment Meter' Media Reveals Public's Trust Level," CBS New York, September 23, 2019, https://newyork.cb slocal.com/2019/09/23/nypd-sentiment-meter-social-media-commissioner-james-oneill/.

17. Frank Rosario and Natalie O'Neill, "De Blasio Gets Policing Advice—from Ex-Cons," *New York Post*, November 21, 2013, https://nypost.com/2013/11/21/de-blasio -hearing-plenty-of-policing-advice-from-ex-cons/; Sally Goldenberg, "Like Old Times: Lhota and de Blasio Argue About Dinkins and Giuliani," *Politico*, October 22, 2013, www.politico.com/states/new-york/albany/story/2013/10/like-old-times-lhota-and-de -blasio-argue-about-dinkins-and-giuliani-000000; Goldman, "Bratton Seeks to Export New Crime-Fighting Miracle"; Michael Howard Saul, "Mayor Bill de Blasio Touts New York City Drop in Crime," *Wall Street Journal*, December 2, 2014, www.wsj.com/articles /mayor-bill-de-blasio-touts-new-york-city-drop-in-crime-1417550271.

18. Elizabeth Glazer, "Mayor's Office of Criminal Justice Strategic Plan: Fiscal Years 2019–2021," New York City Mayor's Office of Criminal Justice, 2019, http://criminaljus tice.cityofnewyork.us/wp-content/uploads/2018/11/Strategic-Plan-2019-2021.pdf.

19. "Adult Arrests 18 and Older by County: Beginning 1970," New York State Division of Criminal Justice Services, 2020. Note: 1993–2019 data are from this source. Arrests for 2020 are from a nonpublished monthly NYPD Criminal Justice Bureau report, published December 2020, and received from the Mayor's Office of Criminal Justice via email.

20. Glazer, "Mayor's Office of Criminal Justice Strategic Plan: Fiscal Years 2019–2021"; New York City's Mayor's Office of Criminal Justice.

21. New York City's Mayor's Office of Criminal Justice.

22. "Adult Arrests 18 and Older by County: Beginning 1970," New York State Division of Criminal Justice Services, 2020, https://data.ny.gov/Public-Safety/Adult-Arrests-18-and-Older-by-County-Beginning-197/rikd-mt35.

23. "Dispositions of Adult Arrests," New York State Division of Criminal Justice Services, 2020, www.criminaljustice.ny.gov/crimnet/ojsa/dispos/nyc.pdf.

24. "Dispositions of Adult Arrests"; New York City's Mayor's Office of Criminal Justice. The 2013 average daily population for New York City's Department of Corrections was 11,696. On April 30, 2020, the jailed population was 3,824.

25. City of New York, "Mayor de Blasio Announces 'Smaller, Safer, Fairer: A Roadmap to Closing Rikers Island,'" news release, June 22, 2017, www1.nyc.gov/office-of-the-mayor/news/427-17/mayor-de-blasio-smaller-safer-fairer—roadmap-closing-rikers-island-.

26. "Making Criminal Justice System Data Available to All New Yorkers," New York City Mayor's Office of Criminal Justice, 2021.

27. "Stop, Question and Frisk Data," City of New York, 2021, www1.nyc.gov/site/nypd/stats/reports-analysis/stopfrisk.page.

28. "Marijuana Possession Arrests," New York City Mayor's Office of Criminal Justice, 2018, https://criminaljustice.cityofnewyork.us/individual_charts/marijuana-possession-arrests/).

29. "Summons Reform: One Year After CJRA," New York City Mayor's Office of Criminal Justice, 2018, https://criminaljustice.cityofnewyork.us/wp-content/uploads/2018/09/summons_ref_factsheet_v3.pdf.

30. "Summons Warrant Fact Sheet," New York City Mayor's Office of Criminal Justice, 2016, https://criminaljustice.cityofnewyork.us/wp-content/uploads/2018/04/warrants-fact-sheet-v5.pdf); "District Attorneys from 4 Boroughs Vacate Nearly 700,000 Warrants Dating Back 10 Years or More," CBS New York, July 26, 2017, https://newyork.cbslocal.com/2017/07/26/district-attorneys-old-warrants/.

31. "Stop, Question and Frisk Data," City of New York, 2021.

32. Tom R. Tyler, *Why People Obey the Law* (New Haven, CT: Yale University Press, 2006); Robert J. Sampson and William J. Wilson, *Great American City: Chicago and the Enduring Neighborhood Effect* (Chicago: University of Chicago Press, 2013).

33. "Interventions: Community Partners—the Crisis Management System," New York City Mayor's Office to Prevent Gun Violence, 2021, www1.nyc.gov/site/peacenyc/interventions/crisis-management.page.

34. "Maps" (Data2Go, 2021), http://www.data2go.nyc.

35. "COVID-19: Data," New York City Department of Health, 2020, www1.nyc.gov/site/doh/covid/covid-19-data-totals.page#deaths.

36. New York City Mayor's Office of Criminal Justice, https://criminaljustice.cityofnewyork.us/programs/ons/; https://criminaljustice.cityofnewyork.us/wp-content/uploads/2021/05/Average-monthly-shootings_1.png.

37. "The Mayor's Action Plan for Neighborhood Safety," New York City Mayor's Office of Criminal Justice, 2018, https://criminaljustice.cityofnewyork.us/programs /map/; Betsy Pearl, "NeighborhoodStat: Strengthening Public Safety Through Community Empowerment," Center for American Progress, October 2, 2019, https://cdn.american progress.org/content/uploads/2019/10/02050005/NYCsafety-brief1.pdf?.

38. "The Mayor's Action Plan for Neighborhood Safety."

39. Sheyla A. Delgado et al., "Reported Crime in MAP Communities Compared with Other NYC Areas. MAP Evaluation Update 5," John Jay College of Criminal Justice Research and Evaluation Center, June 2020, https://johnjayrec.nyc/2020/06/25/mapupdate5/.

40. William Bratton, *Broken Windows and Quality-of-Life Policing in New York City*, New York City Police Department, 2015, www.nyc.gov/html/nypd/downloads/pdf/analy sis_and_planning/qol.pdf.

41. City of New York, "Mayor de Blasio, Commissioner Bratton Unveil New, Groundbreaking Neighborhood Policing Vision," news release, June 25, 2015, www1.nyc .gov/office-of-the-mayor/news/440-15/mayor-de-blasio-commissioner-bratton-new -groundbreaking-neighborhood-policing-vision#/0.

42. "Shootings Fell Sharply in Neighborhoods Operating NYC-Funded 'Cure Violence' Programs, New Study Shows," New York City Mayor's Office of Criminal Justice, October 2, 2017, https://criminaljustice.cityofnewyork.us/press-release/shootings-fell -sharply-in-neighborhoods-operating-nyc-funded-cure-violence-programs-new-study -shows/; Pearl, "NeighborhoodStat."

43. "New York City Jail Population Reduction in the Time of COVID-19," New York City Mayor's Office of Criminal Justice, April 2020, https://criminaljustice.cityofnewyork .us/wp-content/uploads/2020/05/COVID-factsheet_APRIL-30-2020.pdf.

44. "Gun Violence and the Criminal Justice System During COVID," New York City Mayor's Office of Criminal Justice, 2020, https://criminaljustice.cityofnewyork.us /data_reports/.

45. "How Many People Were Rearrested Within a Year?," New York City Mayor's Office of Criminal Justice, 2021; "Index Crimes by County and Agency: Beginning 1990," New York State Division of Criminal Justice Services, 2021; "NYPD Complaint Data Historic: Public Safety," New York City Open Data, 2021.

46. Ashley Southall, "Scrutiny of Social-Distance Policing as 35 of 40 Arrested Are Black," *New York Times*, May 7, 2020, www.nytimes.com/2020/05/07/nyregion/nypd-so cial-distancing-race-coronavirus.html.

47. Dean Meminger and Catalina Gonella, "Over 80 Percent of Social Distancing Summonses Went to Black or Hispanic People, NYPD Says," Spectrum News NY1, May 8, 2020, www.ny1.com/nyc/all-boroughs/news/2020/05/09/most-social-distancing -summonses-went-to-black-or-hispanic-people.

48. New York City Department of Investigation, *Investigation into NYPD Response to the George Floyd Protests*, December 2020, www1.nyc.gov/assets/doi/reports

/pdf/2020/DOIRpt.NYPD%20Reponse.%20GeorgeFloyd%20Protests.12.18.2020
.pdf.

49. "Factsheet: 2020 Shootings and Murders," New York City Mayor's Office of
Criminal Justice, 2020, https://criminaljustice.cityofnewyork.us/wp-content/uploads
/2021/01/2020-Shootings-and-Murder-factsheet_January-2021.pdf.

50. Patrick Sharkey, "City-Level Data," American Violence, 2021, www.americanvio
lence.org.

51. Tanaya Devi and Roland G. Fryer Jr., "Policing the Police: The Impact of Pattern-
or-Practice Investigations on Crime," NBER Working Paper No. W27324, National Bureau of Economic Research, June 2020.

52. Sara Dorn, "Nearly 70 Percent of 2020 Shootings in NYC Are Unsolved:
NYPD," New York Post, January 2, 2021, https://nypost.com/2021/01/02/nearly
-70-percent-of-2020-nyc-shootings-are-unsolved-nypd.

53. Data compiled from monthly press releases found in "Press Releases: NYPD Announces Citywide Crime Statistics for [Insert Month Insert Year]," New York City Police
Department, 2021.

54. Craig McCarthy, Carl Campanile, and Aaron Feis, "NYPD's Own Stats Debunk
Claims of Bail Reform Leading to Spike in Gun Violence," New York Post, July 8, 2020, https://
nypost.com/2020/07/08/nypds-own-stats-debunk-claims-about-bail-reform-link-to-shoot
ings/; "Making Criminal Justice System Data Available to All New Yorkers," New York City
Mayor's Office of Criminal Justice, 2021, https://criminaljustice.cityofnewyork.us/system
-data/); Krystal Rodriguez, Michael Rempel, and Matt Watkins, "The Facts on Crime and Bail
Reform in New York City," Center for Court Innovation, 2021, www.courtinnovation.org/sites
/default/files/media/documents/2021-02/Handout_Bail_Reform_Crime_02032021.pdf.

55. Tina Moore, "NYC Shootings and Homicides Soared in 2020, Crime
Data Shows," New York Post, January 6, 2021, https://nypost.com/2021/01/06/nyc
-shootings-and-homicides-soared-in-2020-crime-data-shows.

56. "Making Criminal Justice System Data Available to All New Yorkers," New York
City Mayor's Office of Criminal Justice, 2021; "Index Crimes by County and Agency: Be-
ginning 1990," New York State Division of Criminal Justice Services, 2021; "Historical
New York City Crime Data," New York City Police Department, 2021.

57. Tracey Meares, "Synthesizing Narratives of Policing and Making a Case for Policing as a Public Good," St. Louis University Law Journal 63, no. 4 (2019), https://scholar
ship.law.slu.edu/lj/vol63/iss4/3; Kim Barker, Mike Baker, and Ali Watkins, "In City After
City, Police Mishandled Black Lives Matter Protests," New York Times, March 20, 2021,
http://www.nytimes.com/2021/03/20/us/protests-policing-george-floyd.html.

58. Daniel S. Nagin, "Deterrence in the Twenty-First Century," Crime and Justice: A
Review of Research 42, no. 1 (2013): 199–263; Daniel S. Nagin, "Deterrence: A Review of
the Evidence by a Criminologist for Economists," Annual Review of Economics 5 (2013):
83–105; Dawn J. Bartusch and Robert J. Sampson, "Legal Cynicism and (Subcultural?)

Tolerance of Deviance: The Neighborhood Context of Racial Differences," *Law and Society Review* 32, no. 4 (1998): 777–804.

59. "Interventions: Community Partners—the Crisis Management System."

60. "June 2020 Adopted Budget, Fiscal Year 2021," New York City Mayor's Office of Management and Budget, 2021; "Current Fiscal Year 2021," New York City Mayor's Office of Management and Budget, 2021; "How Many People Were Rearrested Within a Year?"; City of New York, *Mayor's Management Report: Fiscal 2020*, September 2020; Aubrey Fox and Stephen Koppel, Pretrial Release Without Money: New York City, 1987–2020, New York City Criminal Justice Agency, February 2021.

61. Alexander Gelber, Adam Isen, and Judd B. Kessler, "The Effects of Youth Employment: Evidence from New York City Lotteries," *Quarterly Journal of Economics* 131, no. 1 (2016): 423–60.

62. 2020 update using data from Gelber, Isen, and Kessler, "The Effects of Youth Employment."

63. "Factsheet: 2020 Shootings and Murders"; New York City Department of Health Environment and Health Data Portal, "Health, Housing, and History," 2022, https://a816-dohbesp.nyc.gov/IndicatorPublic/Closerlook/housing/index.html.

64. Charles C. Branas et al., "Citywide Cluster Randomized Trial to Restore Blighted Vacant Land and Its Effects on Violence, Crime, and Fear," *Proceedings of the National Academy of Sciences* 115, no. 2 (2018): 2946–51.

65. Aaron Chalfin et al., "Reducing Crime Through Environmental Design: Evidence from a Randomized Experiment of Street Lighting in New York City," *Journal of Quantitative Criminology* 38, no. 1 (2021), 127–57; Members of the Research Advisory Group, *Reducing Violence Without Police: A Review of Research Evidence*, John Jay College of Criminal Justice Research and Evaluation Center, November 2020, https://johnjayrec.nyc/2020/11/09/av2020.

66. Sara B. Heller et al., "Thinking, Fast and Slow? Some Field Experiments to Reduce Crime and Dropout in Chicago," *Quarterly Journal of Economics* 132, no. 1 (2017): 1–54.

67. Jonathan M.V. Davis and Sara B. Heller, "Rethinking the Benefits of Youth Employment Programs: The Heterogeneous Effects of Summer Jobs," *Review of Economics and Statistics* 102, no. 4 (2020): 664–77.

68. Jeffrey A. Butts and Sheyla A. Delgado, "Repairing Trust: Young Men in Neighborhoods with Cure Violence Programs Report Growing Confidence in Police," John Jay College of Criminal Justice Research and Evaluation Center, October 2017, https://johnjayrec.nyc/2017/10/02/repairing2017/; Danielle Wallace et al., "Desistance and Legitimacy: The Impact of Offender Notification Meetings on Recidivism Among High Risk Offenders," *Justice Quarterly* 33, no. 7 (2016): 1237–64.

69. Jane Jacobs, *The Death and Life of Great American Cities* (New York: Random House Publishing, 1961); Robert J. Sampson, Stephen W. Raudenbush, and Felton Earls, "Neighborhoods and Violent Crime: A Multilevel Study of Collective Efficacy," *Science*

277, no. 5328 (1997): 918–24; Patrick Sharkey, Gerard Torrats-Espinosa, and Delaram Takyar, "Community and the Crime Decline: The Causal Effect of Local Nonprofits on Violent Crime," *American Sociological Review* 82, no. 6 (2017): 1214–40.

70. Barry Friedman, "Disaggregating the Police Function," Working Paper No. 20-03, New York University Law and Economics, April 2020, https://papers.ssrn.com/sol3/papers.cfm?abstract_id=3564469.

71. Rachel Morgan and Jennifer Truman, "Criminal Victimization, 2019," U.S. Department of Justice, Bureau of Justice Statistics, September 2020, www.bjs.gov/content/pub/pdf/cv19.pdf.

72. Danielle Sered, "A New Approach to Victim Services: The Common Justice Demonstration Project," *Federal Sentencing Reporter* 24, no. 1 (2011): 50–53; Danielle Sered, *Until We Reckon: Violence, Mass Incarceration, and a Road to Repair* (New York: The New Press, 2019).

73. Elizabeth Hinton, "George Floyd's Death Is a Failure of Generations of Leadership," *New York Times*, June 2, 2020, www.nytimes.com/2020/06/02/opinion/george-floyd-protests-1960s.html?smid=tw-share. See also www.reclaimtheblock.org and www.blackvisionsmn.org.

16. Who Governs? Safety, Governance, and the Future of Justice

1. Linda K. Mancillas, *Presidents and Mass Incarceration: Choices at the Top, Repercussions at the Bottom* (Santa Barbara, CA: ABC-CLIO, 2018); James Cullen, "The History of Mass Incarceration," The Brennan Center, July 20, 2018, www.brennancenter.org/our-work/analysis-opinion/history-mass-incarceration.

2. National Association of State Budget Officers, *State Expenditure Report*, November 2021, https://www.nasbo.org/reports-data/state-expenditure-report.

3. Lori Dorfman and Vincent Schiraldi, *Off Balance: Youth, Race & Crime in the News*, Justice Policy Institute / Public Health Institute, April 2001, http://www.justicepolicy.org/research/2060.

4. E. Fuller Torrey, *Out of the Shadows: Confronting America's Mental Illness Crisis* (New York: John Wiley & Sons, 1997); H. Carroll, "Psychiatric Bed Supply Need Per Capita," Treatment Advocacy Center, September 2016, https://www.treatmentadvocacycenter.org/storage/documents/backgrounders/bed-supply-need-per-capita.pdf.

5. James Forman Jr., *Locking Up Our Own: Crime and Punishment in Black America* (New York: Farrar, Straus & Giroux, 2017).

6. Ruth Wilson Gilmore, *Golden Gulag: Prisons, Surplus, Crisis, and Opposition in Globalizing California*, 1st ed. (Berkeley: University of California Press, 2006).

7. Karen Brown, "Police Offering Drug Recovery Help: 'We Can't Arrest Our Way Out of This Problem,'" NPR, February 8, 2020, https://www.npr.org/2020/02/08/802318886/police-offering-drug-recovery-help-we-can-t-arrest-our-way-out-of-this-problem; Evan Mintz, "How a Town at the Epicenter of the Opioid Crisis Became a

Model for Recovery," Arnold Ventures, December 3, 2019, https://www.arnoldventures
.org/stories/being-at-the-epicenter-of-the-solution-for-americas-opioid-epidemic; Jason
Cain, "'We Can't Arrest Our Way Out of This'—Why SAFE Supports Pre-Arrest Diversion,"
SAFE Project, January 22, 2019, https://www.safeproject.us/article/we-cant-arrest-our
-way-out-of-this-why-safe-supports-pre-arrest-diversion/.

8. John Irwin, Vincent Schiraldi, and Jason Ziedenberg, "America's One Million
Nonviolent Prisoners," Justice Policy Institute, March 1999, http://www.justicepolicy.org
/images/upload/99-03_REP_OneMillionNonviolentPrisoners_AC.pdf; Judith Greene
and Vincent Schiraldi, "Cutting Correctly: New Prison Policies for Times of Fiscal Crisis,"
Center for Juvenile and Criminal Justice / Justice Policy Institute, February 12, 2002, https://
justicepolicy.org/research/cutting-correctly-new-prison-policies-for-times-of-fiscal-crisis/.

9. Jerome G. Miller, *Search and Destroy: African-American Males in the Criminal
Justice System*, 2nd ed. (New York: Cambridge University Press, 2011); Patrick Sharkey, *Uneasy Peace: The Great Crime Decline, the Renewal of City Life, and the Next War on Violence*,
1st ed. (W.W. Norton, 2018).

10. Jennifer L. Truman, PhD, and Langton Lynn, PhD, "Criminal Victimization,
2014," U.S. Department of Justice, Bureau of Justice Statistics, August 2015.

11. Alliance for Safe and Justice, *Crime Survivors Speak: The First-Ever National
Survey of Victims' Views on Safety and Justice*, Alliance for Safety and Justice, 2016, https://
nicic.gov/crime-survivors-speak-first-ever-national-survey-victims-views-safety-and-jus
ticehttps://allianceforsafetyandjustice.org/crimesurvivorsspeak/.

12. Wesley G. Jennings, Alex R. Piquero, and Jennifer M. Reingle, "On the Overlap Between Victimization and Offending: A Review of the Literature," *Aggression and Violent Behavior* 17, no. 1 (2012): 16–26, https://doi.org/10.1016/j.avb.2011.09.003; Amber L. Beckley
et al., "The Developmental Nature of the Victim-Offender Overlap." *Journal of Developmental and Life-Course Criminology* 4, no. 1 (2018): 24–49, https://doi.org/10.1007/s40865-017-
0068-3; Caitlin Delong and Jessica Reichert, "The Victim-Offender Overlap: Examining the
Relationship Between Victimization and Offending," Illinois Criminal Justice Information
Authority, January 9, 2019, https://icjia.illinois.gov/researchhub/articles/the-victim-of-
fender-overlap-examining-the-relationship-between-victimization-and-offending.

13. Californians for Safety and Justice, *Second Chances and Systems Change: How
Proposition 47 Is Changing California*, Tides Center, March 2017, https://safeandjust.org
/wp-content/uploads/P47_Report_Final.pdf.

14. "Welcome to California's 2018–19 Governor's Budget," California Department of
Finance, January 10, 2018, https://www.ebudget.ca.gov/budget/publication/#/p/2018-19
/BudgetDetail; "Welcome to California's 2022–23 Governor's Budget," California Department of Finance, January 10, 2022, https://www.ebudget.ca.gov/budget/2022-23/#
/BudgetDetail.

15. "Prop 47 Grant Program," California Board of State and Community Corrections, 2020, http://www.bscc.ca.gov/s_bsccprop47/.

16. "Funding and Fiscal Management for the Learning Communities for School Success Program," California Department of Education, October 22, 2020, https://www.cde.ca.gov/fg/fo/r8/fundresults2017-20.asp.

17. National Alliance of Trauma Recovery Centers, *Trauma Recovery Centers: Addressing the Needs of Underserved Crime Survivors*, January 2020, https://alliancefor safetyandjustice.org/wp-content/uploads/2020/10/TRAUMA-RECOVERY-CEN TERSAddressing-the-Needs-of-Underserved-Crime-Survivors.pdf.

18. "TRC Membership Directory," National Alliance of Trauma Recovery Centers, https://nationalallianceoftraumarecoverycenters.org/membership.

19. "Crime Survivors for Safety and Justice," Alliance for Safety and Justice, 2020, https://cssj.org.

20. "Prop 47 Grant Program."

21. "Joint Hearing Assembly Public Safety Committee and Senate Public Safety Committee, Tuesday, February 11th, 2020," California State Assembly, https://www.assembly .ca.gov/media/joint-hearing-assembly-public-safety-committee-senate-public-safety-commit tee-20200211/video.

22. "Joint Hearing Assembly Public Safety Committee and Senate Public Safety Committee."

23. Shirley N. Weber, PhD, "Official Declaration of the Vote Results on November 3, 2020, State Ballot Measures," California Secretary of State, November 3, 2020, https:// www.sos.ca.gov/elections/prior-elections/statewide-election-results/general-election -november-3-2020/statement-vote.

17. Reimagining Judging

1. Kate Stith and José A. Cabranes, *Fear of Judging: Sentencing Guidelines in the Federal Courts* (Chicago: University of Chicago Press, 1998).

2. Stith and Cabranes, *Fear of Judging*.

3. Douglas Berman, "A Common Law for This Age of Federal Sentencing: The Opportunity and Need for Judicial Lawmaking," *Stanford Law and Policy Review* 11, no. 1 (1999): 93–94.

4. U.S. Sentencing Commission, "Survey of Article III Judges," 2002; U.S. Sentencing Commission, "Results of 2014 Survey of United States District Judges," 2015.

5. Michael Tonry, "The Questionable Relevance of Previous Convictions to Punishments for Later Crimes," in *Previous Convictions at Sentencing: Theoretical and Applied Perspectives*, ed. Julian V. Roberts and Andreas von Hirsch (London: Bloomsbury Publishing, 2010), 91–116.

6. Nik DeCosta-Klipa, "Rachael Rollins Blasts Judge for Refusing to Dismiss Charges Against Nonviolent 'Straight Pride Parade' Protestors," *Boston Globe*, September 4, 2016; Jordan Smith, "What Happens When a Reform Prosecutor Stands Up to the Death Penalty," *The Intercept*, December 3, 2019; Angie Ricono and Cyndi Fahrlander, "Missouri

Man Waits for Missouri Supreme Court Ruling, Has Already Spent 26 Years in Prison—Called Innocent by Current Prosecutor," KCTV5, September 21, 2020.

7. Matthew Denis, "Reentry Court Aspires to Give Released Prisoners a Chance to Succeed," *Register-Guard*, April 10, 2019.

8. Russell Patterson, "Punishing Violent Crime," *NYU Law Review* 95, no. 5 (2020): 1521–60.

9. Alice Tihelková, "Framing the 'Scroungers': The Re-Emergence of the Stereotype of the Undeserving Poor and Its Reflection in the British Press," *Brno Studies in English* 41, no. 2 (2015): 121–39.

10. *Miller v. Alabama*, 567 U.S. 460 (2012).

11. *Miller v. Alabama*, 567 U.S. 460 (2012).

12. *Jones v. Mississippi*, 593 U.S. ___ (2021); *Miller v. Alabama*, 567 U.S. 460 (2012).

13. Keri Blakinger and Joseph Neff, "Thousands of Sick Federal Prisoners Sought Compassionate Release. 98 Percent Were Denied," The Marshall Project, October 7, 2020; Victoria Finkle, "How Compassionate? Political Appointments and District Court Judge Responses to Compassionate Release During COVID-19," Georgetown University Law Center, January 22, 2021.

14. Matt Brelis, "DA Rachael Rollins and Defendant Argue COVID-19 Standing Order Was Violated and Arrest Warrant Was in Error," Suffolk County District Attorney's Office, November 12, 2020.

15. Carl Hulse, "Bipartisan Criminal Justice Overhaul Is Haunted by Willie Horton," *New York Times*, January 16, 2016.

16. Adam Liptak, "Why Judges Tilt to the Right," *New York Times*, January 31, 2015.

17. Bryan Stevenson, *Just Mercy: A Story of Justice and Redemption* (New York: Spiegel & Grau, 2015), 14.

18. Terry A. Maroney, "The Persistent Cultural Script of Judicial Dispassion," *California Law Review* 99, no. 629 (2011): 631.

19. "Confirmation Hearing on the Nomination of John G. Roberts, Jr. to Be Chief Justice of the United States," Senate Hearing 109–158 (2005).

20. Linda Greenhouse, "The Thomas Hearings: In Trying to Clarify What He Is Not, Thomas Opens Question of What He Is," *New York Times*, September 13, 1991.

21. Ann Southworth, "Lawyers and the Conservative Counterrevolution," *Law and Social Inquiry* 43, no. 4 (2018): 1698–728.

22. Nancy Gertner, "Judicial Discretion in Sentencing—Real or Imagined?," *Federal Sentencing Reporter* 28, no. 3 (2016): 165–66.

23. Joanna Shepherd, *Jobs, Judges, and Justice: The Relationship Between Professional Diversity and Judicial Decisions*, Demand Justice, 2021. Eighty percent of federal judges are white, and 73 percent are men. Jake Faleschini, Grace Oyenubi, and Danielle Root, "Building a More Inclusive Federal Judiciary," Center for American Progress, October 3, 2019.

24. *United States v. Leviner*, 31 F. Supp. 2d 23 (D. Mass. 1998).

25. Adam J. Kolber, "How to Fix Legal Scholarmush," *Brooklyn Law School* 95, no. 4 (2020): 1191–232.

26. Imposition of a Sentence, 18 U.S. Code § 3553 (1987).

27. Denny Chin, "Sentencing: A Role for Empathy," *University of Pennsylvania Law Review* 160, no. 6 (2012): 1561–84.

28. Perry L. Moriearty, "Framing Justice: Media, Bias, and Legal Decisionmaking," *Maryland Law Review* 69 (2010): 849–909. This seemed to be the residue of the "moral panic" of the 1990s, when the media, politicians, and even judges reflected the view there was a new breed of adolescents who were "godless," even "deviant."

29. Martha L. Minow, "Judging Inside Out," *University of Colorado Law Review* 61 (1990): 795–800.

30. Sharon Brett, Colin Doyle, and Mitali Nagrecha, "Court Culture and Criminal Law Reform," *Duke Law Journal* 69, no. 84 (2020): 106.

31. Chris Guthrie, Jeffrey J. Rachlinski, and Andrew Wistrich, "Blinking on the Bench: How Judges Decide Cases," *Cornell Law Review* 93, no. 1 (2007): 36–37.

32. Chris Guthrie, Jeffrey J. Rachlinski, and Andrew Wistrich, "Inside the Judicial Mind," *Cornell Law Review* 86, no. 4 (2001): 777–830; Mark W. Bennet, "Confronting Cognitive 'Anchoring Effect' and 'Blind Spot' Biases in Federal Sentencing: A Modest Solution for Reforming a Fundamental Flaw," *Journal of Criminal Law and Criminology* 104, no. 3 (2014): 489–534.

33. Gertner, "Judicial Discretion in Sentencing."

34. Nancy Gertner, "Losers' Rules," *Yale Law Journal Online* 122 (2012): 109–24.

35. Andrea Woods, "Federal Judges Are Failing Incarcerated People During the Pandemic," American Civil Liberties Union, September 15, 2020.

36. "The Homogeneous Federal Bench," editorial, *New York Times*, February 6, 2014.

37. Robert Martinson, "What Works? Questions and Answers About Prison Reform," *Public Interest* 35 (1974): 22–54. He subsequently recanted some of his conclusions in Robert Martinson, "New Findings, New Views: A Note of Caution Regarding Sentencing Reform," *Hofstra Law Review* 7 (1979): 243.

38. Laura Hawks et al., *Towards a New Framework for Achieving Decarceration: A Review of the Research on Social Investments*, The Square One Project, October 2021; Amanda Alexander and Danielle Sered, *What Makes a City Safe: Viable Community Safety Strategies That Do Not Rely on Police or Prisons*, The Square One Project, December 2021; Nneka Jones-Tapia, *Harm Reduction at the Center of Incarceration*, The Square One Project, April 2021; James Austin et al., *Reconsidering the "Violent Offender,"* The Square One Project, May 2019.

39. Betsy Pearl, "NeighborhoodStat: Strengthening Public Safety Through Community Empowerment," Center for American Progress, October 2, 2019.

40. *Plessy v. Ferguson*, 163 U.S. 537 (1896); *United States v. Alexander*, 471 F.2d 923 (D.C. Cir. 1973); *United States v. Leviner*, 31 F. Supp. 2d 23 (D. Mass. 1998); Richard

Delgado and Jean Stefancic, "Do Judges Cry? An Essay on Empathy and Fellow-Feeling," *Case Western Reserve Law Review* 70, no. 1 (2019): 51, 50.

41. *United States v. Haynes*, 557 F. Supp. 2d 200, 207 (D. Mass. 2008); *United States v. Bannister*, 786 F. Supp. 2d 617, 689 (E.D. N.Y. 2011). See, generally, Jessica A. Roth, "The 'New' District Court Activism in Criminal Justice Reform," *NYU Annual Survey of American Law* 72, no. 2 (2017): 277–363, addressing the case for reform made in their judicial opinions, articles, and speeches.

42. *United States v. Vasquez*, No. 20-40332 (5th Cir. 2021).

43. Lani Guinier, "The Supreme Court, 2007 Term—Foreword: Demosprudence Through Dissent," *Harvard Law Review* 122, no. 4 (2008): 4–138.

44. James Forman Jr., *Locking Up Our Own: Crime and Punishment in Black America* (New York: Farrar, Straus and Giroux, 2017).

18. Closing the Workhouse: Supporting Radical Campaigns at National Nonprofits

1. INCITE! Women of Color Against Violence, *The Revolution Will Not Be Funded: Beyond the Non-Profit Industrial Complex* (2007; repr., Duke University Press, 2017), 67.

2. INCITE! Women of Color Against Violence, *The Revolution Will Not Be Funded*, 35–36.

3. Dylan Rodríguez, "The Political Logic of the Non-Profit Industrial Complex," in *The Revolution Will Not Be Funded*, 22.

4. Rodríguez, "The Political Logic of the Non-Profit Industrial Complex," 22.

5. In describing the origins of the Close the Workhouse campaign, I intentionally include the names of as many people and organizations as I can, in the hope that it conveys what it takes to make this kind of work possible. If anything, I am leaving people out. Each person I named could name several other people who played a role in the advocacy to close this jail. And if I asked Jamala Rogers or Percy Green, legendary civil rights activists in St. Louis, they could probably name another 150. I do this because campaigns do not revolve around a few heroic key players. People join and drop out; they move on to other jobs and come back; and frequently get burned out. Organizational priorities may change, staffing capacity may change, but the people fighting today are shaped by the legacies of those who fought the previous fight. Campaigns are composed of imperfect human beings, dreaming of a beautiful future.

6. "The Bail Project," The Bail Project, http://www.thebailproject.org/; "Action St. Louis," Action St. Louis, https://actionstl.org/; "National Office," Advancement Project, https://advancementproject.org/home/; "Missourians Organizing for Reform and Empowerment (MORE)," Facebook, https://www.facebook.com/organizemo.

7. ArchCity Defenders et al., "Close the Workhouse: A Plan & a Vision," January 2020.

8. Sam Clancy, "Lewis Reed Files Board Bills to Close 'the Workhouse,' Use Funds on Neighborhood Crime Reduction," *5 On Your Side*, KDSK, June 30, 2020, https://www

.ksdk.com/article/news/crime/the-bill-would-take-funding-earmarked-for-the-workhouse
-and-use-it-for-community-programs-aimed-at-reducing-recidivism-and-violent-crime/63
-b6645d19-25ad-436e-a093-362073254114.

9. Clancy, "Lewis Reed Files Board Bills to Close 'the Workhouse'"; ArchCity Defenders et al., "Close the Workhouse."

10. Shanti Parikh and Jong Bum Kwon, "@Ferguson: Still Here in the Afterlives of Black Death, Defiance, and Joy," *American Ethnologist* 47, no. 2 (May 2020): 107–209.

11. Shereen Marisol Meraji, "Nightly Chaos Disrupts Ferguson Residents' Daily Lives," WBUR, August 19, 2014, https://www.wbur.org/npr/341542530/nightly-chaos
-disrupts-ferguson-residents-daily-lives.

12. Kenya Vaughn, "Tef Poe Reflects on Ferguson," *St. Louis American*, August 8, 2019, https://www.stlamerican.com/entertainment/living_it/tef-poe-reflects-on-ferguson
/article_39f901fe-b95f-11e9-8469-13a0e1fd55c2.html.

13. Vaughn, "Tef Poe Reflects on Ferguson."

14. Inez Bordeaux, "Radicalized at the Workhouse," *Inquest*, October 22, 2021, https://inquest.org/radicalized-at-the-workhouse/.

15. "Close the Workhouse: A Plan to Close the Workhouse and Promote a New Vision for St. Louis," Close the Workhouse, September 2018.

16. "Close the Workhouse," 7.

17. "Close the Workhouse," 8.

18. "Close the Workhouse," 8.

19. "Close the Workhouse," 9.

20. "Close the Workhouse," 9.

21. Email from Rachel Sommer to Thomas Harvey, March 3, 2015.

22. "Decarcerate STL," Facebook, https://www.facebook.com/Decarcerate-STL
-1537790673178601/.

23. *DecarcerateSTL* (blog), https://decarceratestl.wordpress.com/.

24. Email from John to Thomas Harvey re work plan, July 3, 2016.

25. "Ferguson Collaborative to Hold 'Reimagining Public Safety' Town Hall on Sunday," *St. Louis American*, September 16, 2016, https://www.stlamerican.com/news/lo
cal_news/ferguson-collaborative-to-hold-reimagining-public-safety-town-hall-on-sunday
/article_ce58b946-7c1a-11e6-9e56-fbfee8e9060c.html.

26. The Center for Popular Democracy, Law for Black Lives, and Black Youth Project 100, *Freedom to Thrive: Reimagining Safety & Security in Our Communities*, July 2017, https://populardemocracy.org/sites/default/files/Freedom%20To%20Thrive%2C%20
Higher%20Res%20Version.pdf.

27. Tishaura O. Jones, "Shut Down the Workhouse," *St. Louis American*, September 15, 2016, https://www.stlamerican.com/news/columnists/guest_columnists/shut
-down-the-workhouse/article_b6b94806-7aed-11e6-97f4-5732ac284577.html.

28. Danny Wicentowski, "For ArchCity Defenders' New Director, Blake Strode, Home Is Where the Injustice Was," *Riverfront Times*, February 10, 2022, https://m.riverfronttimes.com/stlouis/blake-strode-archcity-defenders/Content?oid=11507467&storyPage=3.

29. Chris King, "Krewson Edges Tishaura by 888 Votes," *St. Louis American*, March 21, 2017, https://www.stlamerican.com/news/local_news/krewson-edges-tishaura-by-888-votes/article_a98cf1de-042a-11e7-b233-8f346c276f7d.html.

30. Mariame Kaba, "For Mother's Day, Activists Are Bailing Black Mamas Out of Jail," *Vice*, May 10, 2017, https://www.vice.com/en/article/paegbb/for-mothers-day-activists-are-bailing-black-mamas-out-of-jail.

31. "#BlackMamaBailoutSTL Raised $13k to Get Moms out of Jail for Mother's Day," St. Louis Public Radio, May 15, 2017, https://news.stlpublicradio.org/government-politics-issues/2017-05-15/blackmamabailoutstl-raised-13k-to-get-moms-out-of-jail-for-mothers-day.

32. Freedom Community Center, www.freedomstl.org.

33. Sophie Hurwitz and Melinda Oliver, "Heat Wave Hitting Workhouse Without A/C Stirs Outrage, Cries for Reform," *St. Louis American*, September 26, 2017, http://www.stlamerican.com/news/local_news/heat-wave-hitting-workhouse-without-a-c-stirs-outrage-cries-for-reform/article_a8c73bea-724f-11e7-8c6b-9373be3ee40a.html.

34. Hurwitz and Oliver, "Heat Wave Hitting Workhouse."

35. "Close the Workhouse."

36. Jessica Karins, "ArchCity Defenders Sues to Close Workhouse, Claims Violations of the First, Eighth and Fourteenth Amendments," *St. Louis American*, November 16, 2017, https://www.stlamerican.com/news/local_news/archcity-defenders-sues-to-close-workhouse-claims-violations-of-the-first-eighth-and-fourteenth-amendments/article_71219276-c8ad-11e7-99a2-2783937d7e63.html.

37. Jenny Simeone-Casas, "Moms Bailed Out of Jail for Mother's Day," *St. Louis American*, September 26, 2017, https://www.stlamerican.com/news/local_news/moms-bailed-out-of-jail-for-mother-s-day/article_a3eaa85c-3b5c-11e7-a3e9-13fe5e39fe0b.html.

38. Jon Swaine, "The Five Leaders Who Failed Ferguson," *The Guardian*, November 27, 2014.

39. "Inmate Population by Day," St. Louis-MO.gov, https://www.stlouis-mo.gov/data/dashboards/inmates/by-day.cfm?date=08%2F01%2F2022&race=all&sex=all&employment=all&maritalStatus=all&topCharge=all#singleDay.

40. "Jones Proposes Workhouse Closure in First Budget Meeting," KMOV4, April 21, 2021, https://web.archive.org/web/20210422050300/https://www.kmov.com/news/jones-proposes-workhouse-closure-in-first-budget-meeting/article_a21cd60a-a2d5-11eb-9014-dba4f540683a.html?style=horizontal_slider.

41. Karins, "ArchCity Defenders Sues to Close Workhouse"; Kira Lerner, "'I Am a Human and I Just Ask to Be Treated as One,'" *The Appeal*, February 19, 2019, https://theappeal.org/st-louis-bail-lawsuit-close-the-workhouse/.

42. Rebecca Rivas, "St. Louis City Board of Aldermen Vote to Close the Workhouse," *St. Louis American*, July 21, 2020, https://www.stlamerican.com/news/local_news/st -louis-city-board-of-aldermen-vote-to-close-the-workhouse/article_6ab53558-c87a-11ea -8895-6b86c9aa4e0e.html.

43. Kayla Reed and Blake Strode, "How to Turn Protest Power into Political Power," *New York Times*, May 22, 2021; Danny Wicentowski, "Kim Gardner Is St. Louis' First Black Circuit Attorney. That Matters—and She's Just Getting Started," *Riverfront Times*, March 1, 2017, https://www.riverfronttimes.com/stlouis/and-justice-for-all/Con tent?oid=3676536.

44. "About Deaconess Center," Deaconess Center for Child Well-Being, https:// deaconesscenter.org/about-deaconess-center/.

45. Close the Workhouse Campaign, "Close the Workhouse Campaign Releases Plan to Permanently Close the City's Infamous Medium Security Jail," September 13, 2018.

46. *Finding Justice*, BET, https://www.bet.com/shows/finding-justice.

47. Associated Press, "Federal Lawsuit Challenging St. Louis' Cash Bail System," ABC30 January 29, 2019, https://abcstlouis.com/news/local/federal-lawsuit -challenging-st-louis-cash-bail-system.

48. Rachel Lippmann, "St. Louis' Cash Bail System Challenged in Court," St. Louis Public Radio, January 28, 2019, https://news.stlpublicradio.org/govern ment-politics-issues/2019-01-28/st-louis-cash-bail-system-challenged-in-court.

49. Sarah Fenske, "Paying Bail in St. Louis? Better Have $45,000 Cash, on a Weekday," *Riverfront Times*, January 31, 2022, https://www.riverfronttimes.com/stlouis /paying-bail-in-st-louis-better-have-45000-cash-on-a-weekday/Content?oid=30074550.

50. Fenske, "Paying Bail in St. Louis?"

51. Fenske, "Paying Bail in St. Louis?"

52. "People Power! St. Louis' Close the Workhouse Coalition Is Fighting to Bring Justice Back to St. Louis," Ben & Jerry's, July 3, 2019, https://www.benjerry.com/whats -new/2019/07/close-the-workhouse-campaign; Rebecca Rivas, "Close the Workhouse Finds Allies in Federal Judge, Ben & Jerry's," *St. Louis American*, June 12, 2019, https:// www.stlamerican.com/news/local_news/close-the-workhouse-finds-allies-in-federal -judge-ben-jerry-s/article_7d71fe32-8d2b-11e9-89df-9b054942af1d.html.

53. "McCarthy: Guilty Until Proven Wealthy: It's Time to Close the Workhouse and End Cash Bail," *St. Louis Post-Dispatch*, June 10, 2019, https://www.stltoday.com/opinion /columnists/mccarthy-guilty-until-proven-wealthy-it-s-time-to-close/article_bc327916 -795e-5121-a4d1-5e434370da89.html; "We're Fighting a Racist, Predatory System; and We're Winning: A Look at the Numbers," Advancement Project, June 27, 2019, https:// advancementproject.org/cashbailbythenumbers/.

54. "People Power!"

19. What Makes a City Safe? Strategies
That Don't Rely on Police or Prisons

1. Albert Reiss and Jeffrey Roth, "Patterns of Violence in American Society," in *Understanding and Preventing Violence: Panel on the Understanding and Control of Violent Behavior*, vol. 1, ed. Albert Reiss and Jeffrey Roth (Washington, DC: National Academies Press, 1993), nap.edu/catalog/1861/understanding-and-preventing-violence-volume-1; Bruce Kennedy et al., "Social Capital, Income Inequality, and Firearm Violent Crime," *Social Science and Medicine* 47, no. 1 (1998): 7–17; Cleopatra H. Caldwell et al., "Racial Discrimination and Racial Identity as Risk or Protective Factors for Violent Behaviors in African American Young Adults," *American Journal of Community Psychology* 33, nos. 1–2 (2004): 91–105.

2. Douglas A. Blackmon, *Slavery by Another Name: The Re-Enslavement of Black Americans from the Civil War to World War II* (New York: Anchor Books, 2009); Christopher Hartney and Linh Vuong, *Created Equal: Racial and Ethnic Disparities in the US Criminal Justice System*, National Council on Crime and Delinquency, March 2009, www.evidentchange.org/sites/default/files/publication_pdf/created-equal.pdf; Alex F. Schwartz, *Housing Policy in the United States* (New York: Routledge, 2010); Ta-Nehisi Coates, "The Case for Reparations," *The Atlantic*, June 2014; Equal Justice Initiative, *Lynching in America: Confronting the Legacy of Racial Terror*, 3rd ed., 2017, eji.org/reports/lynching-in-america; Michelle Alexander, *The New Jim Crow: Mass Incarceration in the Age of Colorblindness* (New York: The New Press, 2010).

3. One Million Experiments, "One Million Experiments: A Virtual Zine Project c/o Project Nio & Interrupting Criminalization," 2021, millionexperiments.com.

4. Grace Lee Boggs, "Solutionaries Are Today's Revolutionaries," *The Boggs Blog*, October 27, 2013, conversationsthatyouwillneverfinish.wordpress.com/2013/10/27/solutionaries-are-todays-revolutionaries-by-grace-lee-boggs.

5. "Social Determinants of Health: Know What Affects Health," Centers for Disease Control and Prevention, 2021, www.cdc.gov/socialdeterminants/index.htm.

6. National Network of Hospital-based Violence Intervention Programs, "Hospital-Based Violence Intervention: Practices and Policies to End the Cycle of Violence," 2019, static1.squarespace.com/static/5d6f61730a2b610001135b79/t/5d83c0d9056f4d4cbdb9acd9/1568915699707/NNHVIP+White+Paper.pdf.

7. National Network, "Hospital-Based Violence Intervention."

8. Paulette Parker, "Living in a Violent Neighborhood Can Give You PTSD, Study Suggests," NPR Michigan, April 3, 2017, stateofopportunity.michiganradio.org/post/living-violent-neighborhood-can-give-you-ptsd-study-suggests.

9. National Network, "Hospital-Based Violence Intervention."

10. National Network, "Hospital-Based Violence Intervention."

11. Kurtis Lee, "In Detroit's Busiest ER, a Man with His Own Dark Past Tries to Halt a Cycle of Violence," *Los Angeles Times*, June 15, 2018, www.latimes.com/nation/la-na-detroit-gun-violence-activists-20180615-htmlstory.html.

12. National Network, "Hospital-Based Violence Intervention."

13. National Network, "Hospital-Based Violence Intervention."

14. Durham Beyond Policing Coalition, *Proposal for a Community-Led Safety and Wellness Task Force*, 2020, durhambeyondpolicing.org/wp-content/uploads/2019/07/Dur ham-Beyond-Policing-Budget-Proposal-2019-2020.pdf.

15. Samuel Corey, "Detroit Teens Reimagine Criminal Justice with Alternative to New Jail," *Detroit Metro Times*, 2018, www.metrotimes.com/news-hits/archives/2018/10/05 /detroit-teens-reimagine-criminal-justice-with-alternative-to-new-jail; Designing Justice and Designing Spaces, "Restorative Justice Youth Design Summit," August 2019, www.detroit justice.org/blog/2019/8/29/report.

16. Saneta deVuono-powell et al., *Who Pays? The True Cost of Incarceration on Families*, Ella Baker Center, Forward Together, and Research Action Design, September 2015, whopaysreport.org/who-pays-full-report.

17. Benita Tsao and Rachel A. Davis, *Community Safety by Design: Preventing Violence Through Land Use*, Prevention Institute for The California Endowment, September 2015, www.preventioninstitute.org/publications/community-safety-design.

18. "Million Dollar Blocks," Chicago's Million Dollar Blocks, n.d., chicagos milliondollarblocks.com; Prisoner's Alliance with Community, *The Non-Traditional Approach to Criminal & Social Justice*, rev. ed., January 1997, static1.squarespace .com/static/58eb0522e6f2e1dfce591dee/t/5edf83f8c692cc7379542d 72/1591706634465/NonTraditionalApproachUpdatedRpt_Scanned.pdf; Center for NuLeadership on Urban Solutions, "The Seven Neighborhood Study Revisited," 2013, static1.squarespace.com/static/58eb0522e6f2e1dfce591dee/t/596e1246d482e9c1 c6b86699/1500385865855/seven-neighborhood+revisited+rpt.pdf; deVuono-powell et al.,*Who Pays?*; Neil Schoenherr, "Cost of Incarceration in the U.S. More than $1 Trillion," *The Source*, September 7, 2016, source.wustl.edu/2016/09/cost-incarceration-u-s-1 -trillion.

19. "Rapid Employment and Development Initiative Chicago," Heartland Alliance, 2020, www.heartlandalliance.org/readi/about.

20. "Rapid Employment and Development Initiative Chicago."

21. Rikha Sharma Rani, "Building Trust Cuts Violence. Cash Also Helps," *New York Times*, February 21, 2017.

22. "News," Second Chance Center, Inc., 2020, www.scccolorado.org/news/cat egories/path-updates.

23. Andrea J. Ritchie, introduction to *The Demand Is Still #DefundPolice*, Interrupting Criminalization, January 2021, static1.squarespace.com/static/5ee39ec764dbd 7179cf1243c/t/60806839979abc1b93aa8695/1619028044655/%23DefundThePolice%2 BUpdate.pdf; City of Chicago, Office of Budget and Management, "2021 Budget Public Engagement Recap," 2021, www.chicago.gov/content/dam/city/sites/budget/2021Budget EngagementRecap.pdf.

24. Natalie Moore, "New Coalition Seeks a Bottom-Up Approach to Transform Chicago's South and West Sides," WBEZ Chicago, December 11, 2020, www.wbez.org /stories/new-coalition-seeks-a-bottoms-up-approach-to-transform-chicagos-south-and -west-sides/28bd4614-b86e-498f-b648-93f1f1cbe560?fbclid=IwAR0sUAmK_7fcxy mhH_eQw0S52BX3jHjBb2IgU3AyzpW2JzfKjqgtk1o92EU.

25. "We Are Equity and Transformation," Equity and Transformation Chicago, 2021, www.eatchicago.org.

26. 482Forward, n.d., https://482forward.org/.

27. Durham Beyond Policing Coalition, *Proposal for a Community-Led Safety and Wellness Task Force.*

28. Alliance Safety and Justice, *Crime Survivors Speak.*

29. "Detroit Youth-Led Healing Hub," Detroit Heals Detroit, 2020, www.de troithealsdetroit.org/l/detroit-youth-led-healing-hub.

30. 482Forward, n.d., https://482forward.org/; "Healing Generations," National Compadres Network, 2017, www.nationalcompadresnetwork.org/institutes/healing -generations.

31. "Crisis Response," Urban Grief, 2020, urbangrief.org.

32. "Our Mission," Mothers in Charge, 2022, https://www.mothersincharge.org /our-mission/.

33. Sara Kershnar et al., *Toward Transformative Justice: A Liberatory Approach to Child Sexual Abuse and Other Forms of Intimate and Community Violence,* generationFIVE, June 2007, www.generationfive.org/wp-content/uploads/2013/07/G5_Toward_Transfor mative_Justice-Document.pdf.

34. Danielle Sered, *Until We Reckon: Violence, Mass Incarceration, and a Road to Repair* (New York: The New Press, 2019).

35. James Gilligan, "Shame, Guilt, and Violence," *Social Research* 70, no. 4 (2003): 1149–80.

36. Nathan James, *Offender Reentry: Correctional Statistics, Reintegration into the Community, and Recidivism,* Congressional Research Service, January 2015, fas.org/sgp /crs/misc/RL34287.pdf.

37. Sered, *Until We Reckon.*

38. Mark S. Umbreit, Robert B. Coates, and Betty Vos, "The Impact of Victim-Offender Mediation: Two Decades of Research," *Federal Probation* 65, no. 3 (2001): 29–35; Christopher Hartney and Linh Vuong, *Created Equal: Racial and Ethnic Disparities in the US Criminal Justice System,* National Council on Crime and Delinquency, March 2009, www.evidentchange.org/sites/default/files/publication_pdf/created-equal .pdf; Sujatha Baliga, Sia Henry, and George Valentine, *Restorative Community Conferencing: A Study of Community Works West's Restorative Justice Youth Diversion Program in Alameda County,* Impact Justice, Summer 2017, impactjustice.org/resources

/restorative-community-conferencing-a-study-of-community-works-wests-restorative-jus
tice-youth-diversion-program-in-alameda-county.

39. Alliance Safety and Justice, *Crime Survivors Speak*.

40. "About Us," FWD.us, 2018, www.fwd.us/about.

41. Rashad Robinson, "Changing Our Narrative About Narrative: The Infrastructure Required for Building Narrative Power," Color of Change, 2019, colorofchange.org
/press_release/changing-our-narrative-about-narrative-the-infrastructure-required-for
-building-narrative-power.

ABOUT THE EDITORS

Jeremy Travis is executive vice president for criminal justice at the Arnold Foundation and the former president of John Jay College of Criminal Justice. He clerked for Ruth Bader Ginsburg and was special counsel to the NYPD commissioner. The author of *But They All Come Back: Facing the Challenges of Prisoner Reentry* and co-editor of *Prisoner Reentry and Crime in America* and *Prisoners Once Removed*, he lives in New York City.

Bruce Western is the Bryce Professor of Sociology and Social Justice and co-director of the Justice Lab at Columbia University. He has been a Guggenheim Fellow, a Russell Sage Foundation Fellow, and a fellow of the Radcliffe Institute of Advanced Study. The author of *Homeward: Life in the Year After Prison* and *Punishment and Inequality in America*, he lives in New York City.

PUBLISHING IN THE PUBLIC INTEREST

Thank you for reading this book published by The New Press. The New Press is a nonprofit, public interest publisher. New Press books and authors play a crucial role in sparking conversations about the key political and social issues of our day.

We hope you enjoyed this book and that you will stay in touch with The New Press. Here are a few ways to stay up to date with our books, events, and the issues we cover:

- Sign up at www.thenewpress.com/subscribe to receive updates on New Press authors and issues and to be notified about local events
- www.facebook.com/newpressbooks
- www.twitter.com/thenewpress
- www.instagram.com/thenewpress

Please consider buying New Press books for yourself; for friends and family; or to donate to schools, libraries, community centers, prison libraries, and other organizations involved with the issues our authors write about.

The New Press is a 501(c)(3) nonprofit organization. You can also support our work with a tax-deductible gift by visiting www.thenewpress.com/donate.